America's Best Low-Tax Retirement Towns

Eve Evans & Richard Fox

VACATION
PUBLICATIONS
HOUSTON

America's Best Low-Tax Retirement Towns

Art Direction and Cover Design: Fred W. Salzmann

Senior Research Associate: Michele Castillo

Research Associates: Sarah Ainsworth, Brad Luebe, Amy Lusignan, Konnett Mays, Robert Reichle, Caitlin Van Allen

Publisher's Note: This book contains information from many sources. Every effort has been made to verify the accuracy and authenticity of the information contained in this book. Although care and diligence have been used in preparation and review, the material is subject to change. It is published for general reference and the publisher does not guarantee the accuracy of the information.

Published by Vacation Publications, Inc.
1502 Augusta Drive, Suite 415
Houston, TX 77057

Library of Congress Catalog Card Number: 2001098608
ISBN 0-9644216-8-2

Printed in the United States of America

VACATION
PUBLICATIONS

America's Best Low-T

CON

ax Retirement Towns

ENTS

INTRODUCTION

If you plan to move to another state to retire, examine the tax burden you'll face when you arrive. Your retirement dreamland could be a tax heaven — or hell.

Taxes are increasingly important to everyone, but retirees have extra cause for concern since their income may be fixed. In a survey by *Where to Retire* magazine, readers cited a low overall tax rate as one of the five most important factors in choosing a place to retire.

Retirees' interest in the tax scene and the lack of readily available information about tax burdens in specific locations promoted us to undertake a unique — and massive — project: to compare the tax burdens in 163 cities in all 50 states.

That's *total* tax burden — all state and local taxes, fees and assessments — including state and local income tax, property tax, personal property tax, sales tax, auto licensing fees and fees or assessments for things like garbage pickup, street and storm drain maintenance and more.

Nowhere else have we seen information as extensive and specific as what is presented in this book. Rather than base our data on the "average" retired couple, we've calculated the tax liabilities for nine different couples, using three income levels and six home values. Most relocating retirees will find that their income and home value fall near those of one of our couples.

For each city, you will find a chart detailing and tallying the taxes due from our couples. Our figures are based on married couples filing jointly who are age 65 or older. We've included tax breaks related to age in our calculations. These additional deductions and exemptions are widespread and frequently quite significant. We suspect that rankings based on tax burdens of residents under the age of 65 could be dramatically different from those herein. All couples are assumed to be relocating across state lines.

We used three income levels — $25,000, $50,000 and $75,000 in gross income — and extrapolated expenditures for each income level from the Consumer Expenditure Survey of people age 65 and older, issued by the U.S. Department of Labor, Bureau of Labor Statistics (BLS). The BLS survey tracks spending habits of this age group. We've estimated the sales taxes for each income level in each city using the expenditures that we extrapolated from the BLS.

We've determined the amount due in state income tax from the rates provided to us by the individual states, taking into account appropriate exemptions, deductions and credits.

Some cities levy a local income tax, although the type of income subject to the tax differs. We have included local income taxes in our calculations.

We have calculated property taxes for six home values ranging from $75,000 to $350,000. For each income, we cite three home values. Since our detailed breakdowns include home value and income level, you can more closely identify your own tax burden. For instance, if you expect to earn about $50,000 a year in retirement, you can look up your estimated tax bill accord-ing to whether you will live in a home valued at $100,000, $150,000 or $200,000.

Don't plan on moving to a home valued at $100,000 or less in cities such as Los Angeles, San Diego, San Francisco, New York or Honolulu. Most homes at that price wouldn't be fit to live in. We've included these home values in our charts to be consistent, but we've also calculated taxes on homes valued at $400,000, $450,000 and $500,000 in order to give a more realistic view of what retirees might expect to pay there.

Personal property taxes are not uncommon, although most cities don't impose a personal property tax on individuals. Items that are taxed vary from city to city. In cities where there are personal property taxes on automobiles, we have calculated these taxes and they appear in the chart.

Finally, registering a vehicle is one cost relocators might overlook. We found that the fees can vary dramatically, so we've broken down automobile registration and renewal fees by gathering the information for two specific cars.

Top Retirement Towns

We recognize that tax considerations are but one of many factors influencing the choice of where to retire. So in this new edition, to help you with your relocation decision, we have included our exclusive list of the 99 best retirement towns in America. You can read more about our favorites under their appropriate state headings.

It's important to note that you'll find some towns that are tax-friendly and others that are not so friendly in our list of the 99 best. These are not Tax Heavens, they are our favorites from an overall quality-of-life standpoint. In the selection process, we visited hundreds of towns from coast to coast and interviewed retirees who had moved there, from out-of-state, at every stop. We collected data on cost of living, health care, crime rate, recreational and cultural opportunities, climate and more. We feel that these college towns, scenic havens, waterfront retreats, historic

Published by *Where to Retire* magazine and Vacation Publications, Inc., 1502 Augusta Drive – Suite 415, Houston, TX 77057, (713) 974-6903. Copyright© 2002 by Vacation Publications, Inc. All rights reserved. No part of this publication may be reproduced without the written consent of Vacation Publications, Inc.

A city's tax climate may not be uniformly favorable or unfavorable across all income levels. Billings, MT, for example, has higher-than-average total tax burdens for higher incomes and lower-than-average total tax burdens for lower incomes.

communities, mountain escapes and city settings offer the country's best retirement lifestyles.

Fact Finding

All of the tax rates, assessment rates, deductions, exemptions, rebates, credits and related facts and data included in this book were supplied to us by local and/or state tax authorities. The same authorities were asked in writing to review our calculations and verify them as correct, or make corrections and return them to us.

The great majority of these public officials were informed and willing to help. In a few cases, however, tax authorities at the local level refused to take or return our calls or respond to letters or faxes. Rather than drop these cities from the study, we have included the unverified rates and prepared our best estimate of the total tax burden.

It's important to note here that the data-gathering part of this study began in the summer of 2001 and continued into late fall of the same year. In fact, it took seven researchers more than five months to collect and verify the information contained in this report. We based our work on the tax year 2000, the latest year for which every state and municipality could supply complete information. Tax rates and qualifiers change frequently, and some of the data herein may already have changed. Nonetheless, this is our fourth study of tax burdens over the last ten years, and while there is fluctuation and a general tendency for rates to increase over time, rankings have remained remarkably consistent. Still, you should use our calculations as a rough guide only, and be sure to inquire about changes in tax rates or planned tax hikes before you relocate.

Many of the cities featured are loca-

tions favored for retirement, while others are urban areas from which large numbers of retirees migrate. Geographically, we cover at least one city from each state, plus Washington, DC.

Book Layout

Our book begins with a brief synopsis of the kinds of taxes you can expect to pay. Next, we've alphabetized our report by state and then by city within the state. The applicable taxes for each city are described in detail. Our comprehensive charts tally it all up and tell you where each city stands in our rankings.

At the end, you'll find our exclusive list of tax heavens and tax hells, plus nine separate rankings of all cities, one for each of our income/home value categories. A rank of #1 means that city has the lowest total tax burden of the 163 cities in the survey. The average total tax burden for each category is also shown.

As we neared completion of this project and our rankings began to take shape, we found more than a few surprises. Perhaps the most significant of these is the fact that a city's tax climate may not be uniformly favorable or unfavorable across all income levels. Billings, MT, for example, has higher-than-average total tax burdens for higher incomes and lower-than-average total tax burdens for lower incomes. Also, note that in some cities only the low-priced homes in each income category earn favorable rankings; in other cities, it may be mid-priced homes that net better rankings.

Perhaps the greatest paradox of all is the fact that some cities widely known for a high cost of living do not have high tax burdens. New York City, for example, has tax burdens that range from much-lower-than-average to about average, depending

on income and home value.

State Income Tax

Many retirees use the presence or absence of a state income tax as a litmus test for a retirement destination. This is a serious miscalculation, as higher sales and property taxes can offset the lack of a state income tax, particularly for retirees with little or no earned income. The lack of a state income tax doesn't necessarily ensure a low total tax burden.

Only a handful of states don't tax personal income. The others levy some sort of income tax, although the taxable income varies. One state may tax only interest and dividends, while another bases its income tax on adjusted gross income calculated for the federal tax return. Most states allow exemptions to reduce gross income. For instance, some states tax Social Security benefits subject to federal taxation, while other states allow your full monthly check to escape taxation.

Some states allow residents to exempt all or part of federal, state or private pensions, while others don't exclude any pension income from taxation.

Of course, tax rates vary from state to state. Some states have graduated rates; for instance, the first $20,000 in taxable income might be taxed at a rate of 5% while the next $5,000 would be taxed at a rate of 6%. Other states tax all income at the same flat rate.

Most states have standard deductions, although these deductions vary. Some are similar to deductions offered on the federal return, while other states offer additional deductions that may be based on age or income.

Most states offer income tax credits or rebates as well. The most common is credit for income taxes paid to other states. We've assumed our couples do not owe income taxes to any other

When inquiring about the presence of a local income tax, word your question to include any local tax, assessment or fee applied to any of your income. Some municipalities go to extremes to avoid calling their tax an income tax.

states. Other credits are often based on low income, for which our couples would not be eligible. In many states, there are a host of credits available that might apply to your situation. We do not attempt to list all of them.

If you're considering several states for retirement, contact state tax offices and request a tax form to determine the full tax bite in each state. Many state Web sites have general tax information, as well as forms, available online. In addition, the Web sites often contain links to city and county sites for additional information.

In order to calculate state and local income tax, it is necessary to make a large number of assumptions about our couples and the nature and source of their income. We will not list these assumptions here, due to space considerations, except for the following:

1) Our couples are age 65, file jointly and take standard deductions rather than itemizing. In some states and under certain circumstances, retirees might reduce their state income tax by filing separately or itemizing deductions.

2) We use three representative gross annual household income levels in our study — $25,000, $50,000 and $75,000. The components of these income totals are extrapolated from the BLS survey. In the survey, income consists of: Wages and salaries; self-employment income; Social Security, private and government retirement; interest, dividends, rental income and other property income; and other income.

3) We do not include the effect of the alternative minimum tax calculation in our analysis of income taxes due.

4) We assume that our couples are full-time residents of the state for which income tax is due.

Local Income Tax

Retirees who relocate to certain U.S. cities may be surprised to learn that they owe income taxes not only to the state but also to the local government. Cities call local income taxes by different names, such as wage taxes or occupational license fees. Just as their names are different, local income taxes are assessed in varying ways.

Some cities tax only earned income. Other cities impose taxes based on a percentage of the amount of state income tax due. Still others tax all income, offering exemptions and deductions like those at the state level.

When inquiring about the presence of a local income tax, word your question to include any local tax, assessment or fee applied to any of your income. Some municipalities go to extremes to avoid calling their tax an income tax.

We have used the same local income tax assumptions as were used in calculating state income tax.

Sales Tax

In all but a handful of states, residents pay some form of sales tax on their purchases. In a few states, a sales tax is replaced by a general excise tax or gross receipts tax on businesses. Since these taxes are also passed on to the consumer, we treat them herein as sales taxes.

Usually, a base sales tax rate is determined by the state. Often, local governments add to that base rate, sometimes significantly.

Our sales tax calculations are based on data extrapolated from the BLS survey, which estimates how much people age 65 and over spend each year on certain items at various income levels.

We estimate the sales tax burden in each city by applying local and state sales taxes to each of the following categories named in the BLS survey: Food at

home (groceries); food away from home; household operations and housekeeping supplies; household furnishings and equipment; apparel and services; transportation; medical services; drugs; medical supplies; entertainment; personal care products and services; and miscellaneous. The BLS survey does not list sales tax as a separate expenditure and, therefore, we have applied sales tax to each category if applicable. This has the effect of inflating sales taxes for all cities, but the methodology has been consistently applied and does not unfairly skew the rankings.

We assume that certain categories — shelter, health insurance, cash contributions and personal insurance and pensions — are universally exempt from sales tax.

We exclude sales tax on utilities from our calculations altogether because it is often difficult to distinguish the basic rate from fees and taxes. Frequently, there are markups in utility bills that we believe are hidden taxes. We recommend that retirees inquire about the typical utility bill for the typical home before relocating.

Generally, residents of a city pay the same sales tax rate on most purchases. However, it is common to find certain items taxed at a different rate. For instance, groceries or drugs may be taxed at a lower rate than clothing, or exempt altogether. Or, there may be an additional tax on food away from home. We've incorporated the applicable varying tax rates in our calculations if the items were included in the BLS survey as a separate category.

In most cases, if any items within a category are taxed, we assume that the whole category is taxed since the BLS survey does not break out all potential components of a category. For example, some cities exempt services from tax but do tax apparel. We assume the entire category of "apparel and ser-

The costs of registering a vehicle and annually renewing license plates are often overlooked by relocators, but these fees can add up (and do, in several states).

vices" is taxable. Therefore, we may overstate sales tax burdens in some cities, but this method is consistently applied to all cities.

The most common items exempt from sales tax are drugs, groceries and medical services.

Property Tax And Other Fees

Property taxes differ widely from state to state and between cities within the same state. Sometimes property taxes vary from neighborhood to neighborhood or even street to street within the same city.

Property taxes may consist of components from several different taxing entities, including the city, county, school district, fire district and others. Property tax rates change annually in many communities.

In most states the property tax is determined by multiplying a property tax rate by an assessed value. Assessment rates are decided either by the state or by local governments. Homes are assessed at such widely varying rates as 1% to 125% of market value, but a low assessment percentage does not translate into lower taxes, as the tax rate may be adjusted to make up the difference.

Some cities appraise property annually, but once every two, three or four years is more common. We assume that the appraised value equals the market value of the home.

In a few cases, municipalities tax homes and the land on which they are built at different rates. We have assumed that the home (or improvement) value is 80% and the land value is 20% of the total market value. Actual allocations will vary significantly depending on the location in question.

Many cities offer tax-saving breaks from the amount of property taxes due, often exempting a certain dollar amount from the home's assessed value. Other exemptions or deductions may be statewide and may be based on age or income. In cities where our couples qualified for these tax breaks, we have included them in our property tax calculations. Some homestead exemptions or credits require one or more years residency. We assume our couples meet these residency requirements, because we believe it is more useful to reflect ongoing, long-term tax burdens than those of year one.

In some cities, services such as garbage pickup, street maintenance and storm drain utility fees are included in your property tax bill. In other locations, residents pay these fees separately. To make our numbers comparable, we have added these additional fees where applicable, and they are included with the property tax amounts in our charts. Homeowner association fees can be significant and we have included them only if all residents of a city or town would be subject to such fees. We do not include fees to register or own pets.

Many cities have property tax deferral programs for seniors and some cities have implemented caps on allowable annual increases in appraised property values for residents. We have not included the effect of either of these programs in our calculations, but both warrant research for potential retirement destinations.

There are often property tax exemptions and deductions available to veterans, widows or people with disabilities that should also be investigated, if applicable.

It is necessary to make many assumptions about our couples and their age and income in order to complete property tax calculations. We will not list these assumptions here, except for the following:

1) We selected three home values for each of the income categories used in the income tax analysis. For income of $25,000, we looked at property tax burdens for homes valued at $75,000, $100,000 and $125,000. For income of $50,000, the home values we used were $100,000, $150,000 and $200,000. For income of $75,000, we figured property tax bills for home values of $150,000, $250,000 and $350,000.

2) We assumed a free-standing, site-built home and lot. The current national median home price is approximately $139,000. We selected a range of homes we believe reflect home-buying capabilities as determined by incomes shown above.

Auto Licensing Fees

The costs of registering a vehicle and annually renewing license plates are often overlooked by relocators, but these fees can add up (and do, in several states). So we contacted every city's department of motor vehicles and asked for all fees related to registration or renewal of an automobile.

In order to show the wide range of vehicle registration costs in different cities, we've given our couples two cars — a 1999 Ford Explorer and a 1999 Oldsmobile Cutlass. Their current market values — $16,950 for the Explorer and $11,875 for the Cutlass — were provided online from nadaguides.com and were taken from the Spring 2001 Retail Consumer and Industry editions of the N.A.D.A. Official Used Car Guides.

At the time of registration, relocators can expect to pay for a state title, which generally ranges from $5 to $50. Other common expenses are plate and inspection fees.

In many states, registration fees are based on the value of the car, but the method for determining value varies from state to state. Some states base their fees on the automobile's weight or model. You should know this specific information about your car before calling to find out registration fees in a particular city.

New residents may also face a tax on automobiles brought into the state. For instance, the Kentucky sales tax rate is 6%. Relocators to that state who paid a sales tax of 6% or greater on their vehicle in another state at the time of purchase are not subject to additional tax. However, people who paid a sales tax of less than 6% to another state are required to pay the difference on the current market value of the car to Kentucky, in the form of a usage tax. We've universally assumed that our couples do not owe additional tax, but we recommend a call to states being considered as potential retirement destinations to determine the impact of this tax, if any.

A few years ago, Florida abolished one very unpopular surprise for newcomers — a $295 impact fee per automobile brought into the state. However, there's still a one-time $100 fee paid by everyone registering a car in Florida. In Texas, a new resident is now assessed a $90 fee upon initial registration of a car in the state.

Annual license plate renewal fees also vary. In many states, the costs decrease as the car depreciates. Other states have a flat renewal fee, regardless of the type or year of the vehicle.

It's important to note here that even though we discuss initial registration fees in our text, our charts reflect the ongoing annual or annualized fees for the first year after registration.

Finally, in many cities, auto licensing fees resemble personal property taxes in size and method of calculation. In most cases, if the tax is verified and assessed by the department of motor vehicles, we discuss it with other auto registration-related taxes. Otherwise, you'll find it noted in the paragraph devoted to personal property taxes.

Personal Property Tax

In addition to a property tax, many local governments tax the personal property of individuals. Items that are taxed vary, even among cities within the same state. Items that are most often taxed are vehicles, including automobiles, boats, motorcycles and motor homes. Usually, but not always, the personal property tax rate in a city or area is the same as the property tax rate there, and items subject to the tax are usually assessed at the same rate as homes.

Many cities levy personal property tax only on mobile homes or mobile home attachments (carports, etc.). Mobile homes may be taxed as real property in some cities and taxed as personal property in other cities. We assume our couples do not own these items.

Intangibles Tax

An intangibles tax is a tax imposed on the value of investments that many retirees depend on for income. Because this tax was not well-known outside the handful of states that levied it, relocating retirees were often shocked to discover its existence after moving, when the first payment was due. That's particularly frustrating because some careful portfolio management might have reduced the tax, had they known about it in advance.

Over the past few years, intangibles taxes have been challenged and overturned by courts in some states, and simply phased out in others. At press time, Florida still imposed an intangibles tax on certain types of investments, and anyone considering Florida retirement is advised to contact the state tax office for details.

How To Use This Book

Unless you are personally involved in local or state taxation or have an academic interest in the national taxation picture, you probably won't read this book cover to cover. Instead, a good place to start is the table of contents, where you can identify cities of interest and find their location in the book.

For each city covered, we have described both the state and local tax picture as it relates to retirees. At the beginning of this description, we reveal any tax heavens, tax hells and top retirement towns in the state.

In a table below this summary, we estimate tax components and total tax burdens for nine different couples. Find the income and home value that most closely resembles your financial situation, and pay closest attention to the tax estimates for that category. At the far right of the table, you can see how this city ranks against all others in total tax burden placed on retirees. Ranking #1 is best (lowest tax burden), and #163 is worst (highest tax burden).

If you don't find a city you're interested in, see if we cover a nearby city of similar size. Usually, but not always, same-state cities of similar size will have similar tax burdens.

Perhaps you're undecided as to your ultimate retirement destination and want to get a quick glance at tax-friendly cities for retirees with your income and expected home value. You may wish to turn immediately to our list of tax heavens and hells on pages 168-169. Or, for an idea of how 163 cities match up for retirees in your income/home value category, turn to the rankings on pages 159-167.

Is your prospective retirement destination a tax heaven or a tax hell? Read on to find out.

ALABAMA

Tax Heavens ⭘	Tax Hells Ψ	Top Retirement Towns
Fairhope	None	Eufaula
		Fairhope

Alabama has a state income tax and a state sales tax.

The state income tax rate is graduated from 2% to 5% depending upon income bracket. For married couples filing jointly, the rate is 2% on the first $1,000 of taxable income; the rate is 4% on the next $5,000 of taxable income; and the rate is 5% on taxable income above $6,000.

In calculating the tax, there is a deduction from adjusted gross income for federal income tax paid. Federal and state pensions are exempt. Private pensions that qualify as a "defined benefit plan" are exempt. Social Security benefits are exempt. There is a $3,000 exemption from adjusted gross income for married couples filing jointly and a standard deduction of 20% of total adjusted gross income not to exceed $4,000 for married couples filing jointly.

Major tax credits or rebates include: Credit for income taxes paid to other states, employer-sponsored basic skills education credit, rural physician credit, coal credit and capital credit. Our couples do not qualify for these programs.

The state sales tax rate is 4%, but local governments can add to this amount.

Our couples relocating to the cities listed below must pay an ad valorem tax based on the year, make and model of each automobile. The tax is $110 for the Explorer and $88 for the Cutlass. Our couples also pay a tag fee of $24 to register each automobile and a title fee of $18 per automobile. Thereafter, on an annual basis, our

ALABAMA TAX TABLE

Instructions

1. Find the Income in the far left column closest to your anticipated retirement income.
2. Find the Home Value closest to the value of the home where you will live in retirement.
3. Follow that row to your estimated Total Tax Burden at age 65 and beyond.

Income	Home Value	Property Tax & Other Fees	Personal Property Tax & Auto Fees	Sales Tax	Local Income Tax	State Income Tax	Total Tax Burden	Rank* From #1-#163
EUFAULA								
$25,000	$75,000	$398	$247	$1,265	-	$373	$2,283	#105
	100,000	492	247	1,265	-	373	2,377	#70
	125,000	586	247	1,265	-	373	2,471	#53
$50,000	$100,000	$492	$247	$1,980	-	$1,174	$3,893	#118
	150,000	680	247	1,980	-	1,174	4,081	#58
	200,000	867	247	1,980	-	1,174	4,268	#37
$75,000	$150,000	$680	$247	$2,465	-	$2,039	$5,431	#75
	250,000	1,055	247	2,465	-	2,039	5,806	#32
	350,000	1,430	247	2,465	-	2,039	6,181	#15
FAIRHOPE								
$25,000	$75,000	$346	$247	$949	-	$373	$1,915	#46
	100,000	436	247	949	-	373	2,005	#27
	125,000	526	247	949	-	373	2,095	#17
$50,000	$100,000	$436	$247	$1,485	-	$1,174	$3,342	#61
	150,000	616	247	1,485	-	1,174	3,522	#29
	200,000	796	247	1,485	-	1,174	3,702	#13
$75,000	$150,000	$616	$247	$1,849	-	$2,039	$4,751	#51
	250,000	976	247	1,849	-	2,039	5,111	#15
	350,000	1,336	247	1,849	-	2,039	5,471	#7 ⭘

*There are 163 cities in this book. The city with the lowest tax burden for an income/home value combination is given the #1 rating; the city with the highest total tax burden is given the #163 rating.

couples will pay an ad valorem tax and a tag fee, per automobile.

Eufaula

Eufaula has no local income tax but does levy a sales tax.

Most purchases are taxed at a rate of 8%. Major consumer categories taxed at a different rate: None. Major consumer categories that are exempt from sales tax include: Drugs and medical services.

Within the city limits of Eufaula, the property tax rate is .044. Homes are assessed at 10% of market value. There are four categories of homestead exemptions available. Property tax does not cover garbage pickup; the additional fee is approximately $135 per year.

Eufaula has no personal property tax for individuals.

Fairhope

Fairhope has no local income tax but does levy a sales tax.

Most purchases are taxed at a rate of 6%. Major consumer categories taxed at a different rate: None. Major consumer categories that are exempt from sales tax include: Drugs and medical services.

Within the city limits of Fairhope, the property tax rate is .0425. Homes are assessed at 10% of market value. There are four categories of homestead exemptions available. Property tax does not cover garbage pickup; the additional fee is approximately $94 per year.

Fairhope has no personal property tax for individuals.

• Alabama's Best Retirement Towns •

Eufaula, Alabama

Eufaula is situated in one of those "you can't get there from here" spots on the Alabama-Georgia border, relatively undiscovered until recent years when the chamber of commerce began publicizing the area's many attractions for retirees. These include the small, bustling antebellum town, with more than 700 buildings on the National Register of Historic Places, and 45,000-acre Lake Eufaula, which offers excellent bass fishing.

Gerald and Patty Creech had lived in Newport Beach, CA, and Denver, CO, and were looking at potential retirement places when they read about Eufaula in Where to Retire magazine.

"I had always loved meeting Southerners and enjoyed traveling in the South," Patty says. "Eufaula is a pretty little town, and if you just drive through it you might wonder why anyone would want to live here. We found it filled with fascinating, well-traveled, cosmopolitan people. You can live in old historic homes, modern residential subdivisions or on the lakefront. It's just a wonderful place. Now when we travel out to California or Colorado, I can't wait to get back home."

Population: 17,000 in city, 26,000 in county.

Climate:

	High	Low
January	57	32
July	91	68

Cost of living: Below average (specific index not available).

Average price of a new home: $122,000

Security: 46.6 crimes per 1,000 residents, higher than the national average of 42.7 crimes per 1,000 residents.

Information: Eufaula/Barbour County Chamber of Commerce, P.O. Box 697, Eufaula, AL 36072-0697, (800) 524-7529 or www.zebra.net/~ebcc.

Fairhope, Alabama

About a 30-minute drive from the hustle and bustle of Mobile, this quiet, pretty town on the eastern shore of Mobile Bay is light years away in terms of traffic, congestion, pollution and crime. Centrally situated among the small bayside communities of Daphne, Montrose and Point Clear, it is the focal point for cultural activities, dining and shopping. There is talk of an enclosed mall coming to the area, but there is no hard-and-fast commitment at this time.

Ric and Kay Lahti settled in the area after retirement and immediately became involved in property-owner activities in their residential subdivision, Lake Forest, and local civic affairs.

"We are delighted to be here. By planning in a responsible way, they're developing a wonderful place for people to live," Kay says of the community, adding that it is a "place where our grandchildren can visit and enjoy a slower, safer lifestyle missing in most communities today."

She cites gorgeous vegetation and great location as examples of its exceptional qualities. And with interstates 10 and 65 just minutes away, it's a great starting point for travel north, east or west. "But you don't have to travel the interstates to stay busy," Kay says. "We're a community on the move."

Population: 10,481 in city, 136,000 in county.

Climate:

	High	Low
January	59	39
July	90	72

Cost of living: Below average (specific index not available).

Average price of a new home: $195,000

Security: 47.2 crimes per 1,000 residents, higher than the national average of 42.7 crimes per 1,000 residents.

Information: Eastern Shore Chamber of Commerce, 327 Fairhope Ave., Fairhope, AL 36532, (334) 928-6387 or www.es chamber.com.

ALASKA

Tax Heavens O
Anchorage

Tax Hells Ψ
None

Top Retirement Towns
None

Alaska has no state income tax and no state sales tax.

Major tax credits or rebates include: Property tax exemption for persons age 65 and older. Our couples qualify for this program.

Since car registration and renewal fees differ within the state, see city information for details.

Anchorage

Anchorage has no local income tax and no sales tax.

Within the city limits of Anchorage, the property tax rate is .01774. Homes are assessed at 100% of market value. Homeowners age 65 and older are exempt from property taxes on up to $150,000 of home value. Property tax does not cover garbage pickup; the additional fee is approximately $180 per year.

Anchorage has a personal property tax rate of .01774. Items subject to the tax include mobile homes. The senior property tax exemption applies to mobile homes. We've assumed our couples do not own any of the items subject to personal property tax.

Our couples relocating to Anchorage pay $5 per automobile for an Alaska title, a $5 lien recording fee per automobile, and a $2 emissions fee per automobile at the time of registration. Persons over 65 are exempt from other registration fees and taxes; in order for both automobiles to qualify for the exemption, one must be titled to the wife and the other to the husband, and the couple must prove Alaska residence. Thereafter, as long as the senior exemption applies to both automobiles, our couples will pay a $2 emissions fee per automobile.

ALASKA TAX TABLE

Instructions

1. Find the Income in the far left column closest to your anticipated retirement income.
2. Find the Home Value closest to the value of the home where you will live in retirement.
3. Follow that row to your estimated Total Tax Burden at age 65 and beyond.

Income	Home Value	Property Tax & Other Fees	Personal Property Tax & Auto Fees	Sales Tax	Local Income Tax	State Income Tax	Total Tax Burden	Rank* From #1-#163
ANCHORAGE								
$25,000	$75,000	$180	$4	-	-	-	$184	#1 O
	100,000	180	4	-	-	-	184	#1 O
	125,000	180	4	-	-	-	184	#1 O
$50,000	$100,000	$180	$4	-	-	-	$184	#1 O
	150,000	180	4	-	-	-	184	#1 O
	200,000	1,067	4	-	-	-	1,071	#1 O
$75,000	$150,000	$180	$4	-	-	-	$184	#1 O
	250,000	1,954	4	-	-	-	1,958	#1 O
	350,000	3,728	4	-	-	-	3,732	#1 O

*There are 163 cities in this book. The city with the lowest tax burden for an income/home value combination is given the #1 rating; the city with the highest total tax burden is given the #163 rating.

ARIZONA

Tax Heavens ○	Tax Hells Ψ	Top Retirement Towns
None	None	Flagstaff
		Green Valley
		Prescott
		Scottsdale
		Sierra Vista
		Tucson

Arizona has a state income tax and a state sales tax.

The state income tax rate is graduated from 2.87% to 5.04% depending upon income bracket. For married couples filing jointly, the rate is 2.87% on the first $20,000 of taxable income; the rate is 3.2% on the next $30,000 of taxable income; the rate is 3.74% on the next $50,000 of taxable income; the rate is 4.72% on the next $200,000 of taxable income; and the rate is 5.04% on taxable income above $300,000.

In calculating the tax, there is no deduction for federal income tax paid. Federal, state and local pensions are exempt up to $2,500. Private pensions are not exempt. Social Security benefits are exempt. There is a $7,200 standard deduction from Arizona adjusted gross income for married couples filing jointly. There is an additional $4,200 exemption from Arizona adjusted gross income for married couples filing jointly. There is a $2,100 exemption from Arizona adjusted gross income for each person age 65 or older.

Major tax credits or rebates include: Credit for income taxes paid to other states, family income tax credit and property tax credit. Our couples do not qualify for these programs.

The state sales tax rate is 5%, but local governments can add to this rate.

Our couples relocating to the cities listed below must pay a vehicle license tax based on year and MSRP of each automobile at the time of registration. The tax is $422 for the Explorer and $350 for the Cutlass. Our couples also pay a registration fee of $8 per automobile, a title fee of $4 per automobile and an air quality fee of $2 per automobile. In Phoenix, there is an additional $25 emissions test per automobile, and in Tucson, there is an additional $10 emissions test per automobile. Thereafter, on an annual basis, our couples will pay a vehicle license tax, registration fee and air quality fee, per automobile. Phoenix requires the

ARIZONA TAX TABLE

Instructions

1. Find the Income in the far left column closest to your anticipated retirement income.
2. Find the Home Value closest to the value of the home where you will live in retirement.
3. Follow that row to your estimated Total Tax Burden at age 65 and beyond.

Income	Home Value	Property Tax & Other Fees	Personal Property Tax & Auto Fees	Sales Tax	Local Income Tax	State Income Tax	Total Tax Burden	Rank* From #1- #163
FLAGSTAFF								
$25,000	$75,000	$765	$505	$991	-	-	$2,261	#104
	100,000	976	505	991	-	-	2,472	#80
	125,000	1,186	505	991	-	-	2,682	#68
$50,000	$100,000	$976	$505	$1,608	-	$587	$3,676	#96
	150,000	1,396	505	1,608	-	587	4,096	#60
	200,000	1,817	505	1,608	-	587	4,517	#49
$75,000	$150,000	$1,396	$505	$2,037	-	$1,339	$5,277	#66
	250,000	2,238	505	2,037	-	1,339	6,119	#41
	350,000	3,079	505	2,037	-	1,339	6,960	#34
GREEN VALLEY								
$25,000	$75,000	$830	$505	$658	-	-	$1,993	#59
	100,000	1,050	505	658	-	-	2,213	#51
	125,000	1,270	505	658	-	-	2,433	#48

Income	Home Value	Property Tax & Other Fees	Personal Property Tax & Auto Fees	Sales Tax	Local Income Tax	State Income Tax	Total Tax Burden	Rank* From #1- #163
GREEN VALLEY continued								
$50,000	$100,000	$1,050	$505	$1,066	-	$587	$3,208	#47
	150,000	1,490	505	1,066	-	587	3,648	#35
	200,000	1,930	505	1,066	-	587	4,088	#31
$75,000	$150,000	$1,490	$505	$1,354	-	$1,339	$4,688	#46
	250,000	2,370	505	1,354	-	1,339	5,568	#25
	350,000	3,250	505	1,354	-	1,339	6,448	#21
PHOENIX								
$25,000	$75,000	$1,055	$530	$987	-	-	$2,572	#138
	100,000	1,336	530	987	-	-	2,853	#125
	125,000	1,617	530	987	-	-	3,134	#105
$50,000	$100,000	$1,336	$530	$1,599	-	$587	$4,052	#122
	150,000	1,897	530	1,599	-	587	4,613	#107
	200,000	2,459	530	1,599	-	587	5,175	#91
$75,000	$150,000	$1,897	$530	$2,030	-	$1,339	$5,796	#90
	250,000	3,021	530	2,030	-	1,339	6,920	#72
	350,000	4,145	530	2,030	-	1,339	8,044	#54
PRESCOTT								
$25,000	$75,000	$746	$505	$1,065	-	-	$2,316	#114
	100,000	945	505	1,065	-	-	2,515	#84
	125,000	1,144	505	1,065	-	-	2,714	#72
$50,000	$100,000	$945	$505	$1,710	-	$587	$3,747	#105
	150,000	1,343	505	1,710	-	587	4,145	#68
	200,000	1,740	505	1,710	-	587	4,542	#53
$75,000	$150,000	$1,343	$505	$2,159	-	$1,339	$5,346	#71
	250,000	2,138	505	2,159	-	1,339	6,141	#42
	350,000	2,933	505	2,159	-	1,339	6,936	#32
SCOTTSDALE								
$25,000	$75,000	$821	$505	$970	-	-	$2,296	#109
	100,000	1,038	505	970	-	-	2,513	#82
	125,000	1,256	505	970	-	-	2,731	#73
$50,000	$100,000	$1,038	$505	$1,562	-	$587	$3,692	#99
	150,000	1,473	505	1,562	-	587	4,127	#65
	200,000	1,908	505	1,562	-	587	4,562	#54
$75,000	$150,000	$1,473	$505	$1,974	-	$1,339	$5,291	#67
	250,000	2,343	505	1,974	-	1,339	6,161	#43
	350,000	3,213	505	1,974	-	1,339	7,031	#37
SIERRA VISTA								
$25,000	$75,000	$851	$505	$985	-	-	$2,341	#119
	100,000	1,092	505	985	-	-	2,582	#94
	125,000	1,334	505	985	-	-	2,824	#82
$50,000	$100,000	$1,092	$505	$1,569	-	$587	$3,753	#106
	150,000	1,576	505	1,569	-	587	4,237	#79
	200,000	2,059	505	1,569	-	587	4,720	#61
$75,000	$150,000	$1,576	$505	$1,981	-	$1,339	$5,401	#74
	250,000	2,542	505	1,981	-	1,339	6,367	#48
	350,000	3,508	505	1,981	-	1,339	7,333	#42

*There are 163 cities in this book. The city with the lowest tax burden for an income/home value combination is given the #1 rating; the city with the highest total tax burden is given the #163 rating.

ARIZONA TAX TABLE

Instructions

1. Find the Income in the far left column closest to your anticipated retirement income.
2. Find the Home Value closest to the value of the home where you will live in retirement.
3. Follow that row to your estimated Total Tax Burden at age 65 and beyond.

Income	Home Value	Property Tax & Other Fees	Personal Property Tax & Auto Fees	Sales Tax	Local Income Tax	State Income Tax	Total Tax Burden	Rank* From #1 - #163
TUCSON								
$25,000	$75,000	$929	$525	$922	-	-	$2,376	#123
	100,000	1,239	525	922	-	-	2,686	#106
	125,000	1,549	525	922	-	-	2,996	#93
$50,000	$100,000	$1,239	$525	$1,492	-	$587	$3,843	#113
	150,000	1,858	525	1,492	-	587	4,462	#100
	200,000	2,478	525	1,492	-	587	5,082	#86
$75,000	$150,000	$1,858	$525	$1,895	-	$1,339	$5,617	#83
	250,000	3,097	525	1,895	-	1,339	6,856	#68
	350,000	4,336	525	1,895	-	1,339	8,095	#60

*There are 163 cities in this book. The city with the lowest tax burden for an income/home value combination is given the #1 rating; the city with the highest total tax burden is given the #163 rating.

emissions test every other year and Tucson requires the emissions test every year.

Flagstaff

Flagstaff has no local income tax but does levy a sales tax.

Most purchases are taxed at a rate of 7.31%. Major consumer categories taxed at a different rate include: Food away from home, which is taxed at a rate of 9.31%. Major consumer categories that are exempt from sales tax include: Groceries, drugs and medical services.

Within the city limits of Flagstaff, the property tax rate is .084151 including the state aid to education deduction for all homeowners. Homes are assessed at 10% of market value. Property tax does not cover garbage pickup; the additional fee is approximately $134 per year.

Flagstaff has a personal property tax rate of .084151. Personal property is assessed at 10% of MSRP. Items subject to the tax include mobile homes. We've assumed our couples do not own any of the items subject to personal property tax.

Green Valley

Green Valley has no local income tax and does not levy an additional sales tax.

Most purchases are taxed at the state rate of 5%. Major consumer categories taxed at a different rate: None. Major consumer categories that are exempt from sales tax include: Groceries, drugs and medical services.

The property tax rate varies widely within Green Valley, but actual taxes paid are generally around a rate of .11 including the state aid to education deduction for all homeowners. Homes are valued at approximately 80% of market value and then assessed at 10% of that value. There is an exemption of up to $2,500 off the assessed value of the property if Arizona adjusted gross income is less than $10,000. Property tax does not cover garbage pickup; the additional fee is approximately $170 per year.

Personal property taxes are paid in Green Valley at a rate of about .11. Personal property is assessed at 10% of MSRP. Items subject to the tax include mobile homes. We've assumed our couples do not own any of the items subject to personal property tax.

Phoenix

Phoenix has no local income tax but does levy a sales tax.

Most purchases are taxed at a rate of 7.5%. Major consumer categories taxed at a different rate: None. Major consumer categories that are exempt from sales tax include: Groceries, drugs and medical services.

In the Paradise Valley Unified School District area of Phoenix, the property tax rate is .112365 including the state aid to education deduction for all homeowners. Homes are assessed at 10% of market value. Property tax does not cover garbage pickup; the additional fee is approximately $212 per year.

In the Paradise Valley Unified School District area, there is a personal property tax rate of .112365. Personal property is assessed at 10% of MSRP. Items subject to the tax include mobile homes. We've assumed our couples do not own any of the items subject to personal property tax.

Prescott

Prescott has no local income tax but does levy a sales tax.

Most purchases are taxed at a rate of 7.7%. Major consumer categories taxed at a different rate include: Groceries, which are taxed at a rate of 2%. Major consumer categories that are exempt from sales tax include: Drugs and medical services.

In tax district 0120, the main tax district in Prescott, the property tax rate is

.079517 including the state aid to education deduction for all homeowners. Homes are assessed at 10% of market value. Property tax does not cover garbage pickup; the additional fee is approximately $150 per year.

In tax district 0120, there is a personal property tax rate of .079517. Personal property is assessed at 10% of MSRP. Items subject to the tax include mobile homes. We've assumed our couples do not own any of the items subject to personal property tax.

Scottsdale

Scottsdale has no local income tax but does levy a sales tax.

Most purchases are taxed at a rate of 7.1%. Major consumer categories taxed at a different rate include: Groceries, which are taxed at a rate of 1.4%. Major consumer categories that are exempt from sales tax include: Drugs and medical services.

Within the city limits of Scottsdale in the Scottsdale school district, the property tax rate is .087007 including the state aid to education deduction for all homeowners. Homes are assessed at 10% of market value. Property tax does not cover garbage pickup; the additional fee is approximately $168 per year.

Within Scottsdale city limits in the Scottsdale school district, there is a personal property tax rate of .087007. Personal property is assessed at 10% of MSRP. Items subject to the tax include mobile homes. We've assumed our couples do not own any of the items subject to personal property tax.

Sierra Vista

Sierra Vista has no local income tax but does levy a sales tax.

Most purchases are taxed at a rate of 7%. Major consumer categories taxed at a different rate include: Groceries, drugs and medical services, which are taxed at a rate of 1.5%. Major consumer categories that are exempt from sales tax: None.

Within the city limits of Sierra Vista, the average property tax rate is .1208 including the state aid to education deduction for all homeowners. Homes are valued at approximately 80% of market value and then assessed at 10% of that value. Property tax does not cover garbage pickup; the additional fee is approximately $126 if paid in advance.

Within the city limits of Sierra Vista, there is a personal property tax rate of .1208. Personal property is assessed based on MSRP and a depreciation schedule. Items subject to the tax include mobile homes. We've assumed our couples do not own any of the items subject to personal property tax.

Tucson

Tucson has no local income tax but does levy a sales tax.

Most purchases are taxed at the state rate of 7%. Major consumer categories taxed at a different rate: None. Major consumer categories that are exempt from sales tax include: Groceries, drugs and medical services.

In tax rate area 0150 of Tucson, the property tax rate is .154857 including the state aid to education deduction for all homeowners. Homes are valued at approximately 80% of market value and then assessed at 10% of that value. There is an exemption of up to $2,500 off the assessed value of the property if Arizona adjusted gross income is less than $10,000. Property tax includes garbage pickup.

Tax rate area 0150 of Tucson has a personal property tax rate of .154857. Personal property is assessed at 10% of MSRP. Items subject to the tax include mobile homes. We've assumed our couples do not own any of the items subject to personal property tax.

• Arizona's Best Retirement Towns •

Flagstaff, Arizona

At 7,000 feet, Flagstaff is one of the highest cities in the country, and many of those who live here think it's also one of the prettiest. "We love to be able to get up in the morning, look at the mountain, and plan our schedule for the day," says Sue Szego (pronounced Zay-go), who with husband Ron retired to Flagstaff from Dallas in 1999. "It is a rare day when we can't do some outdoor activity," she says.

Flagstaff is ideally situated in the midst of several national forests. It is protected from frigid breezes during the winter months by 12,643-foot San Francisco Mountain, which looms on the northern horizon.

Northern Arizona University keeps Flagstaff young and lively. A restored historic downtown and burgeoning residential construction keep the economy healthy.

"We lived all over the country while working for the federal government and came up to Flagstaff every year to hike and ski," Sue says. "When it came time to pick a place to retire, it had to be Flagstaff. We love the mountains, forests and four-season climate. In winter, temperatures are low but there's no humidity, so you don't feel the cold. We don't even have air conditioning. There's no need for it.

"It has a small-town atmosphere, enhanced by Amtrak running right through the center of town. It is absolutely beautiful. I highly recommend it to anyone looking for a place to retire," she adds.

Population: 60,880 in city, 121,625 in county.

Climate:

	High	Low
January	42	15
July	81	50

Cost of living: 107, based on national average of 100.

Average price of a new home: $205,000

Security: 79.1 crimes per 1,000 residents, higher than the national average of 42.7 crimes per 1,000 residents.

Information: Flagstaff Chamber of Commerce, 101 W. Route 66, Flagstaff, AZ 86001, (520) 774-4505 or www.flagstaffchamber.com.

Green Valley, Arizona

Located about midway between the plentiful shopping and dining of Tucson and the galleries and art studios of Tubac, this appropriately named oasis in Arizona's Sonoran high desert has come a long way in some 35 years.

Green Valley was founded as a winter retreat for upper Midwesterners seeking relief from months of cold, icy conditions, but its moderate year-round climate soon began attracting full-time residents. Today, many of its 26,400 inhabitants, mostly retirees, spend their days golfing, hiking and bird-watching. In the evening, they look to the skies for spectacular astronomical displays.

Skip and Dee Gard moved from Genoa, OH, choosing Green Valley over Florida "because of the four-season climate," Skip says. "About 95 percent of the time we have sunshine."

Dee, whose hobbies include tennis, billiards, golf, hiking, square dancing and pinochle, says she never dreamed she would be so active. "I don't have enough time to do all of the things I want to do," she laments. "If you're bored in Green Valley, it's your own fault," Skip says.

Population: 26,400 in city, 835,000 in county.

Climate:

	High	Low
January	65	37
July	98	71

Cost of living: Below average (specific index not available).

Average price of a new home: $135,000

Security: 68.2 crimes per 1,000 residents in Pima County, higher than the national average of 42.7 crimes per 1,000 residents. Specific crime rate not available for Green Valley.

Information: Green Valley Chamber of Commerce, 270 W. Continental Road, Green Valley, AZ 85614, (520) 625-7575 or www.greenvalleyazchamber.com.

Prescott, Arizona

Arizona's mile-high city is located in the center of the state in one of the largest stands of Ponderosa pine in the world. Clean air, a mild four-season climate and near-perfect weather invite outdoor activities, with lakes, hiking trails and equestrian events — the latter a carry-over from the days of the Wild West, when Prescott was a rip-roaring town in the Arizona Territory.

In the last 100 years it has toned down its act, and today its cultural side prevails, as evidenced by Prescott

College, a 110,000-volume public library and an excellent performance hall at Yavapai Community College that attracts symphonies, theater groups and ballet troupes.

Alice O'Brien moved here from Fullerton, CA, "due to its climate, its small-town atmosphere and an enhanced quality of life," she says. "We have been here about five years, and it is really growing, with new golf courses, a mall under construction and more. There's lots of arts and crafts — and theater. We love it."

Population: 37,500 in city, 166,000 in county.

Climate:

	High	Low
January	50	22
July	84	58

Cost of living: 112, based on national average of 100.

Average price of a new home: $247,563

Security: 50.8 crimes per 1,000 residents, higher than the national average of 42.7 crimes per 1,000 residents.

Information: Prescott Chamber of Commerce, 101 S. Cortez, P.O. Box 1147, Prescott, AZ 86302, (928) 778-2193 or www.prescott.org.

Scottsdale, Arizona

When Clark and Sylvia Watkin bought a retirement home "out in the northern fringe of the city" several years ago, "we had coyotes, roadrunners and jack rabbits in our back yard," Clark says. "Today, it is almost in the center city, geographically."

Though population growth and urban sprawl have forever changed this once-peaceful Western desert town, the underlying characteristics that precipitated this growth remain intact: climate, desert and mountains.

These natural amenities, and the opportunity to explore the cultural heritage of the Southwest, drew Sid and Rosemary Bishop from their long-time Edmonds, WA, home. With some 300 sunny days each year, and endless avenues to explore, "including the entire states of Arizona and New Mexico, we have more time and opportunity to enjoy outdoor activities and a less-formal social life," Rosemary says.

Is she glad she made the move? "I

love Scottsdale so much — there is no place I would rather be," she says.

Population: 208,000 in city, 2,696,198 in county.

Climate:

	High	Low
January	65	39
July	105	80

Cost of living: 118, based on national average of 100.

Average price of a new home: $249,000

Security: 42.9 crimes per 1,000 residents, near the national average of 42.7 crimes per 1,000 residents.

Information: Scottsdale Chamber of Commerce, 7343 Scottsdale Mall, Scottsdale, AZ 85251, (480) 945-8481 or www.scottsdalechamber.com.

Sierra Vista, Arizona

Sierra Vista was first settled in the 1950s to provide off-base housing for military personnel stationed at nearby Fort Huachuca. Soon the scenic beauty of the area, its wildlife and bird populations, moderate climate and inexpensive land costs began attracting retiring servicemen, Nature Conservancy devotees and seniors fleeing hostile Northern winter weather.

It can get warm in southern Arizona, but at an elevation of 4,600 feet, this small, pretty oasis in the desert has summertime temperatures that are 8 to 10 degrees cooler than Tucson and a temperate year-round climate with just a dusting of wintertime snow.

John and Millie Tripp came all the way from Herkimer, NY, "for health reasons, a slower pace of living, lower taxes and a warm and friendly people," Millie says. "We found all of that and a lot more. We joined a walking club, the Pacesetters, and now our blood pressures are much lower than before."

"People think of Arizona as desert, but I haven't been anywhere in the state that there aren't mountains," John says. "We visited once, came back five months later and bought a house. Seeing is believing."

Population: 39,995 in city, 123,750 in county.

Climate:

	High	Low
January	58	34
July	89	66

Cost of living: 95, based on national

average of 100.

Average price of a new home: $139,000

Security: 35.7 crimes per 1,000 residents, lower than the national average of 42.7 crimes per 1,000 residents.

Information: Sierra Vista Chamber of Commerce, 21 E. Wilcox Dr., Sierra Vista, AZ 85635, (520) 458-6940 or www.sierra vistachamber.org.

Tucson, Arizona

Tucson still displays vestiges of the days of cowboys and Indians, but it has become a major metropolitan city "not lacking for things to do and enjoy," says Edie Harvey. Edie and her husband, Roger, moved here from Reno, NV, after spending vacations in the area over the years.

As for the desert climate, Edie says, "in this day of air-conditioned cars, homes and public buildings, temperature is not a problem. We play golf and attend to outside activities in early morning and do our inside chores in midday. Summers are livable, and evenings cool off. We only run our air conditioner from about 2 to 10 p.m."

The Harveys, who live in the Sun City Vistoso development of 2,500 homes, "once saw a bobcat come up and look in our front door and a gray fox walking up our sidewalk, and we still hear coyotes howling in the night," Edie says. Still, she advises those considering retirement to spend time here in both summer and winter. "The desert is not for everyone. You like it or you don't," she says.

Population: 475,000 in city, 835,000 in county.

Climate:

	High	Low
January	64	39
July	100	68

Cost of living: 100, based on national average of 100.

Average price of a new home: $159,000

Security: 89.9 crimes per 1,000 residents, higher than the national average of 42.7 crimes per 1,000 residents.

Information: Tucson Metropolitan Chamber of Commerce, 465 W. St. Mary's Road, Tucson, AZ 85701, (520) 792-1212 or www.tucsonchamber.org.

ARKANSAS

Tax Heavens ○
None

Tax Hells ψ
None

Top Retirement Towns
Hot Springs

Arkansas has a state income tax and a state sales tax.

The state income tax rate is graduated from 1% to 7% depending upon income bracket. For married couples filing jointly, the rate is 1% on the first $3,099 of taxable income; the rate is 2.5% on the next $3,100 of taxable income; the rate is 3.5% on the next $3,100 of taxable income; the rate is 4.5% on the next $6,200 of taxable income; the rate is 6% on the next $10,400 of taxable income; and the rate is 7% on taxable income above $25,899.

In calculating the tax, there is no deduction for federal income tax paid. Federal, state and private pensions are not exempt. However, up to $6,000 of pension income is exempt per person. Social Security benefits are exempt. There is a standard deduction of $4,000 from Arkansas adjusted gross income for married couples filing jointly. There is a $40 credit against tax for married couples filing jointly and a $20 credit against tax per person age 65 or older.

Major tax credits or rebates include: Credit for income taxes paid to other states and a special credit for persons age 65 or older who don't claim the $6,000 per year pension exemption. Our couples do not qualify for these programs.

The state sales tax rate is 4.625%, but local governments can add to this amount.

Our couples relocating to the cities listed below must pay a registration fee of $25 per automobile, a title fee of $5 per automobile and miscellaneous fees of $3 per automobile at the time of registration. Thereafter, on an annual basis, our couples will pay a registration fee and miscella-

ARKANSAS TAX TABLE

Instructions

1. Find the Income in the far left column closest to your anticipated retirement income.
2. Find the Home Value closest to the value of the home where you will live in retirement.
3. Follow that row to your estimated Total Tax Burden at age 65 and beyond.

Income	Home Value	Property Tax & Other Fees	Personal Property Tax & Auto Fees	Sales Tax	Local Income Tax	State Income Tax	Total Tax Burden	Rank* From #1-#163
HOT SPRINGS								
$25,000	$75,000	$426	$296	$1,173	-	$2	$1,897	#39
	100,000	634	296	1,173	-	2	2,105	#41
	125,000	842	296	1,173	-	2	2,313	#36
$50,000	$100,000	$634	$296	$1,837	-	$1,058	$3,825	#112
	150,000	1,050	296	1,837	-	1,058	4,241	#80
	200,000	1,466	296	1,837	-	1,058	4,657	#57
$75,000	$150,000	$1,050	$296	$2,282	-	$2,717	$6,345	#109
	250,000	1,882	296	2,282	-	2,717	7,177	#84
	350,000	2,714	296	2,282	-	2,717	8,009	#53
LITTLE ROCK								
$25,000	$75,000	$1,216	$448	$999	-	$2	$2,665	#144
	100,000	1,556	448	999	-	2	3,005	#140
	125,000	1,896	448	999	-	2	3,345	#131
$50,000	$100,000	$1,556	$448	$1,565	-	$1,058	$4,627	#143
	150,000	2,236	448	1,565	-	1,058	5,307	#138
	200,000	2,916	448	1,565	-	1,058	5,987	#126
$75,000	$150,000	$2,236	$448	$1,945	-	$2,717	$7,346	#142
	250,000	3,596	448	1,945	-	2,717	8,706	#135
	350,000	4,956	448	1,945	-	2,717	10,066	#124

*There are 163 cities in this book. The city with the lowest tax burden for an income/home value combination is given the #1 rating; the city with the highest total tax burden is given the #163 rating.

neous fees, per automobile.

Hot Springs

Hot Springs has no local income tax but does levy a sales tax.

Most purchases are taxed at a rate of 7.125%. Major consumer categories taxed at a different rate include: Food away from home, which is taxed at a rate of 10.125%. Major consumer categories that are exempt from sales tax include: Drugs and medical services.

In the Hot Springs School District, the property tax rate is .0416. Homes are assessed at approximately 20% of market value. There is a homestead deduction of $300 off property taxes for homeowners age 65 and over. Property tax does not cover garbage pickup; the additional fee is approximately $102 per year.

In the Hot Springs School District, the personal property tax rate is .0416. Personal property is assessed at 20% of market value. Items subject to the tax include automobiles, boats and RVs.

Little Rock

Little Rock has no local income tax but does levy a sales tax.

Most purchases are taxed at a rate of 6.125%. Major consumer categories taxed at a different rate include: Food away from home, which is taxed at a rate of 8.125%. Major consumer categories that are exempt from sales tax include: Drugs and medical services.

Within the city limits of Little Rock, the property tax rate is .068. Homes are assessed at 20% of market value. Property tax does not cover garbage pickup; the additional fee is approximately $196 per year.

Within the city limits of Little Rock, the personal property tax rate is .068. Personal property is assessed at 20% of market value. Items subject to the tax include automobiles, boats, RVs, motorcycles, all-terrain vehicles and livestock.

• Arkansas' Best Retirement Town •

Hot Springs, Arkansas

Talk of Hot Springs inevitably comes around to Bathhouse Row, the early 20th-century visitor enticement that put the town on the map. But while Bathhouse Row still brings tourists to the community, there are far more important qualities attracting a growing retiree population.

Excellent weather, mountains, lakes, hills and heavily forested terrain are an ideal combination for an outdoor lifestyle, according to Fred and Betty Sims, who moved here from Baton Rouge, LA. Fishing, boating and game hunting keep Fred busy when he isn't working part time at the local horse race track.

"Its size is just about right," says Fred of the town. "Things are building up — but that's good. Hot Springs is different, pleasant. You never get tired of it. There's a lot going on, and you can run up to Little Rock in about an hour if you can't find what you want in Hot Springs."

Another important factor is a low cost of living. "You can save money living here," Fred says. "You can still buy a nice 2,000-square-foot house here for $125,000. Let's see you try that in New Jersey."

Population: 37,500 in city, 86,000 in county.

Climate:

	High	Low
January	50	29
July	89	70

Cost of living: 96, based on national average of 100.

Average price of a new home: $145,000

Security: 94.8 crimes per 1,000 residents, higher than the national average of 42.7 crimes per 1,000 residents.

Information: Greater Hot Springs Chamber of Commerce, P.O. Box 6090, Hot Springs, AR 72902, (800) 467-INFO or http://hotsprings.dina.org.

CALIFORNIA

Tax Heavens O
None

Tax Hells Ψ
None

Top Retirement Towns
Carlsbad
Ojai
Palm Desert
San Juan Capistrano
Temecula

California has a state income tax and a state sales tax.

The state income tax is graduated from 1% to 9.3% depending upon income bracket. For married couples filing jointly, the rate is 1% on the first $10,918 of taxable income; the rate is 2% on the next $14,960 of taxable income; the rate is 4% on the next $14,964 of taxable income; the rate is 6% on the next $15,854 of taxable income; the rate is 8% on the next $14,956 of taxable income; and the rate is 9.3% on taxable income above $71,652.

In calculating the tax, there is no deduction for federal income tax paid.

Federal, state and private pensions are not exempt. Social Security benefits are exempt. There is a $5,622 standard deduction from California adjusted gross income for married couples filing jointly. There is a $150 credit against tax for married couples filing jointly and a $150 credit per person for persons age 65 and older.

Major tax credits or rebates include: Homeowner property tax assistance, which one of our couples qualifies for.

The state sales tax rate is 7.25%, but local governments can add to this rate.

Our couples relocating to the cities listed below must pay a vehicle license fee per automobile of 2% of the vehicle's depreciated value, less a 35% rebate. The license fee is approximately $256 for the Explorer and $213 for the Cutlass. Our couples must also pay a registration fee of $30 per automobile, county fees of approximately $8 per automobile, a non-resident fee of $10 per automobile and a license plate fee of $1 per automobile. Before registration, both automobiles must undergo smog inspection for a fee of approximately $50. Thereafter, on an annual basis, our couples will pay a vehicle license fee with a 67.5% rebate and a $38 renewal fee. Smog inspection is required every other year in some cities.

CALIFORNIA TAX TABLE

Instructions

1. Find the Income in the far left column closest to your anticipated retirement income.
2. Find the Home Value closest to the value of the home where you will live in retirement.
3. Follow that row to your estimated Total Tax Burden at age 65 and beyond.

Income	Home Value	Property Tax & Other Fees	Personal Property Tax & Auto Fees	Sales Tax	Local Income Tax	State Income Tax	Total Tax Burden	Rank* From #1-#163
CARLSBAD								
$25,000	$75,000	$904	$284	$1,020	-	-	$2,208	#95
	100,000	1,171	284	1,020	-	-	2,475	#81
	125,000	1,438	284	1,020	-	-	2,742	#74
$50,000	$100,000	$1,225	$284	$1,652	-	$289	$3,450	#73
	150,000	1,759	284	1,652	-	289	3,984	#51
	200,000	2,292	284	1,652	-	289	4,517	#49
$75,000	$150,000	$1,759	$284	$2,098	-	$1,490	$5,631	#84
	250,000	2,826	284	2,098	-	1,490	6,698	#61
	350,000	3,893	284	2,098	-	1,490	7,765	#49
LOS ANGELES								
$25,000	$75,000	$819	$334	$1,086	-	-	$2,239	#99
	100,000	1,131	334	1,086	-	-	2,551	#88
	125,000	1,444	334	1,086	-	-	2,864	#86

Income	Home Value	Property Tax & Other Fees	Personal Property Tax & Auto Fees	Sales Tax	Local Income Tax	State Income Tax	Total Tax Burden	Rank* From #1 - #163
LOS ANGELES continued								
$50,000	$100,000	$1,186	$334	$1,759	-	$289	$3,568	#83
	150,000	1,811	334	1,759	-	289	4,193	#76
	200,000	2,436	334	1,759	-	289	4,818	#65
$75,000	$150,000	$1,811	$334	$2,233	-	$1,490	$5,868	#95
	250,000	3,061	334	2,233	-	1,490	7,118	#80
	350,000	4,311	334	2,233	-	1,490	8,368	#73
	$400,000	$4,936	$334	$2,233	-	$1,490	$8,993	Not Ranked
	450,000	5,561	334	2,233	-	1,490	9,618	Not Ranked
	500,000	6,186	334	2,233	-	1,490	10,243	Not Ranked
OJAI								
$25,000	$75,000	$1,427	$284	$955	-	-	$2,666	#145
	100,000	1,690	284	955	-	-	2,929	#133
	125,000	1,953	284	955	-	-	3,192	#115
$50,000	$100,000	$1,745	$284	$1,546	-	$289	$3,864	#115
	150,000	2,271	284	1,546	-	289	4,390	#93
	200,000	2,797	284	1,546	-	289	4,916	#75
$75,000	$150,000	$2,271	$284	$1,963	-	$1,490	$6,008	#100
	250,000	3,323	284	1,963	-	1,490	7,060	#78
	350,000	4,376	284	1,963	-	1,490	8,113	#61
PALM DESERT								
$25,000	$75,000	$1,054	$284	$1,020	-	-	$2,358	#120
	100,000	1,334	284	1,020	-	-	2,638	#101
	125,000	1,613	284	1,020	-	-	2,917	#90
$50,000	$100,000	$1,388	$284	$1,652	-	$289	$3,613	#89
	150,000	1,947	284	1,652	-	289	4,172	#73
	200,000	2,506	284	1,652	-	289	4,731	#62
$75,000	$150,000	$1,947	$284	$2,098	-	$1,490	$5,819	#94
	250,000	3,065	284	2,098	-	1,490	6,937	#73
	350,000	4,184	284	2,098	-	1,490	8,056	#55
SAN DIEGO								
$25,000	$75,000	$738	$284	$1,020	-	-	$2,042	#65
	100,000	1,017	284	1,020	-	-	2,321	#64
	125,000	1,295	284	1,020	-	-	2,599	#60
$50,000	$100,000	$1,070	$284	$1,652	-	$289	$3,295	#57
	150,000	1,627	284	1,652	-	289	3,852	#43
	200,000	2,184	284	1,652	-	289	4,409	#41
$75,000	$150,000	$1,627	$284	$2,098	-	$1,490	$5,499	#80
	250,000	2,740	284	2,098	-	1,490	6,612	#56
	350,000	3,853	284	2,098	-	1,490	7,725	#48
	$400,000	$4,410	$284	$2,098	-	$1,490	$8,282	Not Ranked
	450,000	4,966	284	2,098	-	1,490	8,838	Not Ranked
	500,000	5,523	284	2,098	-	1,490	9,395	Not Ranked
SAN FRANCISCO								
$25,000	$75,000	$858	$334	$1,119	-	-	$2,311	#111
	100,000	1,142	334	1,119	-	-	2,595	#97
	125,000	1,426	334	1,119	-	-	2,879	#87
$50,000	$100,000	$1,196	$334	$1,812	-	$289	$3,631	#90
	150,000	1,764	334	1,812	-	289	4,199	#78
	200,000	2,332	334	1,812	-	289	4,767	#63

*There are 163 cities in this book. The city with the lowest tax burden for an income/home value combination is given the #1 rating; the city with the highest total tax burden is given the #163 rating.

CALIFORNIA TAX TABLE

Instructions

1. Find the Income in the far left column closest to your anticipated retirement income.
2. Find the Home Value closest to the value of the home where you will live in retirement.
3. Follow that row to your estimated Total Tax Burden at age 65 and beyond.

Income	Home Value	Property Tax & Other Fees	Personal Property Tax & Auto Fees	Sales Tax	Local Income Tax	State Income Tax	Total Tax Burden	Rank* From #1- #163
SAN FRANCISCO continued								
$75,000	$150,000	$1,764	$334	$2,301	-	$1,490	$5,889	#96
	250,000	2,900	334	2,301	-	1,490	7,025	#77
	350,000	4,036	334	2,301	-	1,490	8,161	#63
	$400,000	$4,604	$334	$2,301	-	$1,490	$8,729	Not Ranked
	450,000	5,172	334	2,301	-	1,490	9,297	Not Ranked
	500,000	5,740	334	2,301	-	1,490	9,865	Not Ranked
SAN JUAN CAPISTRANO								
$25,000	$75,000	$1,010	$334	$1,020	-	-	$2,364	#122
	100,000	1,277	334	1,020	-	-	2,631	#100
	125,000	1,544	334	1,020	-	-	2,898	#89
$50,000	$100,000	$1,331	$334	$1,652	-	$289	$3,606	#88
	150,000	1,865	334	1,652	-	289	4,140	#67
	200,000	2,399	334	1,652	-	289	4,674	#58
$75,000	$150,000	$1,865	$334	$2,098	-	$1,490	$5,787	#89
	250,000	2,933	334	2,098	-	1,490	6,855	#67
	350,000	4,001	334	2,098	-	1,490	7,923	#52
TEMECULA								
$25,000	$75,000	$1,147	$284	$1,020	-	-	$2,451	#130
	100,000	1,445	284	1,020	-	-	2,749	#115
	125,000	1,742	284	1,020	-	-	3,046	#99
$50,000	$100,000	$1,499	$284	$1,652	-	$289	$3,724	#102
	150,000	2,094	284	1,652	-	289	4,319	#86
	200,000	2,688	284	1,652	-	289	4,913	#74
$75,000	$150,000	$2,094	$284	$2,098	-	$1,490	$5,966	#98
	250,000	3,283	284	2,098	-	1,490	7,155	#83
	350,000	4,472	284	2,098	-	1,490	8,344	#72

*There are 163 cities in this book. The city with the lowest tax burden for an income/home value combination is given the #1 rating; the city with the highest Total tax burden is given the #163 rating.

Carlsbad

Carlsbad has no local income tax but does levy a sales tax.

Most purchases are taxed at a rate of 7.75%. Major consumer categories taxed at a different rate: None. Major consumer categories that are exempt from sales tax include: Groceries, drugs and medical services.

Within tax rate area 09000 of Carlsbad, the property tax rate is .0106707. Homes are assessed at either 100% of market value or purchase price plus 2% per year, whichever is lower. There is a home-owner's exemption of $7,000 off assessed value of the home available to all homeowners. Property tax does not cover garbage pickup; the additional fee is approximately $174 per year.

Carlsbad has a personal property tax rate of .0104940 within tax rate area 09000. Personal property is assessed at 100% of market value. Items subject to the tax include boats and aircraft. There is a special tax on racehorses. We've assumed our couples do not own any of the items subject to these taxes.

Los Angeles

Los Angeles has no local income tax but does levy a sales tax.

Most purchases are taxed at a rate of 8.25%. Major consumer categories taxed at a different rate: None. Major consumer categories that are exempt from sales tax include: Groceries, drugs and medical services.

Within the city limits of Los Angeles, the property tax rate is .0125. Homes are assessed at either 100% of market value or purchase price plus 2% per year, whichever is lower. There is a homeowner's exemption of $7,000 off assessed value of the home available to all homeowners. There is a stormwater pollution abatement charge of approximately $23 per year. Property tax includes garbage pickup.

Los Angeles has a personal property tax rate of .01 within the city limits. Personal property is assessed at 100% of market value. Items subject to the tax include boats and aircraft. There is a special tax on racehorses. We've assumed our couples do not own any of the items subject to these taxes.

Ojai

Ojai has no local income tax but does levy a sales tax.

Most purchases are taxed at a rate of 7.25%. Major consumer categories taxed at a different rate: None. Major consumer categories that are exempt from sales tax include: Groceries, drugs and medical services.

Within the city limits of Ojai, the property tax rate is .01052383. Homes are assessed at either 100% of market value or purchase price plus 2% per year, whichever is lower. There is a homeowner's exemption of $7,000 off assessed value of the home available to all homeowners. Additional fees and special assessments are approximately $436 per year. Property tax does not cover garbage pickup; the additional fee is approximately $295 per year. There is a storm drain fee of approximately $35 per year.

Ojai has a personal property tax rate of .01064840. Personal property is assessed at 100% of market value. Items subject to the tax include boats and aircraft. We've assumed our couples do not own any of the items subject to these taxes.

Palm Desert

Palm Desert has no local income tax but does levy a sales tax.

Most purchases are taxed at a rate of 7.75%. Major consumer categories taxed at a different rate: None. Major consumer categories that are exempt from sales tax include: Groceries, drugs and medical services.

Within the Country Club area of Palm Desert, property taxes can vary by parcel, but one property tax rate is .0111830. Homes are assessed at either

100% of market value or purchase price plus 2% per year, whichever is lower. There is a homeowner's exemption of $7,000 off assessed value of the home available to all homeowners. Additional fees and special assessments are approximately $226 per year. Property tax does not cover garbage pickup; the additional fee is approximately $122 per year.

Palm Desert has a personal property tax rate of approximately .0125 to .0150, with the exact rate depending upon location. Personal property is assessed at 100% of market value. Items subject to the tax include boats and aircraft. There is a special tax on racehorses. We've assumed our couples do not own any of the items subject to these taxes.

San Diego

San Diego has no local income tax but does levy a sales tax.

Most purchases are taxed at a rate of 7.75%. Major consumer categories taxed at a different rate: None. Major consumer categories that are exempt from sales tax include: Groceries, drugs and medical services.

Within tax rate area 08001 of San Diego, the property tax rate is .0111289. Homes are assessed at either 100% of market value or purchase price plus 2% per year, whichever is lower. There is a homeowner's exemption of $7,000 off assessed value of the home available to all homeowners. Additional fees and special assessments are approximately $25 per year. There is a storm drain fee of approximately $11 per year. Property tax includes garbage pickup. Very few new homes are currently being built within San Diego city limits now, so the rates we used for our calculations were based on an older home inside the city limits.

San Diego has a personal property tax rate of .0111325 within tax rate area 08001. Personal property is assessed at 100% of market value. Items subject to the tax include boats and aircraft. There is a special tax on racehorses. We've assumed our couples do not own any of the items subject to these taxes.

San Francisco

San Francisco has no local income

tax but does levy a sales tax.

Most purchases are taxed at a rate of 8.5%. Major consumer categories taxed at a different rate: None. Major consumer categories that are exempt from sales tax include: Groceries, drugs and medical services.

Within the city limits of San Francisco, the property tax rate is .01136. Homes are assessed at either 100% of market value or purchase price plus 2% per year, whichever is lower. There is a homeowner's exemption of $7,000 off assessed value of the home available to all homeowners. There is an additional San Francisco School District Facilities fee, but seniors can apply to become exempt from it. Property tax does not cover garbage pickup; the additional fee is approximately $140 per year.

San Francisco has a personal property tax rate of .01136. Personal property is assessed at 100% of market value. Items subject to the tax include boats and aircraft. There is a special tax on racehorses. We've assumed our couples do not own any of the items subject to these taxes.

San Juan Capistrano

San Juan Capistrano has no local income tax but does levy a sales tax.

Most purchases are taxed at a rate of 7.75%. Major consumer categories taxed at a different rate: None. Major consumer categories that are exempt from sales tax include: Groceries, drugs and medical services.

The most common property tax rate in San Juan Capistrano is .0106804. Homes are assessed at either 100% of market value or purchase price plus 2% per year, whichever is lower. There is a homeowner's exemption of $7,000 off assessed value of the home available to all homeowners. There is a sewer maintenance fee of approximately $185 per year. Property tax does not cover garbage pickup; the additional fee is approximately $141 per year. There is also a vector control fee of approximately $2 per year and a Metropolitan Water District (MWD) standby charge of approximately $10 per year. Most people in newer neighborhoods pay a homeowner's association fee of $2,400 to $4,800 per year; we did not include this fee in our calculations.

The most common personal property

tax rate in San Juan Capistrano is .0107663. Personal property is assessed at 100% of market value. Items subject to the tax include boats and aircraft if valued at over $1,350. We've assumed our couples do not own any of the items subject to these taxes.

Temecula

Temecula has no local income tax but does levy a sales tax.

Most purchases are taxed at a rate of 7.75%. Major consumer categories taxed at a different rate: None. Major consumer categories that are exempt from sales tax include: Groceries, drugs and medical services.

A common property tax rate in Temecula is .0112925. Homes are assessed at either 100% of market value or purchase price plus 2% per year, whichever is lower. There is a homeowner's exemption of $7,000 off assessed value of the home available to all homeowners. There is a Rancho California debt fee of $.30 per $100 of assessed land value. Additional assessments and fees total approximately $389 per year. Property tax includes garbage pickup.

Temecula has a personal property tax rate of approximately .0125 to .0150, with the exact rate depending upon location. Personal property is assessed at 100% of market value. Items subject to the tax include boats and aircraft. There is a special tax on racehorses. We've assumed our couples do not own any of the items subject to these taxes.

• California's Best Retirement Towns •

Carlsbad, California

Thirty miles north of San Diego, this picturesque seaside village exudes Old World charm in a New World setting. Upscale planned communities, a picture-perfect environment, and year-round temperate climate are some of the qualities treasured by its residents. Golfers, hikers, sunbathers, fishers and beach-strollers share a popular outdoor lifestyle utilizing its multifaceted recreational sites.

A growth-management plan that reserves 40 percent of the land for open spaces has produced the salutary effect of slowing growth, but resulting high land costs have placed the city off limits to many middle-income families.

Pat and Bill Northridge moved here from north of Los Angeles in 1997, "but we were not expecting so many wonderful benefits," Pat says. She cites "the wildlife and nature's landscaping viewed from forest trails within walking distance of our home, the afternoon farmer's market in the village and the rapid and prodigious growth of everything we've planted in our yard.

"The one negative is the cost of living," Pat says. "It's not cheap to enjoy all of these natural wonders."

Population: 83,000 in city, 3,000,000 in county.

Climate: High Low
January 65 47
July 78 68

Cost of living: Above average (specific index not available).

Average price of a new home: $335,000

Security: 28.8 crimes per 1,000 residents, lower than the national average of 42.7 crimes per 1,000 residents.

Information: Carlsbad Chamber of Commerce, 5620 Paseo del Norte, No. 128, Carlsbad, CA 92008, (760) 931-8400 or www.carlsbad.org.

Ojai, California

Bothered by the elevation and cooler temperatures of their hometown of Lake Isabella in Northern California, Farrell and Lola Smith moved to Ojai in 1999. An "almost-perfect climate" — the product of a soft ocean breeze that keeps summer high temperatures in the low 80s, dropping into the 50s at night — soon became secondary to the enjoyment they found in the town itself.

"It's a complete small town," Farrell says, "with good shopping, beautiful scenery, friendly people and large old oak trees with branches that seem to cover a half acre of land."

Located in a scenic coastal valley only 14 miles from the Pacific Ocean, and in the foothills of the 6,000-foot Topa Topa Mountains, this picture-perfect little village, decked out in its Mexican-mission revival architectural style, offers the best of two worlds.

"We can drive up in the eastern hills where Hollywood stars like Goldie Hawn live, or a few miles west to the ultra-expensive seaside town of Santa Barbara for a heavy dose of culture, but we have everything we need right here," Farrell says. "If you can handle the cost of housing, everything else is easy."

Population: 8,154 in city, 32,867 in Ojai Valley.

Climate: High Low
January 67 37
July 90 55

Cost of living: Above average (specific index not available).

Average price of a new home: $326,000

Security: 28.5 crimes per 1,000 residents, lower than the national average of 42.7 crimes per 1,000 residents.

Information: Ojai Valley Chamber of Commerce, 150 W. Ojai Ave., Ojai, CA 93023, (805) 646-8126 or www.the-ojai.org.

Palm Desert, California

Affluence and celebrity are the visible signs of Palm Desert. Elegant performing arts theaters and museums, posh country club communities (each with its own championship golf course), fashionable upscale boutiques, designer shops and indoor malls, and streets named for Hollywood stars contribute to the glitz and glamour of this playground of the rich and famous.

Not that you have to be rich and famous to live here. Sheldon and Ruth Esko decided to retire here from Chicago in 1998 after vacationing in the area for 15 years. To their delight, they found that a home could be bought for half the price of a similar home in their old neighborhood. "Cost of living is very reasonable for a city that has everything," Sheldon says.

"It's a little warm in summer," says Ruth, searching for something that isn't perfect about the city. "Palm Desert is a wonderful place to retire. It has a very active social climate. Its residents have a youthful outlook and are always looking for new things to do. And there's no limit to things to do. We have wonderful theater, museums and schools. Volunteering opportunities abound."

Population: 40,000 in city, 1,300,000 in county.

Climate:

	High	Low
January	70	38
July	107	77

Cost of living: Above average (specific index not available).

Average price of a new home: $354,000

Security: 64.3 crimes per 1,000 residents, higher than the national average of 42.7 crimes per 1,000 residents.

Information: Palm Desert Chamber of Commerce, 73-710 Fred Waring Drive, Suite 114, Palm Desert, CA 92260, (760) 346-6111 or www.pdcc.org.

San Juan Capistrano, California

A gentle offshore breeze from the Pacific Ocean — only a mile away — keeps summer and winter temperatures in this picturesque little village at a comfortable shirtsleeves level. Streets are filled with visitors who come from around the world to see historic, much-acclaimed Mission San Juan Capistrano. Residents go about their daily lives in a town little changed by time.

Former mayor Gil Jones credits a city council initiative 25 years ago for the low annual growth rate and expansive open spaces that have kept the town impervious to the overcrowding experienced by many Southern California communities.

Les and Marie Blair say they looked all over Southern California before settling in San Juan Capistrano seven years ago. "We love the town, its nearness to the ocean, the friendly people, the mission and historical aspects," Marie says.

"We work with patients with Alzheimer's disease and the Special Olympics, deliver for Meals on Wheels, answer Santa's letters from children and participate in the United Way and the Seniors Club," Les says, describing one aspect of their active lifestyle.

"We run every day, swim in the ocean, do aerobic exercises and win dance contests," Marie laughs, describing another. "I'll stay here forever," Les says.

Population: 32,500 in city, 2,450,000 in county.

Climate:

	High	Low
January	65	50
July	89	73

Cost of living: Above average (specific index not available).

Average price of a new home: $386,000

Security: 18.1 crimes per 1,000 residents, lower than the national average of 42.7 crimes per 1,000 residents.

Information: San Juan Capistrano Chamber of Commerce, P.O. Box 1878, San Juan Capistrano, CA 92693, (949) 493-4700 or www.sanjuanchamber.com.

Temecula, California

Ten years ago Temecula wasn't big enough or sufficiently populated to bother with incorporation. Today it's one of the fastest growing cities in California — and one of the prettiest.

Set in a long, green valley with snowcapped mountains visible in the distance, its historic Old Town, east of Interstate 15, has the Western appeal of Tombstone, AZ. West of the interstate, a 21st-century city of sparkling new commercial buildings and state-of-the-art housing developments is slowly spreading across the rolling landscape.

Linda and Bill Cole, natives of the Midwest, came to a neighboring town for a funeral, drove through Temecula and were so captivated by its small-town Western atmosphere and warm, friendly people that they vowed they would someday return here to live.

"It's a very conscientious place," Linda says. "The town is growing rapidly, but there's plenty of room for growth in the countryside, and officials are planning well. We've never been happier."

Population: 58,650 in city, 1,300,000 in county.

Climate:

	High	Low
January	69	46
July	92	61

Cost of living: Above average (specific index not available).

Average price of a new home: $258,000

Security: 31.3 crimes per 1,000 residents, lower than the national average of 42.7 crimes per 1,000 residents.

Information: Temecula Valley Chamber of Commerce, 27450 Ynez Road, No. 124, Temecula, CA 92590, (909) 676-5090 or www.temecula.org.

COLORADO

Tax Heavens O
Denver

Tax Hells Ψ
None

Top Retirement Towns
Fort Collins

Colorado has a state income tax and a state sales tax.

The state income tax rate is 4.63% of federal taxable income.

In calculating the tax, there is no deduction for federal income tax paid. Federal, state and private pensions and Social Security benefits subject to federal tax are not exempt. However, there is an exclusion of up to $24,000 in taxable pension and Social Security benefits for each taxpayer age 65 or older. There is an interest, dividend and capital gain deduction from

income of up to $2,400 for married couples filing jointly. There is an additional standard deduction of $1,450 for married couples filing jointly.

Major tax credits or rebates include: Credit for income taxes paid to other states, which our couples do not qualify for; property tax/rent and heat credit, which our couples do not qualify for; and state sales tax refund up to $1,148 for full-year residents, married filing jointly, which our couples do qualify for.

The state sales tax rate is 3%, but

local governments can add to this amount.

Our couples relocating to the cities listed below must pay a personal property tax (ownership tax) based on the year and MSRP of each automobile, which is assessed and collected through the Motor Vehicle Division. Our couples also pay a license fee per automobile based on the weight of each automobile and a VIN verification fee of $9 per automobile. An emissions test is required before registration for a fee of $24 in Denver and

COLORADO TAX TABLE

Instructions

1. Find the Income in the far left column closest to your anticipated retirement income.
2. Find the Home Value closest to the value of the home where you will live in retirement.
3. Follow that row to your estimated Total Tax Burden at age 65 and beyond.

Income	Home Value	Property Tax & Other Fees	Personal Property Tax & Auto Fees	Sales Tax	Local Income Tax	State Income Tax†	Total Tax Burden	Rank* From #1-#163
DENVER								
$25,000	$75,000	$529	$514	$969	$138	($364)	$1,786	#30
	100,000	693	514	969	138	(364)	1,950	#23
	125,000	857	514	969	138	(364)	2,114	#22
$50,000	$100,000	$693	$514	$1,569	$138	($323)	$2,591	#10 O
	150,000	1,021	514	1,569	138	(323)	2,919	#8 O
	200,000	1,348	514	1,569	138	(323)	3,246	#7 O
$75,000	$150,000	$1,021	$514	$1,990	$138	$621	$4,284	#21
	250,000	1,676	514	1,990	138	621	4,939	#11
	350,000	2,332	514	1,990	138	621	5,595	#9 O
FORT COLLINS								
$25,000	$75,000	$927	$505	$955	-	($364)	$2,023	#60
	100,000	1,144	505	955	-	(364)	2,240	#53
	125,000	1,360	505	955	-	(364)	2,456	#50
$50,000	$100,000	$1,144	$505	$1,527	-	($323)	$2,853	#23
	150,000	1,577	505	1,527	-	(323)	3,286	#19
	200,000	2,010	505	1,527	-	(323)	3,719	#15
$75,000	$150,000	$1,577	$505	$1,925	-	$621	$4,628	#40
	250,000	2,443	505	1,925	-	621	5,494	#22
	350,000	3,310	505	1,925	-	621	6,361	#19

†State sales tax refund is issued as a reduction of income tax due or as a refund if the credit is greater than the tax liability.
*There are 163 cities in this book. The city with the lowest tax burden for an income/home value combination is given the #1 rating; the city with the highest total tax burden is given the #163 rating.

$15 in Fort Collins. The personal property tax is approximately $278 for the Explorer and $231 for the Cutlass. The license fee is $41 for the Explorer and $41 for the Cutlass. Thereafter, on an annual basis, our couples will pay a personal property tax and a license fee, per automobile. Emissions tests are required every other year in both Denver and Fort Collins.

Denver

Denver has a local income tax and a sales tax.

The local income tax (Occupational Privilege Tax) is $6 per month per person. It applies to each person with earned income of at least $500 per month.

Most purchases are taxed at a rate of 7.3%. Major consumer categories taxed at a different rate include: Food away from home, which is taxed at a rate of 7.8%. Major consumer categories that are exempt from sales tax include: Groceries, drugs and medical services.

Within the city limits of Denver, the property tax rate is .067321. Homes are assessed at 9.74% of market value. There is an additional storm drain fee of approximately $37 per year. Property tax includes garbage pickup.

Denver has a personal property tax on automobiles, as discussed above.

Fort Collins

Fort Collins has no local income tax but does levy a sales tax.

Most purchases are taxed at a rate of 6.8%. Major consumer categories taxed at a different rate include: Groceries, which are taxed at a rate of 2.25%. Major consumer categories that are exempt from sales tax include: Drugs and medical services.

Within the city limits of Fort Collins, the property tax rate is .088970. Homes are assessed at 9.74% of market value. Property tax does not cover garbage pickup; the additional fee is approximately $186 per year. There is also a stormwater fee of approximately $91 per year.

Fort Collins has a personal property tax on automobiles, as discussed above.

• Colorado's Best Retirement Town •

Fort Collins, Colorado

It's hard to improve on a city with a major educational institution such as Colorado State University and panoramic views of the beautiful snow-capped Rocky Mountains. But there's more. A wide, clean river flows through its corporate limits, and there's a strong, diversified economy, outstanding cultural amenities and an active, involved populace intent on finding ways to keep these prized features intact.

Jack and Camille Trolla left the smog, traffic and wall-to-wall people of Southern California to spend their retirement years in Fort Collins. Millie

describes it as "the best decision we ever made."

"Its clean air and warmhearted, hospitable people" are the main reasons she likes the city, she says. "We love to get up in the mornings and see the beautiful blue sky and white clouds floating by."

Outdoors the Trollas enjoy photography, collecting fossils, flying radio-controlled airplanes and hiking on trails around Fort Collins and in Rocky Mountain National Park. When they aren't enjoying the outdoors, they build model planes and trains, attend concerts by the Fort Collins Symphony and drive to

Denver for plays.

Population: 109,000 in city, 200,000 in county.

Climate:

	High	Low
January	41	14
July	86	57

Cost of living: 106, based on national average of 100.

Average price of a new home: $218,000

Security: 43.6 crimes per 1,000 residents, higher than the national average of 42.7 crimes per 1,000 residents.

Information: Fort Collins Chamber of Commerce, 225 S. Meldrum, Fort Collins, CO 80521, (970) 482-3746 or www.fcchamber.org.

CONNECTICUT

Tax Heavens O
None

Tax Hells Ψ
Hartford
New Haven

Top Retirement Towns
None

Connecticut has a state income tax and a state sales tax.

The state income tax rate is graduated from 3% to 4.5% depending upon income bracket. For married couples filing jointly, the rate is 3% on the first $20,000 of taxable income and the rate is 4.5% on taxable income above $20,000.

In calculating the tax, there is no deduction for federal income tax paid. Federal, state and private pensions are not exempt. Some Social Security ben-

efits subject to federal tax are not exempt. There is a personal exemption of up to $24,000 from adjusted gross income for married couples filing jointly.

Major tax credits or rebates include: Credit for income taxes paid to other states, which our couples do not qualify for; property tax credit of up to $500 of Connecticut income tax liability, which some of our couples qualify for; and personal tax credit against income tax due of up to 75% depend-

ing on filing status and income bracket, which our couples do qualify for.

The state sales tax rate is 6%.

Our couples relocating to the cities listed below must pay a registration fee of $70 for two years per automobile, a title fee of $25 per automobile, a plate fee of $5 per automobile, a lien fee of $10 per automobile and a $10 administration fee per automobile at the time of registration. Thereafter, every two years, our couples will pay a registration fee

---

CONNECTICUT TAX TABLE

Instructions

1. Find the Income in the far left column closest to your anticipated retirement income.
2. Find the Home Value closest to the value of the home where you will live in retirement.
3. Follow that row to your estimated Total Tax Burden at age 65 and beyond.

Income	Home Value	Property Tax & Other Fees	Personal Property Tax & Auto Fees	Sales Tax	Local Income Tax	State Income Tax	Total Tax Burden	Rank* From #1- #163
HARTFORD								
$25,000	$75,000	$883	$1,043	$790	-	-	$2,716	#147
	100,000	1,393	1,043	790	-	-	3,226	#145
	125,000	1,904	1,043	790	-	-	3,737	#144
$50,000	$100,000	$2,043	$1,043	$1,279	-	-	$4,365	#132
	150,000	3,065	1,043	1,279	-	-	5,387	#140
	200,000	4,149	1,043	1,279	-	-	6,471	#141
$75,000	$150,000	$3,065	$1,043	$1,624	-	$1,469	$7,201	#137
	250,000	5,829	1,043	1,624	-	1,469	9,965	#151
	350,000	9,189	1,043	1,624	-	1,469	13,325	#154 Ψ
NEW HAVEN								
$25,000	$75,000	$1,685	$779	$790	-	-	$3,254	#158 Ψ
	100,000	2,297	779	790	-	-	3,866	#158 Ψ
	125,000	2,908	779	790	-	-	4,477	#157 Ψ
$50,000	$100,000	$2,447	$779	$1,279	-	-	$4,505	#138
	150,000	3,670	779	1,279	-	-	5,728	#149
	200,000	4,893	779	1,279	-	-	6,951	#150
$75,000	$150,000	$3,670	$779	$1,624	-	$1,469	$7,542	#147
	250,000	6,116	779	1,624	-	1,469	9,988	#152
	350,000	8,563	779	1,624	-	1,469	12,435	#151

*There are 163 cities in this book. The city with the lowest tax burden for an income/home value combination is given the #1 rating; the city with the highest total tax burden is given the #163 rating.

and a clean air fee, per automobile.

Hartford

Hartford has no local income tax and does not levy an additional sales tax.

Most purchases are taxed at the state rate of 6%. Major consumer categories taxed at a different rate: None. Major consumer categories that are exempt from sales tax include: Groceries, drugs and medical services.

Within the city limits of Hartford, the property tax rate is .02919. The portion of the home's market value exceeding $155,300 is taxed at a slightly higher rate. Homes are assessed at 70% of market value. There is a $500 credit against tax for homeowners age 65 or older with gross income up to $31,700. There is an additional homeowner's tax credit of 10% off tax bills, up to $150, for married couples with at least one spouse age 65 or over and with up to $30,000 gross income. Property tax includes garbage pickup.

The personal property tax rate in Hartford is .048. Personal property is assessed at 70% of market value. Items subject to the tax include motor vehicles.

New Haven

New Haven has no local income tax and does not levy an additional sales tax.

Most purchases are taxed at the state rate of 6%. Major consumer categories taxed at a different rate: None. Major consumer categories that are exempt from sales tax include: Groceries, drugs and medical services.

Within the city limits of New Haven, the property tax rate is .03495. Homes are assessed at 70% of market value. There is a homeowner's tax credit of 10% off tax bills, up to $150, for married couples with at least one spouse age 65 or over and with up to $30,000 gross income. Property tax includes garbage pickup.

The personal property tax rate in New Haven is .03495. Personal property is assessed at 70% of market value. Items subject to the tax include motor vehicles.

DELAWARE

Tax Heavens O
Wilmington

Tax Hells Ψ
None

Top Retirement Towns
None

Delaware has a state income tax but no state sales tax.

The state income tax rate is graduated from zero to 5.95% depending upon income bracket. For married couples filing jointly, no tax is paid on the first $2,000 of taxable income; the rate is 2.2% on the next $3,000 of taxable income; the rate is 3.9% on the next $5,000 of taxable income; the rate is 4.8% on the next $10,000 of taxable income; the rate is 5.2% on the next $5,000 of taxable income;

the rate is 5.5% on the next $35,000 of taxable income; and the rate is 5.95% on taxable income above $60,000.

In calculating the tax, there is no deduction for federal income tax paid. Federal, state and private pensions are not exempt, but there is an exclusion of up to $12,500 from pension income per person age 60 or over and up to $2,000 per person under age 60. Social Security benefits are exempt. There is a $6,500 standard deduction from

Delaware adjusted gross income for married couples filing jointly and an additional standard deduction of $2,500 from adjusted gross income per person age 65 or older.

Major tax credits or rebates include: Credit for income taxes paid to other states, which our couples do not qualify for, as well as personal credit of $110 per person against tax and an additional $110 credit against tax per person age 60 or older, both of which our couples do qualify for.

DELAWARE TAX TABLE

Instructions

1. Find the Income in the far left column closest to your anticipated retirement income.
2. Find the Home Value closest to the value of the home where you will live in retirement.
3. Follow that row to your estimated Total Tax Burden at age 65 and beyond.

Income	Home Value	Property Tax & Other Fees	Personal Property Tax & Auto Fees	Sales Tax	Local Income Tax	State Income Tax	Total Tax Burden	Rank* From #1- #163
WILMINGTON								
$25,000	$75,000	$628	$40	-	$44	-	$712	#2 O
	100,000	1,077	40	-	44	-	1,161	#2 O
	125,000	1,525	40	-	44	-	1,609	#3 O
$50,000	$100,000	$1,794	$40	-	$208	-	$2,042	#2 O
	150,000	2,872	40	-	208	-	3,120	#11
	200,000	3,996	40	-	208	-	4,244	#36
$75,000	$150,000	$2,872	$40	-	$401	$1,145	$4,458	#33
	250,000	5,120	40	-	401	1,145	6,706	#62
	350,000	7,368	40	-	401	1,145	8,954	#94

*There are 163 cities in this book. The city with the lowest tax burden for an income/home value combination is given the #1 rating; the city with the highest total tax burden is given the #163 rating.

Wilmington

Wilmington has a local income tax but does not levy a sales tax.

The local income tax rate is 1.25% of wages, salaries and self-employment income.

In the Red Clay School District, the property tax rate is .022479. New homes are assessed at 100% of market value. There is a senior deduction from the school component of property tax if at least one spouse is age 65 or over of up to 50% off school taxes or $500,

whichever is less. Married couples with at least one spouse age 65 or over and with gross income up to $40,000 (including capital gains, pension, annuity and retirement benefits and Social Security benefits) may exempt up to $40,000 off the assessed value of the home. Married couples with at least one spouse age 65 or over and with gross income up to $19,000 may exempt an additional $32,000 off assessed home value. Property tax includes garbage pickup.

Wilmington has no personal property tax for individuals.

Our couples relocating to Wilmington must pay a vehicle document fee per automobile based on the NADA trade-in value of the automobile. The document fee is $602 for the Explorer and $500 for the Cutlass. Our couples must also pay a $25 title fee per automobile and a $20 registration fee per automobile at the time of registration. Thereafter, on an annual basis, our couples will pay a renewal fee per automobile.

FLORIDA

Tax Heavens O

Naples

Tax Hells Ψ

Celebration

Top Retirement Towns

Boca Raton, Bradenton, Celebration, Dade City, DeLand, Gainesville Jupiter-Tequesta, Key West, Lakeland, Leesburg, Longboat Key, Mount Dora, Naples, North Fort Myers, Ocala, Orlando, Ormond Beach, Pensacola, Punta Gorda, St. Augustine, Sanibel Island, Sarasota, Siesta Key, Venice, Vero Beach, Winter Haven

Florida has no state income tax but does have a state sales tax.

Major tax credits or rebates: None.

The state sales tax rate is 6%, but local governments can add to this amount.

Our couples relocating to the cities below must pay a registration fee of $191 for the Explorer and $181 for the Cutlass. This includes an initial registration fee of $100 per automobile, a new license plate fee of $10 per automobile, a title fee for an out-of-state vehicle of $33 per automobile, a fee for recording a lien of $2 per automobile and a registration fee of $46 for the Explorer and $36 for the Cutlass. Thereafter, on an annual basis, our couples will pay a registration fee per automobile.

FLORIDA TAX TABLE

Instructions

1. Find the Income in the far left column closest to your anticipated retirement income.
2. Find the Home Value closest to the value of the home where you will live in retirement.
3. Follow that row to your estimated Total Tax Burden at age 65 and beyond.

Income	Home Value	Property Tax & Other Fees	Personal Property Tax & Auto Fees	Sales Tax	Local Income Tax	State Income Tax	Total Tax Burden	Rank* From #1-#163
BOCA RATON								
$25,000	$75,000	$1,167	$81	$790	-	-	$2,038	#64
	100,000	1,691	81	790	-	-	2,562	#89
	125,000	2,214	81	790	-	-	3,085	#101
$50,000	$100,000	$1,691	$81	$1,279	-	-	$3,051	#35
	150,000	2,738	81	1,279	-	-	4,098	#61
	200,000	3,785	81	1,279	-	-	5,145	#89
$75,000	$150,000	$2,738	$81	$1,624	-	-	$4,443	#32
	250,000	4,832	81	1,624	-	-	6,537	#52
	350,000	6,926	81	1,624	-	-	8,631	#79
BRADENTON								
$25,000	$75,000	$1,313	$81	$790	-	-	$2,184	#93
	100,000	1,840	81	790	-	-	2,711	#110
	125,000	2,368	81	790	-	-	3,239	#121

*There are 163 cities in this book. The city with the lowest tax burden for an income/home value combination is given the #1 rating; the city with the highest total tax burden is given the #163 rating.

FLORIDA TAX TABLE

Instructions

1. Find the Income in the far left column closest to your anticipated retirement income.
2. Find the Home Value closest to the value of the home where you will live in retirement.
3. Follow that row to your estimated Total Tax Burden at age 65 and beyond.

Income	Home Value	Property Tax & Other Fees	Personal Property Tax & Auto Fees	Sales Tax	Local Income Tax	State Income Tax	Total Tax Burden	Rank* From #1 - #163
BRADENTON continued								
$50,000	$100,000	$1,840	$81	$1,279	-	-	$3,200	#46
	150,000	2,895	81	1,279	-	-	4,255	#82
	200,000	3,950	81	1,279	-	-	5,310	#100
$75,000	$150,000	$2,895	$81	$1,624	-	-	$4,600	#39
	250,000	5,005	81	1,624	-	-	6,710	#63
	350,000	7,114	81	1,624	-	-	8,819	#87
CELEBRATION								
$25,000	$75,000	$2,696	$81	$922	-	-	$3,699	#161 Ψ
	100,000	3,112	81	922	-	-	4,115	#160 Ψ
	125,000	3,529	81	922	-	-	4,532	#158 Ψ
$50,000	$100,000	$3,112	$81	$1,492	-	-	$4,685	#147
	150,000	3,946	81	1,492	-	-	5,519	#143
	200,000	4,780	81	1,492	-	-	6,353	#139
$75,000	$150,000	$3,946	$81	$1,895	-	-	$5,922	#97
	250,000	5,613	81	1,895	-	-	7,589	#99
	350,000	7,281	81	1,895	-	-	9,257	#104
DADE CITY								
$25,000	$75,000	$1,450	$81	$790	-	-	$2,321	#115
	100,000	2,114	81	790	-	-	2,985	#138
	125,000	2,779	81	790	-	-	3,650	#140
$50,000	$100,000	$2,114	$81	$1,279	-	-	$3,474	#74
	150,000	3,444	81	1,279	-	-	4,804	#114
	200,000	4,774	81	1,279	-	-	6,134	#130
$75,000	$150,000	$3,444	$81	$1,624	-	-	$5,149	#62
	250,000	6,103	81	1,624	-	-	7,808	#110
	350,000	8,763	81	1,624	-	-	10,468	#133
DELAND								
$25,000	$75,000	$1,090	$81	$790	-	-	$1,961	#56
	100,000	1,692	81	790	-	-	2,563	#90
	125,000	2,294	81	790	-	-	3,165	#109
$50,000	$100,000	$2,012	$81	$1,279	-	-	$3,372	#64
	150,000	3,216	81	1,279	-	-	4,576	#106
	200,000	4,420	81	1,279	-	-	5,780	#118
$75,000	$150,000	$3,216	$81	$1,624	-	-	$4,921	#59
	250,000	5,624	81	1,624	-	-	7,329	#89
	350,000	8,033	81	1,624	-	-	9,738	#115
FORT LAUDERDALE								
$25,000	$75,000	$1,487	$81	$790	-	-	$2,358	#120
	100,000	2,119	81	790	-	-	2,990	#139
	125,000	2,750	81	790	-	-	3,621	#139
$50,000	$100,000	$2,307	$81	$1,279	-	-	$3,667	#95
	150,000	3,570	81	1,279	-	-	4,930	#123
	200,000	4,833	81	1,279	-	-	6,193	#134

Income	Home Value	Property Tax & Other Fees	Personal Property Tax & Auto Fees	Sales Tax	Local Income Tax	State Income Tax	Total Tax Burden	Rank* From #1- #163
FORT LAUDERDALE continued								
$75,000	$150,000	$3,570	$81	$1,624	-	-	$5,275	#65
	250,000	6,097	81	1,624	-	-	7,802	#108
	350,000	8,623	81	1,624	-	-	10,328	#128
GAINESVILLE								
$25,000	$75,000	$1,536	$81	$790	-	-	$2,407	#126
	100,000	2,208	81	790	-	-	3,079	#141
	125,000	2,880	81	790	-	-	3,751	#145
$50,000	$100,000	$2,208	$81	$1,279	-	-	$3,568	#83
	150,000	3,552	81	1,279	-	-	4,912	#119
	200,000	4,896	81	1,279	-	-	6,256	#136
$75,000	$150,000	$3,552	$81	$1,624	-	-	$5,257	#64
	250,000	6,240	81	1,624	-	-	7,945	#115
	350,000	8,929	81	1,624	-	-	10,634	#136
JACKSONVILLE								
$25,000	$75,000	$753	$81	$856	-	-	$1,690	#26
	100,000	1,261	81	856	-	-	2,198	#48
	125,000	1,770	81	856	-	-	2,707	#71
$50,000	$100,000	$1,526	$81	$1,386	-	-	$2,993	#32
	150,000	2,543	81	1,386	-	-	4,010	#55
	200,000	3,560	81	1,386	-	-	5,027	#82
$75,000	$150,000	$2,543	$81	$1,760	-	-	$4,384	#27
	250,000	4,577	81	1,760	-	-	6,418	#50
	350,000	6,612	81	1,760	-	-	8,453	#74
JUPITER								
$25,000	$75,000	$1,196	$81	$790	-	-	$2,067	#71
	100,000	1,732	81	790	-	-	2,603	#98
	125,000	2,269	81	790	-	-	3,140	#107
$50,000	$100,000	$1,732	$81	$1,279	-	-	$3,092	#38
	150,000	2,805	81	1,279	-	-	4,165	#71
	200,000	3,877	81	1,279	-	-	5,237	#97
$75,000	$150,000	$2,805	$81	$1,624	-	-	$4,510	#36
	250,000	4,949	81	1,624	-	-	6,654	#58
	350,000	7,094	81	1,624	-	-	8,799	#86
KEY WEST								
$25,000	$75,000	$884	$81	$987	-	-	$1,952	#52
	100,000	1,244	81	987	-	-	2,312	#62
	125,000	1,603	81	987	-	-	2,671	#67
$50,000	$100,000	$1,349	$81	$1,599	-	-	$3,029	#34
	150,000	2,068	81	1,599	-	-	3,748	#37
	200,000	2,788	81	1,599	-	-	4,468	#44
$75,000	$150,000	$2,068	$81	$2,030	-	-	$4,179	#16
	250,000	3,507	81	2,030	-	-	5,618	#28
	350,000	4,946	81	2,030	-	-	7,057	#40
LAKELAND								
$25,000	$75,000	$1,184	$81	$790	-	-	$2,055	#69
	100,000	1,701	81	790	-	-	2,572	#92
	125,000	2,217	81	790	-	-	3,088	#102

*There are 163 cities in this book. The city with the lowest tax burden for an income/home value combination is given the #1 rating; the city with the highest total tax burden is given the #163 rating.

FLORIDA TAX TABLE

Instructions

1. Find the Income in the far left column closest to your anticipated retirement income.
2. Find the Home Value closest to the value of the home where you will live in retirement.
3. Follow that row to your estimated Total Tax Burden at age 65 and beyond.

Income	Home Value	Property Tax & Other Fees	Personal Property Tax & Auto Fees	Sales Tax	Local Income Tax	State Income Tax	Total Tax Burden	Rank* From #1- #163
LAKELAND continued								
$50,000	$100,000	$1,730	$81	$1,279	-	-	$3,090	#37
	150,000	2,764	81	1,279	-	-	4,124	#63
	200,000	3,798	81	1,279	-	-	5,158	#90
$75,000	$150,000	$2,764	$81	$1,624	-	-	$4,469	#34
	250,000	4,831	81	1,624	-	-	6,536	#51
	350,000	6,899	81	1,624	-	-	8,604	#78
LEESBURG								
$25,000	$75,000	$1,126	$81	$922	-	-	$2,129	#84
	100,000	1,642	81	922	-	-	2,645	#102
	125,000	2,157	81	922	-	-	3,160	#108
$50,000	$100,000	$1,770	$81	$1,492	-	-	$3,343	#62
	150,000	2,801	81	1,492	-	-	4,374	#90
	200,000	3,833	81	1,492	-	-	5,406	#105
$75,000	$150,000	$2,801	$81	$1,895	-	-	$4,777	#52
	250,000	4,865	81	1,895	-	-	6,841	#66
	350,000	6,928	81	1,895	-	-	8,904	#92
LONGBOAT KEY								
$25,000	$75,000	$911	$81	$922	-	-	$1,914	#45
	100,000	1,327	81	922	-	-	2,330	#65
	125,000	1,744	81	922	-	-	2,747	#75
$50,000	$100,000	$1,391	$81	$1,492	-	-	$2,964	#30
	150,000	2,224	81	1,492	-	-	3,797	#38
	200,000	3,058	81	1,492	-	-	4,631	#56
$75,000	$150,000	$2,224	$81	$1,895	-	-	$4,200	#19
	250,000	3,891	81	1,895	-	-	5,867	#36
	350,000	5,558	81	1,895	-	-	7,534	#43
MIAMI								
$25,000	$75,000	$1,297	$81	$856	-	-	$2,234	#98
	100,000	1,982	81	856	-	-	2,919	#132
	125,000	2,666	81	856	-	-	3,603	#137
$50,000	$100,000	$2,399	$81	$1,386	-	-	$3,866	#116
	150,000	3,768	81	1,386	-	-	5,235	#135
	200,000	5,137	81	1,386	-	-	6,604	#143
$75,000	$150,000	$3,768	$81	$1,760	-	-	$5,609	#82
	250,000	6,506	81	1,760	-	-	8,347	#128
	350,000	9,245	81	1,760	-	-	11,086	#139
MOUNT DORA								
$25,000	$75,000	$1,096	$81	$922	-	-	$2,099	#76
	100,000	1,655	81	922	-	-	2,658	#104
	125,000	2,212	81	922	-	-	3,215	#117
$50,000	$100,000	$1,937	$81	$1,492	-	-	$3,510	#78
	150,000	3,052	81	1,492	-	-	4,625	#108
	200,000	4,168	81	1,492	-	-	5,741	#115

Income	Home Value	Property Tax & Other Fees	Personal Property Tax & Auto Fees	Sales Tax	Local Income Tax	State Income Tax	Total Tax Burden	Rank* From #1-#163
MOUNT DORA continued								
$75,000	$150,000	$3,052	$81	$1,895	-	-	$5,028	#60
	250,000	5,284	81	1,895	-	-	7,260	#85
	350,000	7,515	81	1,895	-	-	9,491	#110
NAPLES								
$25,000	$75,000	$810	$81	$790	-	-	$1,681	#24
	100,000	1,143	81	790	-	-	2,014	#30
	125,000	1,476	81	790	-	-	2,347	#41
$50,000	$100,000	$1,261	$81	$1,279	-	-	$2,621	#11
	150,000	1,927	81	1,279	-	-	3,287	#20
	200,000	2,593	81	1,279	-	-	3,953	#24
$75,000	$150,000	$1,927	$81	$1,624	-	-	$3,632	#5 O
	250,000	3,258	81	1,624	-	-	4,963	#12
	350,000	4,589	81	1,624	-	-	6,294	#17
NORTH FORT MYERS								
$25,000	$75,000	$1,172	$81	$790	-	-	$2,043	#66
	100,000	1,666	81	790	-	-	2,537	#87
	125,000	2,159	81	790	-	-	3,030	#96
$50,000	$100,000	$1,666	$81	$1,279	-	-	$3,026	#33
	150,000	2,653	81	1,279	-	-	4,013	#57
	200,000	3,640	81	1,279	-	-	5,000	#79
$75,000	$150,000	$2,653	$81	$1,624	-	-	$4,358	#26
	250,000	4,628	81	1,624	-	-	6,333	#47
	350,000	6,602	81	1,624	-	-	8,307	#68
OCALA								
$25,000	$75,000	$1,297	$81	$790	-	-	$2,168	#90
	100,000	1,851	81	790	-	-	2,722	#112
	125,000	2,404	81	790	-	-	3,275	#125
$50,000	$100,000	$1,851	$81	$1,279	-	-	$3,211	#48
	150,000	2,958	81	1,279	-	-	4,318	#85
	200,000	4,065	81	1,279	-	-	5,425	#106
$75,000	$150,000	$2,958	$81	$1,624	-	-	$4,663	#44
	250,000	5,173	81	1,624	-	-	6,878	#70
	350,000	7,387	81	1,624	-	-	9,092	#99
ORLANDO								
$25,000	$75,000	$1,258	$81	$790	-	-	$2,129	#84
	100,000	1,776	81	790	-	-	2,647	#103
	125,000	2,294	81	790	-	-	3,165	#109
$50,000	$100,000	$1,776	$81	$1,279	-	-	$3,136	#40
	150,000	2,812	81	1,279	-	-	4,172	#73
	200,000	3,848	81	1,279	-	-	5,208	#93
$75,000	$150,000	$2,812	$81	$1,624	-	-	$4,517	#37
	250,000	4,884	81	1,624	-	-	6,589	#53
	350,000	6,956	81	1,624	-	-	8,661	#80
ORMOND BEACH								
$25,000	$75,000	$1,082	$81	$790	-	-	$1,953	#54
	100,000	1,643	81	790	-	-	2,514	#83
	125,000	2,203	81	790	-	-	3,074	#100

*There are 163 cities in this book. The city with the lowest tax burden for an income/home value combination is given the #1 rating; the city with the highest total tax burden is given the #163 rating.

FLORIDA TAX TABLE

Instructions

1. Find the Income in the far left column closest to your anticipated retirement income.
2. Find the Home Value closest to the value of the home where you will live in retirement.
3. Follow that row to your estimated Total Tax Burden at age 65 and beyond.

Income	Home Value	Property Tax & Other Fees	Personal Property Tax & Auto Fees	Sales Tax	Local Income Tax	State Income Tax	Total Tax Burden	Rank* From #1-#163
ORMOND BEACH continued								
$50,000	$100,000	$1,898	$81	$1,279	-	-	$3,258	#52
	150,000	3,019	81	1,279	-	-	4,379	#91
	200,000	4,139	81	1,279	-	-	5,499	#108
$75,000	$150,000	$3,019	$81	$1,624	-	-	$4,724	#48
	250,000	5,259	81	1,624	-	-	6,964	#75
	350,000	7,500	81	1,624	-	-	9,205	#103
PENSACOLA								
$25,000	$75,000	$1,175	$81	$987	-	-	$2,243	#100
	100,000	1,753	81	987	-	-	2,821	#123
	125,000	2,330	81	987	-	-	3,398	#135
$50,000	$100,000	$1,971	$81	$1,599	-	-	$3,651	#94
	150,000	3,127	81	1,599	-	-	4,807	#115
	200,000	4,283	81	1,599	-	-	5,963	#125
$75,000	$150,000	$3,127	$81	$2,030	-	-	$5,238	#63
	250,000	5,438	81	2,030	-	-	7,549	#96
	350,000	7,749	81	2,030	-	-	9,860	#120
PUNTA GORDA								
$25,000	$75,000	$1,165	$81	$922	-	-	$2,168	#90
	100,000	1,588	81	922	-	-	2,591	#96
	125,000	2,012	81	922	-	-	3,015	#95
$50,000	$100,000	$1,588	$81	$1,492	-	-	$3,161	#43
	150,000	2,435	81	1,492	-	-	4,008	#54
	200,000	3,282	81	1,492	-	-	4,855	#68
$75,000	$150,000	$2,435	$81	$1,895	-	-	$4,411	#29
	250,000	4,128	81	1,895	-	-	6,104	#40
	350,000	5,822	81	1,895	-	-	7,798	#50
ST. AUGUSTINE								
$25,000	$75,000	$1,172	$81	$790	-	-	$2,043	#66
	100,000	1,758	81	790	-	-	2,629	#99
	125,000	2,344	81	790	-	-	3,215	#117
$50,000	$100,000	$1,910	$81	$1,279	-	-	$3,270	#54
	150,000	3,081	81	1,279	-	-	4,441	#98
	200,000	4,253	81	1,279	-	-	5,613	#110
$75,000	$150,000	$3,081	$81	$1,624	-	-	$4,786	#54
	250,000	5,425	81	1,624	-	-	7,130	#81
	350,000	7,768	81	1,624	-	-	9,473	#109
ST. PETERSBURG								
$25,000	$75,000	$1,489	$81	$922	-	-	$2,492	#133
	100,000	2,109	81	922	-	-	3,112	#142
	125,000	2,728	81	922	-	-	3,731	#143
$50,000	$100,000	$2,109	$81	$1,492	-	-	$3,682	#98
	150,000	3,348	81	1,492	-	-	4,921	#121
	200,000	4,587	81	1,492	-	-	6,160	#132

Income	Home Value	Property Tax & Other Fees	Personal Property Tax & Auto Fees	Sales Tax	Local Income Tax	State Income Tax	Total Tax Burden	Rank* From #1- #163
ST. PETERSBURG continued								
$75,000	$150,000	$3,348	$81	$1,895	-	-	$5,324	#69
	250,000	5,826	81	1,895	-	-	7,802	#108
	350,000	8,304	81	1,895	-	-	10,280	#127
SANIBEL ISLAND								
$25,000	$75,000	$1,103	$81	$790	-	-	$1,974	#57
	100,000	1,579	81	790	-	-	2,450	#77
	125,000	2,055	81	790	-	-	2,926	#91
$50,000	$100,000	$1,622	$81	$1,279	-	-	$2,982	#31
	150,000	2,574	81	1,279	-	-	3,934	#48
	200,000	3,526	81	1,279	-	-	4,886	#69
$75,000	$150,000	$2,574	$81	$1,624	-	-	$4,279	#20
	250,000	4,479	81	1,624	-	-	6,184	#45
	350,000	6,383	81	1,624	-	-	8,088	#58
SARASOTA								
$25,000	$75,000	$1,381	$81	$922	-	-	$2,384	#124
	100,000	1,816	81	922	-	-	2,819	#122
	125,000	2,250	81	922	-	-	3,253	#122
$50,000	$100,000	$1,816	$81	$1,492	-	-	$3,389	#67
	150,000	2,685	81	1,492	-	-	4,258	#83
	200,000	3,554	81	1,492	-	-	5,127	#88
$75,000	$150,000	$2,685	$81	$1,895	-	-	$4,661	#43
	250,000	4,423	81	1,895	-	-	6,399	#49
	350,000	6,161	81	1,895	-	-	8,137	#62
SIESTA KEY								
$25,000	$75,000	$952	$81	$922	-	-	$1,955	#55
	100,000	1,305	81	922	-	-	2,308	#61
	125,000	1,659	81	922	-	-	2,662	#64
$50,000	$100,000	$1,305	$81	$1,492	-	-	$2,878	#25
	150,000	2,012	81	1,492	-	-	3,585	#33
	200,000	2,719	81	1,492	-	-	4,292	#38
$75,000	$150,000	$2,012	$81	$1,895	-	-	$3,988	#12
	250,000	3,426	81	1,895	-	-	5,402	#19
	350,000	4,839	81	1,895	-	-	6,815	#29
TAMPA								
$25,000	$75,000	$1,363	$81	$889	-	-	$2,333	#118
	100,000	2,000	81	889	-	-	2,970	#136
	125,000	2,638	81	889	-	-	3,608	#138
$50,000	$100,000	$2,113	$81	$1,439	-	-	$3,633	#91
	150,000	3,388	81	1,439	-	-	4,908	#118
	200,000	4,663	81	1,439	-	-	6,183	#133
$75,000	$150,000	$3,388	$81	$1,827	-	-	$5,296	#68
	250,000	5,938	81	1,827	-	-	7,846	#111
	350,000	8,488	81	1,827	-	-	10,396	#130
VENICE								
$25,000	$75,000	$1,123	$81	$922	-	-	$2,126	#82
	100,000	1,561	81	922	-	-	2,564	#91
	125,000	2,000	81	922	-	-	3,003	#94

*There are 163 cities in this book. The city with the lowest tax burden for an income/home value combination is given the #1 rating; the city with the highest total tax burden is given the #163 rating.

FLORIDA TAX TABLE

Instructions

1. Find the Income in the far left column closest to your anticipated retirement income.
2. Find the Home Value closest to the value of the home where you will live in retirement.
3. Follow that row to your estimated Total Tax Burden at age 65 and beyond.

Income	Home Value	Property Tax & Other Fees	Personal Property Tax & Auto Fees	Sales Tax	Local Income Tax	State Income Tax	Total Tax Burden	Rank* From #1- #163
VENICE continued								
$50,000	$100,000	$1,561	$81	$1,492	-	-	$3,134	#39
	150,000	2,438	81	1,492	-	-	4,011	#56
	200,000	3,314	81	1,492	-	-	4,887	#70
$75,000	$150,000	$2,438	$81	$1,895	-	-	$4,414	#30
	250,000	4,190	81	1,895	-	-	6,166	#44
	350,000	5,943	81	1,895	-	-	7,919	#51
VERO BEACH								
$25,000	$75,000	$1,215	$81	$922	-	-	$2,218	#96
	100,000	1,715	81	922	-	-	2,718	#111
	125,000	2,215	81	922	-	-	3,218	#119
$50,000	$100,000	$1,715	$81	$1,492	-	-	$3,288	#56
	150,000	2,714	81	1,492	-	-	4,287	#84
	200,000	3,714	81	1,492	-	-	5,287	#99
$75,000	$150,000	$2,714	$81	$1,895	-	-	$4,690	#47
	250,000	4,713	81	1,895	-	-	6,689	#59
	350,000	6,712	81	1,895	-	-	8,688	#81
WINTER HAVEN								
$25,000	$75,000	$1,376	$81	$790	-	-	$2,247	#103
	100,000	1,984	81	790	-	-	2,855	#126
	125,000	2,593	81	790	-	-	3,464	#136
$50,000	$100,000	$1,984	$81	$1,279	-	-	$3,344	#63
	150,000	3,201	81	1,279	-	-	4,561	#105
	200,000	4,418	81	1,279	-	-	5,778	#117
$75,000	$150,000	$3,201	$81	$1,624	-	-	$4,906	#58
	250,000	5,634	81	1,624	-	-	7,339	#90
	350,000	8,068	81	1,624	-	-	9,773	#118

*There are 163 cities in this book. The city with the lowest tax burden for an income/home value combination is given the #1 rating; the city with the highest total tax burden is given the #163 rating.

Boca Raton

Boca Raton has no local income tax and does not levy an additional sales tax.

Most purchases are taxed at the state rate of 6%. Major consumer categories taxed at a different rate: None. Major consumer categories that are exempt from sales tax include: Drugs, groceries and medical services.

Within the city limits of Boca Raton, the property tax rate is .0209423. Homes are assessed at 100% of market value. There is a homestead exemption of $25,000 off assessed value available to all homeowners who own and reside on the property on January 1st of the tax year. Property tax does not cover garbage pickup; the additional fee is approximately $120 per year.

The personal property tax rate is the same as the real property tax rate. Personal property is assessed at 100% of market value. Items subject to the tax include mobile homes on rented land that are not registered as real property and mobile home attachments. We've assumed our couples do not own any items subject to the tax.

Bradenton

Bradenton has no local income tax and does not levy an additional sales tax.

Most purchases are taxed at the state rate of 6%. Major consumer categories taxed at a different rate: None. Major consumer categories that are exempt from sales tax include: Drugs, groceries and medical services.

For most residents living within the city limits of Bradenton, the property tax rate is .0210956. Homes are assessed at 100% of market value. There is a homestead exemption of

$25,000 off assessed value available to all homeowners who own and reside on the property on January 1st of the tax year. Property tax does not cover garbage pickup; the additional fee is approximately $128 per year. There is also a fire district fee of approximately $130 per year.

The personal property tax rate is the same as the real property tax rate. Personal property is assessed at 100% of market value. Items subject to the tax include mobile homes on rented land that are not registered as real property and mobile home attachments. We've assumed our couples do not own any items subject to the tax.

Celebration

Celebration has no local income tax but does levy a sales tax.

Most purchases are taxed at a rate of 7%. Major consumer categories taxed at a different rate: None. Major consumer categories that are exempt from sales tax include: Drugs, groceries and medical services.

For most residents living in Celebration, the property tax rate is .0166725. Homes are assessed at 100% of just value. There is a homestead exemption of $25,000 off assessed value available to all homeowners who own and reside on the property on January 1st of the tax year. Property tax includes garbage pickup. There is a maintenance fee of approximately $439 per year and a capital bonds and debt service fee that varies by location of approximately $613 per year. In addition, all homeowners in Celebration are subject to a homeowners association fee of approximately $810 per year.

The personal property tax rate is the same as the real property tax rate. Personal property is assessed at 100% of market value. Items subject to the tax include mobile homes on rented land that are not registered as real property and mobile home attachments. We've assumed our couples do not own any items subject to the tax.

Dade City

Dade City has no local income tax and does not levy an additional sales tax.

Most purchases are taxed at the state rate of 6%. Major consumer cat-

egories taxed at a different rate: None. Major consumer categories that are exempt from sales tax include: Drugs, groceries and medical services.

Within the city limits of Dade City, the property tax rate is .026593. Homes are assessed at 100% of market value. There is a homestead exemption of $25,000 off assessed value available to all homeowners who own and reside on the property on January 1st of the tax year. Property tax does not cover garbage pickup; the additional fee is approximately $120 per year.

The personal property tax rate is the same as the real property tax rate. Personal property is assessed at 100% of market value. Items subject to the tax include mobile homes on rented land that are not registered as real property and mobile home attachments. We've assumed our couples do not own any items subject to the tax.

DeLand

DeLand has no local income tax and does not levy an additional sales tax.

Most purchases are taxed at the state rate of 6%. Major consumer categories taxed at a different rate: None. Major consumer categories that are exempt from sales tax include: Drugs, groceries and medical services.

Within the city limits of DeLand, the property tax rate is .02408181. Homes are assessed at 100% of market value. There is a homestead exemption of $25,000 off assessed value available to all homeowners who own and reside on the property on January 1st of the tax year. There is an additional senior homestead exemption of $25,000 off assessed value for the city and county components of property tax if federal adjusted gross income is below $20,000. Property tax does not cover garbage pickup; the additional fee is approximately $134 per year. There is also a stormwater fee of $72 per year.

The personal property tax rate is the same as the real property tax rate. Personal property is assessed at 100% of market value. Items subject to the tax include mobile homes on rented land that are not registered as real property and mobile home attachments. We've assumed our couples do

not own any items subject to the tax.

Fort Lauderdale

Fort Lauderdale has no local income tax and does not levy an additional sales tax.

Most purchases are taxed at the state rate of 6%. Major consumer categories taxed at a different rate: None. Major consumer categories that are exempt from sales tax include: Drugs, groceries and medical services.

In District 0332 of Fort Lauderdale, the property tax rate is .0252650. Homes are assessed at 100% of market value. There is a homestead exemption of $25,000 off assessed value available to all homeowners who own and reside on the property on January 1st of the tax year. There is an additional senior homestead exemption of $25,000 off assessed value for the county component of property tax if federal adjusted gross income is below $20,000. Property tax does not cover garbage pickup; the additional fee is $347 per year. There is a stormwater fee of $27 per year and a fire rescue fee of $38 per year.

The personal property tax rate is the same as the real property tax rate. Personal property is assessed at 100% of market value. Items subject to the tax include mobile homes on rented land that are not registered as real property and mobile home attachments. We've assumed our couples do not own any items subject to the tax.

Gainesville

Gainesville has no local income tax and does not levy an additional sales tax.

Most purchases are taxed at the state rate of 6%. Major consumer categories taxed at a different rate: None. Major consumer categories that are exempt from sales tax include: Drugs, groceries and medical services.

In the St. John's Water District of Gainesville, the property tax rate is .0268816. Homes are assessed at 100% of market value. There is a homestead exemption of $25,000 off assessed value available to all homeowners who own and reside on the property on January 1st of the tax year. Property tax does not cover garbage pickup; the additional fee is approximately $192 per year.

The personal property tax rate is the same as the real property tax rate. Personal property is assessed at 100% of market value. Items subject to the tax include mobile homes on rented land that are not registered as real property and mobile home attachments. We've assumed our couples do not own any items subject to the tax.

Jacksonville

Jacksonville has no local income tax but does levy a sales tax.

Most purchases are taxed at a rate of 6.5%. Major consumer categories taxed at a different rate: None. Major consumer categories that are exempt from sales tax include: Drugs, groceries and medical services.

In the General Services District of Jacksonville, the property tax rate is .0203433. Homes are assessed at 100% of market value. There is a homestead exemption of $25,000 off assessed value available to all home-owners who own and reside on the property on January 1st of the tax year. There is an additional senior homestead exemption of $25,000 off assessed value for the government operation component of property tax if federal adjusted gross income is below $20,000. Property tax includes garbage pickup.

The personal property tax rate is the same as the real property tax rate. Personal property is assessed at 100% of market value. Items subject to the tax include mobile homes on rented land that are not registered as real property and mobile home attachments. We've assumed our couples do not own any items subject to the tax.

Jupiter

Jupiter has no local income tax and does not levy an additional sales tax.

Most purchases are taxed at the state rate of 6%. Major consumer categories taxed at a different rate: None. Major consumer categories that are exempt from sales tax include: Drugs, groceries and medical services.

Within the city limits of Jupiter, the property tax rate is .0214458. Homes are assessed at 100% of market value. There is a homestead exemption of $25,000 off assessed value available to all homeowners who own and reside

on the property on January 1st of the tax year. Property tax does not cover garbage pickup; the additional fee is approximately $80 per year. There is also a stormwater fee of $44 per year.

The personal property tax rate is the same as the real property tax rate. Personal property is assessed at 100% of market value. Items subject to the tax include mobile homes on rented land that are not registered as real property and mobile home attachments. We've assumed our couples do not own any items subject to the tax.

Key West

Key West has no local income tax but does levy a sales tax.

Most purchases are taxed at a rate of 7.5%. Major consumer categories taxed at a different rate: None. Major consumer categories that are exempt from sales tax include: Drugs, groceries and medical services.

Within the city limits of Key West, the property tax rate is .0143878. Homes are assessed at 100% of market value after deductions. There is a homestead exemption of $25,000 off assessed value available to all home-owners who own and reside on the property on January 1st of the tax year. There is an additional senior homestead exemption of $25,000 off assessed value for the county component of property tax if federal adjusted gross income is below $20,000. Property tax does not cover garbage pickup; the additional fee is approximately $270 per year.

The personal property tax rate is the same as the real property tax rate. Personal property is assessed at 100% of market value. Items subject to the tax include mobile homes on rented land that are not registered as real property and mobile home attachments. We've assumed our couples do not own any items subject to the tax.

Lakeland

Lakeland has no local income tax and does not levy an additional sales tax.

Most purchases are taxed at the state rate of 6%. Major consumer categories taxed at a different rate: None. Major consumer categories that are exempt from sales tax include: Drugs, groceries and medical services.

For some residents within the city limits of Lakeland, the property tax rate is .020673. Homes are assessed at 100% of just value. There is a homestead exemption of $25,000 off assessed value available to all home-owners who own and reside on the property on January 1st of the tax year. There is an additional senior homestead exemption of $10,000 off assessed value for the city component of property tax if federal adjusted gross income is below $20,000. Property tax does not cover garbage pickup; the additional fee is approximately $156 per year. There is also a stormwater fee of approximately $24 per year.

The personal property tax rate is the same as the real property tax rate. Personal property is assessed at 100% of market value. Items subject to the tax include mobile homes on rented land that are not registered as real property and mobile home attachments. We've assumed our couples do not own any items subject to the tax.

Leesburg

Leesburg has no local income tax but does levy a sales tax.

Most purchases are taxed at a rate of 7%. Major consumer categories taxed at a different rate: None. Major consumer categories that are exempt from sales tax include: Drugs, groceries and medical services.

Within the city limits of Leesburg, the property tax rate is .020634. Homes are assessed at 100% of market value. There is a homestead exemption of $25,000 off assessed value available to all homeowners who own and reside on the property on January 1st of the tax year. There is an additional senior homestead exemption of $25,000 off assessed value for the county component of property tax if federal adjusted gross income is below $20,000. Property tax does not cover garbage pickup; the additional fee is approximately $222 per year.

The personal property tax rate is the same as the real property tax rate. Personal property is assessed at 100% of market value. Items subject to the tax include mobile homes on rented land that are not registered as real property and mobile home attachments. We've assumed our couples do not own any items subject to the tax.

Longboat Key

Longboat Key has no local income tax but does levy a sales tax.

Most purchases are taxed at a rate of 7%. Major consumer categories taxed at a different rate: None. Major consumer categories that are exempt from sales tax include: Drugs, groceries and medical services.

For most residents living in the town of Longboat Key, the property tax rate is .0166669. Homes are assessed at 100% of market value. There is a homestead exemption of $25,000 off assessed value available to all homeowners who own and reside on the property on January 1st of the tax year. There is an additional senior homestead exemption of $25,000 off assessed value for the city component of property tax if federal adjusted gross income is below $20,000. Property tax does not cover garbage pickup; the additional fee is approximately $141 per year.

The personal property tax rate is the same as the real property tax rate. Personal property is assessed at 100% of market value. Items subject to the tax include mobile homes on rented land that are not registered as real property and mobile home attachments. We've assumed our couples do not own any items subject to the tax.

Miami

Miami has no local income tax but does levy a sales tax.

Most purchases are taxed at a rate of 6.5%. Major consumer categories taxed at a different rate: None. Major consumer categories that are exempt from sales tax include: Drugs, groceries and medical services.

In District 0100 of Miami, the property tax rate is .0273840. Homes are assessed at 100% of market value. There is a homestead exemption of $25,000 off assessed value available to all homeowners who own and reside on the property on January 1st of the tax year. Property tax does not cover garbage pickup; the additional fee is approximately $345 per year.

The personal property tax rate is the same as the real property tax rate.

Personal property is assessed at 100% of market value. Items subject to the tax include mobile homes on rented land that are not registered as real property and mobile home attachments. We've assumed our couples do not own any items subject to the tax.

Mount Dora

Mount Dora has no local income tax but does levy a sales tax.

Most purchases are taxed at a rate of 7%. Major consumer categories taxed at a different rate: None. Major consumer categories that are exempt from sales tax include: Drugs, groceries and medical services.

Within the city limits of Mount Dora, the property tax rate is .022315. Homes are assessed at 100% of market value. There is a homestead exemption of $25,000 off assessed value available to all homeowners who own and reside on the property on January 1st of the tax year. There is an additional senior homestead exemption of $25,000 off assessed value for the county and city components of property tax if federal adjusted gross income is below $20,000. Property tax does not cover garbage pickup; the additional fee is approximately $227 per year. There is also a storm drainage fee of approximately $36 per year.

The personal property tax rate is the same as the real property tax rate. Personal property is assessed at 100% of market value. Items subject to the tax include mobile homes on rented land that are not registered as real property and mobile home attachments. We've assumed our couples do not own any items subject to the tax.

Naples

Naples has no local income tax and does not levy an additional sales tax.

Most purchases are taxed at the state rate of 6%. Major consumer categories taxed at a different rate: None. Major consumer categories that are exempt from sales tax include: Drugs, groceries and medical services.

In District 4 of Naples, the property tax rate is .0133121. Homes are assessed at 100% of market value. There is a homestead exemption of

$25,000 off assessed value available to all homeowners who own and reside on the property on January 1st of the tax year. There is an additional senior homestead exemption of $25,000 off assessed value for the county and city components of property tax if federal adjusted gross income is below $20,000. Property tax does not cover garbage pickup; the additional fee is approximately $177 per year. There is also a stormwater fee of $48 per year and a landfill fee of $38 per year.

The personal property tax rate is the same as the real property tax rate. Personal property is assessed at 100% of market value. Items subject to the tax include mobile homes on rented land that are not registered as real property and mobile home attachments. We've assumed our couples do not own any items subject to the tax.

North Fort Myers

North Fort Myers has no local income tax and does not levy an additional sales tax.

Most purchases are taxed at the state rate of 6%. Major consumer categories taxed at a different rate: None. Major consumer categories that are exempt from sales tax include: Drugs, groceries and medical services.

For most residents living within the North Fort Myers Light/Fire District, the property tax rate is .0197448. Homes are assessed at 100% of market value. There is a homestead exemption of $25,000 off assessed value available to all homeowners who own and reside on the property on January 1st of the tax year. Property tax does not cover garbage pickup; the additional fee is approximately $185 per year.

The personal property tax rate is the same as the real property tax rate. Personal property is assessed at 100% of market value. Items subject to the tax include mobile homes on rented land that are not registered as real property and mobile home attachments. We've assumed our couples do not own any items subject to the tax.

Ocala

Ocala has no local income tax and does not levy an additional sales tax.

Most purchases are taxed at the

state rate of 6%. Major consumer categories taxed at a different rate: None. Major consumer categories that are exempt from sales tax include: Drugs, groceries and medical services.

In District 1001 of Ocala, the property tax rate is .0221448. Homes are assessed at 100% of just value. There is a homestead exemption of $25,000 off assessed value available to all homeowners who own and reside on the property on January 1st of the tax year. Property tax does not cover garbage pickup; the additional fee is approximately $190 per year.

The personal property tax rate is the same as the real property tax rate. Personal property is assessed at 100% of market value. Items subject to the tax include mobile homes on rented land that are not registered as real property and mobile home attachments. We've assumed our couples do not own any items subject to the tax.

Orlando

Orlando has no local income tax and does not levy an additional sales tax.

Most purchases are taxed at the state rate of 6%. Major consumer categories taxed at a different rate: None. Major consumer categories that are exempt from sales tax include: Drugs, groceries and medical services.

In District 08A of Orlando, the property tax rate is .0207207. Homes are assessed at 100% of market value. There is a homestead exemption of $25,000 off assessed value available to all homeowners who own and reside on the property on January 1st of the tax year. Property tax does not cover garbage pickup; the additional fee is approximately $156 per year. There is also a stormwater fee of approximately $66 per year.

The personal property tax rate is the same as the real property tax rate. Personal property is assessed at 100% of market value. Items subject to the tax include mobile homes on rented land that are not registered as real property and mobile home attachments. We've assumed our couples do not own any items subject to the tax.

Ormond Beach

Ormond Beach has no local income tax and does not levy an additional

sales tax.

Most purchases are taxed at the state rate of 6%. Major consumer categories taxed at a different rate: None. Major consumer categories that are exempt from sales tax include: Drugs, groceries and medical services.

Within the city limits of Ormond Beach, the property tax rate is .02240623. Homes are assessed at 100% of market value. There is a homestead exemption of $25,000 off assessed value available to all homeowners who own and reside on the property on January 1st of the tax year. There is an additional senior homestead exemption of $25,000 off assessed value for the city, county, port authority and mosquito control components of property tax if federal adjusted gross income is below $20,000. Property tax does not cover garbage pickup; the additional fee is approximately $146 per year. There is also a stormwater fee of $72 per year.

The personal property tax rate is the same as the real property tax rate. Personal property is assessed at 100% of market value. Items subject to the tax include mobile homes on rented land that are not registered as real property and mobile home attachments. We've assumed our couples do not own any items subject to the tax.

Pensacola

Pensacola has no local income tax but does levy a sales tax.

Most purchases are taxed at a rate of 7.5%. Major consumer categories taxed at a different rate: None. Major consumer categories that are exempt from sales tax include: Drugs, groceries and medical services.

Within the city limits of Pensacola, the property tax rate is .023112. Homes are assessed at 100% of market value. There is a homestead exemption of $25,000 off assessed value available to all homeowners who own and reside on the property on January 1st of the tax year. There is an additional senior homestead exemption of $25,000 off assessed value for the county component of property tax if federal adjusted gross income is below $20,000. Property tax does not cover garbage pickup; the additional fee is approximately

$238 per year.

The personal property tax rate is the same as the real property tax rate. Personal property is assessed at 100% of market value. Items subject to the tax include mobile homes on rented land that are not registered as real property and mobile home attachments. We've assumed our couples do not own any items subject to the tax.

Punta Gorda

Punta Gorda has no local income tax but does levy a sales tax.

Most purchases are taxed at a rate of 7%. Major consumer categories taxed at a different rate: None. Major consumer categories that are exempt from sales tax include: Drugs, groceries and medical services.

Within the city limits of Punta Gorda, the property tax rate is .016935. Homes are assessed at 100% of market value. There is a homestead exemption of $25,000 off assessed value available to all homeowners who own and reside on the property on January 1st of the tax year. Property tax does not cover garbage pickup; the additional fee is approximately $198 per year. There is also an additional fee for homes that are located on canals; harbor access is $250 per lot per year and non-harbor access is $120 per lot per year.

The personal property tax rate is the same as the real property tax rate. Personal property is assessed at 100% of market value. Items subject to the tax include mobile homes on rented land that are not registered as real property and mobile home attachments. We've assumed our couples do not own any items subject to the tax.

St. Augustine

St. Augustine has no local income tax and does not levy an additional sales tax.

Most purchases are taxed at the state rate of 6%. Major consumer categories taxed at a different rate: None. Major consumer categories that are exempt from sales tax include: Drugs, groceries and medical services.

For most residents living within the city limits of St. Augustine, the property tax rate is .0234346. Homes are assessed at 100% of market value.

There is a homestead exemption of $25,000 off assessed value available to all homeowners who own and reside on the property on January 1st of the tax year. There is an additional senior homestead exemption of $25,000 off assessed value for the county component of property tax if federal adjusted gross income is below $20,000. Property tax does not cover garbage pickup; the additional fee is approximately $152 per year.

The personal property tax rate is the same as the real property tax rate. Personal property is assessed at 100% of market value. Items subject to the tax include mobile homes on rented land that are not registered as real property and mobile home attachments. We've assumed our couples do not own any items subject to the tax.

St. Petersburg

St. Petersburg has no local income tax but does levy a sales tax.

Most purchases are taxed at a rate of 7%. Major consumer categories taxed at a different rate: None. Major consumer categories that are exempt from sales tax include: Drugs, groceries and medical services.

In the Downtown Improvement District of St. Petersburg, the property tax rate is .0247806. Homes are assessed at 100% of market value. There is a homestead exemption of $25,000 off assessed value available to all homeowners who own and reside on the property on January 1st of the tax year. Property tax does not cover garbage pickup; the additional fee is approximately $196 per year. There is also a stormwater management fee of approximately $54 per year.

The personal property tax rate is the same as the real property tax rate. Personal property is assessed at 100% of market value. Items subject to the tax include mobile homes on rented land that are not registered as real property and mobile home attachments. We've assumed our couples do not own any items subject to the tax.

Sanibel Island

Sanibel Island has no local income tax and does not levy an additional sales tax.

Most purchases are taxed at the state rate of 6%. Major consumer cat-

egories taxed at a different rate: None. Major consumer categories that are exempt from sales tax include: Drugs, groceries and medical services.

For most residents living on Sanibel Island, the property tax rate is .0190422. Homes are assessed at 100% of market value. There is a homestead exemption of $25,000 off assessed value available to all homeowners who own and reside on the property on January 1st of the tax year. There is an additional senior homestead exemption of $25,000 for the city component of property tax if federal adjusted gross income is below $20,000. Property tax does not cover garbage pickup; the additional fee is approximately $194 per year.

The personal property tax rate is the same as the real property tax rate. Personal property is assessed at 100% of market value. Items subject to the tax include mobile homes on rented land that are not registered as real property and mobile home attachments. We've assumed our couples do not own any items subject to the tax.

Sarasota

Sarasota has no local income tax but does levy a sales tax.

Most purchases are taxed at a rate of 7%. Major consumer categories taxed at a different rate: None. Major consumer categories that are exempt from sales tax include: Drugs, groceries and medical services.

Within the city limits of Sarasota, the property tax rate is .0173812. Homes are assessed at 100% of market value. There is a homestead exemption of $25,000 off assessed value available to all homeowners who own and reside on the property on January 1st of the tax year. Property tax does not cover garbage pickup; the additional fee is approximately $274 per year. There is also a stormwater fee of approximately $73 per year and a fire/rescue fee based on the square footage of the home.

The personal property tax rate is the same as the real property tax rate. Personal property is assessed at 100% of market value. Items subject to the tax include mobile homes on rented land that are not registered as real property and mobile home attach-

ments. We've assumed our couples do not own any items subject to the tax.

Siesta Key

Siesta Key has no local income tax but does levy a sales tax.

Most purchases are taxed at a rate of 7%. Major consumer categories taxed at a different rate: None. Major consumer categories that are exempt from sales tax include: Drugs, groceries and medical services.

For most residents living within the city limits of Siesta Key, the property tax rate is .0141366. Homes are assessed at 100% of market value. There is a homestead exemption of $25,000 off assessed value available to all homeowners who own and reside on the property on January 1st of the tax year. Property tax does not cover garbage pickup; the additional fee is approximately $172 per year. There is also a stormwater fee of approximately $73 per year.

The personal property tax rate is the same as the real property tax rate. Personal property is assessed at 100% of market value. Items subject to the tax include mobile homes on rented land that are not registered as real property and mobile home attachments. We've assumed our couples do not own any items subject to the tax.

Tampa

Tampa has no local income tax but does levy a sales tax.

Most purchases are taxed at a rate of 6.75%. Major consumer categories taxed at a different rate: None. Major consumer categories that are exempt from sales tax include: Drugs, groceries and medical services.

In District TBH of Tampa, the property tax rate is .0254975. Homes are assessed at 100% of market value. There is a homestead exemption of $25,000 off assessed value available to all homeowners who own and reside on the property on January 1st of the tax year. There is an additional senior homestead exemption of $15,000 off assessed value for the county component of property tax if federal adjusted gross income is below $20,000. Property tax does not cover garbage pickup; the additional fee is approximately $201 per year.

The personal property tax rate is

the same as the real property tax rate. Personal property is assessed at 100% of market value. Items subject to the tax include mobile homes on rented land that are not registered as real property and mobile home attachments. We've assumed our couples do not own any items subject to the tax.

Venice

Venice has no local income tax but does levy a sales tax.

Most purchases are taxed at a rate of 7%. Major consumer categories taxed at a different rate: None. Major consumer categories that are exempt from sales tax include: Drugs, groceries and medical services.

For most residents living within the city limits of Venice, the property tax rate is .0175258. Homes are assessed at 100% of market value. There is a homestead exemption of $25,000 off assessed value available to all homeowners who own and reside on the property on January 1st of the tax year. Property tax does not cover garbage pickup; the additional fee is approximately $152 per year. There is also a stormwater fee of approximately $36 per year and an ambulance district fee for standby rescue services of approximately $59 per year.

The personal property tax rate is

the same as the real property tax rate. Personal property is assessed at 100% of market value. Items subject to the tax include mobile homes on rented land that are not registered as real property and mobile home attachments. We've assumed our couples do not own any items subject to the tax.

Vero Beach

Vero Beach has no local income tax but does levy a sales tax.

Most purchases are taxed at a rate of 7%. Major consumer categories taxed at a different rate: None. Major consumer categories that are exempt from sales tax include: Drugs, groceries and medical services.

In the Country Club Pointe area of Vero Beach, the property tax rate is .01998769. Homes are assessed at 100% of market value. There is a homestead exemption of $25,000 off assessed value available to all homeowners who own and reside on the property on January 1st of the tax year. Property tax does not cover garbage pickup; the additional fee is approximately $140 per year. There is also a solid waste landfill fee of approximately $76 per year.

The personal property tax rate is the same as the real property tax rate. Personal property is assessed at 100% of market value. Items subject to the

tax include mobile homes on rented land that are not registered as real property and mobile home attachments. We've assumed our couples do not own any items subject to the tax.

Winter Haven

Winter Haven has no local income tax and does not levy an additional sales tax.

Most purchases are taxed at the state rate of 6%. Major consumer categories taxed at a different rate: None. Major consumer categories that are exempt from sales tax include: Drugs, groceries and medical services.

One of the various property tax rates in Winter Haven is .024335. Homes are assessed at 100% of just value. There is a homestead exemption of $25,000 off assessed value available to all homeowners who own and reside on the property on January 1st of the tax year. Property tax does not cover garbage pickup; the additional fee is approximately $159 per year.

The personal property tax rate is the same as the real property tax rate. Personal property is assessed at 100% of market value. Items subject to the tax include mobile homes on rented land that are not registered as real property and mobile home attachments. We've assumed our couples do not own any items subject to the tax.

• Florida's Best Retirement Towns •

Boca Raton, Florida

Empowered by the will and determination of an enlightened citizenry, protected by effective land-use planning and comprehensive zoning laws, and transformed by a highly successful downtown redevelopment program in the '90s, Boca Raton is one of the most beautiful cities in the world.

By focusing on zero traffic congestion and technology to advance quality of life as two major issues to be addressed in the early years of the new millennium, the "city within a park" has announced its intentions to remain "Beautiful Boca" — and a beautiful place to live.

Stan and Gladys Perlstein retired

here from Philadelphia. "We are enjoying the good life — boating, socializing, not looking at my watch," Gladys says. "They're tearing down old houses and putting up multimillion-dollar homes on the waterfront. And they've made some nice improvements downtown. All of the changes have been for the better. Come and enjoy."

Population: 70,000 in city, 1,093,000 in county.

Climate:

	High	Low
January	76	63
July	90	78

Cost of living: Above average (specific index not available).

Average price of a new home: $300,000

Security: 44.6 crimes per 1,000 residents,

higher than the national average of 42.7 crimes per 1,000 residents.

Information: Greater Boca Raton Chamber of Commerce, 1800 N. Dixie Highway, Boca Raton, FL 33432, (561) 395-4433 or www.bocaratonchamber. com.

Bradenton, Florida

Bordered by rivers, bays, islands and the Gulf of Mexico, this pretty, progressive, art-loving community is reluctantly undergoing a metamorphosis of sorts. While clinging to its sleepy small-town past, it is struggling to absorb the significant socioeconomic expansion and population explosion it has experienced over the last two decades — 44 percent in the '80s and more than 15 percent in the '90s.

Still, housing choices are almost unlimited, from new, upscale planned developments and popular riverside, bayside and Gulf-front condominiums to apartments and historic neighborhood homes within walking distance of the newly renovated downtown.

"It rivals Sarasota in its beauty," says John Quam, who with his wife, Birgit, retired to one of its barrier islands, Anna Maria, from New Jersey in 1997. Birgit loves the weather, "and we don't have any problems with the summers here either," she says. Citing friendly people and a laid-back, relaxing atmosphere as two of its many endearing qualities, she reserves her strongest accolades for its beaches. "I have traveled all over the world," she says, "and Anna Maria Island has the prettiest beaches I've ever seen."

While the rapid growth hasn't negatively impacted their lifestyle, John is concerned that it will. "A lot of people who used to go to Fort Myers and Cape Coral are now coming here," he says. "It's just a matter of time."

Population: 48,659 in city, 264,002 in county.

Climate:

	High	Low
January	71	49
July	91	72

Cost of living: 102, based on national average of 100.

Average price of a new home: $143,700

Security: 71.1 crimes per 1,000 residents, higher than the national average of 42.7 crimes per 1,000 residents.

Information: Manatee Chamber of Commerce, P.O. Box 321, 222 10th St. W., Bradenton, FL 34206, (941) 748-3411 or www.manateechamber.com.

Celebration, Florida

"It doesn't get any better than this" is a hackneyed phrase that perfectly fits this 6-year-old town on the outskirts of Orlando.

Built by a subsidiary of the Walt Disney Corp., and only minutes away from Disney World, it has a complete downtown, school with kindergarten through 12th grade, 1,432-bed hospital, 60,000-square-foot fitness center, 18-hole golf course, parks and a broad mix of pre-1940s architectural-style housing.

When Ernie and Melie Sue Ablang first visited Celebration from their home in Chesapeake City, MD, "there was nothing but ground, a few tents and a scale model," Ernie says. Through a lottery they were selected to be one of the first 300 homeowners in the community.

"We moved into our new home in January 1997," Melie Sue says. "Having your bank, grocery, theater and post office all within walking distance is wonderful. All ages are here, and we love seeing and hearing the children. There are sidewalks everywhere. Children are skating by. Families are walking by. We do a lot of walking at night. We can walk downtown at midnight, and feel perfectly safe doing it."

Population: 3,000 in city, 127,728 in county.

Climate:

	High	Low
January	72	49
July	92	73

Cost of living: Above average (specific index not available).

Average price of a new home: $300,000

Security: 54.1 crimes per 1,000 residents in Osceola County, higher than the national average of 42.7 crimes per 1,000 residents. Specific crime rate not available for Celebration.

Information: Celebration Realty, 700 Celebration Ave., Celebration, FL 34747, (407) 566-HOME or www.celebration fl.com.

Dade City, Florida

Groomed as a "Main Street" community, honored as an outstanding rural community and recognized as a "Tree City USA" community by the National Arbor Day Foundation, this five-star small town evokes memories of a slower-paced, quieter, friendlier America of a half-century ago.

The cool shade of moss-hung oaks and brick-paved streets draw strollers young and old, while casual shoppers browse through antique shops and would-be-diners seek seating in popular restaurants.

Nearby modest and historic homes place many residents within short walking distance of the safe, quaint, restored downtown, while others arrive by automobile from outlying master-planned

golfing communities

Harold and Joan Theiss of Dayton, OH, had a winter home in Summerfield south of Ocala but settled on the Dade City area as their permanent Florida home site. Located in "rolling terrain reminiscent of the Carolinas," Harold says, "Dade City has the convenience without the congestion of coastal areas. In about a half-hour we can be at the Gulf, in Tampa or Lakeland. It's a nice, slow, laid-back community and, by design, there's a slower development pace here than in places a little farther south."

"If you're looking for a retirement community where old people pitch horseshoes and roll bocce balls all day, you're not going to get that here," Joan adds.

Population: 6,000 in city, 285,000 in county.

Climate:

	High	Low
January	75	51
July	92	71

Cost of living: Average (specific index not available).

Average price of a new home: $169,000

Security: 116.1 crimes per 1,000 residents, higher than the national average of 42.7 crimes per 1,000 residents.

Information: Greater Dade City Chamber of Commerce, 14112 Eighth Street, Dade City, FL 33525, (352) 567-3769 or www.dadecitychamber.org.

DeLand, Florida

A short stroll down "The Boulevard" in downtown DeLand invigorates, enlightens and entertains. It is Florida's first official "Main Street" city, but neither population growth nor new construction nor major renovations have much affected the peaceful, tranquil ambiance of this one-time outpost on the St. Johns River, a byway to the Atlantic Ocean.

The 125-year-old city has a youthful vitality engendered by the location of Stetson University, a walk of only a few minutes from the city center. Its Cultural Arts Center is a popular destination for those attending stage productions, Little Symphony performances and other entertainment fare put on by local talent and touring groups.

Al and Jean Reeves relocated from

Rochester, NY, and though they go back each year to visit their son, "we have no desire to return there to live," Jean says, citing the warm climate, beautiful setting, size, attractiveness and convenience of DeLand. "Within five minutes we can get everything we need.

"In winter, it's busy with snowbirds, and getting busier year-round. There's a lot of new development and low-cost housing for seniors. We're glad we made the move," she says. "We still love DeLand."

Population: 20,000 in city, 425,000 in county.

Climate:

	High	Low
January	91	69
July	70	44

Cost of living: Below average (specific index not available).

Average price of a new home: $107,000

Security: 122.5 crimes per 1,000 residents, higher than the national average of 42.7 crimes per 1,000 residents.

Information: DeLand Area Chamber of Commerce, 336 N. Woodland Blvd., DeLand, FL 32720, (904) 734-4331 or www.delandchamber.org.

Gainesville, Florida

Lucille Schlichting moved to Gainesville from Long Island, NY, with her husband, Bill, and even after he passed away, she decided to stay. "It's a wonderful place to live," she says.

"There are outstanding cultural activities at the University of Florida, excellent medical facilities for a community of this size, access to Cedar Key on the Gulf and St. Augustine on the Atlantic within an hour, good-tasting water and many opportunities for volunteer work. And it's much less expensive to live here," Lucille adds.

"We have people from all over the country living here," she says, "and despite their different backgrounds, they form a nice homogenous mix."

Despite a population of 105,400 full-time residents and 46,000 students at the university, the oldest and largest in the state, Lucille finds she can get around the city quite easily. "There is little traffic congestion," she says.

For nature lovers, Alachua County provides a diversity of opportunities, with roughly one-third of the land dedicated to parks, preserves, forests, lakes, rivers and springs. "I would like to drive over to the coast, walk the beaches and watch the sun rise and set," Lucille says. "I'm just too busy."

Population: 105,400 in city, 215,620 in county.

Climate:

	High	Low
January	66	42
July	91	71

Cost of living: Average (specific index not available).

Average price of a new home: $163,000

Security: 81.4 crimes per 1,000 residents, higher than the national average of 42.7 crimes per 1,000 residents.

Information: Gainesville Area Chamber of Commerce, P.O. Box 1187, 235 S. Main St., Suite 206, Gainesville, FL 32602, (352) 334-7100 or www.gainesvillechamber.com.

Jupiter-Tequesta, Florida

These quaint, quiet, slow-paced seaside towns offer a last-chance refuge from the gathering storm of city life as you drive south on I-95 into the quickening tempo of West Palm Beach, Fort Lauderdale and Miami.

One can live on the island, focused on a maritime lifestyle, or in one of a number of master-planned communities, with or without a golf course, or in the 2,300-acre new community of Abacoa, with a baseball winter-training facility, university campus, parks, golf courses and every other amenity needed to avoid contact with the outside world.

It's an improbable move from Grass Valley in Northern California to Jupiter in South Florida, but Bob and Annamarie Broeder did just that, with no regrets. Well, just one: "We enjoyed puttering around in our lawn and garden there, and living in a condominium doesn't allow us to do that here," Annamarie says.

Aside from that minor inconvenience, the Broeders got exactly what they were looking for, and Bob easily ticks off the before-and-after of their move. Good golfing weather and relief from a cold winter climate were among the reasons, "though I might suggest to someone considering retirement here that they rent for three months during the summer to see if they can handle the heat."

Quick access to good medical facilities is a plus. "It was a one-hour trip to the hospital there," he says. "We are five minutes from the Jupiter Medical Center, and they are better equipped to handle seniors." And availability of excellent shopping, dining and other amenities also are important. "We had to drive an hour into Sacramento for good shopping and dining. These towns have many good restaurants, and we're 15 minutes from Palm Beach Gardens Mall," Bob says.

The Broeders still spend the summers in California, and they like being only 30 minutes from West Palm Beach Airport.

Population: 29,000 in city, 1,093,000 in county.

Climate:

	High	Low
January	74	54
July	90	73

Cost of living: Average (specific index not available).

Average price of a new home: $169,900

Security: In Jupiter, 52.3 crimes per 1,000 residents, higher than the national average of 42.7 crimes per 1,000 residents.

Information: Jupiter-Tequesta-Juno Beach Chamber of Commerce, 800 N. U.S. Highway 1, Jupiter, FL 33477, (561) 746-7111 or www.jupiterfl.org.

Key West, Florida

This storied, almost legendary town at the southern tip of the Florida Keys has undergone dramatic change since 1900 when Henry Flagler began building his railroad to bring tourists and settlers to a remote island. The railroad didn't last long, destroyed by the Great Hurricane of 1935, but the government bought up the right-of-way and built U.S. Highway 1 — the Overseas Highway — 113 miles and 42 bridges long.

Growth was immediate, and through the years the island has been home to a multitude of creative writers and artists, including Tennessee Williams, John J. Audubon and Ernest Hemingway. One thing didn't change, however — its size. Real-estate prices are sky-high and rising as physical limitations on growth make the law of supply and demand especially relevant.

Bob and Flo Cornell came here from Cambridge, OH, "for the warm climate, as a remedy for Flo's problem with cold winter weather," Bob says. "There are more people than when we came, it's sometimes hard to find parking, and the trolley going by with its speaker volume up can be annoying. But it's still a great place to live.

"It still has a small-town feel — real quiet. You know your neighbors. If you can afford it, I recommend it," Bob adds.

Population: 28,500 in city, 85,000 in county.

Climate:

	High	Low
January	75	65
July	89	80

Cost of living: Above average (specific index not available).

Average price of a new home: $389,000

Security: 97 crimes per 1,000 residents, higher than the national average of 42.7 crimes per 1,000 residents.

Information: Key West Chamber of Commerce, 402 Wall St., Key West, FL 33040, (305) 294-2587 or www.key westchamber.org.

Lakeland, Florida

Lakeland is a five-star city, its meticulously restored downtown filled with parks, lakes, historic structures and classy cultural venues. You don't have to live in the suburbs to have an attractive environment. Some of the best neighborhoods with fine homes, manicured lawns and lakeside vistas are within walking distance of the town center.

Its single drawback is having to use heavily traveled Interstate 4 to get to Gulf beaches. But with Broadway performances and sporting events at the Lakeland Center and Polk Theatre, Detroit Tigers spring baseball games, and a choice of 29 golf courses in the area, the route to the beach seems a minor problem.

Joe and Nancy Fontaine, lifetime residents of Worcester, MA, visited Lakeland in January 1996 "just to look around," Joe recalls. "It was a spur-of-the-moment anniversary trip. Seven months later, we were living here.

"I went to see the mayor — without an appointment — and checked with the city manager to see what volunteer jobs were available," Joe says. "I look on Lakeland as the capital of Central Florida. It has a good cost of living, fantastic medical facilities and an unbelievable climate. It's a clean, well-run city."

Population: 79,000 in city, 483,924 in county.

Climate:

	High	Low
January	72	50
July	92	73

Cost of living: Average (specific index not available).

Average price of a new home: $127,000

Security: 90.4 crimes per 1,000 residents, higher than the national average of 42.7 crimes per 1,000 residents.

Information: Lakeland Chamber of Commerce, 35 Lake Morton Drive, Lakeland, FL 33802, (863) 688-8551 or www.lakelandchamber.com.

Leesburg, Florida

A quiet, small town with an attractive, rehabilitated downtown, Leesburg is the heart of Lake County, appropriately named for some 1,000 lakes that adorn the countryside.

Dozens of adult and retirement communities, as well as golf course- and marina-based developments, attract retirees to an area where, predictably, golfing, boating and fishing are the recreational favorites. Back-roads bicycling is another popular activity. You can access either coast in just over an hour or drive down to Disney World via Florida's Turnpike in 45 minutes.

When they retired from Wisconsin, Jan and Barney Rae chose the Leesburg area for its "great location, rolling hills, Highland Lakes (a gated, waterfront retirement community) and the town itself," Jan says. "It's a neat, growing city with a wonderful downtown square, lots of activities and festivals.

"Unlike some areas of South Florida, overcrowding is not an issue in Lake County," she adds. "We don't experience it or hear complaints about it."

Population: 17,000 in city, 210,528 in county.

Climate:

	High	Low
January	75	57
July	94	74

Cost of living: Average (specific index not available).

Average price of a new home: $159,000

Security: 86.5 crimes per 1,000 residents, higher than the national average of 42.7 crimes per 1,000 residents.

Information: Leesburg Area Chamber of Commerce, 103 S. Sixth St., Leesburg, FL 34748, (352) 787-2131 or www.lees burgchamber.com.

Longboat Key, Florida

This pristine Gulf Coast island, unequaled in the grandeur of its housing, beautiful landscape and white-sand beaches, might have been just another overpopulated tourist trap had not wise city stewards many years ago revised zoning laws and ordinances to limit growth. Now a permanent, year-round population of 8,000 calls Longboat Key home, a far cry from the 60,000 inhabitants expected under the original plan.

But a combination of limited land and growth restrictions exacts a heavy toll on desirable land costs, and the average cost of housing and property taxes are among the highest in the state of Florida.

Retirees who have made the move say it is well worth the cost. Fran and Len Miller of Wallingford, PA, were "booked here by a travel agent by mistake, but once we saw Longboat, we never wanted to leave," Fran says. "The beautiful white-sand beaches, remarkable landscaping, wonderful and diverse housing and proximity to Sarasota's culture and entertainment all add up to heaven on Earth," she says.

Population: 8,000 in summer and 22,000 in winter in city, 264,002 in Manatee County, 325,957 in Sarasota County.

Climate:

	High	Low
January	72	51
July	90	75

Cost of living: Above average (specific index not available).

Average price of a new home: $600,000

Security: 25.2 crimes per 1,000 residents, lower than the national average of 42.7 crimes per 1,000 residents.

Information: Longboat Key Chamber of Commerce, 6854 Gulf of Mexico Drive, Longboat Key, FL 34228, (941) 383-2466

Mount Dora, Florida

A small, picturesque lakeside town, off the beaten path and exhibiting a little touch of New England, is a good description of this community of 10,000 people, 25 miles north of Orlando. Tree-shaded parks, sidewalk cafes, arts-and-crafts shops and faithfully restored Victorian homes are its trademarks.

Famous as the home of major festivals, it hosts an annual fine arts festival that attracts some 300,000 visitors each February. The spring festival in April celebrates music and literature and fills the IceHouse Theatre and all other available public forums with enthusiastic crowds. And in fall, the largest and oldest cycling event in the country and an annual juried craft fair bring thousands more to the town.

Six-mile-long Lake Dora provides seagoing access through a chain of lakes leading to the St. Johns River and the Atlantic Ocean — and a shortcut to downtown for lakeside boat owners.

John and Billie Keenon looked at retirement sites in six states before moving to Mount Dora from Little Rock, AR, in 1995. "I didn't want to retire to Florida," Billie says, "but it was love at first sight."

"If you're looking for a place to retire," John says, "put it on the top of your list."

Population: 10,000 in city, 210,528 in county.

Climate:

	High	Low
January	72	49
July	92	73

Cost of living: Average (specific index not available).

Average price of a new home: $185,000

Security: 66.6 crimes per 1,000 residents, higher than the national average of 42.7 crimes per 1,000 residents.

Information: Mount Dora Area Chamber of Commerce, 341 Alexander St., Mount Dora, FL 32757, (352) 383-2165 or www.mountdora.com.

Naples, Florida

This beautiful Gulf Coast town has experienced one of the highest population growth rates in the nation over the past two decades, fueled by thousands of incoming retirees. It has the elegance, beauty and sophistication of the five-star Ritz-Carlton and the middle-class appeal of Holiday Inn. There are upscale master-planned golf and country club communities, multimillion-dollar mansions and affordable subdivisions. Its resident mix includes patrons of the Naples Philharmonic Center for the Performing Arts and the Greyhound Track and Everglades Airboat Tours. And, you can get your tan at pricey health resorts and spas or lying on the beach.

Bob and Lois Geschrei retired here from Cincinnati eight years ago and have witnessed tremendous growth, especially in the northern outskirts. "Anyone considering moving here needs to be aware that growth is changing the character of Naples. It's still a great place to be — a lovely community," Bob says. "But it's not going to stop growing. They are tearing down small bungalows here a few blocks from the Gulf, selling the lots for $500,000 and building mega-homes that cost $5 to $6 million."

Population: 21,000 in city, 220,000 in county.

Climate:

	High	Low
January	78	53
July	91	72

Cost of living: Above average (specific index not available).

Average price of a new home: $299,000

Security: 58.5 crimes per 1,000 residents, higher than the national average of 42.7 crimes per 1,000 residents.

Information: Naples Area Chamber of Commerce, 3620 Tamiami Trail N., Naples, FL 34103, (941) 262-6376 or www.napleschamber.org.

North Fort Myers, Florida

North Fort Myers was founded as a bedroom community for Fort Myers in unincorporated Lee County. It was favored by retirees because of low taxes, an uncongested environment and some excellent manufactured housing and golf and country club developments along the waterfront.

Its residents still cross the double bridges over the Caloosahatchee to shop, dine and entertain themselves in Fort Myers, but not out of necessity. U.S. Highway 41 North and State Road 78 out to Pine Island have become heavily commercialized, and new retirement communities seem to spring up along these arteries almost daily.

Shirley and Paul Reitmeier moved here from Anchorage, AK, before the current growth boom started, and Shirley says the "commercial growth and new road construction have enhanced the area. There are more and better restaurants, shopping options and reasonable prices."

Population: 46,478 in city, 420,000 in county.

Climate:

	High	Low
January	74	53
July	91	74

Cost of living: Average (specific index not available).

Average price of a new home: $159,900

Security: 129.1 crimes per 1,000 residents, higher than the national average of 42.7 crimes per 1,000 residents.

Information: North Fort Myers Chamber of Commerce, 2787 N. Tamiami Trail, Suite 100, North Fort Myers, FL 33903, (941) 997-9111 or www.northfortmyers.org.

Ocala, Florida

This still-sleepy small town in north-central Florida has more master-planned developments per capita than any town in the state. Its location means that residents can be in Daytona Beach or Orlando in about an hour or pop up to Gainesville in 45 minutes for a University of Florida sporting event.

Low housing costs and a rural environment are attracting out-of-state retirees like Jerry and Nancy Brown, who moved from Dayton, OH, in 1998 after visiting three times in three months. "We were pretty much sold the first time we came and just wanted to reaffirm our decision," Nancy says.

Jerry, who says he started thinking about possible retirement sites "when I was about 22," says he found that the area "offers all of the activities I like — lakes and rivers to fish in, wonderful golf courses — and great value in housing." He also is enthusiastic about the climate. "It's amazing to me, the conditions in the summertime. I've been here three summers and I keep waiting for it to get bad. It never has."

"We have over 200 days a year when

we need neither heat nor air conditioning," Nancy says. "We call them the comfort days."

Population: 60,000 in city, 245,000 in county.

Climate:

	High	Low
January	70	45
July	92	71

Cost of living: Below average (specific index not available).

Average price of a new home: $120,000

Security: 115.4 crimes per 1,000 residents, higher than the national average of 42.7 crimes per 1,000 residents.

Information: Ocala Marion County Chamber of Commerce, 110 Silver Springs Blvd., Ocala, FL 34470, (352) 629-8051 or www.ocalacc.com.

Orlando, Florida

At the mention of Orlando, your first thought might be of Walt Disney World, but there's a lot more to Orlando than Minnie and Mickey. The metropolitan area is brimming with first-class cultural, educational, recreational and healthcare facilities.

It has award-winning residential neighborhoods and master-planned communities in quiet corners where you'll hardly notice a ripple from the 20 million visitors who pass through the city's portals each year.

Ken Howell, who retired with his wife, Qwen, from Rochester, NY, found Orlando to be "a beautiful city, in constant change. It is so convenient. It has everything we want and need.

"Spend at least a year before going back North, to get adjusted to the weather," Ken advises. "You'll never want to leave again."

Population: 175,000 in city, 825,000 in county.

Climate:

	High	Low
January	71	49
July	91	73

Cost of living: 99, based on national average of 100.

Average price of a new home: $138,000

Security: 136.2 crimes per 1,000 residents, higher than the national average of 42.7 crimes per 1,000 residents.

Information: Orlando Regional Chamber of Commerce, P.O. Box 1234, Orlando, FL 32802-1234, (407) 425-1234 or www. orlando.org.

Ormond Beach, Florida

This peaceful seaside town just north of Daytona Beach has made the transition from the former winter home of the rich and famous — the Vanderbilts, Fords, Astors and Rockefellers all had homes here — to a playground of the happily retired.

Today's retirees live in low-slung, lushly landscaped beachfront homes, attractive master-planned developments along inland rivers and forests, and affordable manufactured-home communities adorned with small lakes, waterfalls and gardens. One can practically walk to the Daytona International Speedway or the recreational choices of Ocala National Forest, and the historical artifacts of St. Augustine can be reached in 30 minutes. The big-city amenities of Orlando and entertainment fare of Walt Disney World are only about an hour away.

Pete and Sharon Petropolis moved from Missouri. "It's a lovely area with a clean, attractive downtown," Sharon says. "We like the fact that it's so easy to access the Halifax River, the nice beaches and I-95 for travel to surrounding towns.

"The Ormond Beach Senior Center is an impressive building, the library is beautiful, and the performing arts center has something every weekend. And I can sit outside and watch the shuttle launches at Kennedy Space Center," she adds.

Population: 34,791 in city, 425,000 in county.

Climate:

	High	Low
January	68	47
July	90	73

Cost of living: Average (specific index not available).

Average price of a new home: $155,000

Security: 44.4 crimes per 1,000 residents, higher than the national average of 42.7 crimes per 1,000 residents.

Information: Ormond Beach Chamber of Commerce, 165 W. Granada Blvd., Ormond Beach, FL 32174, (904) 677-3454 or www.ormondchamber.com.

Pensacola, Florida

Diversity is the key to Pensacola's attraction for retirees from all walks of life, especially retired military who served a hitch in Pensacola and savor the easy access to the naval hospital, commissary and their comrades-in-arms. It's a town that has a storied history under five different flags.

Excellent medical facilities, special senior rates at educational institutions, wonderful cultural offerings, a low cost of living, beautiful beaches and emerald-blue waters are other retiree attractions.

Bob and Katie Galeon visited Pensacola on vacation from their home in Minneapolis, MN, and didn't want to leave. "We stayed as long as we could, looked at potential retirement sites on the west side, north of I-10 and down along the beaches in Gulf Breeze," Bob says. "Availability of housing is a big attraction here — type and location. We love the town, too. Of course, climate was the big incentive."

Population: 61,300 in city, 303,465 in Escambia County and 115,240 in Santa Rosa County.

Climate:

	High	Low
January	60	41
July	90	74

Cost of living: 97, based on national average of 100

Average price of a new home: $159,000

Security: 55.2 crimes per 1,000 residents, higher than the national average of 42.7 crimes per 1,000 residents.

Information: Pensacola Area Chamber of Commerce, 117 W. Garden St., P.O. Box 550, Pensacola, FL 32593-0550, (850) 438-4081 or www.pensacola chamber.com.

Punta Gorda, Florida

This meticulously groomed small town on protected Charlotte Harbor offers canal-front and historic district homes, along with some of the finest master-planned communities on the southwest Gulf coast. It's perfect for boating, fishing, golfing, tennis or simply enjoying a quiet atmosphere. Leonard and Harriet Mielke retired here from Dearborn Heights, MI, and are "totally happy" with their decision. "There's big growth taking place — a lot of new home developments and a few more businesses," Harriet says. "But it's still a real comfortable place to live, a boater's haven with very friendly people. Properties are kept real neat and tidy all over the community."

Population: 13,021 in city, 139,824 in county.

Climate:

	High	Low
January	74	51
July	92	73

Cost of living: Average (specific index not available).

Average price of a new home: $189,000

Security: 24.4 crimes per 1,000 residents, lower than the national average of 42.7 crimes per 1,000 residents.

Information: Charlotte County Chamber of Commerce, 326 W. Marion Ave., Suite 112, Punta Gorda, FL 33950, (941) 639-2222 or www.charlottecounty chamber.org.

St. Augustine, Florida

World famous as the site of Ponce de Leon's legendary fountain of youth, this 435-year-old landmark city has been rediscovered in recent years by retirees. Its attractions include a 144-block historic district, excellent beaches and, more recently, the Saint Johns Development, a master-planned project that includes the World Golf Village.

Bob and Louise Ebbinghaus moved to St. Augustine "to escape the high cost of living and cold winters in New York," Bob says. "Taxes are low and, of course, the winters are much warmer, although the temperature dipped into the 40s last night.

"We have more restaurants, malls and shopping centers, and new developments are going up all over the county," he adds. "Traffic is sometimes bad, but they are building new roads and bridges to ease the problem. We wouldn't move back to New York even if we could afford it."

Population: 12,481 in city, 118,000 in county.

Climate:

	High	Low
January	70	47
July	89	71

Cost of living: Average (specific index not available).

Average price of a new home: $159,000

Security: 85.3 crimes per 1,000 residents, higher than the national average of 42.7 crimes per 1,000 residents.

Information: St. Augustine and St. Johns County Chamber of Commerce, 1 Riberia St., St. Augustine, FL 32084, (904) 829-5681 or www.staugustinecham ber.com.

Sanibel Island, Florida

Almost everyone who lives on this island paradise off the southwest Florida coast is involved in preserving and conserving its wildlife and natural habitats. This dedication has resulted in the most beautiful, ecology-conscious, tropical environment in the state.

It all started when Lee County commissioners decided in the 1970s that this fragile strip of land could sustain a permanent population of 90,000. Residents balked, incorporated and voted to reduce that figure to 9,000. But the limitation on the number of souls who can share the island also has produced some of the highest land costs in Florida.

Devotion to conservation brought Bob and Edie Slayton to the island from River Forest, IL, in 1986. "We knew we wanted to be a part of that kind of community," Bob says. He and Edie quickly got involved by joining the Sanibel-Captiva Conservation Foundation and Audubon Society and served on the Committee of the Islands, which backs pro-conservation candidates for the city council and planning commission.

"If you're a bridge, golf or tennis player, come. If you're an environmental conservationist, please come. But join the Conservation Foundation as soon as you arrive," he urges.

Population: 6,138 in city, 420,000 in county.

Climate:

	High	Low
January	72	52
July	91	73

Cost of living: Above average (specific index not available).

Average price of a new home: $535,000

Security: 30.7 crimes per 1,000 residents, lower than the national average of 42.7 crimes per 1,000 residents.

Information: Sanibel and Captiva Islands Chamber of Commerce, 1159 Causeway Road, Sanibel Island, FL 33957, (800) 850-4170 or www.sanibel-captiva.org.

Sarasota, Florida

Sarasota is a five-star city with everything one might expect to find in a Florida Gulf coast community — and more. The city wraps itself around beautiful Sarasota Bay as if to take maximum advantage of the spectacular views and brilliant sunsets over the waterfront.

Sarasota boasts numerous organizations renowned for delivering exceptional culture, education and entertainment to its residents and visitors. Sam and Susan Kalush retired here in 1993 from Saginaw, MI, after checking out a number of North Carolina locales and other mid-to-south Florida communities.

Sarasota offered "a warm climate, good school system for our daughter, culture, entertainment, good restaurants and proximity to the ocean," Sam says. "Plus the feel of a small town," Susan adds. "I especially love all of the beautiful flowers and birds year-round — egrets and storks in our back yard."

"We have a very comfortable lifestyle here — golfing, fishing, boating," Sam says. "All of the natural things are beautiful, but the contrast with Michigan's gray days of winter, I really like."

Population: 55,000 in city, 325,889 in county.

Climate:

	High	Low
January	72	50
July	91	72

Cost of living: 105, based on national average of 100.

Average price of a new home: $189,950

Security: 71.8 crimes per 1,000 residents, higher than the national average of 42.7 crimes per 1,000 residents.

Information: Sarasota Chamber of Commerce, 1819 Main St., Suite 240, Sarasota, FL 34236, (941) 955-8187 or www.sarasotachamber.org.

Siesta Key, Florida

If it's true that a good vacation spot is a good retirement site, Siesta Key is one of the premier retirement places in America. Some 350,000 visitors descend on the eight-mile-long island each winter, much to the chagrin of its 24,000 permanent winter residents.

But when the snowbirds leave, the island regains its casual, small-town atmosphere, becoming "a little piece of heaven," says Jerry Groom, who with his wife, Kathy, retired here from Lake Forest, IL.

The former Notre Dame football all-American cites its "gorgeous weather and beautiful white-sand beaches" but cautions would-be new residents that "it is getting more expensive. They are tearing down the old dilapidated beach houses and putting up big multimillion-dollar homes," he says.

Population: 12,000 year-round in city, 24,000 in winter, plus 350,000 vacationers; 325,889 in county.

Climate:

	High	Low
January	72	51
July	92	75

Cost of living: Above average (specific index not available).

Average price of a new home: $500,000

Security: 39.7 crimes per 1,000 residents, lower than the national average of 42.7 crimes per 1,000 residents.

Information: Siesta Key Chamber of Commerce, 5100-B Ocean Boulevard, Siesta Key, FL 34242, (888) 837-3969 or www.siestachamber.com.

Venice, Florida

This lush, tropical Gulf coast paradise has been attracting retirees since the National Brotherhood of Locomotive Engineers picked it as their retirement center in 1925. Today, its charm and attractiveness is enhanced by the edicts of a historic district architectural review board that approves and monitors all new construction and renovations in the city.

The downtown is resplendent in its Northern Italian Renaissance architectural style set off by palm-lined sidewalks and cobblestone streets. Housing options include beautiful neighborhoods near the Gulf and along the bay, in tree-shaded locations in town and planned communities east of U.S. Highway 41, only minutes from Interstate 75.

"It's the best decision we ever made," says Gay McCarthy, who with husband Larry retired to Venice from Falmouth, MA, in 1994. "We came from a wonderful community to Venice, which has a real sense of community.

"There's a nice mix of retirees and younger people. The weather is wonderful — a little warm in summer, but after cycling the seasons once, you get used to it. We live here year-round — none of that 'six months here, six months there' routine. I'd give it a 10," Gay says.

Population: 21,246 in city, 325,889 in county.

Climate:

	High	Low
January	72	52
July	90	73

Cost of living: Average (specific index not available).

Average price of a new home: $184,500

Security: 25.5 crimes per 1,000 residents, lower than the national average of 42.7 crimes per 1,000 residents.

Information: Venice Area Chamber of Commerce, Tandem Center, 333 Tamiami Trail S., Suite 225, Venice, FL 34285, (941) 488-2236 or www.venicechamber.com.

Vero Beach, Florida

Nancy and Bob Brost moved here from Buffalo, NY, by way of Hilton Head Island, SC, after a long search for the perfect continuing-care community. They found exactly what they were looking for at Indian River Estates and soon discovered what many other retirees have learned: There's a lot more to Vero Beach than sand and surf.

This small coastal town is bisected by the Indian River. It has a neat and tidy downtown, an easily accessible shopping district, and some beautiful residential neighborhoods along the river and seashore.

"For a small community, it has outstanding arts and cultural organizations and a cosmopolitan population — a nice fit because there's something here for everybody," Nancy says.

Population: 17,900 in city, 111,500 in county.

Climate:

	High	Low
January	73	51
July	90	72

Cost of living: 99, based on national average of 100.

Average price of a new home: $159,500

Security: 66.2 crimes per 1,000 residents, higher than the national average of 42.7 crimes per 1,000 residents.

Information: Indian River County Chamber of Commerce, 1216 21st St., Vero Beach, FL 32960, (561) 567-3491 or www.vero-beach.fl.us/chamber.

Winter Haven, Florida

Winter Haven's Cypress Gardens has been a popular destination for families vacationing in Florida since the 1940s. Many who visited as children have returned to build homes for retirement.

It's a small but pretty city with big-time amenities. Some 50 lakes dot the landscape, many connected by canals that permit boat access throughout much of the city. Other attractions include the Chain O'Lakes Convention Center and Recreation Complex, with a 350-seat performing arts auditorium, and spring training facilities for the Cleveland Indians baseball team. And, of course, Cypress Gardens still features water-ski shows and flower festivals.

Robert Price, who retired here with his wife, Lillie, from Chicago, marvels at the number of lakes and variety of wildlife. "Many of the lakes appear to be unspoiled, much like they must have been thousands of years ago," he says.

Population: 28,972 in city, 479,699 in county.

Climate:

	High	Low
January	73	49
July	92	71

Cost of living: Average (specific index not available).

Average price of a new home: $179,500

Security: 71.1 crimes per 1,000 residents, higher than the national average of 42.7 crimes per 1,000 residents.

Information: Winter Haven Area Chamber of Commerce, 401 Ave. B N.W., Winter Haven, FL 33881, (863) 293-2138 or www.winterhavenfl.com.

GEORGIA

Tax Heavens O	Tax Hells ψ	Top Retirement Towns
Savannah	None	Gainesville Golden Isles Savannah Thomasville

Georgia has a state income tax and a state sales tax.

The state income is graduated from 1% to 6% depending upon income bracket. For married couples filing jointly, the rate is 1% on the first $1,000 of taxable income; the rate is 2% on the next $2,000 of taxable income; the rate is 3% on the next $2,000 of taxable income; the rate is 4% on the next $2,000 of taxable income; the rate is 5% on the next $3,000 of taxable

income; and the rate is 6% on taxable income above $10,000.

In calculating the tax, there is no deduction for federal income tax paid. There is a retirement income exclusion of up to $13,500 for people age 62 or older. Retirement income includes all unearned income and the first $4,000 of earned income for each person age 62 or older. Social Security benefits are exempt. There is a $3,000 deduction from adjusted

gross income for married couples filing jointly. There is a $1,300 deduction per person for residents age 65 or older and a $2,700 exemption per person.

Major tax credits or rebates include: Credit for taxes paid to other states and low income credit. Our couples do not qualify for these programs.

The state sales tax rate is 4%, but local governments can add to this amount.

GEORGIA TAX TABLE

Instructions

1. Find the Income in the far left column closest to your anticipated retirement income.
2. Find the Home Value closest to the value of the home where you will live in retirement.
3. Follow that row to your estimated Total Tax Burden at age 65 and beyond.

Income	Home Value	Property Tax & Other Fees	Personal Property Tax & Auto Fees	Sales Tax	Local Income Tax	State Income Tax	Total Tax Burden	Rank* From #1- #163
ATLANTA								
$25,000	$75,000	$594	$648	$1,001	-	-	$2,243	#100
	100,000	1,061	648	1,001	-	-	2,710	#109
	125,000	1,529	648	1,001	-	-	3,178	#112
$50,000	$100,000	$1,067	$648	$1,595	-	$135	$3,445	#71
	150,000	2,002	648	1,595	-	135	4,380	#92
	200,000	2,938	648	1,595	-	135	5,316	#101
$75,000	$150,000	$2,308	$648	$2,007	-	$1,348	$6,311	#108
	250,000	4,179	648	2,007	-	1,348	8,182	#121
	350,000	6,050	648	2,007	-	1,348	10,053	#123
GAINESVILLE								
$25,000	$75,000	$741	$414	$1,001	-	-	$2,156	#89
	100,000	1,054	414	1,001	-	-	2,469	#79
	125,000	1,367	414	1,001	-	-	2,782	#79
$50,000	$100,000	$1,078	$414	$1,595	-	$135	$3,222	#49
	150,000	1,704	414	1,595	-	135	3,848	#41
	200,000	2,330	414	1,595	-	135	4,474	#45
$75,000	$150,000	$1,924	$414	$2,007	-	$1,348	$5,693	#85
	250,000	3,177	414	2,007	-	1,348	6,946	#74
	350,000	4,430	414	2,007	-	1,348	8,199	#65

Income	Home Value	Property Tax & Other Fees	Personal Property Tax & Auto Fees	Sales Tax	Local Income Tax	State Income Tax	Total Tax Burden	Rank* From #1- #163
ST. SIMONS ISLAND								
$25,000	$75,000	$560	$367	$843	-	-	$1,770	#29
	100,000	835	367	843	-	-	2,045	#35
	125,000	1,109	367	843	-	-	2,319	#38
$50,000	$100,000	$889	$367	$1,348	-	$135	$2,739	#17
	150,000	1,438	367	1,348	-	135	3,288	#21
	200,000	1,986	367	1,348	-	135	3,836	#20
$75,000	$150,000	$1,438	$367	$1,699	-	$1,348	$4,852	#56
	250,000	2,534	367	1,699	-	1,348	5,948	#38
	350,000	3,630	367	1,699	-	1,348	7,044	#39
SAVANNAH								
$25,000	$75,000	$144	$443	$843	-	-	$1,430	#10 O
	100,000	380	443	843	-	-	1,666	#10 O
	125,000	717	443	843	-	-	2,003	#14
$50,000	$100,000	$695	$443	$1,348	-	$135	$2,621	#11
	150,000	1,370	443	1,348	-	135	3,296	#22
	200,000	2,045	443	1,348	-	135	3,971	#25
$75,000	$150,000	$1,902	$443	$1,699	-	$1,348	$5,392	#73
	250,000	3,252	443	1,699	-	1,348	6,742	#65
	350,000	4,602	443	1,699	-	1,348	8,092	#59
THOMASVILLE								
$25,000	$75,000	$730	$375	$685	-	-	$1,790	#31
	100,000	1,010	375	685	-	-	2,070	#36
	125,000	1,291	375	685	-	-	2,351	#42
$50,000	$100,000	$1,066	$375	$1,100	-	$135	$2,676	#14
	150,000	1,628	375	1,100	-	135	3,238	#18
	200,000	2,189	375	1,100	-	135	3,799	#17
$75,000	$150,000	$1,628	$375	$1,391	-	$1,348	$4,742	#50
	250,000	2,751	375	1,391	-	1,348	5,865	#35
	350,000	3,873	375	1,391	-	1,348	6,987	#35

*There are 163 cities in this book. The city with the lowest tax burden for an income/home value combination is given the #1 rating; the city with the highest total tax burden is given the #163 rating.

Atlanta

Atlanta has no local income tax but does levy a sales tax.

Most purchases are taxed at a rate of 7%. Major consumer categories taxed at a different rate include: Groceries, which are taxed at a rate of 3%. Major consumer categories that are exempt from sales tax include: Drugs and medical services.

Within the city limits of Atlanta, the property tax rate is .04677. Homes are assessed at 40% of market value. There are various exemptions off the different components of the property tax. Property tax does not cover garbage pickup; the additional fee is approximately $311 per year.

Atlanta has a personal property tax rate of .04677. Airplanes, boats, jet-skis, mobile homes not fixed on a property, RVs, campers/trailers and automobiles are subject to the tax and assessed at 40% of state-determined depreciated value. Automobile values are determined by the state according to the year, make and model of the automobile. We've assumed automobiles are the only items our couples own that are subject to the personal property tax.

Our couples relocating to Atlanta must pay a title transfer fee of $18 per automobile, a tag fee of $20 per automobile and an emissions fee of $25 per automobile at the time of registration. Thereafter, on an annual basis, our couples will pay a tag fee and an emissions fee, per automobile.

Gainesville

Gainesville has no local income tax but does levy a sales tax.

Most purchases are taxed at a rate of 7%. Major consumer categories taxed at a different rate include: Groceries, which are taxed at a rate of 3%. Major consumer categories that are exempt from sales tax include: Drugs and medical services.

Within the city limits of Gainesville, the local property tax rate is .00965 and the county property tax rate is .00719. Homes are assessed at 100% of market value by Gainesville and 40% of market value by Hall County. There are various exemptions off the different components of property tax. Property tax does not cover garbage pickup; the additional fee is $48 per year. There is also an additional fee for recycling of $36 per year and a fee for landfill service of $34 per year.

Gainesville has a personal property tax rate of .00965, and Hall County has a personal property tax rate of .00719. Aircraft, boats and mobile homes not serving as a primary residence are subject to the tax and assessed at 100% of state-determined depreciated value for Gainesville and 40% of state-determined depreciated value for Hall County. Automobiles are assessed at 40% of state-determined depreciated value and taxed at a rate of .031328. We've assumed automobiles are the only items our couples own that are subject to the personal property tax.

Our couples relocating to Gainesville must pay a title transfer fee of $18 per automobile and a tag fee of $20 per automobile at the time of registration. Thereafter, on an annual basis, our couples will pay a tag fee per automobile.

St. Simons Island

St. Simons Island has no local income tax but does levy a sales tax.

Most purchases are taxed at a rate of 6%. Major consumer categories taxed at a different rate include: Groceries, which are taxed at a rate of 2%. Major consumer categories that are exempt from sales tax include: Drugs and medical services.

Within the city limits of St. Simons Island, the local property tax rate is .02741. Homes are assessed at 40% of market value. There are various exemptions off the different components of property tax. Property tax does not cover garbage pickup; the additional fee is $93 per year.

St. Simons Island has a personal property rate of .02741. Aircraft, boats, motors and motor vehicles are subject to the tax and assessed at 40% of state-determined depreciated value. We've assumed automobiles are the only items our couples own that are subject to the personal property tax.

Our couples relocating to St. Simons Island must pay a title transfer fee of $18 per automobile and a tag fee of $20 per automobile at the time of registration. Thereafter, on an annual basis, our couples will pay a tag fee, per automobile.

Savannah

Savannah has no local income tax but does levy a sales tax.

Most purchases are taxed at a rate of 6%. Major consumer categories taxed at a different rate include: Groceries, which are taxed at a rate of 2%. Major consumer categories that are exempt from sales tax include: Drugs and medical services.

Within the Pooler area of Savannah, the local property tax rate is .033749. Homes are assessed at 40% of market value. There are various exemptions off the different components of property tax. Property tax does not cover garbage pickup; the additional fee is approximately $144 per year.

Within the Pooler area of Savannah, the personal property rate is .033749. Aircraft, boats, motors and motor vehicles are subject to the tax and assessed at 40% of state-determined depreciated value. We've assumed automobiles are the only items our couples own that are subject to the personal property tax.

Our couples relocating to Savannah must pay a title transfer fee of $18 per automobile and a tag fee of $20 per automobile at the time of registration. Thereafter, on an annual basis, our couples will pay a tag fee per automobile.

Thomasville

Thomasville has no local income tax but does levy a sales tax.

Most purchases are taxed at a rate of 5%. Major consumer categories taxed at a different rate include: Groceries, which are taxed at a rate of 1%. Major consumer categories that are exempt from sales tax include: Drugs and medical services.

Within the city limits of Thomasville, the local property tax rate is .02807. Homes are assessed at 40% of market value. There are various exemptions off the different components of property tax. Property tax does not cover garbage pickup; the additional fee is approximately $96 per year.

Thomasville has a personal property rate of .02807. Aircraft, boats, motors and motor vehicles are subject to the tax and assessed at 40% of state-determined depreciated value. We've assumed automobiles are the only items our couples own that are subject to the personal property tax.

Our couples relocating to Thomasville must pay a title transfer fee of $18 per automobile and a tag fee of $20 per automobile at the time of registration. Thereafter, on an annual basis, our couples will pay a tag fee per automobile.

• Georgia's Best Retirement Towns •

Gainesville, Georgia

With 38,000-acre Lake Lanier in its back yard, the cool and scenic Appalachian Mountains just up the road, and the big-city attractions of metropolitan Atlanta a few miles south, this three-college town — home to Brenau University, Gainesville College and Lanier Technical College — has become a magnet for retirees.

Lyn and Marlyn Mortland left North Jackson, OH, and spent more than six years traveling around the country in a motor home before settling in Gainesville in July 1999.

"It's a nice small town with everything you would want — mild winters and long springs and summers," Lyn says. "It has reasonable real estate prices. And it's very convenient. We can be in the mountains in 25 minutes or Atlanta in an hour."

Population: 19,672 in city, 123,571 in county.

Climate:

	High	Low
January	49	29
July	86	67

Cost of living: Below average (specific index not available).

Average price of a new home: $179,900

Security: 99.8 crimes per 1,000 residents, higher than the national average of 42.7 crimes per 1,000 residents.

Information: Greater Hall Chamber of Commerce, P.O. Box 374, Gainesville, GA

30503, (770) 532-6206 or www.ghcc.com.

Golden Isles, Georgia

The Golden Isles — St. Simons, Jekyll and Sea islands — offer their residents a moderate year-round climate and unlimited opportunities for water-related activities.

Moderate and upscale housing options include oceanfront condominiums and country club developments with championship-caliber golf courses. There's a quiet, easygoing lifestyle in a subtropical, underdeveloped environment teeming with shore birds and wildlife.

Because the islands are too small to attract traveling shows and exhibits, residents rely chiefly on their own ingenuity for entertainment. "It's good to have the ability for self-entertainment when you decide to settle in the Golden Isles," Michael Grubich says. He and his wife, Linda, retired here from Austin, TX, five years ago after searching for a "quieter, less congested, more secure lifestyle. We found it here," Michael says.

"Once you come across the causeway from the mainland, you're in a different world. St. Simons is not real touristy. Most of its residents live here permanently," he adds. "We garden, golf and work out. There's a bike trail that crosses the entire island (of St. Simons), and there are great restaurants here. An active newcomers club gets people quickly assimilated into community life."

Population: 700 on Jekyll Island, 700 on Sea Island, 17,250 on St. Simons Island, and 68,000 in the county.

Climate:

	High	Low
January	61	42
July	90	74

Cost of living: Above average (specific index not available).

Average price of a new home: $274,000

Security: 66.5 crimes per 1,000 residents in Glynn County, higher than the national average of 42.7 crimes per 1,000 residents.

Information: The Brunswick-Golden Isles Chamber of Commerce, 4 Glynn Ave., Brunswick, GA 31520, (912) 265-0620 or www.brunswick-georgia.com/chamber.

Savannah, Georgia

This antebellum citadel of elegant Southern living displays the best features of its past in its restored and revitalized 2.5-square-mile historic district. Safe, vibrant suburban neighborhoods south and west offer a wide spectrum of modest to upscale homes, while east and southeast are subtropical islands offering housing choices that include quaint rental cottages, luxurious condominiums and upscale estates.

Gerry and Jeanne Williams moved to The Landings on Skidaway Island after 25 years in the Chicago suburbs. "Our criteria for a retirement home were year-round golf, easy airport access and good health-care facilities," Gerry says. "Savannah has many amenities usually found only in much larger cities — a fine symphony, an outstanding historic district, an excellent art museum and some very good restaurants.

"We knew Savannah was a nice historic town, based on one or two visits, but it was not central to our decision to move to The Landings. After living in the Savannah area awhile, the city is central to our staying here," he says.

Population: 131,510 in city; 232,048 in county.

Climate:

	High	Low
January	60	38
July	91	72

Cost of living: 103, based on national average of 100.

Average price of a new home: $178,000

Security: 84.1 crimes per 1,000 residents, higher than the national average of 42.7 crimes per 1,000 residents.

Information: Savannah Area Chamber of Commerce, 101 E. Bay St., Savannah, GA 31401, (912) 644-6400 or www.savannahchamber.com.

Thomasville, Georgia

Situated in south-central Georgia, Thomasville served as a winter retreat for wealthy Northerners in the late 19th century. Its combination of Old South charm and beautiful old antebellum plantation mansions continue to lure thousands of tourists to the city, many returning to make it their retirement home.

Sharon and Eric Miller retired first to Palm Harbor, FL, from their Missouri home. While visiting a son stationed at Fort Benning, they decided to attend the annual Rose Festival in Thomasville and liked the community so much that they moved here a few months later.

"It's about 30 minutes from Tallahassee for big-city shopping and entertainment," Sharon says. "Thomasville is a small community, but it has a vibrant downtown and lots of cultural things going on."

"It's an upscale community with an excellent medical facility," Eric adds. "My only complaint: It's growing too fast."

Population: 20,000 in city, 45,000 in county.

Climate:

	High	Low
January	63	39
July	92	70

Cost of living: Below average to average (specific index not available).

Average price of a new home: $169,900

Security: 85.6 crimes per 1,000 residents, higher than the national average of 42.7 crimes per 1,000 residents.

Information: Thomasville-Thomas County Chamber of Commerce, 401 S. Broad St., P.O. Box 560, Thomasville, GA 31799, (912) 226-9600 or www.thomasvillechamber.com.

HAWAII

Hawaii has a state income tax and a state excise tax (sales tax).

The state income tax rate is graduated from 1.6% to 8.75% depending upon income bracket. For married couples filing jointly the rate is 1.6% on the first $4,000 of taxable income; the rate is 3.9% on the next $4,000 of taxable income; the rate is 6.8% on the next $8,000 of taxable income; the rate is 7.2% on the next $8,000 of taxable income; the rate is 7.5% on the next $8,000 of taxable income; the rate is 7.8% on the next $8,000 of taxable income; the rate is 8.2% on the next

$20,000 of taxable income; the rate is 8.5% on the next $20,000 of taxable income; and the rate is 8.75% on taxable income over $80,000.

In calculating the tax, there is no deduction for federal income tax paid. Federal and state pensions are exempt. Private pensions are exempt if they do not include employee contributions. Social Security benefits are exempt. There is a $1,900 exemption from Hawaii adjusted gross income for married couples filing jointly. There is a $1,040 personal exemption from adjusted gross income per person and

an additional $1,040 personal exemption per person age 65 and over.

Major tax credits or rebates include: Credit for income taxes paid to other states, which our couples do not qualify for; low-income housing tax credit, which our couples do not qualify for; and low-income refundable tax credit, which one of our couples qualifies for.

The state excise tax rate is 4%. Although this tax is imposed on the seller (unlike sales tax, which is imposed on the buyer), businesses customarily pass the tax on to the buyer.

HAWAII TAX TABLE

Instructions

1. Find the Income in the far left column closest to your anticipated retirement income.
2. Find the Home Value closest to the value of the home where you will live in retirement.
3. Follow that row to your estimated Total Tax Burden at age 65 and beyond.

Income	Home Value	Property Tax & Other Fees	Personal Property Tax & Auto Fees	Sales Tax	Local Income Tax	State Income Tax	Total Tax Burden	Rank* From #1- #163
HONOLULU								
$25,000	$75,000	$100	$225	$662	-	$272	$1,259	#4 O
	100,000	100	225	662	-	272	1,259	#3 O
	125,000	100	225	662	-	272	1,259	#2 O
$50,000	$100,000	$100	$225	$1,027	-	$1,785	$3,137	#41
	150,000	183	225	1,027	-	1,785	3,220	#17
	200,000	365	225	1,027	-	1,785	3,402	#10 O
$75,000	$150,000	$183	$225	$1,277	-	$3,666	$5,351	#72
	250,000	548	225	1,277	-	3,666	5,716	#30
	350,000	913	225	1,277	-	3,666	6,081	#13
	$400,000	$1,095	$225	$1,277	-	$3,666	$6,263	Not Ranked
	450,000	1,278	225	1,277	-	3,666	6,446	Not Ranked
	500,000	1,460	225	1,277	-	3,666	6,628	Not Ranked

*There are 163 cities in this book. The city with the lowest tax burden for an income/home value combination is given the #1 rating; the city with the highest total tax burden is given the #163 rating.

Honolulu

Honolulu has no local income tax and does not levy an additional excise tax.

Most purchases include the 4% state excise tax. Major consumer categories taxed at a different rate: None. Major

consumer categories that are exempt from excise tax include: Drugs.

Within the city limits of Honolulu, the property tax rate is .00365. Homes are assessed at 100% of market value. All properties are subject

to a minimum tax of $100 per year. There is a homeowner's exemption that increases by age. For homeowners age 65-69, the exemption is $100,000. Property tax includes garbage pickup.

Honolulu has no personal property tax for individuals.

Our couples relocating to Honolulu must pay a registration fee per automobile based on the weight of the automobile. They also must pay a license plate fee and a title fee per automobile. Total fee is approximately $125 for the Explorer and $110 for the Cutlass. Thereafter, on an annual basis, our couples will pay a registration fee per automobile.

IDAHO

Tax Heavens O
None

Tax Hells Ψ
None

Top Retirement Towns
Boise
Coeur d'Alene

Idaho has a state income tax and a state sales tax.

The state income tax rate is graduated from 1.9% to 8.1% depending upon income bracket. For married couples filing jointly, the rate is 1.9% on the first $2,044 of taxable income; the rate is 3.9% on the next $2,044 of taxable income; the rate is 4.4% on the next $2,044 of taxable income; the rate is 5.4% on the next $2,044 of taxable income; the rate is 6.4% on the next

$2,044 of taxable income; the rate is 7.4% on the next $5,112 of taxable income; the rate is 7.7% on the next $25,552 of taxable income; and the rate is 8.1% on taxable income above $40,884.

In calculating the tax, there is no deduction for federal income tax paid. Federal pensions are not exempt; however, married couples filing jointly with both spouses age 65 or older qualify for up to a $25,794 deduction,

minus any Social Security or railroad retirement benefits received, from their federal pension income. State and private pensions are not exempt. Social Security benefits are exempt. There is a standard deduction of $10,500 from adjusted gross income for married couples filing jointly with both spouses age 65 or older and a $2,800 exemption per person from adjusted gross income.

There is a $10 permanent building

IDAHO TAX TABLE

Instructions

1. Find the Income in the far left column closest to your anticipated retirement income.
2. Find the Home Value closest to the value of the home where you will live in retirement.
3. Follow that row to your estimated Total Tax Burden at age 65 and beyond.

Income	Home Value	Property Tax & Other Fees	Personal Property Tax & Auto Fees	Sales Tax	Local Income Tax	State Income Tax†	Total Tax Burden	Rank* From #1-#163
BOISE								
$25,000	$75,000	$903	$168	$791	-	($50)	$1,812	#32
	100,000	1,174	168	791	-	(50)	2,083	#37
	125,000	1,444	168	791	-	(50)	2,353	#43
$50,000	$100,000	$1,173	$168	$1,238	-	$1,129	$3,708	#100
	150,000	1,896	168	1,238	-	1,129	4,431	#97
	200,000	2,798	168	1,238	-	1,129	5,333	#102
$75,000	$150,000	$1,896	$168	$1,540	-	$2,949	$6,553	#119
	250,000	3,701	168	1,540	-	2,949	8,358	#129
	350,000	5,507	168	1,540	-	2,949	10,164	#126
COEUR D'ALENE								
$25,000	$75,000	$893	$106	$791	-	($50)	$1,740	#28
	100,000	1,161	106	791	-	(50)	2,008	#29
	125,000	1,430	106	791	-	(50)	2,277	#34
$50,000	$100,000	$1,161	$106	$1,238	-	$1,129	$3,634	#92
	150,000	1,877	106	1,238	-	1,129	4,350	#88
	200,000	2,771	106	1,238	-	1,129	5,244	#98
$75,000	$150,000	$1,877	$106	$1,540	-	$2,949	$6,472	#113
	250,000	3,665	106	1,540	-	2,949	8,260	#124
	350,000	5,454	106	1,540	-	2,949	10,049	#122

†Grocery tax credit is issued as a reduction of income tax due or as a refund if the credit is greater than the tax liability.
*There are 163 cities in this book. The city with the lowest tax burden for an income/home value combination is given the #1 rating; the city with the highest total tax burden is given the #163 rating.

fund tax for each Idaho income tax return filed.

Major tax credits or rebates include: Credit for income taxes paid to other states, which our couples do not qualify for; and grocery credit of $15 per person, plus $15 per person age 65 or older, which our couples do qualify for.

The state sales tax rate is 5%.

Since car registration and renewal fees differ within the state, see city information for details.

Boise

Boise has no local income tax and does not levy an additional sales tax.

Most purchases are taxed at the state rate of 5%. Major consumer categories taxed at a different rate: None. Major consumer categories that are exempt from sales tax include: Drugs and medical services.

In the southeast area of Boise, the property tax rate is .018055802. Homes are assessed at 100% of market value. There is a homeowner's exemption of 50% up to $50,000 off assessed value of the home, not including the land value. There is a sliding-scale exemption of up to $1,200 for persons age 65 and over with income up to $20,050. Property tax does not cover garbage pickup; the additional fee is approximately $90 per year.

In the southeast area of Boise, there is a personal property tax rate of .018055802. Personal property is assessed at 100% of market value. Items subject to the tax include mobile homes. The homeowner's exemptions also apply to mobile homes. We've assumed our couples do not own any of the items subject to the personal property tax.

Our couples relocating to Boise must pay a registration fee based on the age and weight of the vehicle of $52 per automobile, a county highway fee of $22 per automobile, a plate fee of $6 per automobile, a title fee of $11 per automobile, miscellaneous fees of $4 per automobile and a $12 emission test fee per automobile. Thereafter, on an annual basis, our couples will pay a registration fee based on the age and weight of the vehicle, county highway fee, miscellaneous fees and an emission test fee, per automobile.

Coeur d'Alene

Coeur d'Alene has no local income tax and does not levy an additional sales tax.

Most purchases are taxed at a rate of 5%. Major consumer categories taxed at a different rate: None. Major consumer categories that are exempt from sales tax include: Drugs and medical services.

One of the property tax rates in Coeur d'Alene is .017886813. Homes are assessed at 100% of market value. There is a homeowner's exemption of 50% up to $50,000 off assessed value of the home, not including the land value. There is a sliding-scale exemption of up to $1,200 for persons age 65 and over with income up to $20,050. Property tax does not cover garbage pickup; the additional fee is approximately $57 per year. There is also a street light service fee of approximately $31 per year.

One of the personal property tax rates in Coeur d'Alene is .017886813. Personal property is assessed at 100% of market value. Items subject to the tax include unaffixed mobile homes. The homeowner's exemptions also apply to mobile homes. We've assumed our couples do not own any of the items subject to the personal property tax.

Our couples relocating to Coeur d'Alene must pay a registration fee based on the age and weight of the vehicle of $52 per automobile, a $6 plate fee per automobile, a title fee of $11 per automobile and miscellaneous fees of $4 per automobile. Thereafter, on an annual basis, our couples will pay a registration fee based on the age and weight of the vehicle and miscellaneous fees, per automobile.

• Idaho's Best Retirement Towns •

Boise, Idaho

Boise was a well-kept secret until recent years when it was discovered by California retirees seeking an alternative to the high cost of living in their native state. What they found was a clean, progressive city with a river and 25-mile-long greenbelt running through it.

Other attractions include a recreational wonderland of mountains, forests and picturesque valleys, outstanding educational and medical facilities at Boise State University, two highly rated regional medical centers and V.A. hospital, and a healthy environment with happy, friendly people — despite the fact that some feel they are being taken over by Californians.

Jerry and Carol Larson retired here from Anchorage, AK, and they love Boise. "It has a lot to offer, especially for those who enjoy the outdoors. We golf, go camping and fishing, and spend a lot of time in the mountains. We're also big Boise State fans," he says. "It's growing too fast, but it's still a great place to live."

Population: 168,258 in city, 283,357 in county.

Climate:

	High	Low
January	36	22
July	90	58

Cost of living: 100, based on national average of 100.

Average price of a new home: $125,785

Security: 47.6 crimes per 1,000 residents, higher than the national average of 42.7 crimes per 1,000 residents.

Information: Boise Metro Chamber of Commerce, 250 S. Fifth St., Boise, ID 83702, (208) 472-5200 or www.boisechamber.org.

Coeur d'Alene, Idaho

This is a region of lakes, rivers, mountains and forests that retains much of the rugged wilderness mystique Lewis and Clark must have experienced on their Northwest Passage expedition.

Shirlee and Dick Wandrocke moved here from Newport Beach, CA, and spend a great deal of time exploring the outdoors. "We go out on the lake (Lake Coeur d'Alene has a 135-mile shoreline) as much as we can, we take our travel trailer to the wonderful campgrounds around the state, get out in the woods with our pets, and cross-country ski in wintertime," Shirlee says.

"The population has grown, but they are still protecting a lot of the wilderness, working to ease traffic congestion and revitalizing downtown," she adds.

Population: 32,200 in city, 104,200 in county.

Climate:

	High	Low
January	35	22
July	86	52

Cost of living: Above average (specific index not available).

Average price of a new home: $129,669

Security: 67 crimes per 1,000 residents, higher than the national average of 42.7 crimes per 1,000 residents.

Information: Coeur d'Alene Area Chamber of Commerce, P.O. Box 850, 1621 N. Third St., Coeur d'Alene, ID 83816, (877) 782-9232 or www.coeur dalenechamber.com.

ILLINOIS

Tax Heavens O
None

Tax Hells Ψ
None

Top Retirement Towns
None

Illinois has a state income tax and a state sales tax.

The state income tax rate is 3%. In calculating the tax, there is no deduction for federal income tax paid. Federal, state and private pensions are exempt. Social Security benefits are exempt.

There is a $2,000 personal exemption from adjusted gross income per person and a $1,000 exemption from adjusted gross income per person age 65 or older.

Major tax credits or rebates include: Credit for income taxes paid to other states, which our couples do not quali-

fy for; education expense credit, which our couples do not qualify for; and property tax credit, which some of our couples qualify for.

The state sales tax rate is 6.25%, but local governments can add to this amount.

ILLINOIS TAX TABLE

Instructions

1. Find the Income in the far left column closest to your anticipated retirement income.
2. Find the Home Value closest to the value of the home where you will live in retirement.
3. Follow that row to your estimated Total Tax Burden at age 65 and beyond.

Income	Home Value	Property Tax & Other Fees	Personal Property Tax & Auto Fees	Sales Tax	Local Income Tax	State Income Tax[†]	Total Tax Burden	Rank[*] From #1-#163
CHICAGO								
$25,000	$75,000	$843	$168	$1,301	-	-	$2,312	#112
	100,000	1,324	168	1,301	-	-	2,793	#118
	125,000	1,804	168	1,301	-	-	3,273	#124
$50,000	$100,000	$1,324	$168	$2,054	-	$417	$3,963	#119
	150,000	2,284	168	2,054	-	369	4,875	#117
	200,000	3,245	168	2,054	-	321	5,788	#119
$75,000	$150,000	$2,284	$168	$2,586	-	$1,036	$6,074	#102
	250,000	4,205	168	2,586	-	940	7,899	#112
	350,000	6,126	168	2,586	-	844	9,724	#114

[†]Credit for property tax paid is issued as a reduction of income tax due.
[*]There are 163 cities in this book. The city with the lowest tax burden for an income/home value combination is given the #1 rating; the city with the highest total tax burden is given the #163 rating.

Chicago

Chicago has no local income tax but does levy an additional sales tax.

Most purchases are taxed at a rate of 8.75%. Major consumer categories taxed at a different rate include: Groceries and drugs, which are taxed at a rate of 2%; and food away from home, which is taxed at a rate of 9.75%. Major consumer categories that are exempt from sales tax: None.

Within the city limits of Chicago, the

median tax rate is .08536. Homes are assessed at 10% of market value then multiplied by an equalization factor of 2.2505. There is a homestead exemption of $4,500 off assessed value of the home available to all resident homeowners and a senior citizen exemption of an additional $2,500 off the assessed value of the home available to all resident homeowners age 65 or older. There is also a circuit breaker rebate program based on gross income and

the amount of the property tax bill. Property tax includes garbage pickup.

Chicago has no personal property tax for individuals.

Our couples relocating to Chicago must pay a registration fee of $54 per automobile, a title fee of $65 per automobile, and a wheel tax of $30 per automobile. Thereafter, on an annual basis, our couples will pay a registration fee and a wheel tax, per automobile.

INDIANA

Tax Heavens O
None

Tax Hells Ψ
Indianapolis

Top Retirement Towns
None

Indiana has a state income tax and a state sales tax.

The state income tax rate is 3.4%. In calculating the tax, there is no deduction for federal income tax paid. Federal pensions are exempt up to $2,000. State and private pensions are not exempt. Social Security benefits are exempt. There is a $1,000 exemption per person and an additional $1,000 exemption per person if age 65 or older. There is an additional exemption of $500 per person age 65 or older with federal adjusted gross income less than $40,000. There is a homeowner's residential property tax deduction of up to $2,500 for property tax paid on principal residence and a renter's deduction of up to $2,000 for rent paid on principal residence.

Major tax credits or rebates include: Credit for income taxes paid to other states, credit for local taxes paid outside the state and unified tax credit for the elderly. Our couples do not qualify for these programs.

The state sales tax rate is 5%.

INDIANA TAX TABLE

Instructions

1. Find the Income in the far left column closest to your anticipated retirement income.
2. Find the Home Value closest to the value of the home where you will live in retirement.
3. Follow that row to your estimated Total Tax Burden at age 65 and beyond.

Income	Home Value	Property Tax & Other Fees	Personal Property Tax & Auto Fees	Sales Tax	Local Income Tax	State Income Tax	Total Tax Burden	Rank* From #1- #163
INDIANAPOLIS								
$25,000	$75,000	$2,117	$410	$674	$56	$273	$3,530	#160 Ψ
	100,000	2,853	410	674	53	259	4,249	#161 Ψ
	125,000	3,590	410	674	53	259	4,986	#161 Ψ
$50,000	$100,000	$2,853	$410	$1,091	$206	$1,003	$5,563	#159 Ψ
	150,000	4,326	410	1,091	206	1,003	7,036	#160 Ψ
	200,000	5,798	410	1,091	206	1,003	8,508	#161 Ψ
$75,000	$150,000	$4,326	$410	$1,382	$371	$1,802	$8,291	#155 Ψ
	250,000	7,270	410	1,382	371	1,802	11,235	#159 Ψ
	350,000	10,214	410	1,382	371	1,802	14,179	#159 Ψ

*There are 163 cities in this book. The city with the lowest tax burden for an income/home value combination is given the #1 rating; the city with the highest total tax burden is given the #163 rating.

Indianapolis

Indianapolis has a local income tax but does not levy an additional sales tax.

The local income tax rate is .7% of Indiana taxable income calculated on the state income tax return.

Most purchases are taxed at the state rate of 5%. Major consumer categories taxed at a different rate: Food away from home, which is taxed at a rate of 6%. Major consumer categories that are exempt from sales tax include: Drugs, groceries and medical services.

For most residents within the area of Lawrence Township, the property tax rate is .1228. Homes are assessed at 33.3% of true tax value. This is approximately 80% of market value for new homes and approximately 30% for older homes. Property tax amounts shown are estimates and are determined in a calculation that is based on discounted reproduction cost and depreciation. There are several exemptions available for homeowners, some of which have age, income and residency requirements. Property tax does not cover garbage pickup; the additional fee is approximately $32 per year.

Indianapolis has a personal property tax based on depreciated value set by the state. Items subject to the tax include boats, boat trailers over 3,000 pounds, trucks over 11,000 pounds, truck campers, travel trailers, RVs, campers, ATVs, snowmobiles and motor homes. We've assumed our couples do not own any of the items subject to the personal property tax.

Our couples relocating to Indianapolis must pay an annual excise fee based on the year, make and model of the vehicle of approximately $225 for the Explorer and approximately $185 for the Cutlass, and a title fee of $11 per automobile at the time of registration. Thereafter, on an annual basis, our couples will pay an excise tax fee per automobile.

IOWA

<table>
<tr><td>**Tax Heavens O**
None</td><td>**Tax Hells ψ**
Des Moines</td><td>**Top Retirement Towns**
None</td></tr>
</table>

Iowa has a state income tax and a state sales tax.

The state income tax rate is graduated from .35% to 8.98%, depending upon income bracket. For married couples filing jointly, the rate is .35% on the first $1,162 of taxable income; the rate is .72% on the next $1,162 of taxable income; the rate is 2.43% on the next $2,324 of taxable income; the rate is 4.5% on the next $5,810 of taxable income; the rate is 6.12% on the next $6,972 of taxable income; the rate is 6.48% on the next $5,810 of taxable income; the rate is 6.8% on the next $11,620 of taxable income; the rate is

7.92% on the next $17,430 of taxable income; and the rate is 8.98% on taxable income above $52,290.

In calculating the tax, there is a deduction from adjusted gross income for federal income tax paid. Federal, state and private pensions are not exempt; however, there is a pension/retirement income exclusion of up to $10,000 for married couples age 55 or older filing jointly or separately. Some Social Security benefits subject to federal tax are not exempt. There is a $3,630 standard deduction from adjusted gross income for married couples filing jointly. There is a $40 credit against tax per

person for married couples filing jointly and an additional $20 credit against tax per person age 65 and older.

There is also an alternate method for income tax calculation that may yield a lower tax due for some taxpayers, particularly lower-income taxpayers. This method does not reduce tax liability for our couples.

Major tax credits or rebates include: Credit for income taxes paid to other states and earned income credit. Our couples do not qualify for these programs.

The state sales tax rate is 5%, but local governments can add to this amount.

IOWA TAX TABLE

Instructions

1. Find the Income in the far left column closest to your anticipated retirement income.
2. Find the Home Value closest to the value of the home where you will live in retirement.
3. Follow that row to your estimated Total Tax Burden at age 65 and beyond.

Income	Home Value	Property Tax & Other Fees	Personal Property Tax & Auto Fees	Sales Tax	Local Income Tax	State Income Tax	Total Tax Burden	Rank* From #1-#163
DES MOINES								
$25,000	$75,000	$1,795	$428	$790	-	-	$3,013	#154 ψ
	100,000	2,405	428	790	-	-	3,623	#153
	125,000	3,014	428	790	-	-	4,232	#153
$50,000	$100,000	$2,405	$428	$1,279	-	$1,051	$5,163	#156 ψ
	150,000	3,623	428	1,279	-	1,051	6,381	#156 ψ
	200,000	4,843	428	1,279	-	1,051	7,601	#156 ψ
$75,000	$150,000	$3,623	$428	$1,624	-	$2,446	$8,121	#154 ψ
	250,000	6,061	428	1,624	-	2,446	10,559	#154 ψ
	350,000	8,499	428	1,624	-	2,446	12,997	#153

*There are 163 cities in this book. The city with the lowest tax burden for an income/home value combination is given the #1 rating; the city with the highest total tax burden is given the #163 rating.

Des Moines

Des Moines has no local income tax but does levy an additional sales tax.

Most purchases are taxed at a rate of 6%. Major consumer categories taxed at a different rate: None. Major consumer categories that are exempt from sales tax include: Drugs, groceries and medical services.

Within the Des Moines School District, the property tax rate for tax year 1999 is .04332624. At the time of publication, the rate for tax year 2000 had not yet been determined. Homes are assessed at 56.2641% of market value in tax year 1999. There is a homestead exemption of $4,850 off assessed value for all homeowners.

Property tax on new homes (not including land values) is abated for five years. We assumed that our couples did not buy new homes. Property tax does not cover garbage pickup; the additional fee is approximately $123 per year. There is also a storm water drain fee of approximately $54 per year.

Des Moines has no personal property tax for individuals.

Our couples relocating to Des Moines must pay a registration fee based on year, make and model of each automobile. The registration fee is $234 for the Explorer and $194 for the Cutlass. Our couples also pay a $15 title fee per automobile and a $5 lien fee per automobile at the time of registration. Thereafter, on an annual basis, our couples will pay a registration fee per automobile.

KANSAS

Tax Heavens O
None

Tax Hells Ψ
None

Top Retirement Towns
None

Kansas has a state income tax and a state sales tax.

The state income tax rate is graduated from 3.5% to 6.45% depending upon income bracket. For married couples filing jointly, the rate is 3.5% on the first $30,000 of taxable income; the rate is 6.25% on the next $30,000 of taxable income; and the rate is 6.45% on taxable income above $60,000.

In calculating the tax, there is no deduction for federal income tax paid. Federal and state pensions are exempt from tax. Private pensions are not exempt. Social Security benefits subject to federal tax are not exempt. There is a $2,250 personal exemption per person from adjusted gross income. There is also a $7,400 standard deduction from adjusted gross income for married couples filing jointly when both are age 65 or older.

Major tax credits or rebates include: Credit for income taxes paid to other states, earned income credit, which our couples do not qualify for; and food sales tax refund, which one of our couples qualifies for.

The state sales tax rate is 4.9%, but local governments can add to this amount.

Our couples relocating to the city listed below must pay a registration fee of $28.50 per automobile, a title fee of $7 per automobile and an inspection fee of $10 per automobile at the time of registration. Thereafter, on an annual basis, our couples will pay a registration fee per automobile.

KANSAS TAX TABLE

Instructions

1. Find the Income in the far left column closest to your anticipated retirement income.
2. Find the Home Value closest to the value of the home where you will live in retirement.
3. Follow that row to your estimated Total Tax Burden at age 65 and beyond.

Income	Home Value	Property Tax & Other Fees	Personal Property Tax & Auto Fees	Sales Tax	Local Income Tax	State Income Tax	Total Tax Burden	Rank* From #1- #163
WICHITA								
$25,000	$75,000	$1,060	$457	$976	-	$53	$2,546	#136
	100,000	1,370	457	976	-	53	2,856	#127
	125,000	1,679	457	976	-	53	3,165	#109
$50,000	$100,000	$1,370	$457	$1,514	-	$1,035	$4,376	#133
	150,000	1,988	457	1,514	-	1,035	4,994	#127
	200,000	2,607	457	1,514	-	1,035	5,613	#110
$75,000	$150,000	$1,988	$457	$1,883	-	$2,957	$7,285	#141
	250,000	3,226	457	1,883	-	2,957	8,523	#131
	350,000	4,464	457	1,883	-	2,957	9,761	#117

*There are 163 cities in this book. The city with the lowest tax burden for an income/home value combination is given the #1 rating; the city with the highest total tax burden is given the #163 rating.

Wichita

Wichita has no local income tax but does levy a sales tax.

Most purchases are taxed at a rate of 5.9%. Major consumer categories taxed at a different rate: None. Major consumer categories that are exempt from sales tax include: Drugs.

In the Wichita School District, the property tax rate is .107622. Homes are assessed at 11.5% of market value. There is a homestead exemption that is determined on a sliding scale for homeowners age 55 or older with an income less than $25,000. Property tax does not cover garbage pickup; the additional fee is approximately $132 per year.

Wichita has a personal property tax rate of .107622 within the USD 259 school district. Mobile homes are assessed at 11.5% of market value, boats and trailers are assessed at 30% of market value, and automobiles are assessed based on year, make and model of the automobile.

KENTUCKY

Tax Heavens O
None

Tax Hells Ψ
None

Top Retirement Towns
None

Kentucky has a state income tax and a state sales tax.

The state income is graduated from 2% to 6% depending upon income bracket. For married couples filing jointly, the rate is 2% on the first $3,000 of taxable income; the rate is 3% on the next $1,000 of taxable income; the rate is 4% on the next $1,000 of taxable income; the rate is 5% on the next $3,000 of taxable

income; and the rate is 6% on taxable income above $8,000.

In calculating the tax, there is no deduction for federal income paid. Federal, state and local pensions are exempt. There is an exemption of up to $36,414 of private pension income. Social Security benefits are exempt. There is a $1,700 standard deduction for married couples filing jointly.

Major tax credits or rebates

include: Credit for income taxes paid to other states, which our couples do not qualify for; personal exemption credit, which our couples do qualify for; and a low-income tax credit, which several of our couples qualify for.

The state sales tax rate is 6%.

Since car registration and renewal fees differ within the state, see city information for details.

KENTUCKY TAX TABLE

Instructions

1. Find the Income in the far left column closest to your anticipated retirement income.
2. Find the Home Value closest to the value of the home where you will live in retirement.
3. Follow that row to your estimated Total Tax Burden at age 65 and beyond.

Income	Home Value	Property Tax & Other Fees	Personal Property Tax & Auto Fees	Sales Tax	Local Income Tax	State Income Tax	Total Tax Burden	Rank* From #1- #163
LEXINGTON								
$25,000	$75,000	$480	$358	$790	-	-	$1,628	#18
	100,000	723	358	790	-	-	1,871	#20
	125,000	965	358	790	-	-	2,113	#21
$50,000	$100,000	$723	$358	$1,279	$292	$859	$3,511	#79
	150,000	1,207	358	1,279	292	859	3,995	#53
	200,000	1,691	358	1,279	292	859	4,479	#46
$75,000	$150,000	$1,207	$358	$1,624	$717	$2,238	$6,144	#105
	250,000	2,175	358	1,624	717	2,238	7,112	#79
	350,000	3,144	358	1,624	717	2,238	8,081	#57
LOUISVILLE								
$25,000	$75,000	$593	$451	$790	$77	-	$1,911	#43
	100,000	892	451	790	77	-	2,210	#50
	125,000	1,191	451	790	77	-	2,509	#57
$50,000	$100,000	$892	$451	$1,279	$365	$859	$3,846	#114
	150,000	1,490	451	1,279	365	859	4,444	#99
	200,000	2,088	451	1,279	365	859	5,042	#83
$75,000	$150,000	$1,490	$451	$1,624	$706	$2,238	$6,509	#116
	250,000	2,686	451	1,624	706	2,238	7,705	#104
	350,000	3,883	451	1,624	706	2,238	8,902	#91

*There are 163 cities in this book. The city with the lowest tax burden for an income/home value combination is given the #1 rating; the city with the highest total tax burden is given the #163 rating.

Lexington

Lexington has a local income tax but does not levy an additional sales tax.

The local income tax is composed of an occupational license fee of 2.75%, which is applied to wages, salaries and

self-employment income.

In calculating the tax, federal, state and private pensions are exempt.

Social Security benefits are exempt.

In calculating the occupational license fee, the first $3,000 of earned income is exempt for taxpayers age 65 or older.

Most purchases are taxed at the state rate of 6%. Major consumer categories taxed at a different rate: None. Major consumer categories that are exempt from sales tax include: Drugs, groceries and medical services.

Within the city limits of Lexington in District 1, the property tax rate is .009685. Homes are assessed at 100% of market value. There is a homestead exemption of $25,400 off assessed value for homeowners age 65 or older. Property tax includes garbage pickup.

Lexington has a personal property tax of .01123 for automobiles. Additional items subject to the tax are trucks, boats, boat trailers, motorcycles and recreational automobiles and are taxed at varying rates. Personal property is assessed at 100% of the N.A.D.A. or appropriate guide trade-in value.

Our couples relocating to Lexington must pay a usage tax on automobiles, which is 6% of the current trade-in value and is paid when the automobile is initially registered in the state. If a vehicle owner paid a usage or sales tax in another state when the automobile was purchased that was equal to or greater than the Kentucky usage tax, there is no additional charge. If a vehicle owner paid a usage or sales tax to another state that was less than the Kentucky usage tax, they are required to pay the difference. We've assumed our couples have paid tax equal to or greater than the Kentucky usage tax. Our couples will pay titling fees of $43 per automobile, $21 per automobile for recording a lien and $28 per automobile for registration and miscellaneous fees at the time of registration. Thereafter, on an annual basis, our couples will pay a registration fee per automobile.

Louisville

Louisville has a local income tax but does not levy an additional sales tax.

The local income tax is composed of an occupational license tax of 2.2%, which is applied to wages, salaries and self-employment income.

In calculating the tax, federal, state and private pensions are exempt. Social Security benefits are exempt.

Most purchases are taxed at the state rate of 6%. Major consumer categories taxed at a different rate: None. Major consumer categories that are exempt from sales tax include: Drugs, groceries and medical services.

Within the city limits of Louisville, the property tax rate is .011961. Homes are assessed at 100% of market value. There is a homestead exemption of $25,400 off assessed value for homeowners age 65 or older. Property tax includes garbage pickup.

Louisville has a personal property tax of .01767 for automobiles. Additional items subject to the tax are boats, boat trailers and recreational vehicles. Personal property is assessed at 100% of the N.A.D.A. or appropriate guide trade-in value.

Our couples relocating to Louisville must pay a usage tax on automobiles, which is 6% of the current trade-in value and is paid when the automobile is initially registered in the state. If a vehicle owner paid a usage or sales tax in another state when the automobile was purchased that was equal to or greater than the Kentucky usage tax, there is no additional charge. If a vehicle owner paid a usage or sales tax to another state that was less than the Kentucky usage tax, they are required to pay the difference. We've assumed our couples have paid tax equal to or greater than the Kentucky usage tax. Our couples will pay a title fee of $6 per automobile, $22 per automobile for registration and miscellaneous fees, a $21 lien filing fee per automobile and $11 per automobile for emissions testing. Thereafter, on an annual basis, our couples will pay a registration fee and for emissions testing.

LOUISIANA

Tax Heavens O
None

Tax Hells Ψ
None

Top Retirement Towns
Natchitoches

Louisiana has a state income tax and a state sales tax.

The state income tax rate is graduated from 0% to 6% depending upon income bracket. For married couples filing jointly, the rate is 0% on the first $9,000 of taxable income; the rate is 2% on the next $11,000 of taxable income; the rate is 4% on the next $80,000 of taxable income; and the rate is 6% on taxable income above $100,000.

In calculating the tax, there is a deduction for federal income tax paid. Federal and state pension incomes are exempt. Social Security benefits are exempt. There is a deduction of up to $12,000 of all other pension income for married couples filing jointly, both age 65 or older. There is an adjustment to income for federal tax applicable to exempt pension income and Social Security benefits.

Major tax credits or rebates include: Credit for income taxes paid to other states, which our couples do not qualify for; tax credit of $20 per person if age 65 or older, which our couples do qualify for.

The state sales tax rate is 4%, but local governments can add to this amount.

Since car registration fees differ within the state, see city information for details.

LOUISIANA TAX TABLE

Instructions

1. Find the Income in the far left column closest to your anticipated retirement income.
2. Find the Home Value closest to the value of the home where you will live in retirement.
3. Follow that row to your estimated Total Tax Burden at age 65 and beyond.

Income	Home Value	Property Tax & Other Fees	Personal Property Tax & Auto Fees	Sales Tax	Local Income Tax	State Income Tax	Total Tax Burden	Rank* From #1- #163
BATON ROUGE								
$25,000	$75,000	$235	$22	$1,370	-	-	$1,627	#17
	100,000	477	22	1,370	-	-	1,869	#19
	125,000	720	22	1,370	-	-	2,112	#20
$50,000	$100,000	$477	$22	$2,148	-	$204	$2,851	#22
	150,000	962	22	2,148	-	204	3,336	#23
	200,000	1,447	22	2,148	-	204	3,821	#18
$75,000	$150,000	$962	$22	$2,687	-	$961	$4,632	#41
	250,000	1,931	22	2,687	-	961	5,601	#27
	350,000	2,902	22	2,687	-	961	6,572	#22
NATCHITOCHES								
$25,000	$75,000	$284	$22	$1,334	-	-	$1,640	#21
	100,000	574	22	1,334	-	-	1,930	#22
	125,000	864	22	1,334	-	-	2,220	#30
$50,000	$100,000	$574	$22	$2,042	-	$204	$2,842	#21
	150,000	1,154	22	2,042	-	204	3,422	#25
	200,000	1,734	22	2,042	-	204	4,002	#27
$75,000	$150,000	$1,154	$22	$2,534	-	$961	$4,671	#45
	250,000	2,314	22	2,534	-	961	5,831	#33
	350,000	3,474	22	2,534	-	961	6,991	#36
NEW ORLEANS								
$25,000	$75,000	$235	$333	$1,343	-	-	$1,911	#43
	100,000	659	333	1,343	-	-	2,335	#66
	125,000	1,083	333	1,343	-	-	2,759	#76

Income	Home Value	Property Tax & Other Fees	Personal Property Tax & Auto Fees	Sales Tax	Local Income Tax	State Income Tax	Total Tax Burden	Rank* From #1-#163
NEW ORLEANS continued								
$50,000	$100,000	$659	$333	$2,108	-	$204	$3,304	#58
	150,000	1,507	333	2,108	-	204	4,152	#69
	200,000	2,356	333	2,108	-	204	5,001	#80
$75,000	$150,000	$1,507	$333	$2,644	-	$961	$5,445	#76
	250,000	3,204	333	2,644	-	961	7,142	#82
	350,000	4,901	333	2,644	-	961	8,839	#90

*There are 163 cities in this book. The city with the lowest tax burden for an income/home value combination is given the #1 rating; the city with the highest total tax burden is given the #163 rating.

Baton Rouge

Baton Rouge has no local income tax but does levy a sales tax.

Most purchases are taxed at a rate of 9%. Major consumer categories taxed at a different rate include: Drugs, which are taxed at a rate of 3%; and groceries, which are taxed at a rate of 6%. Major consumer categories that are exempt from sales tax include: Medical services.

Within the city limits of Baton Rouge, the property tax rate is .09698. Homes are assessed at 10% of market value. There is a homestead exemption of $7,500 off market value for homes assessed at $75,000 or less. The exemption is not available for the city component of property tax and is available to all homeowners. Property tax does not cover garbage pickup; the additional fee is approximately $180 per year.

Baton Rouge has no personal property tax for individuals.

Our couples relocating to Baton Rouge must pay a use tax based on the NADA current loan value of each automobile. The tax rate is 9%, however, the state will give credit to new residents of up to 4% based on sales tax previously paid to another state. We've assumed a 4% credit on the use tax since this is the most common credit given. The use tax would be approximately $610 for the Explorer and $423 for the Cutlass. Our couples also pay a plate fee of $24 for the Explorer and $20 for the Cutlass, $19 per automobile for a title fee and $8 per automobile for a handling fee at the time of registration. Thereafter, our couples will pay a plate fee per automobile every two years.

Natchitoches

Natchitoches has no local income tax but does levy a sales tax.

Most purchases are taxed at a rate of 8%. Major consumer categories taxed at a different rate: None. Major consumer categories that are exempt from sales tax include: Medical services.

For the City of Natchitoches, the property tax rate is .116. Homes are assessed at 10% of market value. There is a homestead exemption of $7,500 off market value for homes assessed at $75,000 or less. The exemption is not available for the city component of property tax and is available to all homeowners. Property tax does not cover garbage pickup; the additional fee is approximately $156 per year.

Natchitoches has no personal property tax for individuals.

Our couples relocating to Natchitoches must pay a use tax based on the NADA current loan value of each automobile. The tax rate is 8%, however, the state will give credit to new residents of up to 4% based on sales tax previously paid to another state. We've assumed a 4% credit on the use tax since this is the most common credit given. The use tax would be approximately $488 for the Explorer and $338 for the Cutlass. Our couples also pay a license fee of $24 for the Explorer and $20 for the Cutlass, $19 per automobile for a title fee and $8 per automobile for a handling fee at the time of registration. Thereafter, our couples will pay a license fee per automobile every two years.

New Orleans

New Orleans has no local income tax but does levy a sales tax.

Most purchases are taxed at a rate of 9%. Major consumer categories taxed at a different rate include: Drugs and groceries, which are both taxed at a rate of 4.5%. Major consumer categories that are exempt from sales tax include: Medical services.

For the City of New Orleans, the property tax rate is .16969. Homes are assessed at 10% of market value. There is a homestead exemption of $7,500 off market value for homes assessed at $75,000 or less. The exemption is not available for the police and fire component of property tax and is available to all homeowners. Property tax does not cover garbage pickup; the additional fee is approximately $156 per year.

New Orleans has a personal property tax rate of .16969. Personal property is assessed at 15% of the value calculated by the parish assessors. Items subject to the tax include automobiles and motorcycles.

Our couples relocating to New Orleans must pay a use tax based on the NADA current loan value of each automobile. The tax rate is 9%, however, the state will give credit to new residents of up to 4% based on sales tax previously paid to another state. We've assumed a 4% credit on the use tax since this is the most common credit given. The use tax would be approximately $610 for the Explorer and $423 for the Cutlass. Our couples also pay a plate fee of $24 for the Explorer and $20 for the Cutlass, $19 per automobile for a title fee and $8 per automobile for a handling fee at the time of registration. Thereafter, our couples will pay a plate fee per automobile every two years.

Natchitoches, Louisiana

This rustic, close-knit town fronting on Cane River Lake and surrounded by rolling hills and deep national forests is attracting retirees from around the world. Ruth and Leland Malcolm spent 12 years in Bahrain, and Ken and Donna Bates had lived in Turkey before deciding to make Natchitoches (pronounced Nak-uh-tish) their retirement home.

David and Carolyn Graham moved only about 300 miles from Germantown, TN, but couldn't imagine living anywhere else. "It's a wonderful place to live," David says. "The people are remarkable — so friendly, helpful and courteous. We are planting our roots even deeper by adding onto our house."

The Grahams stay busily involved with church music, historic preservation and arts and crafts. David has served as chairman of the Melrose Plantation Arts and Crafts Festival, an annual event featuring over 200 outstanding artist-vendors and attracting some 25,000 visitors each year. "There's never a dull moment," David says.

Population: 17,141 in city, 37,377 in parish.

Climate:

	High	Low
January	57	35
July	94	72

Cost of living: Below average (specific index not available).

Average price of a new home: $120,000

Security: 68.3 crimes per 1,000 residents, higher than the national average of 42.7 crimes per 1,000 residents.

Information: Natchitoches Area Chamber of Commerce, P.O. Box 3, Natchitoches, LA 71458, (318) 352-6894 or www. natchitocheschamber.org.

MAINE

Tax Heavens O
None

Tax Hells Ψ
None

Top Retirement Towns
Camden

Maine has a state income tax and a state sales tax.

The state income tax is graduated from 2% to 8.5% depending upon income bracket. For married couples filing jointly, the rate is 2% on the first $8,249 of taxable income; the rate is 4.5% on the next $8,250 of taxable income; the rate is 7% on the next $16,500 of taxable income; and the rate is 8.5% on taxable income above $32,999.

In calculating the tax, there is no deduction for federal income tax paid. There is a federal, state and private pension income exclusion of up to $6,000 per person age 65 or older if included in federal adjusted gross income. The $6,000 must be reduced by any Social Security benefits received, whether taxable or not. Social Security benefits are exempt. There is a $2,850 personal exemption per person from adjusted gross income. There is a $7,350 standard deduction from adjusted gross income for married couples filing jointly, plus an additional deduction of $1,700 if both are age 65 or older.

Major tax credits or rebates include: Credit for income taxes paid to other states, low income credit, elderly and disabled credit, and earned income credit. Our couples do not qualify for these programs.

The state sales tax rate is 5%.

MAINE TAX TABLE

Instructions

1. Find the Income in the far left column closest to your anticipated retirement income.
2. Find the Home Value closest to the value of the home where you will live in retirement.
3. Follow that row to your estimated Total Tax Burden at age 65 and beyond.

Income	Home Value	Property Tax & Other Fees	Personal Property Tax & Auto Fees	Sales Tax	Local Income Tax	State Income Tax	Total Tax Burden	Rank* From #1-#163
CAMDEN								
$25,000	$75,000	$1,279	$595	$689	-	$7	$2,570	#137
	100,000	1,682	595	689	-	7	2,973	#137
	125,000	2,085	595	689	-	7	3,376	#133
$50,000	$100,000	$1,682	$595	$1,115	-	$868	$4,260	#131
	150,000	2,489	595	1,115	-	868	5,067	#129
	200,000	3,295	595	1,115	-	868	5,873	#123
$75,000	$150,000	$2,489	$595	$1,411	-	$2,690	$7,185	#135
	250,000	4,102	595	1,411	-	2,690	8,798	#139
	350,000	5,715	595	1,411	-	2,690	10,411	#131

*There are 163 cities in this book. The city with the lowest tax burden for an income/home value combination is given the #1 rating; the city with the highest total tax burden is given the #163 rating.

Camden

Camden has no local income tax and does not levy an additional sales tax.

Most purchases are taxed at the state rate of 5%. Major consumer categories taxed at a different rate include: Food away from home, which is taxed at 7%. Major consumer categories that are exempt from sales tax include: Drugs, groceries and medical services.

Within the Camden city limits, the property tax rate is .01613. Homes are assessed at 100% of market value. There is a homestead exemption of $7,000 off the assessed value of an owner-occupied home. Property tax does not include garbage pickup; the additional fee is approximately $182 per year.

Camden has a personal property tax called the vehicle excise tax, the rate of which is based on the age of the vehi-cle. Vehicles are assessed at 100% of MSRP. Items subject to the tax include automobiles, RVs and trucks. Boats are subject to the tax but at a different rate.

In addition to the vehicle excise tax, our couples relocating to Camden must pay a registration fee of $25 per automobile and a title fee of $15 per automobile at the time of registration. Thereafter, on an annual basis, our couples will pay a registration fee per automobile.

Camden, Maine

The beauty of the seaside area, its small-town atmosphere and ease of getting around are qualities Ina Doban likes about Camden. She and her husband, Al, made the move from Hagerstown, MD. Since MBNA, a national credit card issuer, moved here a few years ago, things have gotten even better, according to Ina.

"They (MBNA) brought a lot of benefits to the town, and young people don't have to leave to find good-paying jobs. Everything has been done with care and concern for the town's welfare," Ina says. "Taxes, utilities and real estate costs are rather high, but it's worth the extra cost," she says. The winters are longer but no harsher than Hagerstown, and the Dobans warm up in Scottsdale, AZ, frequently heading to the Southwest in the winter months.

Population: 5,100 in city, 37,500 in county.

Climate:	High	Low
January	32	14
July	75	55

Cost of living: Above average (specific index not available).

Average price of a new home: $229,000

Security: 10.8 crimes per 1,000 residents, lower than the national average of 42.7 crimes per 1,000 residents.

Information: Camden-Rockport-Lincolnville Chamber of Commerce, P.O. Box 919, Camden, ME 04843, (207) 236-4404 or www.camdenme.org.

MARYLAND

Maryland has a state income tax and a state sales tax.

The state income tax rate is graduated from 3% to 4.85% depending upon income bracket. For married couples filing jointly, the rate is 3% on the first $3,000 of taxable income and the rate is 4.85% on taxable income above $3,000.

In calculating the tax, there is no deduction for federal income tax paid.

There is a federal, state and private pension income exclusion of up to $16,500 per person age 65 or older. Social Security benefits are exempt. There is a $1,850 personal exemption per person from adjusted gross income and a $1,000 personal exemption per person from adjusted gross income for people age 65 or older. There is a variable standard deduction from adjusted gross income for married couples filing jointly that is based on income. There is also a $1,200 two-income deduction for married couples filing jointly.

Major tax credits or rebates include: Credit for income taxes paid to other states, earned income credit and poverty level credits. Our couples do not qualify for these programs.

The state sales tax rate is 5%.

MARYLAND TAX TABLE

Instructions

1. Find the Income in the far left column closest to your anticipated retirement income.
2. Find the Home Value closest to the value of the home where you will live in retirement.
3. Follow that row to your estimated Total Tax Burden at age 65 and beyond.

Income	Home Value	Property Tax & Other Fees	Personal Property Tax & Auto Fees	Sales Tax	Local Income Tax	State Income Tax	Total Tax Burden	Rank* From #1- #163
BALTIMORE								
$25,000	$75,000	$1,290	$84	$650	-	-	$2,024	#61
	100,000	1,290	84	650	-	-	2,024	#33
	125,000	1,290	84	650	-	-	2,024	#15
$50,000	$100,000	$2,412	$84	$1,052	$443	$811	$4,802	#153
	150,000	3,540	84	1,052	443	811	5,930	#152
	200,000	4,746	84	1,052	443	811	7,136	#152
$75,000	$150,000	$4,824	$84	$1,345	$1,047	$1,992	$9,292	#161 Ψ
	250,000	6,030	84	1,345	1,047	1,992	10,498	#153
	350,000	8,442	84	1,345	1,047	1,992	12,910	#152

*There are 163 cities in this book. The city with the lowest tax burden for an income/home value combination is given the #1 rating; the city with the highest total tax burden is given the #163 rating.

Baltimore

Baltimore has a local income tax but does not levy an additional sales tax.

The local income tax is 2.48% of Maryland taxable income.

Most purchases are taxed at the state rate of 5%. Major consumer categories taxed at a different rate: None. Major consumer categories that are exempt from sales tax include: Groceries, drugs, medical supplies and medical services.

In the area of Roland Park, the property tax rate is .0603. Homes are assessed at 40% of market value. There is a homestead property tax credit available if an appraisal results in an increase of more than 10% on the state portion or 4% on the city portion of the assessed value per year. There is also a homeowner's property tax credit for taxes that exceed a percentage of a homeowner's gross income and only applies to the first $150,000 of assessed value less any homestead credit. Property tax includes garbage pickup.

Baltimore has no personal property tax for individuals.

Our couples relocating to Baltimore may have to pay an excise titling tax per automobile depending on the amount of the tax paid in the state in which the automobile was purchased. If a vehicle owner paid a sales tax in another state when the automobile was purchased that was equal to or greater than the Maryland sales tax, the excise tax fee is $100. If a vehicle owner paid sales tax to another state that was less than the Maryland sales tax, they are required to pay the difference. Our couples also pay a registration fee of $35 for the Cutlass and $49 for the Explorer, a title fee of $20 per automobile, a security interest filing fee of $20 per automobile and a lien-recording fee of $20 per automobile. Thereafter, our couples will pay a registration fee of $70 for the Cutlass and $97 for the Explorer every two years.

MASSACHUSETTS

Tax Heavens O
None

Tax Hells Ψ
Cape Cod (Barnstable)

Top Retirement Towns
None

Massachusetts has a state income tax and a state sales tax.

There are two state income tax rates depending upon type of income. For most income, including earned income, interest income and dividend income, the rate is 5.85% of taxable income. For certain short-term capital gains, the rate is 12% of taxable income.

In calculating the tax, there is no deduction for federal income tax paid. Federal, state and local government pension income is exempt. Private pension income is not exempt. Social Security benefits are exempt. There is a $200 exemption for married couples filing jointly from interest earned from Massachusetts banks. There is a deduction of up to $2,000 per person for payments made to Social Security, Medicare, railroad, federal or Massachusetts retirement systems. There is a personal exemption from 5.85% income of $8,800 total for married couples filing jointly. There is $700 age deduction from 5.85% income per person for persons age 65 or older.

Major tax credits or rebates include: Credit for taxes paid to another state, no-tax status credit and a limited-income credit. Our lowest income level qualifies for the no-tax status credit.

The state sales tax rate is 5%.

Our couples relocating to the cities below must pay a vehicle excise tax (personal property tax) based on the year and MSRP of each automobile. The vehicle excise tax is $491 for the Explorer and $408 for the Cutlass at the time of initial registration. Our couples also pay a registration fee of $30 for two years per automobile, a title fee of

MASSACHUSETTS TAX TABLE

Instructions

1. Find the Income in the far left column closest to your anticipated retirement income.
2. Find the Home Value closest to the value of the home where you will live in retirement.
3. Follow that row to your estimated Total Tax Burden at age 65 and beyond.

Income	Home Value	Property Tax & Other Fees	Personal Property Tax & Auto Fees	Sales Tax	Local Income Tax	State Income Tax	Total Tax Burden	Rank* From #1-#163
BOSTON								
$25,000	$75,000	$986	$687	$658	-	-	$2,331	#116
	100,000	1,315	687	658	-	-	2,660	#105
	125,000	1,644	687	658	-	-	2,989	#92
$50,000	$100,000	$1,315	$687	$1,066	-	$1,423	$4,491	#137
	150,000	1,973	687	1,066	-	1,423	5,149	#131
	200,000	2,630	687	1,066	-	1,423	5,806	#120
$75,000	$150,000	$1,973	$687	$1,354	-	$2,728	$6,742	#125
	250,000	3,288	687	1,354	-	2,728	8,057	#119
	350,000	4,603	687	1,354	-	2,728	9,372	#106
CAPE COD (BARNSTABLE)								
$25,000	$75,000	$1,557	$687	$658	-	-	$2,902	#151
	100,000	1,963	687	658	-	-	3,308	#150
	125,000	2,370	687	658	-	-	3,715	#142
$50,000	$100,000	$1,963	$687	$1,066	-	$1,423	$5,139	#155 Ψ
	150,000	2,777	687	1,066	-	1,423	5,953	#153
	200,000	3,591	687	1,066	-	1,423	6,767	#148
$75,000	$150,000	$2,777	$687	$1,354	-	$2,728	$7,546	#149
	250,000	4,405	687	1,354	-	2,728	9,174	#144
	350,000	6,032	687	1,354	-	2,728	10,801	#138

*There are 163 cities in this book. The city with the lowest tax burden for an income/home value combination is given the #1 rating; the city with the highest total tax burden is given the #163 rating.

$50 per automobile and a $29 fee for emissions and safety tests per automobile. Thereafter, our couples will pay a vehicle excise tax and an emissions testing fee on an annual basis and a registration fee every two years, per automobile.

Boston

Boston has no local income tax and does not levy an additional sales tax.

Most purchases are taxed at the state rate of 5%. Major consumer categories that are taxed at a different rate: None. Major consumer purchases that are exempt from sales tax include: Drugs, groceries and medical services. Purchases of apparel are exempt up to $175 per item.

Within Boston city limits, the property tax rate is .01315. Homes are assessed at 100% of market value.

There is an elderly exemption available to homeowners age 70 or older who meet certain income, residency and net worth requirements. Property tax includes garbage pickup.

Boston has a personal property tax on homes other than the owner's primary residence. The personal property tax is .01315 within Boston city limits. The structure of a secondary residence is assessed at 10% of market value. We've assumed our couples own a primary residence in Boston.

Cape Cod (Barnstable)

Cape Cod has no local income tax and does not levy an additional sales tax.

Most purchases are taxed at the state rate of 5%. Major consumer categories that are taxed at a different rate: None. Major consumer purchases that are exempt from sales tax include: Drugs, groceries and medical services. Purchases of apparel are exempt up to $175 per item.

In the area of Barnstable Township, the property tax rate is .01589. Homes are assessed at 100% of market value. There is an elderly exemption available to homeowners age 70 or older who meet certain income, residency and net worth requirements. Residents pay a Land Bank Fund fee of 3% of property taxes owed. Property tax does not cover garbage pickup; the additional fee is approximately $336 per year.

Cape Cod has a personal property tax on homes other than the owner's primary residence. The personal property tax is .01589 within Barnstable Township. The structure of a secondary residence is assessed at 10% of market value. We've assumed our couples own a primary residence in Barnstable.

MICHIGAN

Tax Heavens O	Tax Hells Ψ	Top Retirement Towns
Petoskey	None	Petoskey

Michigan has a state income tax and a state sales tax.

The state income tax rate is 4.2% of taxable income. In calculating the tax, there is no deduction for federal income tax paid. Federal, state, and local government pensions are exempt. Up to $69,840 of private pension income is excluded for married couples filing jointly. Social Security benefits are exempt. There is an interest/dividends/capital gains deduction of up to $7,785 per person for persons 65 and older. This deduction must first be reduced by any pension deduction taken. There is a $2,900 personal exemption per person from adjusted gross income plus an exemption for persons age 65 or older of $1,800 per person from adjusted gross income.

Major tax credits or rebates include: Credit for taxes paid to other states, which our couples do not qualify for; city income tax credit, which our couples do qualify for if city income tax was paid; and homestead property tax credit, which our couples do qualify for.

The state sales tax rate is 6%.

Our couples relocating to the cities listed below must pay a registration fee of $102 for the Explorer and $91 for the Cutlass and a title fee of $11 per automobile. Thereafter, on an annual basis, our couples will pay a registration fee per automobile.

MICHIGAN TAX TABLE

Instructions

1. Find the Income in the far left column closest to your anticipated retirement income.
2. Find the Home Value closest to the value of the home where you will live in retirement.
3. Follow that row to your estimated Total Tax Burden at age 65 and beyond.

Income	Home Value	Property Tax & Other Fees	Personal Property Tax & Auto Fees	Sales Tax	Local Income Tax	State Income Tax†	Total Tax Burden	Rank* From #1- #163
DETROIT								
$25,000	$75,000	$1,812	$173	$790	$66	($937)	$1,904	#41
	100,000	2,416	173	790	66	(1,200)	2,245	#54
	125,000	3,019	173	790	66	(1,200)	2,848	#83
$50,000	$100,000	$2,416	$173	$1,279	$548	($173)	$4,243	#129
	150,000	3,623	173	1,279	548	(707)	4,916	#120
	200,000	4,831	173	1,279	548	(707)	6,124	#129
$75,000	$150,000	$3,623	$173	$1,624	$1,188	$606	$7,214	#138
	250,000	6,039	173	1,624	1,188	444	9,468	#147
	350,000	8,455	173	1,624	1,188	444	11,884	#149
PETOSKEY								
$25,000	$75,000	$1,613	$173	$790	-	($502)	$2,074	#73
	100,000	1,624	173	790	-	(961)	1,626	#7 O
	125,000	2,122	173	790	-	(1,200)	1,885	#8 O
$50,000	$100,000	$1,624	$173	$1,279	-	$452	$3,528	#80
	150,000	2,587	173	1,279	-	(466)	3,573	#31
	200,000	3,260	173	1,279	-	(662)	4,050	#30
$75,000	$150,000	$2,587	$173	$1,624	-	$1,378	$5,762	#88
	250,000	4,273	173	1,624	-	521	6,591	#54
	350,000	6,240	173	1,624	-	521	8,558	#77

†Credit for local income tax paid is issued as a reduction of state income tax due and credit for property tax paid is issued as a refund if the credit is greater than the tax liability.

*There are 163 cities in this book. The city with the lowest tax burden for an income/home value combination is given the #1 rating; the city with the highest total tax burden is given the #163 rating.

Detroit

Detroit has a local income tax but does not levy an additional sales tax.

The local income tax rate is 2.85% of taxable income for residents and 1.425% of taxable income for non-residents who work in the city limits. Federal, state, and private pensions are exempt. Social Security benefits are exempt. There is a $750 exemption per person plus a $750 exemption per person if age 65 or older.

Most purchases are taxed at the state rate of 6%. Major consumer categories taxed at a different rate: None. Major consumer categories that are exempt from sales tax include: Drugs, groceries and medical services.

Within the city limits of Detroit, the property tax rate is .483114. Homes are assessed at 50% of market value. There is a poverty exemption program available if gross income is $15,628 or less. Property tax includes garbage pickup.

Detroit has no personal property tax for individuals.

Petoskey

Petoskey has no local income tax and does not levy an additional sales tax.

Most purchases are taxed at the state rate of 6%. Major consumer categories taxed at a different rate: None. Major consumer categories that are exempt from sales tax include: Drugs, groceries and medical services.

Within the city limits of Petoskey, the property tax rate is .03671440 for homeowners who qualify for the homestead exemption and .05466750 for homeowners who do not qualify for the homestead exemption. Homes are assessed at 50% of market value, however, taxable value may not equal assessed value. Property tax amounts shown are estimates and were provided by local taxing authorities. Property tax does not cover garbage pickup; the additional fee is approximately $275 per year.

Petoskey has no personal property tax for individuals.

• Michigan's Best Retirement Town •

Petoskey, Michigan

It's not your typical sunny retirement town, but this quaint village on a rolling hillside above Little Traverse Bay in northwest Michigan has attracted a goodly number of retirees and today has one of the fastest growth rates in the state.

Many are summer or second-home residents who enjoy participating in such activities as fishing, boating, golfing and visiting with their neighbors. They usually head south to Arizona, Florida or the Rio Grande Valley of Texas to wait out the snow and cold of winter. But with plenty of fuel and firewood to keep them warm, others are content to stay on year-round, reveling in festive wintertime activities and the opportunity to join their neighbors in the over-70 ski club on beautifully blanketed slopes.

"We don't participate much in outdoor winter activities," says Dick Wise, who retired here with his wife, Betty, from Detroit. "But we love the holiday season, when the town puts on its prettiest face."

Population: 7,200 year-round (25,000 during summer) in city, 23,000 in county.

Climate:

	High	Low
January	28	15
July	77	59

Cost of living: Above average (specific index not available).

Average price of a new home: $250,000

Security: 12.7 crimes per 1,000 residents, lower than the national average of 42.7 crimes per 1,000 residents.

Information: Petoskey Regional Chamber of Commerce, 401 E. Mitchell St., Petoskey, MI 49770, (231) 347-4150 or www.petoskey.com.

MINNESOTA

Tax Heavens ○
None

Tax Hells Ψ
Minneapolis

Top Retirement Towns
None

Minnesota has a state income tax and a state sales tax.

The state income tax is graduated from 5.35% to 7.85% depending upon income bracket. For married couples filing jointly, the rate is 5.35% on the first $25,680 of taxable income; the rate is 7.05% on the next $76,350 of taxable income; and the rate is 7.85% on taxable income above $102,030.

In calculating the tax, there is no deduction for federal income tax paid. Federal, state and private pensions are not exempt. Social Security benefits subject to federal tax are not exempt.

There is a $2,800 personal exemption per person from adjusted gross income. There is a $9,050 standard deduction from adjusted gross income for married couples filing jointly when both are age 65 or older. There are age 65 or older/disabled subtractions for singles or couples meeting certain income requirements.

Major tax credits or rebates include: Credit for taxes paid to other states, which our couples do not qualify for; and a marriage credit, which one of our couples qualifies for.

The state sales tax rate is 6.5%, but local

governments can add to this amount.

Our couples relocating to the city listed below must pay to register and annually renew their automobiles based on the base value of the automobile. The registration tax is $189 for the Explorer and $189 for the Cutlass. Our couples must also pay a title fee of $4 per automobile, a public safety vehicle fee of $4 per automobile, a license fee of $3 per automobile and a filing fee of $7 per automobile. Thereafter, on an annual basis, our couples will pay a registration tax, a public safety fee, a filing fee and a license fee, per automobile.

MINNESOTA TAX TABLE

Instructions

1. Find the Income in the far left column closest to your anticipated retirement income.
2. Find the Home Value closest to the value of the home where you will live in retirement.
3. Follow that row to your estimated Total Tax Burden at age 65 and beyond.

Income	Home Value	Property Tax & Other Fees	Personal Property Tax & Auto Fees	Sales Tax	Local Income Tax	State Income Tax	Total Tax Burden	Rank* From #1-#163	
MINNEAPOLIS									
$25,000	$75,000	$1,178	$225	$892	-	-	$2,295	#108	
	100,000	1,677	225	892	-	-	2,794	#119	
	125,000	2,279	225	892	-	-	3,396	#134	
$50,000	$100,000	$1,677	$225	$1,454	-	$1,454	$4,810	#154	Ψ
	150,000	2,913	225	1,454	-	1,454	6,046	#154	Ψ
	200,000	4,181	225	1,454	-	1,454	7,314	#155	Ψ
$75,000	$150,000	$2,913	$225	$1,806	-	$3,627	$8,571	#157	Ψ
	250,000	5,449	225	1,806	-	3,627	11,107	#157	Ψ
	350,000	7,985	225	1,806	-	3,627	13,643	#156	Ψ

*There are 163 cities in this book. The city with the lowest tax burden for an income/home value combination is given the #1 rating; the city with the highest total tax burden is given the #163 rating.

Minneapolis

Minneapolis has no local income tax but does levy a sales tax.

Most purchases are taxed at a rate of 7%. Major consumer categories taxed at a different rate include: Food away from home, which is taxed at a rate of 10%. Major consumer categories that are exempt from sales tax include: Drugs, groceries, apparel and services,

and medical services.

Within the city limits of Minneapolis, there are two property tax rates based on different components; the property tax rate based on tax capacity (taxable value) is 1.44406 and the tax rate based on market value is .0015310. To calculate tax capacity (taxable value), homes are assessed at 1% of the first $76,000 of market value of the home plus

1.65% of market value in excess of $76,000. There is an education homestead credit of up to $390 available to all residents that is applied to the tax capacity component of tax. Property tax does not include garbage pickup; the additional fee is approximately $213 per year.

Minneapolis has no personal property tax for individuals.

MISSISSIPPI

		Top Retirement Towns
None	None	Hattiesburg
		Oxford

Mississippi has a state income tax and a state sales tax.

The state income tax rate is graduated from 3% to 5% depending upon income bracket. For married couples filing jointly, the rate is 3% on the first $5,000 of taxable income; the rate is 4% on the next $5,000 of taxable income; and the rate is 5% on taxable income above $10,000.

In calculating the tax, there is no deduction for federal income tax paid. Federal, state and private pensions are exempt. Social Security benefits are exempt. There is a $4,600 standard deduction from adjusted gross income for married couples filing jointly. There is a $12,000 exemption for married couples filing jointly. There is an addi-

tional $1,500 exemption for each person age 65 or older.

Major tax credits or rebates include: Credit for taxes paid to other states. Our couples do not qualify for this program.

The state sales tax rate is 7%.

Since car registration and renewal fees differ within the state, see city information for details.

MISSISSIPPI TAX TABLE

Instructions

1. Find the Income in the far left column closest to your anticipated retirement income.
2. Find the Home Value closest to the value of the home where you will live in retirement.
3. Follow that row to your estimated Total Tax Burden at age 65 and beyond.

Income	Home Value	Property Tax & Other Fees	Personal Property Tax & Auto Fees	Sales Tax	Local Income Tax	State Income Tax	Total Tax Burden	Rank* From #1- #163
HATTIESBURG								
$25,000	$75,000	$359	$955	$1,138	-	-	$2,452	#131
	100,000	768	955	1,138	-	-	2,861	#128
	125,000	1,176	955	1,138	-	-	3,269	#123
$50,000	$100,000	$768	$955	$1,781	-	$78	$3,582	#86
	150,000	1,585	955	1,781	-	78	4,399	#94
	200,000	2,402	955	1,781	-	78	5,216	#95
$75,000	$150,000	$1,585	$955	$2,214	-	$970	$5,724	#86
	250,000	3,220	955	2,214	-	970	7,359	#91
	350,000	4,854	955	2,214	-	970	8,993	#96
OXFORD								
$25,000	$75,000	$405	$789	$1,138	-	-	$2,332	#117
	100,000	761	789	1,138	-	-	2,688	#107
	125,000	1,116	789	1,138	-	-	3,043	#98
$50,000	$100,000	$761	$789	$1,781	-	$78	$3,409	#69
	150,000	1,472	789	1,781	-	78	4,120	#62
	200,000	2,183	789	1,781	-	78	4,831	#66
$75,000	$150,000	$1,472	$789	$2,214	-	$970	$5,445	#76
	250,000	2,894	789	2,214	-	970	6,867	#69
	350,000	4,316	789	2,214	-	970	8,289	#67
VICKSBURG								
$25,000	$75,000	$302	$414	$1,153	-	-	$1,869	#36
	100,000	585	414	1,153	-	-	2,152	#44
	125,000	867	414	1,153	-	-	2,434	#49

Income	Home Value	Property Tax & Other Fees	Personal Property Tax & Auto Fees	Sales Tax	Local Income Tax	State Income Tax	Total Tax Burden	Rank* From #1- #163
VICKSBURG continued								
$50,000	$100,000	$585	$414	$1,806	-	$78	$2,883	#26
	150,000	1,150	414	1,806	-	78	3,448	#27
	200,000	1,716	414	1,806	-	78	4,014	#28
$75,000	$150,000	$1,150	$414	$2,243	-	$970	$4,777	#52
	250,000	2,282	414	2,243	-	970	5,909	#37
	350,000	3,413	414	2,243	-	970	7,040	#38

*There are 163 cities in this book. The city with the lowest tax burden for an income/home value combination is given the #1 rating; the city with the highest total tax burden is given the #163 rating.

Hattiesburg

Hattiesburg has no local income tax and does not levy an additional sales tax.

Most purchases are taxed at the state rate of 7%. Major consumer categories taxed at a different rate include: Food away from home, which is taxed at a rate of 9%. Major consumer categories that are exempt from sales tax include: Drugs and medical services.

Within the Hattiesburg city limits, the property tax rate is .16345. Owner-occupied homes are assessed at 10% of market value. The regular homestead exemption is a scaled tax credit of up to $240 on the first $6,000 of a home's assessed value and is available to all homeowners. There is also an elderly exemption of $6,000 off the assessed value of a home for residents age 65 or older. Only one of these exemptions can be taken at once; we've assumed our couples take the elderly exemption. Property tax does not cover garbage pickup; the additional fee is approximately $114 per year.

Hattiesburg has no personal property tax for individuals.

Our couples relocating to Hattiesburg must pay an ad valorem tax based on the state's valuation of each car. The tax due upon initial registration is $643 for the Explorer and $426 for the Cutlass. Our couples also pay a $10 registration fee per automobile, a $5 title fee per automobile and a $15 privilege tax per automobile. Thereafter, on an annual basis, our couples will pay an ad valorem tax, a privilege tax and a renewal fee, per automobile.

Oxford

Oxford has no local income tax and does not levy an additional sales tax.

Most purchases are taxed at the state rate of 7%. Major consumer categories taxed at a different rate include: Food away from home, which is taxed at a rate of 9%. Major consumer categories that are exempt from sales tax include: Drugs and medical services.

Within the Oxford city limits, the property tax rate is .1422. Owner-occupied homes are assessed at 10% of market value. The regular homestead exemption is a scaled tax credit of up to $240 on the first $6,000 of a home's assessed value and is available to all homeowners. There is also an elderly exemption of $6,000 off the assessed value of a home for residents age 65 or older. Only one of these exemptions can be taken at once; we've assumed our couples take the elderly exemption. Property tax does not cover garbage pickup; the additional fee is approximately $192 per year.

Oxford has no personal property tax for individuals.

Our couples relocating to Oxford must pay an ad valorem tax based on the state's valuation of each car. The tax due upon initial registration is $476 for the Explorer and $395 for the Cutlass. Our couples also pay a $10 registration fee per automobile, a $5 title fee per automobile and a $15 privilege tax per automobile. Thereafter, on an annual basis, our couples will pay an ad valorem tax, a privilege tax and a renewal fee, per automobile.

Vicksburg

Vicksburg has no local income tax and does not levy an additional sales tax.

Most purchases are taxed at the state rate of 7%. Major consumer categories taxed at a different rate include: Food away from home, which is taxed at a rate of 10%. Major consumer categories that are exempt from sales tax include: Drugs and medical services.

Within the Vicksburg city limits, the property tax rate is .11315. Owner-occupied homes are assessed at 10% of market value. The regular homestead exemption is a scaled tax credit of up to $240 on the first $6,000 of a home's assessed value and is available to all homeowners. There is also an elderly exemption of $6,000 off the assessed value of a home for residents age 65 or older. Only one of these exemptions can be taken at once; we've assumed our couples take the elderly exemption. Property tax does not cover garbage pickup; the additional fee is approximately $132 per year.

Vicksburg has no personal property tax for individuals.

Our couples relocating to Vicksburg must pay an ad valorem tax based on the state's valuation of each car. The tax due upon initial registration is $231 for the Explorer and $192 for the Cutlass. Our couples also pay a $10 registration fee per automobile, a $5 title fee per automobile and a $15 privilege tax per automobile. Thereafter, on an annual basis, our couples will pay an ad valorem tax, a privilege tax and a renewal fee, per automobile.

Hattiesburg, Mississippi

Tom and Jane Moseley moved to Hattiesburg from Atlanta and are so pleased with their decision that they painted a delightful portrait of the city on their personal Web site. Not only does the city offer all of the amenities anyone could want, its residents are "some of the friendliest people we ever met," says Tom, who moved frequently during a 30-year career with IBM.

Their list of Hattiesburg's exceptional qualities includes its location near the Gulf beaches and New Orleans, a low cost of living, moderate four-season climate, outstanding medical and educational facilities (it is the home of Forrest Medical Center and the University of Southern Mississippi), and the wide range of cultural activities, excellent golf courses and other recreational outlets.

Population: 50,000 in city plus 19,000 college and university students, 100,000 in Lamar and Forrest counties.

Climate:

	High	Low
January	58	34
July	92	71

Cost of living: Below average (specific index not available).

Average price of a new home: $139,000

Security: 72 crimes per 1,000 residents, higher than the national average of 42.7 crimes per 1,000 residents.

Information: Area Development Partnership, P.O. Box 751, Hattiesburg, MS 39403-0751, (800) 238-4288 or www.hattiesburg-adp.org.

Oxford, Mississippi

Best known as the home of the University of Mississippi (Ole Miss) and award-winning authors William Faulkner and John Grisham, among others, Oxford is a bastion of Southern culture and tradition and repository of literary and historical heritage.

Frank and Mary Poole retired here from Baton Rouge, LA, in 1999, "and we love it," says Mary. They immediately became involved with Oxford Newcomers, a multitalented group with clubs focusing on books, investments, bridge, lunch, gardens and golf.

Mary cites university activities where residents can see theater productions such as "Porgy and Bess" for $7 or attend a brown bag luncheon lecture by a local or visiting notable. In addition to the concerts and theatrical performances on campus, a local choral group and band provide opportunities for residents to both perform and be entertained. "This is an extremely musically talented town," Mary adds.

Population: 10,500 in city, 34,000 in county.

Climate:

	High	Low
January	55	36
July	91	72

Cost of living: Below average (specific index not available).

Average price of a new home: $164,900

Security: 28.1 crimes per 1,000 residents, lower than the national average of 42.7 crimes per 1,000 residents.

Information: Oxford-Lafayette County Chamber of Commerce, P.O. Box 147, Oxford, MS 38655, (662) 234-4651 or http://chamber.oxfordms.com.

MISSOURI

Tax Heavens O
None

Tax Hells Ψ
None

Top Retirement Towns
None

Missouri has a state income tax and a state sales tax.

The state income tax rate is graduated from 1.5% to 6% depending upon income bracket. For all filers, the rate is 1.5% on the first $1,000 of taxable income; the rate is 2% on the next $1,000 of taxable income; the rate is 2.5% on the next $1,000 of taxable income; the rate is 3% on the next $1,000 of taxable income; the rate is 3.5% on the next $1,000 of taxable income; the rate is 4% on the next $1,000 of taxable income; the rate is 4.5% on the next $1,000 of taxable income; the rate is 5% on the next $1,000 of taxable income; the rate is 5.5% on the next $1,000 of taxable income; and the rate is 6% on taxable income above $9,000. Taxable income is calculated individually by spouse, even if filing jointly.

In calculating the tax, there is a deduction of up to $10,000 for married couples filing jointly for federal income tax liability. Federal, state and private pensions are not exempt. However, there is a pension exemption of up to $6,000 from federal and state pension income and up to $4,000 from private pension income. Total pension exemption, including government and private pensions, cannot exceed $6,000, and eligibility is subject to certain income limitations. Social Security benefits subject to federal tax are not exempt. There is a standard deduction of $9,050 from adjusted gross income for married couples filing jointly, both age 65 or older. There is a $4,200 exemption from adjusted gross income for married couples filing jointly.

Major tax credits or rebates include: Credit for taxes paid to other states, which our couples do not qualify for; pharmaceutical tax credit if age 65 or older, which our couples do qualify for; and property tax credit, which some of our couples qualify for.

The state sales tax rate is 4.225%, but local governments can add to this amount.

Our couples relocating to the cities listed below must pay to register their automobiles based on horsepower. The registration fee is $39 for the Explorer and $24 for the Cutlass. Our couples must also pay a $9 title fee per automobile. Thereafter, on an annual basis, our couples will pay a license renewal fee per automobile.

MISSOURI TAX TABLE

Instructions

1. Find the Income in the far left column closest to your anticipated retirement income.
2. Find the Home Value closest to the value of the home where you will live in retirement.
3. Follow that row to your estimated Total Tax Burden at age 65 and beyond.

Income	Home Value	Property Tax & Other Fees	Personal Property Tax & Auto Fees	Sales Tax	Local Income Tax	State Income Tax[†]	Total Tax Burden	Rank[*] From #1- #163
BRANSON								
$25,000	$75,000	$797	$465	$1,151	-	($498)	$1,915	#46
	100,000	995	465	1,151	-	(648)	1,963	#25
	125,000	1,194	465	1,151	-	(648)	2,162	#27
$50,000	$100,000	$995	$465	$1,800	-	$845	$4,105	#124
	150,000	1,392	465	1,800	-	845	4,502	#102
	200,000	1,788	465	1,800	-	845	4,898	#72
$75,000	$150,000	$1,392	$465	$2,240	-	$2,381	$6,478	#115
	250,000	2,184	465	2,240	-	2,381	7,270	#86
	350,000	2,977	465	2,240	-	2,381	8,063	#56
KANSAS CITY								
$25,000	$75,000	$1,005	$742	$991	$35	($648)	$2,125	#81
	100,000	1,340	742	991	35	(648)	2,460	#78
	125,000	1,675	742	991	35	(648)	2,795	#80

[†]Property tax credit and pharmaceutical drug credit are issued as a reduction of income tax due or as a refund if the credit is greater than the tax liability.

[*]There are 163 cities in this book. The city with the lowest tax burden for an income/home value combination is given the #1 rating; the city with the highest total tax burden is given the #163 rating.

MISSOURI TAX TABLE

Instructions

1. Find the Income in the far left column closest to your anticipated retirement income.
2. Find the Home Value closest to the value of the home where you will live in retirement.
3. Follow that row to your estimated Total Tax Burden at age 65 and beyond.

Income	Home Value	Property Tax & Other Fees	Personal Property Tax & Auto Fees	Sales Tax	Local Income Tax	State Income Tax†	Total Tax Burden	Rank* From #1-#163
KANSAS CITY continued								
$50,000	$100,000	$1,340	$742	$1,573	$166	$845	$4,666	#145
	150,000	2,010	742	1,573	166	845	5,336	#139
	200,000	2,680	742	1,573	166	845	6,006	#127
$75,000	$150,000	$2,010	$742	$1,972	$321	$2,381	$7,426	#145
	250,000	3,350	742	1,972	321	2,381	8,766	#138
	350,000	4,690	742	1,972	321	2,381	10,106	#125

†Property tax credit and pharmaceutical drug credit are issued as a reduction of income tax due or as a refund if the credit is greater than the tax liability.

*There are 163 cities in this book. The city with the lowest tax burden for an income/home value combination is given the #1 rating; the city with the highest total tax burden is given the #163 rating.

Branson

Branson has no local income tax but does levy a sales tax.

Most purchases are taxed at a rate of 7.225%. Major consumer categories taxed at a different rate include: Food away from home, which is taxed at a rate of 7.725%. Major consumer categories that are exempt from sales tax include: Drugs and medical services.

Within the city limits of Branson, the property tax rate is .041713 for homes. Homes are assessed at 19% of market value. There is a senior citizen tax rebate for residents age 65 and older who are married filing jointly with a household income of up to $27,000. Property tax does not cover garbage pickup; the additional fee is approximately $203 per year.

Branson has a personal property tax rate of .04173. Personal property is assessed at 33.3% of NADA current market value. Items subject to the personal property tax include automobiles, boats, motors, trailers, farm equipment and farm animals.

Kansas City

Kansas City has a local income tax and a sales tax.

The local income tax rate is 1% of earned income, consisting of wages and salaries and self-employment income.

Most purchases are taxed at a rate of 6.6%. Major consumer categories taxed at a different rate include: Food away from home, which is taxed at a rate of 8.35%; and groceries, which are taxed at a rate of 3.6%. Major consumer cat-egories that are exempt from sales tax include: Drugs and medical services.

In Blue Springs in the Grain Valley school district, the property tax rate is .070528 for homes. Homes are assessed at 19% of market value. There is a senior citizen tax rebate for residents age 65 and older who are married filing jointly with a household income of up to $27,000. Property tax includes garbage pickup.

Kansas City has a personal property tax rate of .070528 within Jackson County. Personal property is assessed at 33.3% of NADA current market value. Items subject to the personal property tax include airplanes, automobiles, boats, farm equipment, farm animals, motorcycles, motors, RVs, trailers and trucks.

MONTANA

Tax Heavens O
Billings

Tax Hells Ψ
None

Top Retirement Towns
None

Montana has a state income tax and does not levy a state sales tax.

The state income tax rate is graduated from 2% to 11% depending upon income bracket. For married couples filing jointly, the rate is 2% on the first $2,100 of taxable income; the rate is 3% on the next $2,100 of taxable income; the rate is 4% on the next $4,100 of taxable income; the rate is 5% on the next $4,200 of taxable income; the rate is 6% on the next $4,200 of taxable income; the rate is 7% on the next $4,100 of taxable income; the rate is 8% on the next $8,400 of taxable income; the rate is 9% on the next $12,500 of taxable income; the rate is 10% on the next $31,300 of taxable income; and the rate is 11% on taxable income above $73,000.

In calculating the tax, there is no deduction for federal income tax paid. Federal, state and private pensions are exempt up to $3,600 per person if federal adjusted gross income is less than $30,000. Some Social Security benefits are not exempt. There is a 20% standard deduction of adjusted gross income, subject to a minimum deduction of $2,780 and maximum of $6,260 for married couples filing jointly. There is a $1,670 personal exemption per person from adjusted gross income, plus a $1,670 age exemption per person if age 65 or older.

Major tax credits or rebates include: Credit for income taxes paid to other states, which our couples do not qualify for; and elderly homeowner/renter credit, which some of our couples qualify for.

MONTANA TAX TABLE

Instructions

1. Find the Income in the far left column closest to your anticipated retirement income.
2. Find the Home Value closest to the value of the home where you will live in retirement.
3. Follow that row to your estimated Total Tax Burden at age 65 and beyond.

Income	Home Value	Property Tax & Other Fees	Personal Property Tax & Auto Fees	Sales Tax	Local Income Tax	State Income Tax[†]	Total Tax Burden	Rank[*] From #1-#163
BILLINGS								
$25,000	$75,000	$950	$588	$0	-	$11	$1,549	#14
	100,000	1,240	588	-	-	(215)	1,613	#6 O
	125,000	1,531	588	-	-	(506)	1,613	#4 O
$50,000	$100,000	$1,240	$588	$0	-	$1,508	$3,336	#60
	150,000	1,821	588	-	-	1,508	3,917	#47
	200,000	2,401	588	-	-	1,508	4,497	#48
$75,000	$150,000	$1,821	$588	$0	-	$4,430	$6,839	#128
	250,000	2,982	588	-	-	4,430	8,000	#117
	350,000	4,143	588	-	-	4,430	9,161	#102

[†]Elderly homeowner/renter credit is issued as a reduction of income tax due or as a refund if the credit is greater than the tax liability.

[*]There are 163 cities in this book. The city with the lowest tax burden for an income/home value combination is given the #1 rating; the city with the highest total tax burden is given the #163 rating.

Billings

Billings has no local income tax and no sales tax.

In the Billings School District 2, property taxes are determined in a complex calculation, which takes into account the reappraisal value of a home. There is an elderly homeowner income rebate for homeowners 65 years of age and older who meet certain income requirements, which is taken as a reduction of state income tax due or a refund. There is also a property tax assistance program for homeowners who meet certain income requirements. Property tax does not cover garbage pickup; the additional fee is approximately $79 per year.

Billings has no personal property tax for individuals.

Our couples relocating to Billings must pay a county option tax, which is based on the depreciated value of the automobile and is $103 for the

Explorer and $72 for the Cutlass. Our couples must also pay a registration fee of $18 per automobile, a new design plate fee of $2 per automobile and a title fee of $7 per automobile at the time of registration. In addition to the above fees, there is a personal property tax of $287 for the Explorer and $203 for the Cutlass at the time of registration. Thereafter, on an annual basis, our couples will pay a registration flat rate (this fee replaces the personal property tax), a county option tax and a registration fee, per automobile.

NEBRASKA

Tax Heavens O
Omaha

Tax Hells Ψ
None

Top Retirement Towns
None

Nebraska has a state income tax and a state sales tax.

The state income tax is graduated from 2.51% to 6.68% depending upon income bracket. For married couples filing jointly, the rate is 2.51% for the first $4,000 of taxable income; the rate is 3.49% for the next $26,000 of taxable income; the rate is 5.01% for the next $16,750 of taxable income; and the rate

is 6.68% on taxable income above $46,750.

In calculating the tax, there is no deduction for federal income tax paid. Federal, state and private pensions are not exempt. Social Security benefits subject to federal tax are not exempt. There is a $9,050 standard deduction from adjusted gross income for married couples filing jointly when both

are age 65 or older.

Major tax credits or rebates include: Credit for income taxes paid to other states, which our couples do not qualify for; and personal exemption credit against tax of up to $91 per person, which our couples do qualify for.

The state sales tax rate is 5%, but local governments can add to this amount.

NEBRASKA TAX TABLE

Instructions

1. Find the Income in the far left column closest to your anticipated retirement income.
2. Find the Home Value closest to the value of the home where you will live in retirement.
3. Follow that row to your estimated Total Tax Burden at age 65 and beyond.

Income	Home Value	Property Tax & Other Fees	Personal Property Tax & Auto Fees	Sales Tax	Local Income Tax	State Income Tax	Total Tax Burden	Rank* From #1-#163
OMAHA								
$25,000	$75,000	$0	$553	$845	-	-	$1,398	#9 O
	100,000	320	553	845	-	-	1,718	#11
	125,000	767	553	845	-	-	2,165	#28
$50,000	$100,000	$1,788	$553	$1,368	-	$948	$4,657	#144
	150,000	2,682	553	1,368	-	948	5,551	#144
	200,000	3,576	553	1,368	-	948	6,445	#140
$75,000	$150,000	$2,682	$553	$1,748	-	$2,773	$7,756	#151
	250,000	4,470	553	1,748	-	2,773	9,544	#148
	350,000	6,258	553	1,748	-	2,773	11,332	#142

*There are 163 cities in this book. The city with the lowest tax burden for an income/home value combination is given the #1 rating; the city with the highest total tax burden is given the #163 rating.

Omaha

Omaha has no local income tax but does levy a sales tax.

Most purchases are taxed at a rate of 6.5%. Major consumer categories taxed at a different rate: None. Major consumer categories that are exempt from sales tax include: Groceries, drugs, medical services and medical supplies.

In the Omaha School District 100, the property tax rate is .0188197. Homes are assessed at 95% of market value.

There is a homestead exemption of up to $78,000 off assessed value for homeowners age 65 or older, depending on income. Property tax includes garbage pickup.

Omaha has no personal property tax for individuals.

Our couples relocating to Omaha must pay a motor vehicle tax of $270 for the Explorer and $234 for the Cutlass. The motor vehicle tax is based on the value of the automobile and is set by

the state. Our couples must also pay a wheel tax of $20 per automobile, a plate fee of $3 per automobile, a registration fee of $20 per automobile, a title fee of $17 per automobile and a motor vehicle fee of $20 for the first automobile registered and $5 for each additional automobile at the time of registration. Thereafter, on an annual basis, our couples will pay a motor vehicle tax, a wheel tax, a motor vehicle fee and a registration fee, per automobile.

NEVADA

Tax Heavens O
None

Tax Hells Ψ
None

Top Retirement Towns
Las Vegas
Reno

Nevada has no state income tax but does have a state sales tax.

The state sales tax rate is 2%, but local governments can add to this amount.

Since car registration and renewal fees differ within the state, see city information for details.

Las Vegas

Las Vegas has no local income tax but does levy a sales tax.

Most purchases are taxed at a rate of 7.25%. Major consumer categories taxed at a different rate: None. Major consumer categories that are exempt from sales tax include: Drugs, groceries and medical services.

NEVADA TAX TABLE

Instructions

1. Find the Income in the far left column closest to your anticipated retirement income.
2. Find the Home Value closest to the value of the home where you will live in retirement.
3. Follow that row to your estimated Total Tax Burden at age 65 and beyond.

Income	Home Value	Property Tax & Other Fees	Personal Property Tax & Auto Fees	Sales Tax	Local Income Tax	State Income Tax	Total Tax Burden	Rank* From #1- #163
LAS VEGAS								
$25,000	$75,000	$979	$590	$955	-	-	$2,524	#135
	100,000	1,264	590	955	-	-	2,809	#121
	125,000	1,549	590	955	-	-	3,094	#103
$50,000	$100,000	$1,264	$590	$1,546	-	-	$3,400	#68
	150,000	1,834	590	1,546	-	-	3,970	#49
	200,000	2,403	590	1,546	-	-	4,539	#52
$75,000	$150,000	$1,834	$590	$1,963	-	-	$4,387	#28
	250,000	2,973	590	1,963	-	-	5,526	#24
	350,000	4,112	590	1,963	-	-	6,665	#24
RENO								
$25,000	$75,000	$1,042	$590	$955	-	-	$2,587	#140
	100,000	1,343	590	955	-	-	2,888	#130
	125,000	1,645	590	955	-	-	3,190	#114
$50,000	$100,000	$1,343	$590	$1,546	-	-	$3,479	#75
	150,000	1,946	590	1,546	-	-	4,082	#59
	200,000	2,549	590	1,546	-	-	4,685	#59
$75,000	$150,000	$1,946	$590	$1,963	-	-	$4,499	#35
	250,000	3,152	590	1,963	-	-	5,705	#29
	350,000	4,358	590	1,963	-	-	6,911	#30

*There are 163 cities in this book. The city with the lowest tax burden for an income/home value combination is given the #1 rating; the city with the highest total tax burden is given the #163 rating.

In the Las Vegas tax district 200, the property tax rate is .032546. Homes are assessed at 35% of taxable value. There is a senior citizen rebate of up to $500 for homeowners age 62 or older with a gross income of less than $23,156. Property tax does not cover garbage pickup; the additional fee is approximately $125 per year.

Las Vegas has no personal property tax for individuals.

Our couples relocating to Las Vegas must pay a governmental services tax based on the value of each automobile, a supplemental governmental services tax of one-fourth of the governmental services tax per automobile and a registration fee of $33 per automobile. The governmental services tax is $216 for the Cutlass and $260 for the Explorer. The supplemental governmental services tax is $54 for the Cutlass and $65 for the Explorer. Our couples must also pay a title fee of $20 per automobile, a VIN inspection fee of $1 per automobile and a prison industries fee of $1 per automobile at the time of registration. Thereafter, on an annual basis, our couples will pay a governmental services tax, a supplemental governmental services tax and a registration fee, per automobile.

Reno

Reno has no local income tax but does levy a sales tax.

Most purchases are taxed at a rate of 7.25%. Major consumer categories taxed at a different rate: None. Major consumer categories that are exempt from sales tax include: Drugs, groceries, and medical services.

In Reno's Boca Water TMUGWB area, the property tax rate is .034461. Homes are assessed at 35% of market value. There is a senior citizen rebate of up to $500 for homeowners age 62 or older with a gross income of less than $23,156. Property tax does not cover garbage pickup; the additional fee is approximately $137 per year.

Reno has no personal property tax for individuals.

Our couples relocating to Reno must pay a governmental services tax based on the value of each automobile, a supplemental governmental services tax of one-fourth of the governmental services tax per automobile and a registration fee of $33 per automobile. The governmental services tax is $216 for the Cutlass and $260 for the Explorer. The supplemental governmental services tax is $54 for the Cutlass and $65 for the Explorer. Our couples must also pay a title fee of $20 per automobile, a VIN inspection fee of $1 per automobile and a prison industries fee of $1 per automobile at the time of registration. Thereafter, on an annual basis, our couples will pay a governmental services tax, a supplemental governmental services tax and a registration fee, per automobile.

• Nevada's Best Retirement Towns •

Las Vegas, Nevada

The gaming capital of the world has, in recent years, become the retirement home of choice for thousands of Americans from all walks of life. The big draw for Terry and Claudia Culp was "its small-town feel in a city with amenities serving more than 400,000 residents," Terry says. The Culps, who relocated from Buffalo, NY, also found the cost of living to be lower in Las Vegas and praise the "good transportation in and out of the city."

While the famous gambling Strip gets most of the press, the city's setting in a diverse landscape that includes desert and mountain vistas, lakes Mead and Powell, Hoover Dam and, in the distance, the Grand Canyon, provides a much larger source of entertainment for relocating retirees who look beyond the city.

Terry and Claudia spend a good deal of time exploring the hinterlands, and Terry says that paints a far different picture of the area than the one commonly seen in casinos. "There's a lot more to Las Vegas than meets the eye," he says.

Population: 400,000 in city, 1,300,000 in county.

Climate:	High	Low
January	57	33
July	106	76

Cost of living: Above average (specific index not available).

Average price of a new home: $173,900

Security: 51.8 crimes per 1,000 residents, higher than the national average of 42.7 crimes per 1,000 residents.

Information: Las Vegas Chamber of Commerce, 3720 Howard Hughes Parkway, Las Vegas, NV 89109, (702) 735-1616 or www.lvchamber.com.

Reno, Nevada

Somewhat less known than the other gambling mecca of Nevada, the so-called "biggest little city in the world" sits at about 4,500 feet on a high desert plateau, cloistered by the majestic 10,000-foot peaks of the Sierra Nevada.

Its scenic setting and allure as an affordable center of entertainment attract a growing number of retirees from neighboring California as well as large eastern cities. In summer, golfing, hiking, cruising Lake Tahoe and exploring the surrounding small towns, mountains and valleys are favorite pastimes, while winter offers opportunities for downhill and cross-country skiing.

Ray and Maureen Wilburn of Sacramento, CA, were looking for a lower cost of living and a change of pace. "We wanted a change in our lifestyle after retirement," Ray says. "We were looking for new horizons, new challenges. You can go to a different show every night, and eat at a different restaurant every day. If you can't find enough to do in Reno, you aren't looking very hard."

Population: 154,600 in city, 366,700 in county.

Climate:	High	Low
January	45	20
July	92	51

Cost of living: 107, based on national average of 100.

Average price of a new home: $159,900

Security: 55.7 crimes per 1,000 residents, higher than the national average of 42.7 crimes per 1,000 residents.

Information: Reno-Sparks Chamber of Commerce, P.O. Box 3499, Reno, NV 89505, (775) 337-3030 or www.reno-sparkschamber.org.

NEW HAMPSHIRE

Tax Heavens O
Portsmouth

Tax Hells Ψ
None

Top Retirement Towns
None

New Hampshire has no state income tax but does levy an interest and dividends tax. New Hampshire has no state sales tax.

The state interest and dividends tax rate is 5%. In calculating the tax, there is no deduction for federal income tax paid. Interest from United States government obligations, New Hampshire state and municipal bonds, individual retirement accounts, and dividends representing capital gains or return of capital is exempt from tax. There is a $1,200 personal exemption per person for persons age 65 or older and an exemption of the first $4,800 of taxable income for married couples filing jointly.

Major tax credits or rebates: None.

NEW HAMPSHIRE TAX TABLE

Instructions
1. Find the Income in the far left column closest to your anticipated retirement income.
2. Find the Home Value closest to the value of the home where you will live in retirement.
3. Follow that row to your estimated Total Tax Burden at age 65 and beyond.

Income	Home Value	Property Tax & Other Fees	Personal Property Tax & Auto Fees	Sales Tax	Local Income Tax	State Income Tax	Total Tax Burden	Rank* From #1- #163
PORTSMOUTH								
$25,000	$75,000	$1,268	$549	-	-	-	$1,817	#33
	100,000	1,690	549	-	-	-	2,239	#52
	125,000	2,113	549	-	-	-	2,662	#64
$50,000	$100,000	$1,690	$549	-	-	-	$2,239	#3 O
	150,000	2,535	549	-	-	-	3,084	#10 O
	200,000	3,380	549	-	-	-	3,929	#23
$75,000	$150,000	$2,535	$549	-	-	$203	$3,287	#3 O
	250,000	4,226	549	-	-	203	4,978	#13
	350,000	5,916	549	-	-	203	6,668	#25

*There are 163 cities in this book. The city with the lowest tax burden for an income/home value combination is given the #1 rating; the city with the highest total tax burden is given the #163 rating.

Portsmouth

Portsmouth has no local income tax and no sales tax.

Within the city limits of Portsmouth, the property tax rate is .02817. Homes are assessed at 60% of market value. There is an elderly tax exemption of $100,000 to $200,000 off assessed value for persons age 65 or older with federal adjusted gross income of $35,000 or less and assets of less than $60,000 (excluding home value). Property tax includes garbage pickup.

Portsmouth has no personal property tax for individuals.

Our couples relocating to Portsmouth must pay a city registration fee based on the year and list price of each automobile, a state registration fee of $31 per automobile, a state title fee of $20 per automobile and a state plate fee of $5 per automobile at the time of registration. The city registration fee is $332 for the Explorer and $277 for the Cutlass. Thereafter, on an annual basis, our couples will pay a city registration fee and a state registration fee, per automobile.

NEW JERSEY

Tax Heavens O
None

Tax Hells ψ
Newark

Top Retirement Towns
Cape May
Ocean County (Toms River)

New Jersey has a state income tax and a state sales tax.

The state income tax rate is graduated from 1.4% to 6.37% depending upon income bracket. For married couples filing jointly, the rate is 1.4% on the first $20,000 of taxable income; the rate is 1.75% on the next $30,000 of taxable income; the rate is 2.45% on the next $20,000 of taxable income; the rate is 3.5% on the next $10,000 of taxable income; the rate is 5.525% on the next $70,000 of taxable income; and the rate is 6.37% on taxable income above $150,000.

In calculating the tax, there is no deduction for federal income tax paid.

There is an exclusion of up to $12,500 on federal, state and private pensions from adjusted gross income for married couples filing jointly with both spouses age 65 or older. There is another retirement income exclusion for married couples filing jointly if one spouse is age 65 or older and the entire pension exclusion was not used. The amount of the exclusion varies and is subject to certain limitations. Social Security benefits are exempt. There is a $1,000 personal exemption per person from New Jersey adjusted gross income plus an additional $1,000 exemption per person age 65 or older.

Major tax credits or rebates include: Credit for income taxes paid to other states, which our couples do not qualify for, and homestead property tax deduction or credit, which our couples do qualify for.

The state sales tax rate is 6%.

Our couples relocating to the cities listed below must pay a registration fee based on the weight and year of each automobile. The registration fee is $61 for the Explorer and $36 for the Cutlass. Our couples also pay a title fee of $40 per automobile at the time of registration. Thereafter, on an annual basis, our couples will pay a registration fee per automobile.

NEW JERSEY TAX TABLE

Instructions

1. Find the Income in the far left column closest to your anticipated retirement income.
2. Find the Home Value closest to the value of the home where you will live in retirement.
3. Follow that row to your estimated Total Tax Burden at age 65 and beyond.

Income	Home Value	Property Tax & Other Fees	Personal Property Tax & Auto Fees	Sales Tax	Local Income Tax	State Income Tax†	Total Tax Burden	Rank* From #1-#163
CAPE MAY								
$25,000	$75,000	$1,276	$97	$790	-	($50)	$2,113	#79
	100,000	1,570	97	$790	-	(50)	2,407	#74
	125,000	1,663	97	790	-	(50)	2,500	#56
$50,000	$100,000	$1,644	$97	$1,279	-	$224	$3,244	#51
	150,000	2,381	97	1,279	-	224	3,981	#50
	200,000	2,820	97	1,279	-	224	4,420	#42
$75,000	$150,000	$2,431	$97	$1,624	-	$638	$4,790	#55
	250,000	3,905	97	1,624	-	626	6,252	#46
	350,000	5,379	97	1,624	-	600	7,700	#47
NEWARK								
$25,000	$75,000	$2,236	$97	$790	-	($50)	$3,073	#155 ψ
	100,000	3,147	97	790	-	(50)	3,984	#159 ψ
	125,000	4,059	97	790	-	(50)	4,896	#160 ψ
$50,000	$100,000	$3,147	$97	$1,279	-	$224	$4,747	#151
	150,000	4,971	97	1,279	-	205	6,552	#158 ψ
	200,000	6,795	97	1,279	-	179	8,350	#159 ψ

†Property tax credit or deduction is issued as a reduction of income tax due or as a refund if the credit is greater than the tax liability.

*There are 163 cities in this book. The city with the lowest tax burden for an income/home value combination is given the #1 rating; the city with the highest total tax burden is given the #163 rating.

Income	Home Value	Property Tax & Other Fees	Personal Property Tax & Auto Fees	Sales Tax	Local Income Tax	State Income Tax[†]	Total Tax Burden	Rank[*] From #1- #163
NEWARK continued								
$75,000	$150,000	$5,371	$97	$1,624	-	$594	$7,686	#150
	250,000	9,019	97	1,624	-	531	11,271	#160 ψ
	350,000	12,666	97	1,624	-	513	14,900	#161 ψ
TOMS RIVER								
$25,000	$75,000	$1,278	$97	$790	-	($50)	$2,115	#80
	100,000	1,870	97	790	-	(50)	2,707	#108
	125,000	2,463	97	790	-	(50)	3,300	#126
$50,000	$100,000	$2,220	$97	$1,279	-	$224	$3,820	#111
	150,000	3,056	97	1,279	-	224	4,656	#111
	200,000	4,241	97	1,279	-	215	5,832	#121
$75,000	$150,000	$3,456	$97	$1,624	-	$628	$5,805	#93
	250,000	5,826	97	1,624	-	586	8,133	#120
	350,000	8,197	97	1,624	-	545	10,463	#132

†Property tax credit or deduction is issued as a reduction of income tax due or as a refund if the credit is greater than the tax liability.
*There are 163 cities in this book. The city with the lowest tax burden for an income/home value combination is given the #1 rating; the city with the highest total tax burden is given the #163 rating.

Cape May

Cape May has no local income tax and does not levy an additional sales tax.

Most purchases are taxed at the state rate of 6%. Major consumer categories taxed at a different rate: None. Major consumer categories that are exempt from sales tax include: Drugs, groceries and medical services.

Within the city limits of Cape May, the property tax rate is .0169. Homes are assessed at 87.22% of market value. There is a homestead rebate program, which ranges from $100 to $500 depending upon income, filing status and the amount of property tax or rent paid. There is also an elderly exemption of $250 credit on property taxes due for homeowners age 65 or older with an income of less than $10,000 (excluding Social Security or governmental pension, whichever is higher). There is also a SAVER rebate that is available to residents occupying principal home on October 1st. Property tax does not cover garbage pickup; the additional fee is approximately $320 per year.

Cape May has no personal property tax for individuals.

Newark

Newark has no local income tax and does not levy an additional sales tax.

Most purchases are taxed at the state rate of 6%. Major consumer categories taxed at a different rate: None. Major consumer categories that are exempt from sales tax include: Drugs, groceries and medical services.

Within the city limits of Newark, the property tax rate is .2488. Homes are assessed at 14.66% of market value. There is a homestead rebate program, which ranges from $100 to $500 depending upon income, filing status and the amount of property tax or rent paid. There is also an elderly exemption of $250 credit on property taxes due for homeowners age 65 or older with an income of less than $10,000 (excluding Social Security or governmental pension, whichever is higher). There is also a SAVER rebate that is available to residents occupying principal home on October 1st. Property tax includes garbage pickup.

Newark has no personal property tax for individuals.

Ocean County (Toms River)

Toms River has no local income tax and does not levy an additional sales tax.

Most purchases are taxed at the state rate of 6%. Major consumer categories taxed at a different rate: None. Major consumer categories that are exempt from sales tax include: Drugs, groceries and medical services.

In the Toms River Fire District 2 of Dover Township, the property tax rate is .02585. Homes are assessed at 91.7% of market value. There is a homestead rebate program, which ranges from $100 to $500 depending upon income, filing status and the amount of property tax or rent paid. There is also an elderly exemption of $250 credit on property taxes due for homeowners age 65 or older with an income of less than $10,000 (excluding Social Security or governmental pension, whichever is higher). There is also a SAVER rebate that is available to residents occupying principal home on October 1st. Property tax includes garbage pickup.

Toms River has no personal property tax for individuals.

Cape May, New Jersey

"Cape May is ideal for many migrating species," says Dr. Paul Kerlinger, director of the Cape May Bird Observatory, referring to the loons, egrets, ospreys, falcons, sandpipers and terns that touch down on seasonal flights between northern and southern habitats.

But it's a sentiment shared by many migrating retirees, mostly from heavily populated East Coast communities, who are looking for a quieter, gentler place to spend their golden years.

Jane and Jim Bonner retired here from Philadelphia after vacationing in their 1912 seaside cottage for many years. "It has been a nice experience for us," Jane says. "It has a small-town, rural atmosphere with very little commercialism. There are more than 600 Victorian homes. Many have been converted to bed-and-breakfast inns to accommodate the main industry, tourism.

"For recreation, it's sun and sea, beach activities, sailing and boating. And there are lots of golf courses in the county," she says.

Population: 4,300 in city, 105,000 in county.

Climate:	High	Low
January	40	26
July	83	77

Cost of living: Above average (specific index not available).

Average price of a new home: $194,500

Security: 60.5 crimes per 1,000 residents, higher than the national average of 42.7 crimes per 1,000 residents.

Information: Chamber of Commerce of Greater Cape May, P.O. Box 556, Cape May, NJ 08204, (609) 884-5508 or www.capemaychamber.com. Cape May County Chamber of Commerce, P.O. Box 74, Cape May Court House, NJ 08210, (609) 465-7181 or www.cmc cofc.com.

Ocean County (Toms River), New Jersey

Situated less than 70 miles south of New York City and 50 miles east of Philadelphia, Ocean County is a potpourri of pine forests, wildlife refuges, bays, inlets and barrier islands. Its sandy coastline runs for 140 miles and is dotted with picturesque seaside hamlets.

Once a summer and holiday getaway, part-time retreats have become year-round retirement homes for the fastest-growing segment of the population. Boating, fishing, bird-watching and beach activities are supplemented by outings to historical sites and cultural events in surrounding towns, shopping trips to New York City and occasional visits to Atlantic City casinos.

Tom and Shirley Smathers of Cleveland, OH, were regular summer visitors to Toms River, the county seat. "We never got enough of the seashore when we vacationed here," Tom says. "Now we spend six months soaking up the sun and six months socializing and soaking up culture indoors."

"It's a wonderful place to live," Shirley adds.

Population: 10,000 in Toms River, 500,000 in county.

Climate:	High	Low
January	40	19
July	85	62

Cost of living: Above average (specific index not available.)

Average price of a new home: $275,000

Security: 25.9 crimes per 1,000 residents in Ocean County, lower than the national average of 42.7 crimes per 1,000 residents.

Information: Toms River-Ocean County Chamber of Commerce, 1200 Hooper Ave., Toms River, NJ 08753, (732) 349-0220 or www.oc-chamber.com.

NEW MEXICO

Tax Heavens O	**Tax Hells Ψ**	**Top Retirement Towns**
Santa Fe	None	Las Cruces
		Ruidoso
		Santa Fe

New Mexico has a state income tax and a state gross receipts tax (sales tax).

The state income tax is graduated from 1.7% to 8.2% depending upon income bracket. For married couples filing jointly, the rate is 1.7% on the first $8,000 of taxable income; the rate is 3.2% on the next $8,000 of taxable income; the rate is 4.7% on the next $8,000 of taxable income; the rate is 6% on the next $16,000 of taxable income; the rate is 7.1% on the next $24,000 of taxable income; the rate is 7.9% on the next $36,000 of taxable income; and the rate is 8.2% on taxable income above $100,000.

In calculating the tax, there is no deduction for federal income tax paid. Federal, state and private pensions are not exempt. Social Security benefits subject to federal tax are not exempt. There is a $9,050 standard deduction from adjusted gross income for married couples filing jointly when both are age 65 or older. There is a personal exemption of $2,800 per person. There is an additional deduction ranging from $1,000 to $8,000 per person for married couples filing jointly, both age 65 or older, with federal adjusted gross income of $51,000 or less.

Major tax credits or rebates include: Credit for taxes paid to other states and credit for disabled taxpayers. Our couples do not qualify for these programs.

The state gross receipts tax rate is 5%, but local governments can add to this amount. Although this tax is imposed on the seller (unlike a sales tax which is imposed on the buyer), businesses customarily pass the tax on to the buyer.

Our couples relocating to the cities listed below must pay a registration fee of $45 per automobile and a transfer fee of $5 per automobile at the time of registration. In addition, sales tax of 3% is due at the time of registration unless at least 3% was paid in another state when the automobile was purchased. Thereafter, on an annual basis, our couples will pay a registration fee per automobile.

NEW MEXICO TAX TABLE

Instructions

1. Find the Income in the far left column closest to your anticipated retirement income.
2. Find the Home Value closest to the value of the home where you will live in retirement.
3. Follow that row to your estimated Total Tax Burden at age 65 and beyond.

Income	Home Value	Property Tax & Other Fees	Personal Property Tax & Auto Fees	Sales Tax	Local Income Tax	State Income Tax	Total Tax Burden	Rank* From #1- #163
ALBUQUERQUE								
$25,000	$75,000	$1,057	$90	$961	-	-	$2,108	#77
	100,000	1,392	90	961	-	-	2,443	#76
	125,000	1,728	90	961	-	-	2,779	#78
$50,000	$100,000	$1,392	$90	$1,492	-	$524	$3,498	#77
	150,000	2,063	90	1,492	-	524	4,169	#72
	200,000	2,734	90	1,492	-	524	4,840	#67
$75,000	$150,000	$2,063	$90	$1,855	-	$2,988	$6,996	#133
	250,000	3,405	90	1,855	-	2,988	8,338	#127
	350,000	4,746	90	1,855	-	2,988	9,679	#113
LAS CRUCES								
$25,000	$75,000	$713	$90	$1,054	-	-	$1,857	#35
	100,000	941	90	1,054	-	-	2,085	#38
	125,000	1,169	90	1,054	-	-	2,313	#36
$50,000	$100,000	$941	$90	$1,636	-	$524	$3,191	#45
	150,000	1,397	90	1,636	-	524	3,647	#34
	200,000	1,853	90	1,636	-	524	4,103	#34

Income	Home Value	Property Tax & Other Fees	Personal Property Tax & Auto Fees	Sales Tax	Local Income Tax	State Income Tax	Total Tax Burden	Rank* From #1-#163
LAS CRUCES continued								
$75,000	$150,000	$1,397	$90	$2,034	-	$2,988	$6,509	#116
	250,000	2,310	90	2,034	-	2,988	7,422	#94
	350,000	3,222	90	2,034	-	2,988	8,334	#71
RUIDOSO								
$25,000	$75,000	$664	$90	$1,189	-	-	$1,943	#51
	100,000	859	90	1,189	-	-	2,138	#43
	125,000	1,054	90	1,189	-	-	2,333	#39
$50,000	$100,000	$859	$90	$1,845	-	$524	$3,318	#59
	150,000	1,249	90	1,845	-	524	3,708	#36
	200,000	1,639	90	1,845	-	524	4,098	#32
$75,000	$150,000	$1,249	$90	$2,294	-	$2,988	$6,621	#120
	250,000	2,029	90	2,294	-	2,988	7,401	#92
	350,000	2,809	90	2,294	-	2,988	8,181	#64
SANTA FE								
$25,000	$75,000	$415	$90	$1,065	-	-	$1,570	#15
	100,000	565	90	1,065	-	-	1,720	#12
	125,000	716	90	1,065	-	-	1,871	#7
$50,000	$100,000	$565	$90	$1,652	-	$524	$2,831	#20
	150,000	866	90	1,652	-	524	3,132	#12
	200,000	1,167	90	1,652	-	524	3,433	#11
$75,000	$150,000	$866	$90	$2,054	-	$2,988	$5,998	#99
	250,000	1,467	90	2,054	-	2,988	6,599	#55
	350,000	2,069	90	2,054	-	2,988	7,201	#41

*There are 163 cities in this book. The city with the lowest tax burden for an income/home value combination is given the #1 rating; the city with the highest total tax burden is given the #163 rating.

Albuquerque

Albuquerque has no local income tax but does levy a gross receipts tax (sales tax).

Most purchases are taxed at a rate of 5.8125%. Major consumer categories taxed at a different rate: None. Major consumer categories that are exempt from gross receipts tax: Drugs.

For residents within the MRGCD district of Albuquerque, the property tax rate is .040655. Homes are assessed at 100% of market value. Taxable value is one-third of assessed value. There is a head-of-household exemption of $2,000 off taxable value. Property tax does not cover garbage pickup; the additional fee is approximately $132 per year.

Albuquerque has no personal property tax for individuals.

Las Cruces

Las Cruces has no local income tax but does levy a gross receipts tax (sales tax).

Most purchases are taxed at a rate of 6.375%. Major consumer categories taxed at a different rate: None. Major consumer categories that are exempt from gross receipts tax: Drugs.

Within the city limits of Las Cruces, the property tax rate is .027376. Homes are assessed at 100% of market value. Taxable value is one-third of assessed value. There is a head-of-household exemption of $2,000 off taxable value. Property tax does not cover garbage pickup; the additional fee is approximately $83 per year.

Las Cruces has no personal property tax for individuals.

Ruidoso

Ruidoso has no local income tax but does levy a gross receipts tax (sales tax).

Most purchases are taxed at a rate of 7.1875%. Major consumer categories taxed at a different rate: None. Major consumer categories that are exempt from gross receipts tax: Drugs.

In the Village of Ruidoso, the property tax rate is .026003. Homes are assessed at 90% of market value. Taxable value is one-third of assessed value. There is a head-of-household exemption of $2,000 off taxable value. Property tax does not cover garbage pickup; the additional fee is approximately $131 per year.

Ruidoso has no personal property tax for individuals.

Santa Fe

Santa Fe has no local income tax but does levy a gross receipts tax (sales tax).

Most purchases are taxed at a rate of 6.4375%. Major consumer categories taxed at a different rate: None. Major consumer categories that are exempt from gross receipts tax include: Drugs.

For most residents within the city limits of Santa Fe, the property tax rate is .018042. Homes are assessed at 100% of market value. Taxable value is one-third of assessed value. There is a head-of-household exemption of $2,000 off taxable value. Property tax covers garbage pickup.

Santa Fe has no personal property tax for individuals.

• New Mexico's Best Retirement Towns •

Las Cruces, New Mexico

A diverse culture, New Mexico State University, high desert climate, low cost of living, open spaces and year-round outdoor activities are major attractions drawing retirees to this fertile oasis in southern New Mexico.

Mexican-Spanish influences are clearly reflected in the dominant adobe-style architecture of its homes and buildings, Southwestern-themed arts and crafts, celebrations such as the annual Enchilada Festival, and the preponderance of Spanish heard on the streets.

Ed and Winnie Jacobs from Reston, VA, came to Las Cruces looking for a warmer climate and found this high desert oasis had everything they sought. "It's a very welcoming town that runs on volunteer services," Winnie says. "If you like history, museums, gorgeous untrampled scenery and multi-ethnic cultural activities, you'll love Las Cruces."

Population: 85,400 in city, 180,464 in county.

Climate:

	High	Low
January	57	26
July	98	70

Cost of living: 98.6, based on national average of 100.

Average price of a new home: $98,500

Security: 84.7 crimes per 1,000 residents, higher than the national average of 42.7 crimes per 1,000 residents.

Information: Greater Las Cruces Chamber of Commerce, P.O. Drawer 519, Las Cruces, NM 88004-0519, (505) 524-1968 or www.lascruces.org.

Ruidoso, New Mexico

At 6,800 feet of elevation, protected by the 12,000-foot peaks of the Sierra Blanca Mountains, this rustic alpine village offers clean air, a peaceful low-crime environment and plenty of opportunities for outdoor recreation.

Once known best as a vacation destination, many of its visitors have returned to make it their retirement home. Cree Meadows Country Club, the Links at Sierra Blanca, Ski Apache, Ruidoso Downs and the Inn of the Mountain Gods Resort and Casino are noted sources of entertainment for growing numbers of retirees.

Sue and Bob Macfarlane moved here from El Paso, TX. "We love the four seasons," Sue says. "Outdoor activities include golfing, hiking, fishing, horseback riding and skiing. We've met some wonderful, friendly people. Most of them are retirees who chose to live here and are looking for new friends. There's a large diversity of backgrounds and professions that makes for a very interesting social scene."

Population: 9,800 in city, 17,000 in county.

Climate:

	High	Low
January	49	17
July	78	47

Cost of living: Below average (specific index not available).

Average price of a new home: $189,000

Security: 37.4 crimes per 1,000 residents, lower than the national average of 42.7 crimes per 1,000 residents.

Information: Ruidoso Valley Chamber of Commerce, 720 Sudderth Drive, P.O. Box 698, Ruidoso, NM 88355, (800) 253-2255 or www.ruidoso.net/chamber.

Santa Fe, New Mexico

On a sunny winter afternoon in this charming high desert town, you may be enjoying a snowball fight with grandchildren while your next-door neighbors are sunning in the adobe-walled privacy of their back yards. A few miles away, the snow-covered slopes of the Sangre de Cristo Mountains are likely to be populated with downhill skiers and snowboarders.

Outdoor activities complement the attractions of this multicultural capital city steeped in the traditions of its Spanish, American Indian and Mexican heritage. Adobe architecture, American Indian cultural influences, a strong focus on the arts with special emphasis on handicrafts, and a friendly, informal atmosphere — not to mention many great restaurants — set the city apart from other small towns in America.

"It's not a small town at all," says Tom Coburn, who with wife Martha moved here from Boston on the advice of friends who had relocated earlier. "We have lived in major cities across the country, and Santa Fe has more to offer than many much larger metropolitan areas. The number and quality of cultural offerings is staggering. They have opera, ballet, symphony and art galleries and openings almost daily, it seems."

"But more than that, we love the adobe architecture, the native festivals and the whole Southwestern feel of the city," Martha says. "We like to explore the desert, visit the pueblos and drive up to Taos for the art shows. It's a wonderful setting for a special town."

Population: 68,000 in city, 130,000 in county.

Climate:

	High	Low
January	43	20
July	87	58

Cost of living: 118, based on national average of 100.

Average price of a new home: $204,000

Security: 72.7 crimes per 1,000 residents, higher than the national average of 42.7 crimes per 1,000 residents.

Information: Santa Fe County Chamber of Commerce, P.O. Box 1928, 510 N. Guadalupe St., Santa Fe, NM 87504, (505) 983-7317 or www.santafechamber.com.

NEW YORK

Tax Heavens O
New York City

Tax Hells ψ
Syracuse

Top Retirement Towns
None

New York has a state income tax and a state sales tax.

The state income tax rate is graduated from 4% to 6.85% depending upon income bracket. For married couples filing jointly, the rate is 4% on the first $16,000 of taxable income; the rate is 4.5% on the next $6,000 of taxable income; the rate is 5.25% on the next $4,000 of taxable income; the rate is 5.90% on the next $14,000 of taxable income; and the rate is 6.85% on income above $40,000.

In calculating the tax, there is no deduction for federal income tax paid.

Federal and state pensions are exempt. Private pensions are not exempt, but there is an exclusion of up to $20,000 of private pension income per person. Social Security benefits are exempt. There is a $13,000 standard deduction from adjusted gross income for married couples filing jointly.

Major tax credits or rebates include: Credit for income taxes paid to other states, household income tax credit and real property tax credit. One of our couples qualifies for the household tax credit, but none of our couples qualify

for the other programs.

The state sales tax rate is 4%, but local governments can add to this amount.

Our couples relocating to the cities listed below must pay a registration fee of $54 per automobile every two years, a plate fee of $6 per automobile and a title fee of $5 per automobile at the time of registration. New York City imposes a $30 city vehicle use fee every two years. Thereafter, our couples will pay a renewal fee and, possibly, a city vehicle use fee per automobile, every two years.

NEW YORK TAX TABLE

Instructions

1. Find the Income in the far left column closest to your anticipated retirement income.
2. Find the Home Value closest to the value of the home where you will live in retirement.
3. Follow that row to your estimated Total Tax Burden at age 65 and beyond.

Income	Home Value	Property Tax & Other Fees	Personal Property Tax & Auto Fees	Sales Tax	Local Income Tax	State Income Tax	Total Tax Burden	Rank* From #1- #163
BUFFALO								
$25,000	$75,000	$539	$57	$1,040	-	-	$1,636	#20
	100,000	996	57	1,040	-	-	2,093	#39
	125,000	1,453	57	1,040	-	-	2,550	#59
$50,000	$100,000	$1,606	$57	$1,683	-	$364	$3,710	#101
	150,000	2,825	57	1,683	-	364	4,929	#122
	200,000	4,045	57	1,683	-	364	6,149	#131
$75,000	$150,000	$3,168	$57	$2,151	-	$1,435	$6,811	#127
	250,000	5,607	57	2,151	-	1,435	9,250	#145
	350,000	8,046	57	2,151	-	1,435	11,689	#146
NEW YORK CITY								
$25,000	$75,000	$199	$87	$1,073	-	-	$1,359	#7 O
	100,000	368	87	1,073	-	-	1,528	#5 OO
	125,000	537	87	1,073	-	-	1,697	#5 O
$50,000	$100,000	$593	$87	$1,736	$150	$364	$2,930	#28
	150,000	1,043	87	1,736	150	364	3,380	#24
	200,000	1,493	87	1,736	150	364	3,830	#19
$75,000	$150,000	$1,170	$87	$2,219	$885	$1,435	$5,796	#90
	250,000	2,070	87	2,219	885	1,435	6,696	#60
	350,000	2,970	87	2,219	885	1,435	7,596	#44

*There are 163 cities in this book. The city with the lowest tax burden for an income/home value combination is given the #1 rating; the city with the highest total tax burden is given the #163 rating.

NEW YORK TAX TABLE

Instructions

1. Find the Income in the far left column closest to your anticipated retirement income.
2. Find the Home Value closest to the value of the home where you will live in retirement.
3. Follow that row to your estimated Total Tax Burden at age 65 and beyond.

Income	Home Value	Property Tax & Other Fees	Personal Property Tax & Auto Fees	Sales Tax	Local Income Tax	State Income Tax	Total Tax Burden	Rank* From #1-#163
NEW YORK CITY continued								
	400,000	$3,421	$87	$2,219	$885	$1,435	$8,047	Not Ranked
	450,000	3,871	87	2,219	885	1,435	8,497	Not Ranked
	500,000	4,321	87	2,219	885	1,435	8,947	Not Ranked
SYRACUSE								
$25,000	$75,000	$709	$57	$910	-	-	$1,676	#23
	100,000	1,311	57	910	-	-	2,278	#57
	125,000	1,913	57	910	-	-	2,880	#88
$50,000	$100,000	$2,114	$57	$1,473	-	$364	$4,008	#121
	150,000	3,720	57	1,473	-	364	5,614	#147
	200,000	5,325	57	1,473	-	364	7,219	#153
$75,000	$150,000	$4,171	$57	$1,882	-	$1,435	$7,545	#148
	250,000	7,382	57	1,882	-	1,435	10,756	#155 Ψ
	350,000	10,593	57	1,882	-	1,435	13,967	#158 Ψ

*There are 163 cities in this book. The city with the lowest tax burden for an income/home value combination is given the #1 rating; the city with the highest total tax burden is given the #163 rating.

Buffalo

Buffalo has no local income tax but does levy a sales tax.

Most purchases are taxed at a rate of 8%. Major consumer categories taxed at a different rate: None, although clothing costing less than $110 per item is exempt from the state portion of sales tax effective March 2000. Major consumer categories that are exempt from sales tax include: Drugs, groceries, medical services and medical supplies.

In Buffalo, the property tax rate is .02439. Homes are assessed at 100% of market value. There is an elderly exemption of up to 50% off property tax due for homeowners age 65 or older with a gross income of less than $28,900. There is a School Tax Relief program (STAR), which is available to all residents of New York that exempts a maximum of $20,100 of the full value of a home from property taxes. For residents of New York that meet certain income qualifications, there is an enhanced STAR; it exempts a maximum of $34,160 of the full value of a home from property taxes. Property tax includes garbage pickup.

Buffalo has no personal property tax for individuals.

New York City

New York City has a local income tax and levies a sales tax.

The local income tax rate is graduated from 3.021% to 3.7791% depending upon income bracket. For married couples filing jointly, the rate is 3.021% on the first $21,600 of taxable income; the rate is 3.6651% on the next $23,400 of taxable income; the rate is 3.7221% on the next $45,000 of taxable income; and the rate is 3.7791% on income above $90,000.

In calculating the tax, the same exemptions and deductions are available as those offered at the state level.

Major tax credits or rebates include: Household income credit, which some of our couples qualify for, and school tax credit, which all of our couples qualify for.

Most purchases are taxed at a rate of 8.25%. Major consumer categories taxed at a different rate: None, although clothing costing less than $110 per item is exempt from the state portion of sales tax effective March 2000. Major consumer categories that are exempt from sales tax include: Drugs, groceries, medical services and medical supplies.

In Manhattan, the property tax rate is .11255. Homes are assessed at 8% of market value for Class I (one-, two- or three-family) homes. There is an elderly exemption of up to 50% off property tax due for homeowners age 65 or older with a gross income of less than $28,900. There is a School Tax Relief program (STAR), which is available to all residents of New York that exempts a maximum of $20,100 of the full value of a home from property taxes. For residents of New York that meet certain income qualifications, there is an enhanced STAR; it exempts a maximum of $34,160 of the full value of a home from property taxes. Property tax includes garbage pickup.

New York City has no personal property tax for individuals.

Syracuse

Syracuse has no local income tax but does levy a sales tax.

Most purchases are taxed at a rate of

7%. Major consumer categories taxed at a different rate: None, although clothing costing less than $110 per item is exempt from the state portion of sales tax effective March 2000. Major consumer categories that are exempt from sales tax include: Drugs, groceries, medical services and medical supplies.

In Syracuse, the property tax rate is .03211. Homes are assessed at 100% of market value. There is an elderly exemption of up to 50% off property tax due for homeowners age 65 or older with a gross income of less than $28,900. There is a School Tax Relief program (STAR), which is available to all residents of New York that exempts a maximum of $20,100 of the full value of a home from property taxes. For residents of New York that meet certain income qualifications, there is an enhanced STAR; it exempts a maximum of $34,160 of the full value of a home from property taxes. Property tax includes garbage pickup.

Syracuse has no personal property tax for individuals.

NORTH CAROLINA

Tax Heavens O
None

Tax Hells ψ
None

Top Retirement Towns
Asheville
Brevard
Chapel Hill
Edenton
Hendersonville
New Bern
Pinehurst
Waynesville
Wilmington

North Carolina has a state income tax and a state sales tax.

The state income tax is graduated from 6% to 7.75% depending upon income bracket. For married couples filing jointly, the rate is 6% on the first $21,250 of taxable income; the rate is 7% on the next $78,750 of taxable income; and the rate is 7.75% on taxable income above $100,000.

In calculating the tax, there is no deduction for federal income tax paid.

Social Security benefits are exempt. There is an exclusion of up to $4,000 in federal, state and local government pensions per person and an exclusion of up to $2,000 in private pensions per person, but no more than $4,000 in total retirement benefits (not including Social Security) may be deducted per person. There is a $6,200 standard deduction from adjusted gross income for married couples filing jointly when both are age 65 or older. There is a per-

sonal exemption of $2,500 per person for married couples filing jointly.

Major tax credits or rebates include: Credit for income taxes paid to other states and credit for disabled taxpayers. Our couples do not qualify for these programs.

The state sales tax rate is 4%, but local governments can add to this amount. Since car registration and renewal fees differ within the state, see city information for details.

NORTH CAROLINA TAX TABLE

Instructions
1. Find the Income in the far left column closest to your anticipated retirement income.
2. Find the Home Value closest to the value of the home where you will live in retirement.
3. Follow that row to your estimated Total Tax Burden at age 65 and beyond.

Income	Home Value	Property Tax & Other Fees	Personal Property Tax & Auto Fees	Sales Tax	Local Income Tax	State Income Tax	Total Tax Burden	Rank* From #1-#163
ASHEVILLE								
$25,000	$75,000	$1,043	$441	$843	-	$115	$2,442	#127
	100,000	1,390	441	843	-	115	2,789	#117
	125,000	1,738	441	843	-	115	3,137	#106
$50,000	$100,000	$1,390	$441	$1,348	-	$1,383	$4,562	#141
	150,000	2,085	441	1,348	-	1,383	5,257	#136
	200,000	2,780	441	1,348	-	1,383	5,952	#124
$75,000	$150,000	$2,085	$441	$1,699	-	$3,029	$7,254	#140
	250,000	3,475	441	1,699	-	3,029	8,644	#134
	350,000	4,865	441	1,699	-	3,029	10,034	#121
BREVARD								
$25,000	$75,000	$1,015	$375	$949	-	$115	$2,454	#132
	100,000	1,305	375	949	-	115	2,744	#114
	125,000	1,595	375	949	-	115	3,034	#97

Income	Home Value	Property Tax & Other Fees	Personal Property Tax & Auto Fees	Sales Tax	Local Income Tax	State Income Tax	Total Tax Burden	Rank* From #1- #163
BREVARD continued								
$50,000	$100,000	$1,305	$375	$1,485	-	$1,383	$4,548	#140
	150,000	1,886	375	1,485	-	1,383	5,129	#130
	200,000	2,466	375	1,485	-	1,383	5,709	#114
$75,000	$150,000	$1,886	$375	$1,849	-	$3,029	$7,139	#134
	250,000	3,047	375	1,849	-	3,029	8,300	#125
	350,000	4,208	375	1,849	-	3,029	9,461	#108
CHAPEL HILL								
$25,000	$75,000	$1,133	$486	$843	-	$115	$2,577	#139
	100,000	1,511	486	843	-	115	2,955	#135
	125,000	1,889	486	843	-	115	3,333	#129
$50,000	$100,000	$1,511	$486	$1,348	-	$1,383	$4,728	#150
	150,000	2,267	486	1,348	-	1,383	5,484	#141
	200,000	3,022	486	1,348	-	1,383	6,239	#135
$75,000	$150,000	$2,267	$486	$1,699	-	$3,029	$7,481	#146
	250,000	3,778	486	1,699	-	3,029	8,992	#140
	350,000	5,289	486	1,699	-	3,029	10,503	#134
EDENTON								
$25,000	$75,000	$898	$353	$949	-	$115	$2,315	#113
	100,000	1,169	353	949	-	115	2,586	#95
	125,000	1,440	353	949	-	115	2,857	#85
$50,000	$100,000	$1,169	$353	$1,485	-	$1,383	$4,390	#134
	150,000	1,712	353	1,485	-	1,383	4,933	#124
	200,000	2,254	353	1,485	-	1,383	5,475	#107
$75,000	$150,000	$1,712	$353	$1,849	-	$3,029	$6,943	#131
	250,000	2,797	353	1,849	-	3,029	8,028	#118
	350,000	3,882	353	1,849	-	3,029	9,113	#101
HENDERSONVILLE								
$25,000	$75,000	$749	$314	$949	-	$115	$2,127	#83
	100,000	986	314	949	-	115	2,364	#67
	125,000	1,224	314	949	-	115	2,602	#61
$50,000	$100,000	$986	$314	$1,485	-	$1,383	$4,168	#126
	150,000	1,461	314	1,485	-	1,383	4,643	#109
	200,000	1,936	314	1,485	-	1,383	5,118	#87
$75,000	$150,000	$1,461	$314	$1,849	-	$3,029	$6,653	#121
	250,000	2,411	314	1,849	-	3,029	7,603	#100
	350,000	3,361	314	1,849	-	3,029	8,553	#76
NEW BERN								
$25,000	$75,000	$812	$340	$843	-	$115	$2,110	#78
	100,000	1,072	340	843	-	115	2,370	#69
	125,000	1,332	340	843	-	115	2,630	#63
$50,000	$100,000	$1,072	$340	$1,348	-	$1,383	$4,143	#125
	150,000	1,592	340	1,348	-	1,383	4,663	#112
	200,000	2,112	340	1,348	-	1,383	5,183	#92
$75,000	$150,000	$1,592	$340	$1,699	-	$3,029	$6,660	#122
	250,000	2,632	340	1,699	-	3,029	7,700	#103
	350,000	3,672	340	1,699	-	3,029	8,740	#84

*There are 163 cities in this book. The city with the lowest tax burden for an income/home value combination is given the #1 rating; the city with the highest total tax burden is given the #163 rating.

NORTH CAROLINA TAX TABLE

Instructions

1. Find the Income in the far left column closest to your anticipated retirement income.
2. Find the Home Value closest to the value of the home where you will live in retirement.
3. Follow that row to your estimated Total Tax Burden at age 65 and beyond.

Income	Home Value	Property Tax & Other Fees	Personal Property Tax & Auto Fees	Sales Tax	Local Income Tax	State Income Tax	Total Tax Burden	Rank* From #1- #163
PINEHURST								
$25,000	$75,000	$671	$298	$949	-	$115	$2,033	#63
	100,000	895	298	949	-	115	2,257	#55
	125,000	1,119	298	949	-	115	2,481	#54
$50,000	$100,000	$895	$298	$1,485	-	$1,383	$4,061	#123
	150,000	1,343	298	1,485	-	1,383	4,509	#103
	200,000	1,790	298	1,485	-	1,383	4,956	#77
$75,000	$150,000	$1,343	$298	$1,849	-	$3,029	$6,519	#118
	250,000	2,238	298	1,849	-	3,029	7,414	#93
	350,000	3,133	298	1,849	-	3,029	8,309	#69
WAYNESVILLE								
$25,000	$75,000	$833	$346	$843	-	$115	$2,137	#86
	100,000	1,098	346	843	-	115	2,402	#72
	125,000	1,363	346	843	-	115	2,667	#66
$50,000	$100,000	$1,098	$346	$1,348	-	$1,383	$4,175	#127
	150,000	1,628	346	1,348	-	1,383	4,705	#113
	200,000	2,158	346	1,348	-	1,383	5,235	#96
$75,000	$150,000	$1,628	$346	$1,699	-	$3,029	$6,702	#124
	250,000	2,688	346	1,699	-	3,029	7,762	#106
	350,000	3,748	346	1,699	-	3,029	8,822	#88
WILMINGTON								
$25,000	$75,000	$1,279	$405	$843	-	$115	$2,642	#143
	100,000	1,549	405	843	-	115	2,912	#131
	125,000	1,819	405	843	-	115	3,182	#113
$50,000	$100,000	$1,549	$405	$1,348	-	$1,383	$4,685	#147
	150,000	2,089	405	1,348	-	1,383	5,225	#134
	200,000	2,629	405	1,348	-	1,383	5,765	#116
$75,000	$150,000	$2,089	$405	$1,699	-	$3,029	$7,222	#139
	250,000	3,169	405	1,699	-	3,029	8,302	#126
	350,000	4,249	405	1,699	-	3,029	9,382	#107

*There are 163 cities in this book. The city with the lowest tax burden for an income/home value combination is given the #1 rating; the city with the highest total tax burden is given the #163 rating.

Asheville

Asheville has no local income tax but does levy a sales tax.

Most purchases are taxed at a rate of 6%. Major consumer categories taxed at a different rate include: Groceries, which are taxed at a rate of 2%. Major consumer categories that are exempt from sales tax include: Drugs and medical services.

Within the city limits of Asheville, the property tax rate is .0139. Homes are assessed at 100% of market value. There is an elderly exemption of $20,000 off assessed value for persons age 65 or older with a gross income of less than $15,000. Property tax includes garbage pickup.

Asheville has a personal property tax rate of .0139. Personal property is assessed at 100% of current market value. Items subject to the tax include motor vehicles, aircraft, mobile homes, watercraft and watercraft engines.

Our couples relocating to Asheville must pay a highway use tax of $150 per automobile, a title fee of $35 per automobile and a registration fee of $20 per automobile at the time of registration. The highway use tax is 3% of the value of the vehicle as set by the state, up to a maximum tax of $150. Thereafter, on an annual basis, our couples will pay a registration fee per automobile.

Brevard

Brevard has no local income tax but does levy a sales tax.

Most purchases are taxed at a rate of 6%. Major consumer categories taxed at a different rate: None. Major consumer categories that are exempt from sales tax include: Drugs and medical services.

Within the city limits of Brevard, the property tax rate is .01161. Homes are assessed at 100% of market value. There is a senior citizen exemption of $20,000 off assessed value for persons age 65 or older with a gross income of less than $15,000. Property tax does not cover garbage pickup; the additional fee is approximately $144 per year.

Brevard has a personal property tax rate of .01161. Personal property is assessed at 100% of current market value. Items subject to the tax include motor vehicles, aircraft, mobile homes, watercraft and watercraft engines.

Our couples relocating to Brevard must pay a highway use tax of $150 per automobile, a title fee of $35 per automobile and a registration fee of $20 per automobile at the time of registration. The highway use tax is 3% of the value of the vehicle as set by the state, up to a maximum tax of $150. Thereafter, on an annual basis, our couples will pay a registration fee per automobile.

Chapel Hill

Chapel Hill has no local income tax but does levy a sales tax.

Most purchases are taxed at a rate of 6%. Major consumer categories taxed at a different rate: Groceries, which are taxed at a rate of 2%. Major consumer categories that are exempt from sales tax include: Drugs, medical services and groceries.

For residents in the Orange County portion of Chapel Hill, the property tax rate is .01511. Homes are assessed at 100% of market value. There is a senior citizen exemption of $20,000 off assessed value for persons age 65 or older with a gross income of less than $15,000. Property tax includes garbage pickup.

Chapel Hill has a personal property tax rate of .01511 within Orange County. Personal property is assessed at 100% of NADA average retail value

(current market value). Items subject to the tax include motor vehicles, aircraft, mobile homes, watercraft and watercraft engines.

Our couples relocating to Chapel Hill must pay a highway use tax of $150 per automobile, a title fee of $35 per automobile and a registration fee of $25 per automobile at the time of registration. The highway use tax is 3% of the current value of the vehicle as set by the state, up to a maximum tax of $150. Thereafter, on an annual basis, our couples will pay a registration fee per automobile.

Edenton

Edenton has no local income tax but does levy a sales tax.

Most purchases are taxed at a rate of 6%. Major consumer categories taxed at a different rate: None. Major consumer categories that are exempt from sales tax include: Drugs and medical services.

Within the city limits of Edenton, the property tax rate is .01085. Homes are assessed at 100% of market value. There is an elderly exemption of $20,000 off assessed value for persons age 65 or older with a gross income of less than $15,000. Property tax does not cover garbage pickup; the additional fee is approximately $84 per year. Edenton has a personal property tax rate of .01085. Personal property is assessed at 100% of current market value. Items subject to the tax include motor vehicles, aircraft, mobile homes, watercraft and watercraft engines.

Our couples relocating to Edenton must pay a highway use tax of $150 per automobile, a title fee of $35 per automobile and a plate fee of $20 per automobile at the time of registration. The highway use tax is 3% of the current value of the vehicle as set by the state, up to a maximum tax of $150. Thereafter, on an annual basis, our couples will pay a registration fee per automobile.

Hendersonville

Hendersonville has no local income tax but does levy a sales tax.

Most purchases are taxed at a rate of 6%. Major consumer categories taxed at a different rate: None. Major consumer categories that are exempt from sales tax include: Drugs and medical

services.

Within the city limits of Hendersonville, the property tax rate is .0095. Homes are assessed at 100% of market value. There is an elderly exemption of $20,000 off assessed value for persons age 65 or older with a gross income of less than $15,000. Property tax does not cover garbage pickup; the additional fee is approximately $36 per year.

Hendersonville has a personal property tax rate of .0095. Personal property is assessed at 100% of NADA current market value. Items subject to the tax include motor vehicles, aircraft, mobile homes, watercraft and watercraft engines.

Our couples relocating to Hendersonville must pay a highway use tax of $150 per automobile, a title fee of $35 per automobile and a plate fee of $20 per automobile at the time of registration. The highway use tax is 3% of the current value of the vehicle as set by the state, up to a maximum tax of $150. Thereafter, on an annual basis, our couples will pay a plate fee per automobile.

New Bern

New Bern has no local income tax but does levy a sales tax.

Most purchases are taxed at a rate of 6%. Major consumer categories taxed at a different rate: Groceries, which are taxed at a rate of 2%. Major consumer categories that are exempt from sales tax include: Drugs and medical services.

Within the city limits of New Bern, the property tax rate is .0104. Homes are assessed at 100% of market value. There is an elderly exemption of $20,000 off assessed value for persons 65 or older with a gross income of less than $15,000. Property tax includes garbage pickup. There is an additional recycling fee of approximately $32 per year.

New Bern has a personal property tax rate of .0104. Personal property is assessed at 100% of current market value. Items subject to the tax include motor vehicles, aircraft, mobile homes, watercraft and watercraft engines.

Our couples relocating to New Bern must pay a highway use tax of $150 per automobile, a title fee of $35 per automobile and a registration fee of $20 per automobile at the time of registration. The highway use tax is 3% of the value of the vehicle as set by the state, up to a maximum tax of $150. Thereafter, on an annual basis, our couples will pay a registration fee per automobile.

Pinehurst

Pinehurst has no local income tax but does levy a sales tax.

Most purchases are taxed at a rate of 6%. Major consumer categories taxed at a different rate: None. Major consumer categories that are exempt from sales tax include: Drugs and medical services.

Within the village of Pinehurst, the property tax rate is .00895. Homes are assessed at 100% of market value. There is an elderly exemption of $20,000 off assessed value for persons age 65 or older with a household gross income of less than $15,000. Property tax includes garbage pickup.

Pinehurst has a personal property tax rate of .00895. Personal property is assessed at 100% of NADA current market value. Items subject to the tax include motor vehicles, aircraft, mobile homes, watercraft and watercraft engines.

Our couples relocating to Pinehurst must pay a highway use tax of $150 per automobile, a title fee of $35 per automobile and a registration fee of $20 per automobile at the time of registration. The highway use tax is 3% of the value of the vehicle as set by the state, up to a maximum tax of $150. Thereafter, on

an annual basis, our couples will pay a registration fee per automobile.

Waynesville

Waynesville has no local income tax but does levy a sales tax.

Most purchases are taxed at a rate of 6%. Major consumer categories taxed at a different rate: Groceries, which are taxed at a rate of 2%. Major consumer categories that are exempt from sales tax include: Drugs and medical services.

Within the town of Waynesville, the property tax rate is .0106. Homes are assessed at 100% of market value. There is an elderly exemption of $20,000 off assessed value for persons age 65 or older with a gross income of less than $15,000. Property tax includes garbage pickup. There is a landfill fee of $38 per year.

Waynesville has a personal property tax rate of .0106. Personal property is assessed at 100% of current market value. Items subject to the tax include motor vehicles, aircraft, mobile homes, watercraft and watercraft engines.

Our couples relocating to Waynesville must pay a highway use tax of $150 per automobile, a title fee of $35 per automobile, and a registration fee of $20 per automobile at the time of registration. The highway use tax is 3% of the value of the vehicle as set by the state, up to a maximum tax of $150. Thereafter, on an annual basis, our couples will pay a registration fee per

automobile.

Wilmington

Wilmington has no local income tax but does levy a sales tax.

Most purchases are taxed at a rate of 6%. Major consumer categories taxed at a different rate: Groceries, which are taxed at a rate of 2%. Major consumer categories that are exempt from sales tax include: Drugs and medical services.

Within the city limits of Wilmington, the property tax rate is .0108. Homes are assessed at 100% of market value. There is an elderly exclusion of $20,000 off assessed value for persons age 65 or older with a household gross income of less than $15,000. Property tax does not cover garbage pickup; the additional fee is approximately $409 per year.

Wilmington has a personal property tax rate of .0108. Personal property is assessed at 100% of current market value. Items subject to the tax include motor vehicles, aircraft, mobile homes, watercraft and watercraft engines.

Our couples relocating to Wilmington must pay a highway use tax of $150 per automobile, a title fee of $35 per automobile and a registration fee of $20 per automobile at the time of registration. The highway use tax is 3% of the current value of the vehicle as set by the state, up to a maximum tax of $150. Thereafter, on an annual basis, our couples will pay a plate fee per automobile.

• North Carolina's Best Retirement Towns •

Asheville, North Carolina

Asheville is the quintessential highland retirement town. Rivers, forests, inviting mountain vistas and moderate year-round temperatures encourage outdoor activities — hiking, snow-skiing, whitewater rafting — in all seasons.

An extensive slate of cultural, educational and social opportunities are made possible by the University of North Carolina's Center for Creative Retirement, College for Seniors and Leadership Asheville Seniors program. The Folk Art Center and YMI Cultural Center attract large audiences to presentations of local crafts and perform-

ing arts productions.

Nearby Cherokee, Flat Rock, Pisgah National Forest and Great Smoky Mountains National Park entice residents to embark on one-day outings or longer forays to discover the treasures hidden in their mountain coves and villages.

Maryanne and David Harlan came all the way across the country from their homes in New Mexico — Santa Fe and Alamogordo — to settle in Asheville. "We were very impressed with the city and beautiful surrounding mountains," David says. "It has culture, beauty and open, friendly people.

"Asheville is a unique city," he says. "There's something here for everybody, with its strong cultural climate, exceptional educational opportunities and great recreational resources. We call Asheville the Santa Fe of North Carolina."

Population: 68,000 in city, 195,000 in county.

Climate:

	High	Low
January	45	26
July	84	64

Cost of living: 103, based on national average of 100.

Average price of a new home: $210,000

Security: 83.7 crimes per 1,000 residents, higher than the national average of 42.7 crimes per 1,000 residents.

Information: Asheville Area Chamber of Commerce, 151 Haywood St., Asheville, NC 28801, (800) 280-0005 or www.exploreasheville.com.

Brevard, North Carolina

Brevard Music Center's annual six-week summer music festival is world-renowned, visited by hundreds of thousands of people in its 60-year history. Lesser-known attractions of this picturesque village in the mountains of western North Carolina are its moderate year-round temperatures and low humidity, low crime and low cost of living.

At 2,230 feet, there are spectacular scenic vistas of the Blue Ridge Mountains, French Broad River and waterfalls that cascade majestically down the colorful slopes of the Blue Ridge range to the valley below.

Barbara Cronin, who retired here with husband Jack from Princeton, MA, embraced the town's musical tradition wholeheartedly. She has season tickets to the music festival, is organist and choir director at her church, and sings in a 12-person Friday morning vocal group.

Barbara's love of music is matched only by her love of the people she has met since moving here. "The most unusual thing about Brevard is its nice, loving, kind, thoughtful people," Barbara says. "Strangers smile at strangers. You don't find that everywhere."

Population: 7,500 in city, 29,000 in county.

Climate:
	High	Low
January	50	25
July	85	61

Cost of living: Below average (specific index not available).

Average price of a new home: $169,000

Security: 40.6 crimes per 1,000 residents, lower than the national average of 42.7 crimes per 1,000 residents.

Information: Brevard-Transylvania Chamber of Commerce, 35 W. Main St., Brevard, NC 28712, (800) 648-4523 or www.brevardncchamber.org.

Chapel Hill, North Carolina

Best known as the home of the University of North Carolina Tar Heels, and affectionately called "blue heaven" by its legions of alumni and supporters, Chapel Hill is increasingly well-known as a magnet for relocating retirees seeking more than a place in the sun.

Its main attractions, besides the multifaceted educational, cultural and athletic offerings of the university, are a midstate location offering same-day access to mountains, beaches and major metropolitan areas, a renowned medical complex, outstanding continuing-care facilities, master-planned communities and historic neighborhoods.

Dexter and Carole Winters moved to Chapel Hill from Alexandria, VA, after looking at Charlottesville, VA, and Raleigh, NC, as well as Clemson, SC, and Athens, GA. "We wanted the flavor, fare and youthful vitality of a college town," Dexter says, "and it had to be in the Southeast. Chapel Hill was our favorite of all the towns we visited."

Adds Carole, "It has some of the prettiest old neighborhoods we saw in our travels, and it's an exciting place to be, even when the Tar Heels aren't playing at home. We love the Playmakers performances and other cultural events brought in by the university."

Population: 46,000 in city, including about 25,000 students, and 100,000 in county.

Climate:
	High	Low
January	49	26
July	89	65

Cost of living: Above average (specific index not available).

Average price of a new home: $295,000

Security: 67.6 crimes per 1,000 residents, higher than the national average of 42.7 crimes per 1,000 residents.

Information: Chapel Hill-Carrboro Chamber of Commerce, 104 S. Estes Dr., Chapel Hill, NC 27514, (919) 967-7075 or www.chapelhillcarrboro.org.

Edenton, North Carolina

Founded in 1722, this Colonial seaport on the banks of Albemarle Sound evokes imagery of a time known only from the pages of early American history.

Scores of restored 18th-century homes, churches and public buildings mark the town's historical authenticity. Visitors from North and South are seen to pause in their touring, reflecting on the dramas that unfolded here when the town was young and merchant ships plied its waters laden with goods from England and Europe.

Bob and Carole Zembraski drove down U.S. Highway 17 from their home in Ridgefield, CT, and sized up several locations in the Carolinas as potential retirement homes but kept coming back to Edenton, Bob says. He describes Edenton as "a scenic little town, right on the water, with a pretty, working downtown — not a real touristy town, even though very historic."

In addition to Edenton's compelling physical attractiveness, they found the townspeople extremely warm, friendly and caring. "I don't know if it's because it's in the Bible belt, but there's a goodness here you don't find in a lot of places," he says. "We have more friends here than we had after 30 years in Connecticut. We couldn't have made a better choice, and we've never regretted it for a minute."

Population: 5,300 in city, 14,500 in county.

Climate:
	High	Low
January	51	32
July	88	70

Cost of living: Below average (specific index not available).

Average price of a new home: $139,000

Security: 63.1 crimes per 1,000 residents, higher than the national average of 42.7 crimes per 1,000 residents.

Information: Edenton-Chowan Chamber of Commerce, 116 E. King St., Edenton, NC 27932, (800) 775-0111 or www.co.chowan.nc.us/commerce.htm.

Hendersonville, North Carolina

On a plateau about 2,500 feet above sea level, between the Blue Ridge and Great Smoky Mountains of western North Carolina, this town was for years a summer retreat for sweltering coastal lowlanders. In recent years it has become a haven for retirees moving out of the cities in search of a quieter, safer environment.

Recreational opportunities abound in nearby forests, mountains and rivers. And in the neighboring communities of Flat Rock and Brevard, music, art and theater provide a diverse array of cultural events that attract visitors from across the nation to festivals and playhouses.

Bill and Barbara Johnson moved from Rockville, MD, in February 1997 after vacationing here in 1987 and '89. "We found out we really liked the place," Barbara says. "We wanted a mild winter, a cool summer and a house in the mountains on a golf course."

Though Hendersonville is growing at a rapid rate — a 35 percent increase in the last 10 years — it retains "a small-town atmosphere, with friendly people, beautiful developments, remote scenic surroundings and an unhurried pace — all of the things we were looking for in retirement," Bill says.

Population: 10,000 in city, 83,000 in county.

Climate:

	High	Low
January	48	26
July	84	62

Cost of living: Average (specific index not available).

Average price of a new home: $145,000

Security: 112.1 crimes per 1,000 residents, higher than the national average of 42.7 crimes per 1,000 residents.

Information: Greater Hendersonville Chamber of Commerce, 330 N. King St., Hendersonville, NC 28792, (828) 692-1413 or www.hendersonvillechamber.org.

New Bern, North Carolina

Scenic beauty, a four-season climate, boating and other water-related activities, a historical past preserved, and outstanding housing developments are some of the reasons given by retirees who left their homes in New York, Pennsylvania, Ohio and Maryland to retire to this pretty waterfront town in eastern North Carolina.

Others came because they fell in love with the area while in military service at nearby Cherry Point Marine Air Station or Camp Lejeune Marine Base. Whatever the reason, relocating retirees are finding this hamlet at the confluence of the Trent and Neuse rivers has everything they are seeking.

Ed and Linda Stuckrath drove south from their home in Annapolis in search of a quieter, less congested place to spend their golden years. "When we arrived in New Bern, got out and walked the downtown streets, we were sold," Ed says. "The people smiled, waved and said 'hi.' We fell in love immediately with the town and the friendly people."

Ed, a former Navy officer, and Linda had set proximity to the ocean as a priority for their retirement home. "Two years, and we haven't been to the ocean yet," he laughs. Ed says it's hard to believe that there's always something special going on in a town of such small size.

"Changes are taking place — all positive. New roads and bridges have improved transportation, though we've never had a problem with traffic congestion. There's a new airport and a lot of new restaurants. It's a wonderful place. You can't go wrong," he says.

Population: 22,500 in city, 91,000 in county.

Climate:

	High	Low
January	55	35
July	89	71

Cost of living: Average (specific index not available).

Average price of a new home: $159,900

Security: 82.3 crimes per 1,000 residents, higher than the national average of 42.7 crimes per 1,000 residents.

Information: New Bern Area Chamber of Commerce, 316 S. Front St., New Bern, NC 28560, (252) 637-3111 or www.newbernchamber.com.

Pinehurst, North Carolina

To golfers, Pinehurst is a household word. To horsemen, it is famed for horse shows, harness racing and fox hunting, all nurtured by the soft earth and open spaces of the surrounding sandhills.

Whatever your favorite sport might be — running with the hounds or chasing the little white ball — you will cherish the genteel lifestyle in this quaint Southern town where a 62-degree average yearly temperature dictates that a majority of waking hours be spent outdoors.

Charlie and Marjean Fischer discovered Pinehurst in the 1960s and '70s while vacationing from their home in the Greenville-Spartanburg area of South Carolina. The combination of some 40 golf courses and a year-round mild climate lured them here permanently after retirement in 1994.

Founded in the late 19th century, the village is filled with historical treasures. Marjean includes among village highlights the arts, culture (including summer concerts) and community college courses offered to seniors at "bargain-basement prices."

Charlie and Marjean perform volunteer services at First Healthcare, which Charlie describes as "one of the 100 best hospitals in the country." Pinehurst's location is also a big plus. "Charlotte, Raleigh and Fayetteville are all nearby, and you can be at the beach or in the mountains in under two hours," Charlie says.

Population: 7,400 in city, 73,200 in county.

Climate:

	High	Low
January	55	33
July	91	67

Cost of living: Average (specific index not available).

Average price of a new home: $269,900

Security: 24.2 crimes per 1,000 residents, lower than the national average of 42.7 crimes per 1,000 residents.

Information: Sandhills Area Chamber of Commerce, 10677 Highway 15-501, Southern Pines, NC 28387, (910) 692-3926 or www.sandhills.net.

Waynesville, North Carolina

Tucked between the Great Smoky Mountains National Park to the north and the Pisgah National Forest to the south, this slow-paced hamlet in western North Carolina is luring retirees with its visitor-friendly downtown, four-season climate, one of the lowest crime rates in North Carolina, and an excellent health-care facility in Haywood County Regional Medical Center.

Residents can choose to live in town at 2,700 feet of elevation or in a mile-high scenic mountain retreat overlooking the town. John and Erika Elshoff came up from Treasure Island, FL, in the 1980s and bought a vacation home one mile above sea level on Eagles Nest Mountain. When they retired in 1993 they sold their home and bought one at 3,500 feet. "That high elevation is fine when you come here for the summer, but not for year-round living," John says.

Erika describes the view from their home as "breathtakingly beautiful." She likes the fact that there is "no crime, or very little," and she extols the "natural weather cycle of warm, pleasant summers and very mild winters without the crush of harsh weather. This is a place for golfing, horseback riding, fly-fishing and gardening," she says.

Population: 9,750 in city, 52,800 in county.

Climate:

	High	Low
January	47	23
July	82	59

Cost of living: Below average (specific index not available).

Average price of a new home: $159,000

Security: 31.2 crimes per 1,000 residents, lower than the national average of 42.7 crimes per 1,000 residents.

Information: Haywood County Chamber of Commerce, 73 Walnut St., P.O. Drawer 600, Waynesville, NC 28786, (877) 456-3073 or www.haywood-nc.com.

Wilmington, North Carolina

This lovely town has a restored, historic waterfront on the Cape Fear River, a vibrant downtown area, pretty neighborhoods of architecturally significant homes, and miles of white, sandy beaches only minutes from the city center.

Its cultural directory lists 75 organizations involved in perpetuation of the arts, including 11 theater companies, perhaps not surprising for a city with a burgeoning motion picture industry. A regional medical center, two community colleges and the University of North Carolina at Wilmington add cultural, social and educational appeal to the community.

Howard and Elisabeth Loving made some 20 moves during Howard's Navy career and chose Wilmington over Charleston, SC, and Maryland's Eastern Shore because of its "history, beauty and wonderful people," Elisabeth says. "They reach out to you. You feel so welcomed by your neighbors and the community."

Howard says that despite its size and location, "Wilmington is cosmopolitan in many respects. Its museums and educational and cultural fare are exceptional. Accessibility can't be compared."

Population: 71,000 in city, 156,196 in county.

Climate:

	High	Low
January	55	34
July	88	71

Cost of living: Above average (specific index not available).

Average price of a new home: $175,000

Security: 114 crimes per 1,000 residents, higher than the national average of 42.7 crimes per 1,000 residents.

Information: Greater Wilmington Chamber of Commerce, 1 Estell Lee Place, Wilmington, NC 28401, (910) 762-2611 or www.wilmingtonchamber.org.

NORTH DAKOTA

Tax Heavens O
None

Tax Hells Ψ
None

Top Retirement Towns
None

North Dakota has a state income tax and a state sales tax.

There are two methods that can be used to calculate income tax in North Dakota. The state income tax rate using the short-form method is 14% of federal income tax liability before subtracting any federal tax credits.

The state income tax rate using the long-form method is graduated from 2.67% to 12% depending upon income bracket. For married couples filing jointly, the rate is 2.67% on the first $3,000 of taxable income; the rate is 4% on the next $2,000 of taxable income; the rate is 5.33% on the next $3,000 of

taxable income; the rate is 6.67% on the next $7,000 of taxable income; the rate is 8% on the next $10,000 of taxable income; the rate is 9.33% on the next $10,000 of taxable income; the rate is 10.67% on the next $15,000 of taxable income; and the rate is 12% on taxable income above $50,000.

In calculating the tax using the long form method, there is a deduction for federal income tax paid. Federal and state pensions are not exempt, but there is an exclusion for some of these pensions of up to $5,000 with certain limitations. Private pension income is not exempt. Social Security benefits subject

to federal tax are not exempt. There is a standard deduction of up to $600 for interest income received from financial institutions located in North Dakota for married couples filing jointly. There is an additional exemption of $300 from income for married couples filing jointly.

Major tax credits or rebates include: Credit for taxes paid to other states, credit for long-term care insurance and credit for contribution to qualifying North Dakota private high school or college. Our couples do not qualify for these programs.

The state sales tax rate is 5%, but local governments can add to this amount.

NORTH DAKOTA TAX TABLE

Instructions
1. Find the Income in the far left column closest to your anticipated retirement income.
2. Find the Home Value closest to the value of the home where you will live in retirement.
3. Follow that row to your estimated Total Tax Burden at age 65 and beyond.

Income	Home Value	Property Tax & Other Fees	Personal Property Tax & Auto Fees	Sales Tax	Local Income Tax	State Income Tax	Total Tax Burden	Rank* From #1-#163
FARGO								
$25,000	$75,000	$1,767	$128	$856	-	-	$2,751	#148
	100,000	2,323	128	856	-	-	3,307	#149
	125,000	2,878	128	856	-	-	3,862	#148
$50,000	$100,000	$2,323	$128	$1,386	-	$563	$4,400	#135
	150,000	3,434	128	1,386	-	563	5,511	#142
	200,000	4,545	128	1,386	-	563	6,622	#145
$75,000	$150,000	$3,434	$128	$1,760	-	$1,465	$6,787	#126
	250,000	5,656	128	1,760	-	1,465	9,009	#141
	350,000	7,878	128	1,760	-	1,465	11,231	#140

*There are 163 cities in this book. The city with the lowest tax burden for an income/home value combination is given the #1 rating; the city with the highest total tax burden is given the #163 rating.

Fargo

Fargo has no local income tax but does levy a sales tax.

Most purchases are taxed at a rate of 6.5%. Major consumer categories taxed at a different rate: None. Major consumer categories that are exempt from sales tax include: Groceries, medical services and drugs.

In Fargo School District 1, the property tax rate is .49375. Homes are assessed at 50% of market value. Taxable value is 9% of assessed value. There is a homestead credit for homeowners age 65 or older with gross income less than $14,000 (after medical expenses) and with assets of $50,000 or less, excluding the first $80,000 of mar-

ket value of the home. Property tax does not cover garbage pickup; the additional fee is approximately $77 per year. Residents also pay approximately $24 per year in forestry fees.

Fargo has no personal property tax for individuals.

Our couples relocating to Fargo must pay a registration fee of $72 for the

Explorer and $52 for the Cutlass, a title fee of $5 per automobile and a service charge fee of $8 per automobile. Thereafter, on an annual basis, our couples will pay a registration fee and a service charge fee, per automobile.

OHIO

Tax Heavens O
None

Tax Hells Ψ
None

Top Retirement Towns
None

Ohio has a state income tax and a state sales tax.

The state income tax rate is graduated from .691% to 6.98% depending upon income bracket. For married couples filing jointly, the rate is .691% on the first $5,000 of taxable income; the rate is 1.383% on the next $5,000 of taxable income; the rate is 2.766% on the next $5,000 of taxable income; the rate is 3.458% on the next $5,000 of taxable income; the rate is 4.148% on the next $20,000 of taxable income; the rate is 4.841% on the next $40,000 of taxable income; the rate is 5.531% on the next $20,000 of taxable income;

the rate is 6.422% on the next $100,000 of taxable income; and the rate is 6.98% on taxable income above $200,000.

In calculating the tax, there is no deduction for federal income tax paid. Social Security benefits are exempt. There is a $1,100 personal exemption per person.

Major tax credits or rebates include: Credit for income taxes paid to other states; pension income credit from tax due of up to $200 for federal, state and private pensions for married couples filing jointly; senior citizen tax credit of $50 for married couples filing jointly

when one or both persons are age 65 or older; exemption tax credit of $20 per person; and joint filing credit of up to $650 from tax for married couples filing jointly if both spouses have earned income of at least $500 included in Ohio adjusted gross income. Our couples qualify for all these programs except for credit for income taxes paid to other states.

The state sales tax rate is 5%, but local governments can add to this amount.

Since car registration and renewal fees differ within the state, see city information for details.

OHIO TAX TABLE

Instructions

1. Find the Income in the far left column closest to your anticipated retirement income.
2. Find the Home Value closest to the value of the home where you will live in retirement.
3. Follow that row to your estimated Total Tax Burden at age 65 and beyond.

Income	Home Value	Property Tax & Other Fees	Personal Property Tax & Auto Fees	Sales Tax	Local Income Tax	State Income Tax	Total Tax Burden	Rank* From #1- #163
CINCINNATI								
$25,000	$75,000	$1,430	$106	$790	$73	-	$2,399	#125
	100,000	1,898	106	790	73	-	2,867	#129
	125,000	2,366	106	790	73	-	3,335	#130
$50,000	$100,000	$1,898	$106	$1,279	$349	$592	$4,224	#128
	150,000	2,834	106	1,279	349	592	5,160	#132
	200,000	3,771	106	1,279	349	592	6,097	#128
$75,000	$150,000	$2,834	$106	$1,624	$674	$1,614	$6,852	#129
	250,000	4,707	106	1,624	674	1,614	8,725	#137
	350,000	6,580	106	1,624	674	1,614	10,598	#135
CLEVELAND								
$25,000	$75,000	$953	$106	$922	$70	-	$2,051	#68
	100,000	1,270	106	922	70	-	2,368	#68
	125,000	1,588	106	922	70	-	2,686	#69
$50,000	$100,000	$1,270	$106	$1,492	$332	$592	$3,792	#109
	150,000	1,905	106	1,492	332	592	4,427	#96
	200,000	2,540	106	1,492	332	592	5,062	#84
$75,000	$150,000	$1,905	$106	$1,895	$642	$1,614	$6,162	#106
	250,000	3,175	106	1,895	642	1,614	7,432	#95
	350,000	4,445	106	1,895	642	1,614	8,702	#82

Income	Home Value	Property Tax & Other Fees	Personal Property Tax & Auto Fees	Sales Tax	Local Income Tax	State Income Tax	Total Tax Burden	Rank* From #1- #163
COLUMBUS								
$25,000	$75,000	$1,117	$86	$757	$70	-	$2,030	#62
	100,000	1,489	86	757	70	-	2,402	#72
	125,000	1,862	86	757	70	-	2,775	#77
$50,000	$100,000	$1,489	$86	$1,226	$332	$592	$3,725	#103
	150,000	2,234	86	1,226	332	592	4,470	#101
	200,000	2,978	86	1,226	332	592	5,214	#94
$75,000	$150,000	$2,234	$86	$1,557	$642	$1,614	$6,133	#104
	250,000	3,723	86	1,557	642	1,614	7,622	#101
	350,000	5,212	86	1,557	642	1,614	9,111	#100

*There are 163 cities in this book. The city with the lowest tax burden for an income/home value combination is given the #1 rating; the city with the highest total tax burden is given the #163 rating.

Cincinnati

Cincinnati has a local income tax and a local sales tax.

The local income tax rate is 2.1%, which is applied to wages, salaries and self-employment income.

Most purchases are taxed at a rate of 6%. Major consumer categories taxed at a different rate: None. Major consumer categories that are exempt from sales tax include: Drugs, groceries and medical services.

Within the Cincinnati School District, the effective property tax rate is .06114. Homes are assessed at 35% of market value. There is a reduction of 10% of property taxes due for all homeowners. There is a reduction of 2.5% of property taxes due for all owner-occupied homes. There is also a homestead deduction available to homeowners age 65 or older whose combined total gross income is $23,300 or less. Property tax includes garbage pickup. There is a storm water fee of approximately $25 per year. Cincinnati has no personal property tax.

Our couples relocating to Cincinnati must pay a registration and plate fee of approximately $44 per automobile, an emissions test fee of approximately $20 per automobile, a title fee of $5 per automobile and an inspection fee of $4 per automobile at the time of registration. Thereafter, on an annual basis, our couples will pay a registration/plate fee per automobile. Our couples will also pay an emissions test fee per automobile every two years.

Cleveland

Cleveland has a local income tax and a local sales tax.

The local income tax rate is 2%, which is applied to wages, salaries and self-employment income.

Most purchases are taxed at a rate of 7%. Major consumer categories taxed at a different rate: None. Major consumer categories that are exempt from sales tax include: Drugs, groceries and medical services.

Within the Highland Heights area of Cleveland, the property tax rate is .04147. Homes are assessed at 35% of market value. There is a reduction of 10% of property tax due for all homeowners. There is a reduction of 2.5% of property taxes due for all owner-occupied homes. There is also a homestead deduction available to homeowners age 65 or older whose combined total gross income is $23,300 or less. Property tax includes garbage pickup.

Cleveland has no personal property tax.

Our couples relocating to Cleveland must pay a registration and plate fee of approximately $44 per automobile, an emissions test fee of approximately $20 per automobile, a title fee of $5 per automobile and an inspection fee of $4 per automobile at the time of registration. Thereafter, on an annual basis, our couples will pay a registration/plate fee per automobile. Our couples will also pay an emissions test fee per automobile every two years.

Columbus

Columbus has a local income tax and a local sales tax.

The local income tax rate is 2%, which is applied to wages, salaries, rental income and self-employment income.

Most purchases are taxed at a rate of 5.75%. Major consumer categories taxed at a different rate: None. Major consumer categories that are exempt from sales tax include: Drugs, groceries and medical services.

Within the Columbus city limits, the effective property tax rate is .048628. Homes are assessed at 35% of market value. There is a reduction of 10% of property taxes due for all homeowners. There is a reduction of 2.5% of property taxes due for all owner-occupied homes. There is also a homestead deduction available to homeowners age 65 or older whose combined total gross income is $23,300 or less. Property tax includes garbage pickup.

Columbus has no personal property tax.

Our couples relocating to Columbus must pay a registration and plate fee of approximately $44 per automobile, a title fee of $5 per automobile and an inspection fee of $4 per automobile at the time of registration. Thereafter, on an annual basis, our couples will pay a registration/plate fee per automobile.

OKLAHOMA

Tax Heavens O	Tax Hells Ψ	Top Retirement Towns
None	None	None

Oklahoma has a state income tax and a state sales tax.

There are two methods for determining the amount of state income tax due. Using Method I, the state income tax rate is graduated from .5% to 6.75% depending upon income bracket. For married couples filing jointly with taxable income of up to $2,000, the rate is .5%; up to $5,000, the tax is $10 plus 1% of the amount above $2,000; up to $7,500, the tax is $40 plus 2% of the amount above $5,000; up to $9,800, the tax is $90 plus 3% of the amount above $7,500; up to $12,200, the tax is $159 plus 4% of the amount above $9,800; up to $15,000, the tax is $255 plus 5% of the amount above $12,200; up to $21,000, the tax is $395 plus 6% of the amount above $15,000; $21,000 or above, the tax is $755 plus 6.75% of the amount above $21,000.

Using Method II, the income brackets and tax amounts stay the same as

Method I for income of up to $7,500; up to $8,900, the tax is $90 plus 3% of the amount above $7,500; up to $10,400, the tax is $132 plus 4% of the amount above $8,900; up to $12,000, the tax is $192 plus 5% of the amount above $10,400; up to $13,250, the tax is $272 plus 6% of the amount above $12,000; up to $15,000, the tax is $347 plus 7% of the amount above $13,250; up to $18,000, the tax is $469.50 plus 8% of the amount above $15,000; up to $24,000, the tax is $709.50 plus 9% of the amount above $18,000; $24,000 or above, the tax is $1,249.50 plus 10% of the amount above $24,000.

In calculating the tax, there is a deduction for federal income tax paid only if Method II is used. Federal and state pensions are exempt up to $5,500 per person. Private pensions are not exempt, although there is a retirement income exclusion up to $4,400 per qualifying individual if age 65 or older

for married couples filing jointly with an Oklahoma adjusted gross income of $50,000 or less. Social Security benefits are exempt. There is a 15% standard deduction of Oklahoma adjusted income for married couples filing jointly, with a minimum deduction of $1,000 and a maximum of $2,000. There is a $1,000 personal exemption per person and an additional $1,000 personal exemption per person for married couples filing jointly age 65 or older whose federal adjusted gross income does not exceed $25,000. There is a partial exemption of interest received from a bank, credit union or savings and loan located in Oklahoma, up to $200 for a married couple filing jointly even if only one spouse received interest income.

Major tax rebates or credits include: Credit for income taxes paid to other states, a low-income property tax credit and sales tax relief credit. Several of

OKLAHOMA TAX TABLE

Instructions

1. Find the Income in the far left column closest to your anticipated retirement income.
2. Find the Home Value closest to the value of the home where you will live in retirement.
3. Follow that row to your estimated Total Tax Burden at age 65 and beyond.

Income	Home Value	Property Tax & Other Fees	Personal Property Tax & Auto Fees	Sales Tax	Local Income Tax	State Income Tax[†]	Total Tax Burden	Rank[*] From #1-#163
OKLAHOMA CITY								
$25,000	$75,000	$917	$185	$1,233	-	($41)	$2,294	#107
	100,000	1,197	185	1,233	-	(41)	2,574	#93
	125,000	1,476	185	1,233	-	(41)	2,853	#84
$50,000	$100,000	$1,197	$185	$1,927	-	$1,105	$4,414	#136
	150,000	1,756	185	1,927	-	1,105	4,973	#125
	200,000	2,315	185	1,927	-	1,105	5,532	#109
$75,000	$150,000	$1,756	$185	$2,412	-	$3,071	$7,424	#144
	250,000	2,874	185	2,412	-	3,071	8,542	#132
	350,000	3,992	185	2,412	-	3,071	9,660	#112

[†]Sales tax relief credit is issued as a reduction of income tax due or as a refund if the credit is greater than the tax liability.
[*]There are 163 cities in this book. The city with the lowest tax burden for an income/home value combination is given the #1 rating; the city with the highest total tax burden is given the #163 rating.

our couples qualify for the sales tax relief credit, but none of our couples qualify for the other programs.

The state sales tax rate is 4.5%, but local governments can add to this amount.

Oklahoma City

Oklahoma City has no local income tax but does levy a sales tax.

Most purchases are taxed at a rate of 7.875%. Major consumer categories taxed at a different rate: None. Major consumer categories that are exempt from sales tax include: Drugs, medical services and medical supplies.

In the Oklahoma City School District, the property tax rate is .10166. Homes are assessed at 11% of market value. There is a homestead deduction of $1,000 off assessed value and an additional homestead deduction of $1,000 off assessed value available to homeowners with a gross income of $20,000 or less. There is also an elderly exemption, which is a refund of real estate tax over 1% of income with a maximum refund of $200 available to homeowners who are age 65 or older or disabled with a gross income of $10,000 or less. Property tax does not cover garbage pickup; the additional fee is approximately $147 per year. There is also a drainage fee of $33 per year.

Oklahoma City has no personal property tax for individuals.

Our couples relocating to Oklahoma City must pay a registration fee per automobile based on the age of the automobile. The registration fee is $91 for the Explorer and $91 for the Cutlass. Our couples also pay a title fee of $11 per automobile and $7 per automobile in miscellaneous fees. Thereafter, on an annual basis, our couples will pay a renewal fee and some miscellaneous fees, per automobile.

OREGON

Tax Heavens O
Ashland
Bend
Grants Pass
Lincoln City

Tax Hells Ψ
None

Top Retirement Towns
Ashland
Bend
Eugene
Grants Pass
Lincoln City

Oregon has a state income tax and no state sales tax.

The state income tax is graduated from 5% to 9% depending upon income bracket. For married couples filing jointly, the rate is 5% on the first $4,900 of taxable income; the rate is 7% on the next $7,300 of taxable income; and the rate is 9% on taxable income above $12,200.

In calculating the tax, there is a deduction of up to $3,000 for federal income tax paid. Federal pensions for service after October 1, 1991 and state and private pensions are not exempt. Social Security benefits are exempt. There is a $5,000 standard deduction for married couples filing jointly when both are age 65 or older.

Major tax credits or rebates include: Credit for income taxes paid to other states, which our couples do not qualify for; exemption tax credit of $139 per person, which our couples qualify for; and retirement income credit, which some of our couples qualify for.

Our couples relocating to the cities listed below must pay $47 to register each automobile. Thereafter, on an annual basis, our couples will pay a license renewal fee per automobile.

OREGON TAX TABLE

Instructions
1. Find the Income in the far left column closest to your anticipated retirement income.
2. Find the Home Value closest to the value of the home where you will live in retirement.
3. Follow that row to your estimated Total Tax Burden at age 65 and beyond.

Income	Home Value	Property Tax & Other Fees	Personal Property Tax & Auto Fees	Sales Tax	Local Income Tax	State Income Tax	Total Tax Burden	Rank* From #1- #163
ASHLAND								
$25,000	$75,000	$1,199	$60	$77	-	-	$1,336	#6 O
	100,000	1,520	60	77	-	-	1,657	#9 O
	125,000	1,842	60	77	-	-	1,979	#12
$50,000	$100,000	$1,520	$60	$122	-	$1,900	$3,602	#87
	150,000	2,163	60	122	-	1,900	4,245	#81
	200,000	2,806	60	122	-	1,900	4,888	#71
$75,000	$150,000	$2,163	$60	$144	-	$4,015	$6,382	#110
	250,000	3,448	60	144	-	4,015	7,667	#102
	350,000	4,734	60	144	-	4,015	8,953	#93
BEND								
$25,000	$75,000	$1,126	$60	-	-	-	$1,186	#3 O
	100,000	1,427	60	-	-	-	1,487	#4 O
	125,000	1,729	60	-	-	-	1,789	#6 O
$50,000	$100,000	$1,427	$60	-	-	$1,900	$3,387	#66
	150,000	2,030	60	-	-	1,900	3,990	#52
	200,000	2,633	60	-	-	1,900	4,593	#55
$75,000	$150,000	$2,030	$60	-	-	$4,015	$6,105	#103
	250,000	3,235	60	-	-	4,015	7,310	#87
	350,000	4,441	60	-	-	4,015	8,516	#75

Income	Home Value	Property Tax & Other Fees	Personal Property Tax & Auto Fees	Sales Tax	Local Income Tax	State Income Tax	Total Tax Burden	Rank* From #1-#163
EUGENE								
$25,000	$75,000	$1,396	$60	-	-	-	$1,456	#11
	100,000	1,719	60	-	-	-	1,779	#15
	125,000	2,041	60	-	-	-	2,101	#18
$50,000	$100,000	$1,719	$60	-	-	$1,900	$3,679	#97
	150,000	2,364	60	-	-	1,900	4,324	#87
	200,000	3,009	60	-	-	1,900	4,969	#78
$75,000	$150,000	$2,364	$60	-	-	$4,015	$6,439	#112
	250,000	3,654	60	-	-	4,015	7,729	#105
	350,000	4,944	60	-	-	4,015	9,019	#97
GRANTS PASS								
$25,000	$75,000	$1,258	$60	-	-	-	$1,318	#5 O
	100,000	1,576	60	-	-	-	1,636	#8 O
	125,000	1,895	60	-	-	-	1,955	#11
$50,000	$100,000	$1,576	$60	-	-	$1,900	$3,536	#81
	150,000	2,213	60	-	-	1,900	4,173	#75
	200,000	2,851	60	-	-	1,900	4,811	#64
$75,000	$150,000	$2,213	$60	-	-	$4,015	$6,288	#107
	250,000	3,488	60	-	-	4,015	7,563	#97
	350,000	4,762	60	-	-	4,015	8,837	#89
LINCOLN CITY								
$25,000	$75,000	$1,325	$60	-	-	-	$1,385	#8 O
	100,000	1,684	60	-	-	-	1,744	#13
	125,000	2,042	60	-	-	-	2,102	#19
$50,000	$100,000	$1,684	$60	-	-	$1,900	$3,644	#93
	150,000	2,401	60	-	-	1,900	4,361	#89
	200,000	3,118	60	-	-	1,900	5,078	#85
$75,000	$150,000	$2,401	$60	-	-	$4,015	$6,476	#114
	250,000	3,834	60	-	-	4,015	7,909	#114
	350,000	5,268	60	-	-	4,015	9,343	#105
PORTLAND								
$25,000	$75,000	$1,408	$60	-	-	-	$1,468	#12
	100,000	1,801	60	-	-	-	1,861	#18
	125,000	2,194	60	-	-	-	2,254	#31
$50,000	$100,000	$1,801	$60	-	-	$1,900	$3,761	#108
	150,000	2,587	60	-	-	1,900	4,547	#104
	200,000	3,373	60	-	-	1,900	5,333	#102
$75,000	$150,000	$2,587	$60	-	-	$4,015	$6,662	#123
	250,000	4,158	60	-	-	4,015	8,233	#122
	350,000	5,729	60	-	-	4,015	9,804	#119

*There are 163 cities in this book. The city with the lowest tax burden for an income/home value combination is given the #1 rating; the city with the highest total tax burden is given the #163 rating.

Ashland

Ashland has no local income tax and no sales tax, with the exception of a 5% tax on food away from home.

Within the city limits of Ashland, the property tax rate is .015121. Homes are assessed at 85% of market value. There are no exemptions or deductions off the property tax. Property tax does not cover garbage pickup; the additional fee is approximately $150 per year. Additional fees include a $23 storm drain fee and a $61 street fee.

Ashland has no personal property tax for individuals.

Bend

Bend has no local income tax and no sales tax.

Within the city limits of Bend, the property tax rate is .0146987. Homes are assessed at approximately 82% of market value. There are no exemptions or deductions off the property tax. Property tax does not cover garbage pickup; the additional fee is approximately $222 per year.

Bend has no personal property tax for individuals.

Eugene

Eugene has no local income tax and no sales tax.

Within the city limits of Eugene, the property tax rate is .0181433. New homes are assessed at 78.92% of market value. Actual property tax due may be affected by Measure 5 limitations on the tax rates and the local option exemptions to those limitations. Property tax does not cover garbage pickup; the additional fee is approximately $345 per year. There is also a storm water fee of approximately $84 per year.

Eugene has no personal property tax for individuals.

Grants Pass

Grants Pass has no local income tax and no sales tax.

Within the city limits of Grants Pass, the property tax rate is .0146472. Homes are assessed at approximately 87% of market value. There are no exemptions or deductions off the property tax. Property tax does not cover garbage pickup; the additional fee is approximately $300 per year.

Grants Pass has no personal property tax for individuals.

Lincoln City

Lincoln City has no local income tax and no sales tax.

Within the city limits of Lincoln City, the property tax rate is .01648. Homes are assessed at 87% of market value. There are no exemptions or deductions off the property tax. Property tax does not cover garbage pickup; the additional fee is approximately $250 per year.

Lincoln City has no personal property tax for individuals.

Portland

Portland has no local income tax and no sales tax.

Within the city limits of Portland, the property tax rate is .02095. Homes are assessed at 75% of market value. There are no exemptions or deductions off the property tax. Property tax does not cover garbage pickup; the additional fee is approximately $230 per year.

• Oregon's Best Retirement Towns •

Ashland, Oregon

Ashland sits just off Interstate 5 at the south end of the Rogue River Valley, 15 miles north of the California border and at 2,000 feet of elevation. Attracted by its beauty, culture and entertainment, thousands of visitors come annually to stroll its colorful tree-lined Main Street, hang out in popular Lithia Park, ski 7,533-foot Mount Ashland or simply savor the sights and sounds of this scenic wonderland.

From February through October, nearly 500,000 visitors come to plays produced by the Oregon Shakespeare Festival, a highly successful Ashland fixture since 1935. Proximity to California makes the town a popular destination for retirees seeking a lower cost of living — but who, in the process of moving to Ashland, drive up living costs with large proceeds from the sale of their expensive former homes.

Bob and Jeanne Arago retired here from Walnut Creek, CA, in 1997 after visiting potential retirement sites from coast to coast. "Its beautiful setting, high intellectual convergence, strong community support for seniors and great entertainment and recreation" were the attractions, Bob says. "In short, the high quality of life."

Population: 19,200 in city, 172,800 in county.

Climate:

	High	Low
January	46	29
July	87	51

Cost of living: Above average (specific index not available).

Average price of a new home: $196,000

Security: 45.9 crimes per 1,000 residents, higher than the national average of 42.7 crimes per 1,000 residents.

Information: Ashland Chamber of Commerce, P.O. Box 1360, 110 E. Main St., Ashland, OR 97520, (541) 482-3486 or www.ashlandchamber.com.

Bend, Oregon

Located at 3,600 feet in the high desert of central Oregon, this small gem — bordered on the west by Deschutes National Forest, the Cascade Mountain Range and the lava-strewn Deschutes River — abounds in recreational possibilities. Fishing, hunting, golfing and snow skiing are the outdoor activities of choice for many residents. Skiers fill the slopes of 9,000-foot Mount Bachelor from October through June, sometimes coming down from a morning run to play an afternoon round of golf.

In town, diners fill sidewalk cafes until late evening, and on star-filled nights you might catch a reflection of nearby snowcapped mountains in Mirror Pond.

Max and Sandra Jacobs moved from Laguna Beach, CA, in 1994 "before the big rush of growth," Max says. That growth, primarily in the retail sector, "hasn't really affected our lifestyle that much — a little more traffic, but these problems are being addressed.

"It's not cheap anymore, but relative to Southern California, it's very affordable. We bought a 2.5-acre lot for $24,000 in 1989, and similar lots are going for $100,000 now," he says. "We've seen a lot of growth, but it's still a lovely environment."

Population: 50,649 in city, 110,810 in county.

Climate:

	High	Low
January	42	22
July	81	45

Cost of living: 105, based on national average of 100.

Average price of a new home: $169,000

Security: 83 crimes per 1,000 residents, higher than the national average of 42.7 crimes per 1,000 residents.

Information: Bend Chamber of Commerce, 777 N.W. Wall St., Bend, OR

Eugene, Oregon

Start with a clean, modern city and an active, enlightened population of less than 134,000, mix in the first-class University of Oregon, add the Hult Center (one of the best performing arts centers in the Northwest), place the Pacific Ocean an hour west and the Cascade Mountains on the east, sprinkle in pretty rivers, streams, forests and scenic vistas, and you have Eugene.

Sharon Munson says she and husband Keith "started all over here after years in Anchorage. It's a wonderful, friendly college town with a great quality of life. I even like the rainy winters," she says. "It's a good time to hibernate."

Location is another big plus for the Munsons. "It's an easy place to travel from for half-day drives up and down the coast," she says. "We take about six trips a year to Ashland for the Oregon Shakespeare Festival. We are crazy about it here."

Population: 133,460 in city, 313,100 in county.

Climate:

	High	Low
January	46	33
July	82	51

Cost of living: 110, based on national average of 100.

Average price of a new home: $249,000

Security: 78.9 crimes per 1,000 residents, higher than the national average of 42.7 crimes per 1,000 residents.

Information: Eugene Area Chamber of Commerce, 1401 Willamette St., Eugene, OR 97401, (541) 484-1314 or www.eugenechamber.com.

Grants Pass, Oregon

Set in the scenic splendor of the Rogue River Valley and protected to the west by the 5,000-foot peaks of the Siskiyou Mountains, this one-time favorite vacation spot of famed western writer Zane Grey is little changed, in many ways, from its frontier days. Surrounded by lakes, rivers and forests, it has long been a popular destination for hunters and fishermen. In recent years it has become a retirement destination favored by Californians seeking a less stressful, less costly lifestyle.

Renee Smith retired here with husband Richard from the San Francisco Bay area. "I am living in my favorite vacation spot all year," she says. "It has a small-town '50s and '60s flavor, slow-paced and relaxed. There's very little crime, and a good, safe feeling.

"Tourism has become a big thing in helping to revitalize downtown. It's very beautiful," she says. "Though it can get cold in winter and hot in summer, there's a generally mild four-season climate with low humidity."

Population: 20,565 in city, 68,000 in county.

Climate:

	High	Low
January	48	33
July	90	53

Cost of living: Above average (specific index not available).

Average price of a new home: $130,000

Security: 92.2 crimes per 1,000 residents, higher than the national average of 42.7 crimes per 1,000 residents.

Information: Grants Pass-Josephine County Chamber of Commerce, 1995 N.W. Vine St., P.O. Box 970, Grants Pass, OR 97528, (800) 547-5927 or www. grantspasschamber.org.

Lincoln City, Oregon

Perched on a bluff overlooking the Pacific, this small town provides a scenic haven for retirees and visitors — the latter contingent considerably increased by the introduction of the Chinook Winds Casino and Convention Center a few years back.

"It's a nice small town with a relaxed atmosphere," says Bill Kacy, who with wife Mary retired to Lincoln City from Austin, TX. "You can indulge your interest in water sports at the ocean or on Devil's Lake east of town.

"The primary draw for us was clean air. We've been told the EPA air standard for the United States was established on Cascade Head, site of our home just north of Lincoln City," he says. "The weather is temperate, rarely getting above 75 degrees or below freezing. And you can play golf year-round, even in the rainy season."

Population: 6,850 in city, 45,000 in county.

Climate:

	High	Low
January	54	37
July	68	53

Cost of living: Above average (specific index not available).

Average price of a new home: $154,900

Security: 102.5 crimes per 1,000 residents, higher than the national average of 42.7 crimes per 1,000 residents.

Information: Lincoln City Chamber of Commerce, 4039 N.W. Logan Road, Lincoln City, OR 97367, (541) 994-3070 or www.lcchamber.com.

PENNSYLVANIA

Tax Heavens O
None

Tax Hells Ψ
Philadelphia
Pittsburgh

Top Retirement Towns
Lancaster

Pennsylvania has a state income tax and a state sales tax.

The state income tax rate is 2.8%. In calculating the tax, there is no deduction for federal income tax paid. Federal, state and private pensions are exempt. Social Security benefits are exempt.

Major tax credits or rebates include: Credit for income taxes paid to other states, which our couples do not qualify for; and tax forgiveness credit, which

PENNSYLVANIA TAX TABLE

Instructions

1. Find the Income in the far left column closest to your anticipated retirement income.
2. Find the Home Value closest to the value of the home where you will live in retirement.
3. Follow that row to your estimated Total Tax Burden at age 65 and beyond.

Income	Home Value	Property Tax & Other Fees	Personal Property Tax & Auto Fees	Sales Tax	Local Income Tax	State Income Tax	Total Tax Burden	Rank* From #1- #163
LANCASTER								
$25,000	$75,000	$2,008	$72	$726	$55	-	$2,861	#150
	100,000	2,618	72	726	55	-	3,471	#151
	125,000	3,227	72	726	55	-	4,080	#152
$50,000	$100,000	$2,618	$72	$1,183	$186	$622	$4,681	#146
	150,000	3,836	72	1,183	186	622	5,899	#150
	200,000	5,055	72	1,183	186	622	7,118	#151
$75,000	$150,000	$3,836	$72	$1,473	$341	$1,251	$6,973	#132
	250,000	6,274	72	1,473	341	1,251	9,411	#146
	350,000	8,711	72	1,473	341	1,251	11,848	#147
PHILADELPHIA								
$25,000	$75,000	$1,983	$72	$846	$172	-	$3,073	#155 Ψ
	100,000	2,644	72	846	172	-	3,734	#156 Ψ
	125,000	3,306	72	846	172	-	4,396	#155 Ψ
$50,000	$100,000	$2,644	$72	$1,381	$790	$622	$5,509	#158 Ψ
	150,000	3,967	72	1,381	790	622	6,832	#159 Ψ
	200,000	5,289	72	1,381	790	622	8,154	#158 Ψ
$75,000	$150,000	$3,967	$72	$1,719	$1,526	$1,251	$8,535	#156 Ψ
	250,000	6,611	72	1,719	1,526	1,251	11,179	#158 Ψ
	350,000	9,256	72	1,719	1,526	1,251	13,824	#157 Ψ
PITTSBURGH								
$25,000	$75,000	$2,940	$72	$846	$121	-	$3,979	#162 Ψ
	100,000	3,920	72	846	121	-	4,959	#163 Ψ
	125,000	4,900	72	846	121	-	5,939	#163 Ψ
$50,000	$100,000	$3,920	$72	$1,381	$497	$622	$6,492	#162 Ψ
	150,000	5,880	72	1,381	497	622	8,452	#163 Ψ
	200,000	7,840	72	1,381	497	622	10,412	#163 Ψ
$75,000	$150,000	$5,880	$72	$1,719	$943	$1,251	$9,865	#163 Ψ
	250,000	9,800	72	1,719	943	1,251	13,785	#163 Ψ
	350,000	13,720	72	1,719	943	1,251	17,705	#163 Ψ

*There are 163 cities in this book. The city with the lowest tax burden for an income/home value combination is given the #1 rating; the city with the highest total tax burden is given the #163 rating.

one of our couples qualifies for.

The state sales tax rate is 6% but local governments can add to this amount.

Since car registration and renewal fees differ within the state, see city information for details.

Lancaster

Lancaster has a local income tax but does not levy an additional sales tax.

The local income city wage tax rate is 1% of wages, salaries and self-employment income for residents and 0% of wages, salaries and self-employment income for non-residents who work inside the Lancaster city limits. In addition, there is an occupation tax of $10 per wage earner.

Most purchases are taxed at the state rate of 6%. Major consumer categories taxed at a different rate: None. Major consumer categories that are exempt from sales tax include: Apparel and services, drugs, groceries and medical services.

Within the Lancaster city limit, the property tax rate is .026553. Homes are assessed at 91.8% of market value. There is a property tax rebate of up to $500 for homeowners age 65 or older with a gross income of less than $15,000 (excluding 50% of their Social Security income). Property tax does not cover garbage pickup; the additional fee is approximately $180 per year.

Lancaster has no personal property tax for individuals.

Our couples relocating to Lancaster must pay a registration fee of $36 per automobile, a lien fee of $5 per automobile and a title fee of $23 per automobile at the time of registration. Thereafter, on an annual basis, our couples will pay a renewal fee per automobile.

Philadelphia

Philadelphia has a local income tax and a sales tax.

The local income tax rate is 4.5635% of wages, salaries and self-employment income for residents and 3.9672% of wages, salaries and self-employment income for non-residents who work inside the Philadelphia city limits. In addition, there is a one-time Business Privilege License fee of $200 per self-employed wage earner. Philadelphia also has a school income tax, which applies to unearned income including certain types of interest and dividends. The rate is 4.5635%.

Most purchases are taxed at a rate of 7%. Major consumer categories taxed at a different rate: None. Major consumer categories that are exempt from sales tax include: Apparel and services, drugs, groceries and medical services.

Within the Philadelphia city limit, the property tax rate is .08264. Homes are assessed at 32% of market value. There is a property tax rebate of up to $500 for homeowners age 65 or older with a gross income of less than $15,000 (excluding 50% of their Social Security income). Property tax includes garbage pickup.

Our couples relocating to Philadelphia must pay a registration fee of $36 per automobile, a lien fee of $5 per automobile and a title fee of $23 per automobile at the time of registration. They must also pay approximately $44 for an emissions test per automobile. Thereafter, on an annual basis, our couples will pay a renewal fee per automobile.

Pittsburgh

Pittsburgh has a local income tax and a sales tax.

The local income tax rate is 2.875% of wages, salaries and net self-employment income for residents and 1% of wages, salaries and net self-employment income for non-residents who work inside the Pittsburgh city limits. In addition, there is an occupational privilege tax of $10 per wage earner. There is a Business Privilege Tax of .6% on gross receipts, but there is an exclusion of $20,000 from gross receipts.

Most purchases are taxed at a rate of 7%. Major consumer categories taxed at a different rate: None. Major consumer categories that are exempt from sales tax include: Apparel and services, drugs, groceries and medical services.

Within the Pittsburgh city limit, the property tax rate is .15680. Homes are assessed at 25% of market value. There is a property tax rebate of up to $500 for homeowners age 65 or older with a gross income of less than $15,000 (excluding 50% of their Social Security income). There is also a rollback of assessed value to 1993 value, based on certain age, income and residency requirements. Property tax includes garbage pickup.

Pittsburgh has no personal property tax for individuals.

Our couples relocating to Pittsburgh must pay a registration fee of $36 per automobile, a lien fee of $5 per automobile and a title fee of $23 per automobile at the time of registration. They must also pay approximately $28 for an emissions test per automobile. Thereafter, on an annual basis, our couples will pay a renewal fee per automobile.

• Pennsylvania's Best Retirement Town •

Lancaster, Pennsylvania

In terms of location, it could almost be a bedroom community of Philadelphia, but the serene and peaceful environment of Lancaster is light years away from the frenetic pace and atmosphere of its big eastern neighbor.

In a landscape dotted with the manicured farms and homes of Amish, Mennonite and other sectarian families,

those who retire to the Pennsylvania Dutch Country have found their lives influenced and enriched by the 19th-century customs and mores of these hardworking people.

The pretty, historic town has its own strong appeal, providing a variety of cultural, educational and social opportunities — opera, theater, symphony and university activities among them.

Fred and Patricia Howell came east from Cleveland, OH, looking for "smaller crowds, less crime and more congenial neighbors," Fred says. "We were intrigued by the honest lifestyle of the Amish," says Patricia, "and felt their goodness and industriousness might have a salutary effect on our lives. It has," she says. "We have never felt better, physically. Our lives are fuller, and we have never been happier."

Population: 65,000 in city, 466,000 in county.

Climate:	High	Low
January	37	19
July	85	63

Cost of living: 96, based on national average of 100.

Average price of a new home: $149,900

Security: 49.8 crimes per 1,000 residents, higher than the national average of 42.7 crimes per 1,000 residents.

Information: Lancaster Chamber of Commerce and Industry, 100 S. Queen St., P.O. Box 1558, Lancaster, PA 17608-1558, (717) 397-3531 or www.lcci. com.

RHODE ISLAND

Tax Heavens O
None

Tax Hells Ψ
Providence

Top Retirement Towns
None

Rhode Island has a state income tax and a state sales tax.

The state income tax rate is 26% of federal income tax liability.

Major tax credits or rebates include: Credit for income taxes paid to other states, which our couples do not qualify for; and property tax relief credit, which some of our couples qualify for.

RHODE ISLAND TAX TABLE

Instructions

1. Find the Income in the far left column closest to your anticipated retirement income.
2. Find the Home Value closest to the value of the home where you will live in retirement.
3. Follow that row to your estimated Total Tax Burden at age 65 and beyond.

Income	Home Value	Property Tax & Other Fees	Personal Property Tax & Auto Fees	Sales Tax	Local Income Tax	State Income Tax†	Total Tax Burden	Rank* From #1- #163
PROVIDENCE								
$25,000	$75,000	$1,354	$2,273	$846	-	$18	$4,491	#163 Ψ
	100,000	1,922	2,273	846	-	(232)	4,809	#162 Ψ
	125,000	2,489	2,273	846	-	(232)	5,376	#162 Ψ
$50,000	$100,000	$1,922	$2,273	$1,381	-	$1,046	$6,622	#163 Ψ
	150,000	3,057	2,273	1,381	-	1,046	7,757	#162 Ψ
	200,000	4,193	2,273	1,381	-	1,046	8,893	#162 Ψ
$75,000	$150,000	$3,057	$2,273	$1,719	-	$2,720	$9,769	#162 Ψ
	250,000	5,328	2,273	1,719	-	2,720	12,040	#161 Ψ
	350,000	7,599	2,273	1,719	-	2,720	14,311	#160 Ψ

†Property tax relief is issued as a reduction of income tax due or as a refund if the credit is greater than the tax liability.
*There are 163 cities in this book. The city with the lowest tax burden for an income/home value combination is given the #1 rating; the city with the highest total tax burden is given the #163 rating.

The state sales tax rate is 7%.

Providence

Providence has no local income tax and does not levy an additional sales tax.

Most purchases are taxed at the state rate of 7%. Major consumer categories taxed at a different rate: None. Major consumer categories that are exempt from sales tax include: Medical services, drugs, groceries, apparel and services.

Within the Providence city limits, the property tax rate is .03494. Homes are assessed at 100% of market value. There is a homestead deduction of 35% off assessed value available to all homeowners and an elderly exemption of $10,000 off assessed value available to homeowners age 65 or older who collect Social Security and have been residents of the city for at least three years. Property tax includes garbage pickup.

Providence has no personal property tax for individuals; however, it does have an excise tax on vehicles, which is essentially the same as the personal property tax in several other states. The tax rate is .07678 and is assessed on 100% of the NADA current market value.

Our couples relocating to Providence must pay a registration fee of $60 per automobile that covers registration for a two-year period, a title fee of $25 per automobile and an emissions test fee of $47 per automobile every two years. Thereafter, every two years, our couples will pay a registration fee and an emissions test fee, per automobile.

SOUTH CAROLINA

Tax Heavens ⭘
Beaufort
Clemson
Hilton Head
Myrtle Beach

Tax Hells Ψ
None

Top Retirement Towns
Aiken
Beaufort
Charleston
Clemson
Greenville
Hilton Head Island
Myrtle Beach

South Carolina has a state income tax and a state sales tax.

The state income tax rate is graduated from 2.5% to 7% depending upon income bracket. For married couples filing jointly, the rate is 2.5% on the first $2,360 of taxable income; the rate is 3% on the next $2,360 of taxable income; the rate is 4% on the next $2,360 of taxable income; the rate is 5% on the next $2,360 of taxable income; the rate is 6% on the next $2,360 of taxable income; and the rate is 7% on taxable income above $11,800.

In calculating the tax, there is no deduction for federal income tax paid. Federal, state and private pension income is not exempt. However, there is a retirement income deduction of up to $10,000 per resident age 65 or older. Social Security benefits are exempt. There is an age deduction of up to $15,000 per resident if age 65 or older; this deduction is reduced by any retirement deduction claimed by each person.

Major tax credits or rebates include: Credit for income taxes paid to other states, which our couples do not qualify for, and two wage-earner credit when both spouses work, which our couples do qualify for.

The state sales tax rate is 5%, but local governments can add to this amount.

Our couples relocating to the cities listed below must pay a $20 registration fee (which is the senior citizen rate) to register each automobile and a $5 title fee per automobile. Thereafter, every two years, our couples will pay a renewal fee per automobile.

Aiken
Aiken has no local income tax but does levy a sales tax.

SOUTH CAROLINA TAX TABLE

Instructions
1. Find the Income in the far left column closest to your anticipated retirement income.
2. Find the Home Value closest to the value of the home where you will live in retirement.
3. Follow that row to your estimated Total Tax Burden at age 65 and beyond.

Income	Home Value	Property Tax & Other Fees	Personal Property Tax & Auto Fees	Sales Tax	Local Income Tax	State Income Tax	Total Tax Burden	Rank* From #1- #163
AIKEN								
$25,000	$75,000	$294	$845	$949	-	-	$2,088	#75
	100,000	484	845	949	-	-	2,278	#57
	125,000	673	845	949	-	-	2,467	#52
$50,000	$100,000	$484	$845	$1,485	-	-	$2,814	#19
	150,000	862	845	1,485	-	-	3,192	#14
	200,000	1,407	845	1,485	-	-	3,737	#16
$75,000	$150,000	$862	$845	$1,849	-	$624	$4,180	#17
	250,000	1,952	845	1,849	-	624	5,270	#17
	350,000	3,042	845	1,849	-	624	6,360	#18
BEAUFORT								
$25,000	$75,000	$255	$806	$791	-	-	$1,852	#34
	100,000	425	806	791	-	-	2,022	#31
	125,000	596	806	791	-	-	2,193	#29

Income	Home Value	Property Tax & Other Fees	Personal Property Tax & Auto Fees	Sales Tax	Local Income Tax	State Income Tax	Total Tax Burden	Rank* From #1- #163
BEAUFORT continued								
$50,000	$100,000	$425	$806	$1,238	-	-	$2,469	#6 O
	150,000	766	806	1,238	-	-	2,810	#5 O
	200,000	1,259	806	1,238	-	-	3,303	#9 O
$75,000	$150,000	$766	$806	$1,540	-	$624	$3,736	#8 O
	250,000	1,752	806	1,540	-	624	4,722	#8 O
	350,000	2,737	806	1,540	-	624	5,707	#10 O
CHARLESTON								
$25,000	$75,000	$261	$936	$949	-	-	$2,146	#88
	100,000	432	936	949	-	-	2,317	#63
	125,000	604	936	949	-	-	2,489	#55
$50,000	$100,000	$432	$936	$1,485	-	-	$2,853	#23
	150,000	776	936	1,485	-	-	3,197	#15
	200,000	1,287	936	1,485	-	-	3,708	#14
$75,000	$150,000	$776	$936	$1,849	-	$624	$4,185	#18
	250,000	1,799	936	1,849	-	624	5,208	#16
	350,000	2,821	936	1,849	-	624	6,230	#16
CLEMSON								
$25,000	$75,000	$217	$732	$949	-	-	$1,898	#40
	100,000	345	732	949	-	-	2,026	#34
	125,000	473	732	949	-	-	2,154	#25
$50,000	$100,000	$345	$732	$1,485	-	-	$2,562	#9 O
	150,000	602	732	1,485	-	-	2,819	#6 O
	200,000	1,014	732	1,485	-	-	3,231	#5 O
$75,000	$150,000	$602	$732	$1,849	-	$624	$3,807	#9 O
	250,000	1,426	732	1,849	-	624	4,631	#7 O
	350,000	2,250	732	1,849	-	624	5,455	#6 O
GREENVILLE								
$25,000	$75,000	$277	$1,011	$791	-	-	$2,079	#74
	100,000	504	1,011	791	-	-	2,306	#60
	125,000	730	1,011	791	-	-	2,532	#58
$50,000	$100,000	$504	$1,011	$1,238	-	-	$2,753	#18
	150,000	956	1,011	1,238	-	-	3,205	#16
	200,000	1,591	1,011	1,238	-	-	3,840	#21
$75,000	$150,000	$956	$1,011	$1,540	-	$624	$4,131	#15
	250,000	2,226	1,011	1,540	-	624	5,401	#18
	350,000	3,495	1,011	1,540	-	624	6,670	#26
HILTON HEAD								
$25,000	$75,000	$428	$674	$791	-	-	$1,893	#38
	100,000	557	674	791	-	-	2,022	#31
	125,000	685	674	791	-	-	2,150	#24
$50,000	$100,000	$557	$674	$1,238	-	-	$2,469	#6 O
	150,000	813	674	1,238	-	-	2,725	#3 O
	200,000	1,221	674	1,238	-	-	3,133	#3 O
$75,000	$150,000	$813	$674	$1,540	-	$624	$3,651	#6 O
	250,000	1,629	674	1,540	-	624	4,467	#5 O
	350,000	2,445	674	1,540	-	624	5,283	#5 O

*There are 163 cities in this book. The city with the lowest tax burden for an income/home value combination is given the #1 rating; the city with the highest total tax burden is given the #163 rating.

SOUTH CAROLINA TAX TABLE

Instructions

1. Find the Income in the far left column closest to your anticipated retirement income.
2. Find the Home Value closest to the value of the home where you will live in retirement.
3. Follow that row to your estimated Total Tax Burden at age 65 and beyond.

Income	Home Value	Property Tax & Other Fees	Personal Property Tax & Auto Fees	Sales Tax	Local Income Tax	State Income Tax	Total Tax Burden	Rank* From #1- #163
MYRTLE BEACH								
$25,000	$75,000	$305	$773	$791	-	-	$1,869	#36
	100,000	441	773	791	-	-	2,005	#27
	125,000	578	773	791	-	-	2,142	#23
$50,000	$100,000	$441	$773	$1,238	-	-	$2,452	#5 O
	150,000	715	773	1,238	-	-	2,726	#4 O
	200,000	1,193	773	1,238	-	-	3,204	#4 O
$75,000	$150,000	$715	$773	$1,540	-	$624	$3,652	#7 O
	250,000	1,671	773	1,540	-	624	4,608	#6 O
	350,000	2,627	773	1,540	-	624	5,564	#8 O

*There are 163 cities in this book. The city with the lowest tax burden for an income/home value combination is given the #1 rating; the city with the highest total tax burden is given the #163 rating.

Most purchases are taxed at a rate of 6%. However, persons age 85 or older qualify for a reduced rate of 5%. Major consumer categories taxed at a different rate: None. Major consumer categories that are exempt from sales tax include: Drugs and medical services.

Within the city limits of Aiken, the property tax rate is .2725. Homes are assessed at 4% of market value if owner-occupied. There is a homestead deduction of $50,000 off market value for homeowners age 65 or older who have been residents for one year. We've assumed that our couples qualify for this exemption. There is a $100,000 exemption off market value for a portion of the school operations levy after the homestead deduction has been taken, which effectively lowers the total property tax rate in Aiken to .1893 for the first $100,000 of a home's market value. Property tax does not cover garbage pickup; the additional fee is approximately $105 per year.

Aiken has a personal property tax rate of .2725. Personal property is assessed at 10.5% of market value. Items subject to the tax include vehicles, aircraft, campers, motors and watercraft.

Beaufort

Beaufort has no local income tax and does not levy an additional sales tax.

Most purchases are taxed at the state rate of 5%. However, persons age 85 or older qualify for a reduced rate of 4%. Major consumer categories taxed at a different rate: None. Major consumer categories that are exempt from sales tax include: Drugs and medical services.

Within the city limits of Beaufort, the property tax rate is .2463. Homes are assessed at 4% of market value if owner-occupied. There is a homestead deduction of $50,000 off market value for homeowners age 65 or older who have been residents for one year. We've assumed that our couples qualify for this exemption. There is a $100,000 exemption off market value for a portion of the school operations levy after the homestead deduction has been taken, which effectively lowers the total property tax rate in Beaufort to .1706 for the first $100,000 of a home's market value. Property tax does not cover garbage pickup; the additional fee is approximately $84 per year.

Beaufort has a personal property tax rate of .2463. Most personal property is assessed at 10.5% of market value except for automobiles, which are assessed by the county according to their year, make and model. Items subject to the tax include vehicles, aircraft, campers, motors and watercraft. Personal property tax also includes a $10 paving fee per automobile.

Charleston

Charleston has no local income tax but does levy a sales tax.

Most purchases are taxed at a rate of 6%. However, persons age 85 or older qualify for a reduced rate of 5%. Major consumer categories taxed at a different rate: None. Major consumer categories that are exempt from sales tax include: Drugs and medical services.

Within the city limits of Charleston, the property tax rate is .3437. Homes are assessed at 4% of market value if owner-occupied. There is a homestead deduction of $50,000 off market value for homeowners age 65 or older who have been residents for one year. We've assumed that our couples qualify for this exemption. There is a $100,000 exemption off market value for a portion of the school operations levy after the homestead deduction has been taken, which effectively lowers the total property tax rate in Charleston to .2597 for the first $100,000 of a home's market value. There is a sales tax credit of .181% of the home's market value after homestead deduction against the county component of property tax and a credit of .171% of market value after homestead deduction against the city component of property tax. Property tax does not cover garbage pickup; the additional fee is approximately $89 per year.

Charleston has a personal property tax rate of .3437. Personal property is assessed at 10.5% of market value. There is a credit available that reduces personal property tax. Items subject to the tax include vehicles, aircraft, campers, motors and watercraft.

Clemson

Clemson has no local income tax but does levy a sales tax.

Most purchases are taxed at a rate of 6%. However, persons age 85 or older qualify for a reduced rate of 5%. Major consumer categories taxed at a different rate: None. Major consumer categories that are exempt from sales tax include: Drugs and medical services.

Within the city limits of Clemson, the property tax rate is .2692. Homes are assessed at 4% of market value if owner-occupied. There is a homestead deduction of $50,000 off market value for homeowners age 65 or older who have been residents for one year. We've assumed that our couples qualify for this exemption. There is a $100,000 exemption off market value for a portion of the school operations levy after the homestead deduction has been taken, which effectively lowers the total property tax rate in Clemson to .1913 for the first $100,000 of a home's market value. There is a sales tax credit of .1124% of the home's market value after homestead deduction against the county component of property tax and a credit of .1402% of market value after homestead deduction against the city component of property tax. Property tax does not cover garbage pickup; the additional fee is approximately $89 per year.

Clemson has a personal property tax rate of .2692. Personal property is assessed at 10.5% of market value. There is a credit available that reduces personal property tax. Items subject to the tax include vehicles, aircraft, campers, motors and watercraft.

Greenville

Greenville has no local income tax and does not levy an additional

sales tax.

Most purchases are taxed at the state rate of 5%. However, persons age 85 or older qualify for a reduced rate of 4%. Major consumer categories taxed at a different rate: None. Major consumer categories that are exempt from sales tax include: Drugs and medical services.

Within the city limits of Greenville, the property tax rate is .3174. Homes are assessed at 4% of market value if owner-occupied. There is a homestead deduction of $50,000 off market value for homeowners age 65 or older who have been residents for one year. We've assumed that our couples qualify for this exemption. There is a $100,000 exemption off market value for a portion of the school operations levy after the homestead deduction has been taken, which effectively lowers the total property tax rate in Greenville to .2263 for the first $100,000 of a home's market value. Property tax does not cover garbage pickup; the additional fee is approximately $30 per year. There is also a storm water fee of approximately $21 per year.

Greenville has a personal property tax rate of .3174. Personal property is assessed at 10.5% of market value. Items subject to the tax include vehicles, aircraft, campers, motors and watercraft. There is also a $15 county road maintenance fee per automobile added to the vehicle tax notice.

Hilton Head

Hilton Head has no local income tax and does not levy an additional sales tax.

Most purchases are taxed at the state rate of 5%. However, persons age 85 or older qualify for a reduced rate of 4%. Major consumer categories taxed at a different rate: None. Major consumer categories that are exempt from sales tax include: Drugs and medical services.

For most residents of Hilton Head, the property tax rate is .204. Homes are assessed at 4% of market value if owner-occupied. There is a homestead deduction of $50,000 off market value for homeowners age 65 or older who have been residents for one year. We've assumed that our couples qualify for this exemption. There is a

$100,000 exemption off market value for a portion of the school operations levy after the homestead deduction has been taken, which effectively lowers the total property tax rate in Hilton Head to .1283 for the first $100,000 of a home's market value. Property tax does not cover garbage pickup; the additional fee is approximately $300 per year.

Hilton Head has a personal property tax rate of .204. Most personal property is assessed at 10.5% of market value except for automobiles, which are assessed by the county according to their year, make and model. Items subject to the tax include vehicles, aircraft, campers, motors and watercraft. Personal property tax also includes a $10 paving fee per automobile.

Myrtle Beach

Myrtle Beach has no local income tax and does not levy an additional sales tax.

Most purchases are taxed at the state rate of 5%. However, persons age 85 or older qualify for a reduced rate of 4%. Major consumer categories taxed at a different rate: None. Major consumer categories that are exempt from sales tax include: Drugs and medical services.

Within the city limits of Myrtle Beach, the property tax rate is .239. Homes are assessed at 4% of market value if owner-occupied. There is a homestead deduction of $50,000 off market value for homeowners age 65 or older who have been residents for one year. We've assumed that our couples qualify for this exemption. There is a $100,000 exemption off market value for a portion of the school operations levy after the homestead deduction has been taken, which effectively lowers the total property tax rate in Myrtle Beach to .1367 for the first $100,000 of a home's market value. Property tax does not cover garbage pickup; the additional fee is approximately $168 per year.

Myrtle Beach has a personal property tax rate of .239. Personal property is assessed at 10.5% of market value. Items subject to the tax include vehicles, aircraft, campers, motors and watercraft. Personal property tax also includes a $15 road fee per automobile.

Aiken, South Carolina

This one-time "polo capital of the world" still draws thousands to its triple crown horse races, but its multiple non-equestrian attractions are the big draws for relocating retirees.

While still working, teachers Jan and Buck Mizelle drew up a list of the things they wanted in a retirement town. Every spring break they took off from their hometown of Springfield, VA, to search for their idyllic future home.

"We looked at many places east of the Mississippi, south of Virginia and north of Florida before finally discovering Aiken," Jan says. "It has everything we were looking for — a small town with year-round residents, four-season climate, easygoing lifestyle, good medical and cultural amenities, good shopping (including Augusta, GA, only 15 minutes away) and a wonderful, mixed-ages subdivision.

"Whoever you are, wherever you're from, you're welcome in Aiken," she adds.

Population: 25,600 in city, 135,400 in county.

Climate:

	High	Low
January	57	33
July	92	69

Cost of living: Below average (specific index not available).

Average price of a new home: $144,900

Security: 50.2 crimes per 1,000 residents, higher than the national average of 42.7 crimes per 1,000 residents.

Information: Aiken Chamber of Commerce, P.O. Box 892, Aiken, SC 29802, (800) 542-4536 or http://chamber.aiken. net.

Beaufort, South Carolina

"Beautiful Beaufort" is more than a catch phrase to distinguish the pronunciation from that other Beaufort in North Carolina. It perfectly describes this picture-perfect antebellum town and its lush, semitropical, coastal setting.

Causeways lead to quiet, secluded offshore islands north, east and south of town. Narrow streets lined with live oaks and palms, Lowcountry homes and verdant golfing fairways bordered by salt marshes and crossed by tidal creeks beckon retirees to master-planned communities designed to blend naturally with the environment.

Bowen and Judy King had lived in Texas, Louisiana and North Carolina before discovering the charms of Beaufort and its surrounding sea islands last year. Describing the suddenness and finality of their decision to retire here, Bowen says, "We drove into Dataw (an offshore island just south of Beaufort) and the fat lady sang. We bought a house the next day.

"We came here for the warm weather. We found that, plus vibrant people with a young mental outlook, great golf and a lifestyle that suits us better than any place we've ever lived," he says.

Population: 14,967 in city, 118,337 in county.

Climate:

	High	Low
January	59	39
July	90	73

Cost of living: Average (specific index not available).

Average price of a new home: $230,000

Security: 77.8 crimes per 1,000 residents, higher than the national average of 42.7 crimes per 1,000 residents.

Information: Greater Beaufort Chamber of Commerce, 1108 Carteret St., P.O. Box 910, Beaufort, SC 29901, (800) 638-3525 or www.beaufortsc.org.

Charleston, South Carolina

Known best for its prominent part in Colonial American history, this vibrant, living history museum has taken on a role as the educational, medical and cultural center of coastal South Carolina. In the process, through wise stewardship by an enlightened citizenry, it has retained much of its Old World charm.

Take a ride in an open-air bus or horse-drawn carriage along its cobblestone streets past stately mansions, old churches and ornate public buildings, and you will experience a sense of its memorable past. From the Isle of Palms north to Kiawah and Seabrook islands south, retirees are flocking to the metro Charleston area.

Lured from their New Canaan, CT, home by the grace, beauty and storied history of Charleston, Charles and Carolyn Betz were captivated by the maritime forests, tidal creeks and marshes of Seabrook. They quickly became immersed in the social, cultural and governmental affairs of the island, volunteering their time and energies in Habitat for Humanity, a natural history club, aquarium and property owners association — "still finding time for golfing, boating and lots of playtime activities," Charles says.

"It has been wonderful. If you're considering a move to Seabrook, do it quickly," he advises. "Costs are going up dramatically — an average of 30 percent in the last two years. The island will probably be built out in 10 years."

Population: 88,133 in city, 316,483 in county.

Climate:

	High	Low
January	58	38
July	90	73

Cost of living: 102, based on national average of 100.

Average price of a new home: $139,900

Security: 78 crimes per 1,000 residents, higher than the national average of 42.7 crimes per 1,000 residents.

Information: Charleston Metro Chamber, 81 Mary St., Charleston, SC 29403, (843) 577-2510 or www.charlestonchamber. net.

Clemson, South Carolina

Football fans know Clemson as the home of the Clemson University Tigers, perennial national power, who play their home games in dreaded Death Valley Stadium. In fact, university activities — educational, cultural and athletic — dominate this small town of about 12,500 residents and 18,000 students.

Rolling hills, a string of lakes and the nearby Blue Ridge Mountains provide outdoor recreational possibilities for a growing retiree population. David and Julia Wise (she a native of Cheltenham, England) moved 26 times during David's long U.S. Air Force career. After four months in Beaufort, SC, they tried a cooler climate — Cascade, CO — but abandoned its isolation for the moderate weather and more diverse social and cultural atmosphere of Clemson.

"It's a small village — charming, safe and friendly," Julia says. University concerts, proximity to Atlanta and the Amtrak station stop are things she likes best about the town.

Population: 12,500 in city, 100,000 in county.

Climate:

	High	Low
January	50	30
July	88	68

Cost of living: Below average (specific index not available).

Average price of a new home: $168,500

Security: 29 crimes per 1,000 residents, lower than the national average of 42.7 crimes per 1,000 residents.

Information: Clemson Area Chamber of Commerce, P.O. Box 1622, Clemson, SC 29633-1622, (800) 542-0746 or www.clemsonchamber.org.

Greenville, South Carolina

This once-sleepy Southern village in the foothills of the Blue Ridge Mountains was awakened in recent years by the introduction of multinational companies to its small industrial base. Thousands of new jobs, a booming construction industry and an ever-expanding retail-commercial complex followed.

Despite concerns about the rapid growth, retirees still find much to like about the town. A quaint, tree-lined downtown has undergone major renovation, bringing shoppers and diners to its colorful boutiques and more than 60 restaurants along Main Street.

The Peace Center for the Performing Arts anchors a lively arts scene, while Furman and Bob Jones universities provide forums for educational, cultural and sporting activities. With easy access to interstate highways in all directions, you can be in Atlanta, Charlotte, Asheville or Columbia in less than two hours or exploring the scenic byways of the Blue Ridge Mountains in under an hour.

Art and Catherine Fallis made Greenville their retirement home, moving from Atlanta to be nearer their daughter. "It's still a small town, but it has big-city amenities," Art says. "We like the location. It's an easy drive down to Garden City Beach, SC, or up to Hendersonville, NC. There's a lot to do here — and it has a nice four-season cli-

mate. It's a real nice place to live," he adds.

Population: 60,000 in city, 353,000 in county.

Climate:

	High	Low
January	50	30
July	88	68

Cost of living: Below average (specific index not available).

Average price of a new home: $143,741

Security: 92.1 crimes per 1,000 residents, higher than the national average of 42.7 crimes per 1,000 residents.

Information: Greater Greenville Chamber of Commerce, 24 Cleveland St., Greenville, SC 29601, (864) 242-1050 or www.greenvillechamber.org.

Hilton Head Island, South Carolina

As night falls on this normally busy-as-a-beehive barrier island off South Carolina's southern coast, it is accompanied by a quiet calm and almost impenetrable darkness that obscures many of the telltale signs of man's habitation. Even though heavily developed, a thick canopy of natural vegetation, mandated and monitored by local government officials, and a total ban on commercial signage protects and maintains the pristine beauty of this popular resort.

Most of the island's homes are hidden behind the gates and walls of more than a dozen "plantations" — the name given to mammoth-sized master-planned communities. Twenty-four golf courses help ensure a preponderance of open spaces. White-masted sailboats can be seen plying the island's shallow coves and inlets.

Wally and Gerda Hollinger could have thrown a rock across the border from Savannah, GA, their home of 20 years, to their new home. "We are both fitness fanatics," Wally says, "and this is the perfect place for golfing and biking.

"There's a very safe feel to the atmosphere here," he adds, "and the warmest, friendliest neighbors you can imagine. No one tries to impress anyone. No pressure — no stresses."

Population: 30,377 year-round and 150,000 in summer in city; 120,937 in county.

Climate:

	High	Low
January	60	38
July	90	72

Cost of living: Above average (specific index not available).

Average price of a new home: $329,000

Security: 53.6 crimes per 1,000 residents, higher than the national average of 42.7 crimes per 1,000 residents.

Information: Hilton Head Island Chamber of Commerce, P.O. Box 5647, Hilton Head Island, SC 29938, (800) 523-3373 or www.hiltonheadchamber.com.

Myrtle Beach, South Carolina

A town of nearly 35,000 permanent residents that invites 12 million nonresidents to share its beaches, restaurants and golf courses may be considered hospitable to a fault. The Grand Strand, with Myrtle Beach in the anchor position, started out as a local, family-style, summertime beach resort. Today it is a four-season destination, having added year-round live entertainment to its familiar repertoire of sun, sand and golf. Hordes of older Americans and Canadians now descend on its shores during the off-season.

Charles Gary, who retired here with wife Betty from Lakehurst, NJ, appreciates "the weather, Brookgreen Gardens, its proximity to Charleston and the North Carolina mountains." When not enjoying fishing, boating, golf and tennis, the Garys attend Central Carolina University activities and volunteer for the chamber of commerce, Long Bay Symphony and Bike-the-Neck, a program to build a bike trail down to Georgetown, SC.

"There's something here for everybody," Charles says.

Population: 34,672 in city, 180,000 in county.

Climate:

	High	Low
January	53	34
July	86	72

Cost of living: 98, based on national average of 100.

Average price of a new home: $169,900

Security: 190.5 crimes per 1,000 residents, higher than the national average of 42.7 crimes per 1,000 residents.

Information: Myrtle Beach Chamber of Commerce, P.O. Box 2115, Myrtle Beach, SC 29578, (843) 626-7444 or www.mbchamber.com.

SOUTH DAKOTA

Tax Heavens O	Tax Hells ψ	Top Retirement Towns
None	None	None

South Dakota has no state income tax but does have a state sales tax. The state sales tax rate is 4%, but local governments can add to this amount.

Sioux Falls

Sioux Falls has no local income tax but does levy a sales tax.

Most purchases are taxed at a rate of 6%. Major consumer categories taxed at a different rate include: Food away from home, which is taxed at a rate of 7%; and groceries, which are taxed at a rate of 5%. Major consumer categories that are exempt from sales tax include: Drugs and medical services.

Within the Sioux Falls city limits, the property tax rate is .0236. Homes are assessed at 100% of market value. There is a tax reduction available to owner-occupied homes that reduces the property tax rate to .0157. Property tax does not cover garbage pickup; the additional fee is approximately $204 per year.

There is no personal property tax in Sioux Falls.

Our couples relocating to Sioux Falls are subject to an automobile excise tax, which is 3% of the purchase price and is paid when the vehicle is initially registered in the state. If a vehicle owner paid a sales or excise tax in another state when the automobile was purchased, the previously paid amount is deducted from the South Dakota excise tax due. We've assumed our couples have paid a tax greater than or equal to the South Dakota excise tax. Our couples will pay $64 to cover the plates, tags, wheel tax and solid waste disposal fees per automobile. They will also pay a $5 title transfer fee per automobile and a $5 lien fee per automobile. Thereafter, on an annual basis, our couples will pay a registration fee, wheel tax and solid waste disposal fee, per automobile.

SOUTH DAKOTA TAX TABLE

Instructions

1. Find the Income in the far left column closest to your anticipated retirement income.
2. Find the Home Value closest to the value of the home where you will live in retirement.
3. Follow that row to your estimated Total Tax Burden at age 65 and beyond.

Income	Home Value	Property Tax & Other Fees	Personal Property Tax & Auto Fees	Sales Tax	Local Income Tax	State Income Tax	Total Tax Burden	Rank* From #1- #163
SIOUX FALLS								
$25,000	$75,000	$1,382	$128	$938	-	-	$2,448	#128
	100,000	1,774	128	938	-	-	2,840	#124
	125,000	2,167	128	938	-	-	3,233	#120
$50,000	$100,000	$1,774	$128	$1,475	-	-	$3,377	#65
	150,000	2,559	128	1,475	-	-	4,162	#70
	200,000	3,344	128	1,475	-	-	4,947	#76
$75,000	$150,000	$2,559	$128	$1,840	-	-	$4,527	#38
	250,000	4,129	128	1,840	-	-	6,097	#39
	350,000	5,699	128	1,840	-	-	7,667	#46

*There are 163 cities in this book. The city with the lowest tax burden for an income/home value combination is given the #1 rating; the city with the highest total tax burden is given the #163 rating.

TENNESSEE

Tax Heavens O	Tax Hells Ψ	Top Retirement Towns
Paris	None	Maryville
		Paris

Tennessee has no state earned income tax but does levy an interest and dividends tax. Tennessee has a state sales tax.

The state interest and dividends tax rate is 6%, and it applies to income from stocks, bonds and notes receivable. In calculating the tax, there is no deduction for federal income tax paid. Interest from CDs, savings accounts, money market accounts and credit union accounts is exempt from tax. Interest from bonds issued by the federal, Tennessee or a local government in Tennessee is exempt from tax. Interest from commercial paper maturing in six months or less is exempt from tax. Dividends from Tennessee or national banks, from state or federal savings and loans situated in Tennessee, from credit unions, and from insurance companies licensed to do business in Tennessee are exempt from tax. There is a $2,500 exemption for married couples filing jointly. Married couples filing jointly with a gross income of less than $27,000 are exempt from tax. We've assumed our couples do not owe interest and dividends tax.

Major tax credits or rebates: None.

The state sales tax amount is 6% but local governments can add to this amount.

Since car registration and renewal fees differ within the state, see city information for details.

Maryville

Maryville has no local income tax but does levy a sales tax.

Most purchases are taxed at a rate of 8.25%. Major consumer categories that are exempt from sales tax include: Drugs and medical services.

Within the Maryville city limits, the

TENNESSEE TAX TABLE

Instructions

1. Find the Income in the far left column closest to your anticipated retirement income.
2. Find the Home Value closest to the value of the home where you will live in retirement.
3. Follow that row to your estimated Total Tax Burden at age 65 and beyond.

Income	Home Value	Property Tax & Other Fees	Personal Property Tax & Auto Fees	Sales Tax	Local Income Tax	State Income Tax	Total Tax Burden	Rank* From #1-#163
MARYVILLE								
$25,000	$75,000	$879	$48	$1,305	-	-	$2,232	#97
	100,000	1,173	48	1,305	-	-	2,526	#86
	125,000	1,466	48	1,305	-	-	2,819	#81
$50,000	$100,000	$1,173	$48	$2,042	-	-	$3,263	#53
	150,000	1,759	48	2,042	-	-	3,849	#42
	200,000	2,345	48	2,042	-	-	4,435	#43
$75,000	$150,000	$1,759	$48	$2,542	-	-	$4,349	#24
	250,000	2,931	48	2,542	-	-	5,521	#23
	350,000	4,104	48	2,542	-	-	6,694	#27
MEMPHIS								
$25,000	$75,000	$1,359	$156	$1,305	-	-	$2,820	#149
	100,000	1,783	156	1,305	-	-	3,244	#147
	125,000	2,206	156	1,305	-	-	3,667	#141
$50,000	$100,000	$1,783	$156	$2,042	-	-	$3,981	#120
	150,000	2,629	156	2,042	-	-	4,827	#116
	200,000	3,475	156	2,042	-	-	5,673	#113

*There are 163 cities in this book. The city with the lowest tax burden for an income/home value combination is given the #1 rating; the city with the highest total tax burden is given the #163 rating.

TENNESSEE TAX TABLE

Instructions

1. Find the Income in the far left column closest to your anticipated retirement income.
2. Find the Home Value closest to the value of the home where you will live in retirement.
3. Follow that row to your estimated Total Tax Burden at age 65 and beyond.

Income	Home Value	Property Tax & Other Fees	Personal Property Tax & Auto Fees	Sales Tax	Local Income Tax	State Income Tax	Total Tax Burden	Rank* From #1- #163
MEMPHIS continued								
$75,000	$150,000	$2,629	$156	$2,542	-	-	$5,327	#70
	250,000	4,321	156	2,542	-	-	7,019	#76
	350,000	6,014	156	2,542	-	-	8,712	#83
PARIS								
$25,000	$75,000	$765	$116	$1,305	-	-	$2,186	#94
	100,000	980	116	1,305	-	-	2,401	#71
	125,000	1,195	116	1,305	-	-	2,616	#62
$50,000	$100,000	$980	$116	$2,042	-	-	$3,138	#42
	150,000	1,410	116	2,042	-	-	3,568	#30
	200,000	1,840	116	2,042	-	-	3,998	#26
$75,000	$150,000	$1,410	$116	$2,542	-	-	$4,068	#14
	250,000	2,270	116	2,542	-	-	4,928	#10 O
	350,000	3,130	116	2,542	-	-	5,788	#12

*There are 163 cities in this book. The city with the lowest tax burden for an income/home value combination is given the #1 rating; the city with the highest total tax burden is given the #163 rating.

property tax rate is .0469. Homes are assessed at 25% of market value. There is a property tax relief credit of $99 for homeowners age 65 or older with a gross income of less than $11,510. Property tax includes garbage pickup.

Maryville has no personal property tax for individuals.

Our couples relocating to Maryville must pay a registration fee of $32 per automobile plus a $1 mailing fee per automobile. Thereafter, on an annual basis, our couples will pay a renewal fee per automobile.

Memphis

Memphis has no local income tax but does levy a sales tax.

Most purchases are taxed at a rate of 8.25%. Major consumer categories that are exempt from sales tax include: Drugs and medical services.

Within the Memphis city limits, the property tax rate is .0677. Homes are assessed at 25% of market value. There is a property tax relief credit of $147 for homeowners age 65 or older with a gross income of less than $11,510. Property tax does not cover garbage pickup; the additional fee is approximately $90 per year.

Memphis has no personal property tax for individuals.

Our couples relocating to Memphis must pay a registration fee of $88 per automobile. Thereafter, on an annual basis, our couples will pay a renewal fee per automobile.

Paris

Paris has no local income tax but does levy a sales tax. Most purchases are taxed at a rate of 8.25%. Major consumer categories that are exempt from sales tax include: Drugs and medical services.

Within the Paris city limits, the property tax rate is .0344. Homes are assessed at 25% of market value. There is a property tax relief credit of $99 for homeowners age 65 or older with a gross income of less than $11,510. Property tax does not cover garbage pickup; the additional fee is approximately $120 per year.

Paris has no personal property tax for individuals.

Our couples relocating to Paris must pay a registration fee of $58 per automobile and a title fee of $8 per automobile. Thereafter, on an annual basis, our couples will pay a renewal fee per automobile.

• Tennessee's Best Retirement Towns •

Maryville, Tennessee

Only 20 miles south of Knoxville, this small college town has a stronger connection to Great Smoky Mountains National Park, roughly the same distance south. The park forms the backdrop for a number of master-planned communities favored by relocating retirees. There are miles of hiking and biking trails, an abundance of lakes and rivers, and a wild and scenic mountainous landscape.

Ed and Faye Crick settled into Royal Oaks Country Club, outside the Maryville town limits, from Fort Washington, MD, after a 10-year search for their retirement home. "Maryville deserves its top billing," says Ed, who never tires of the view. "The mountains are a scenic wonder, the tax structure is very good and the four-season climate allows me to spend a lot of time playing golf. We're here for the duration."

Population: 24,000 in city, 100,000 in county.

Climate:

	High	Low
January	47	30
July	87	68

Cost of living: Below average (specific index not available).

Average price of a new home: $135,900

Security: 34.7 crimes per 1,000 residents, lower than the national average of 42.7 crimes per 1,000 residents.

Information: Blount County Chamber of Commerce, 201 S. Washington St., Maryville, TN 37804-5728, (865) 983-2241 or www.chamber.blount.tn.us.

Paris, Tennessee

This small, quiet town in rural northwest Tennessee has a popularity boosted by its proximity (about a 15-minute drive) to Kentucky Lake, a Tennessee Valley Authority project with a 2,100-mile shoreline. But the town itself is the centerpiece and drawing card for many relocating retirees. With a restored downtown, the courthouse square bustles with activity, and rarely does a storefront stay vacant any length of time.

Paris is blessed by a mix of new residents who bring their considerable strengths, talents and skills to diverse local issues and concerns, says Mary Walker, who settled here with husband Al from Philadelphia, PA. They immediately got involved in numerous clubs and social and civic affairs.

"There's a strong sense of community and an abiding interest in history, aided by the heritage center," Mary says. "It's a good, safe place to live with a low cost of living. And it's the givingest town I've ever lived in," she adds.

Population: 10,000 in city, 32,000 in county.

Climate:

	High	Low
January	44	24
July	89	68

Cost of living: Below average (specific index not available).

Average price of a new home: $159,500

Security: 28.2 crimes per 1,000 residents in Henry County, lower than the national average of 42.7 crimes per 1,000 residents.

Information: Paris-Henry County Chamber of Commerce, P.O. Box 8, Paris, TN 38242, (901) 642-3431 or www.paris.tn.org/chamber.htm.

TEXAS

Texas has no state income tax but does have a state sales tax. Major credits or rebates: None.

The state sales tax rate is 6.25% but local governments can add to this amount.

Since car registration and renewal fees differ within the state, see city information for details.

TEXAS TAX TABLE

Instructions

1. Find the Income in the far left column closest to your anticipated retirement income.
2. Find the Home Value closest to the value of the home where you will live in retirement.
3. Follow that row to your estimated Total Tax Burden at age 65 and beyond.

Income	Home Value	Property Tax & Other Fees	Personal Property Tax & Auto Fees	Sales Tax	Local Income Tax	State Income Tax	Total Tax Burden	Rank* From #1- #163	
AUSTIN									
$25,000	$75,000	$703	$143	$1,086	-	-	$1,932	#49	
	100,000	1,287	143	1,086	-	-	2,516	#85	
	125,000	1,896	143	1,086	-	-	3,125	#104	
$50,000	$100,000	$1,287	$143	$1,759	-	-	$3,189	#44	
	150,000	2,506	143	1,759	-	-	4,408	#95	
	200,000	3,725	143	1,759	-	-	5,627	#112	
$75,000	$150,000	$2,506	$143	$2,233	-	-	$4,882	#57	
	250,000	4,945	143	2,233	-	-	7,321	#88	
	350,000	7,383	143	2,233	-	-	9,759	#116	
BROWNSVILLE									
$25,000	$75,000	$1,921	$140	$1,086	-	-	$3,147	#157	ψ
	100,000	2,618	140	1,086	-	-	3,844	#157	ψ
	125,000	3,314	140	1,086	-	-	4,540	#159	ψ
$50,000	$100,000	$2,618	$140	$1,759	-	-	$4,517	#139	
	150,000	4,011	140	1,759	-	-	5,910	#151	
	200,000	5,405	140	1,759	-	-	7,304	#154	ψ
$75,000	$150,000	$4,011	$140	$2,233	-	-	$6,384	#111	
	250,000	6,798	140	2,233	-	-	9,171	#143	
	350,000	9,585	140	2,233	-	-	11,958	#150	
DALLAS									
$25,000	$75,000	$264	$142	$1,086	-	-	$1,492	#13	
	100,000	775	142	1,086	-	-	2,003	#26	
	125,000	1,164	142	1,086	-	-	2,392	#45	
$50,000	$100,000	$775	$142	$1,759	-	-	$2,676	#14	
	150,000	1,940	142	1,759	-	-	3,841	#40	
	200,000	3,106	142	1,759	-	-	5,007	#81	

Income	Home Value	Property Tax & Other Fees	Personal Property Tax & Auto Fees	Sales Tax	Local Income Tax	State Income Tax	Total Tax Burden	Rank* From #1-#163
DALLAS continued								
$75,000	$150,000	$1,940	$142	$2,233	-	-	$4,315	#23
	250,000	4,272	142	2,233	-	-	6,647	#57
	350,000	6,603	142	2,233	-	-	8,978	#95
GEORGETOWN								
$25,000	$75,000	$1,514	$143	$955	-	-	$2,612	#142
	100,000	2,125	143	955	-	-	3,223	#144
	125,000	2,737	143	955	-	-	3,835	#147
$50,000	$100,000	$2,125	$143	$1,546	-	-	$3,814	#110
	150,000	3,348	143	1,546	-	-	5,037	#128
	200,000	4,571	143	1,546	-	-	6,260	#137
$75,000	$150,000	$3,348	$143	$1,963	-	-	$5,454	#78
	250,000	5,794	143	1,963	-	-	7,900	#113
	350,000	8,240	143	1,963	-	-	10,346	#129
HOUSTON								
$25,000	$75,000	$951	$143	$1,086	-	-	$2,180	#92
	100,000	1,546	143	1,086	-	-	2,775	#116
	125,000	2,145	143	1,086	-	-	3,374	#132
$50,000	$100,000	$1,546	$143	$1,759	-	-	$3,448	#72
	150,000	2,744	143	1,759	-	-	4,646	#110
	200,000	3,966	143	1,759	-	-	5,868	#122
$75,000	$150,000	$2,744	$143	$2,233	-	-	$5,120	#61
	250,000	5,424	143	2,233	-	-	7,800	#107
	350,000	8,339	143	2,233	-	-	10,715	#137
KERRVILLE								
$25,000	$75,000	$1,684	$140	$1,086	-	-	$2,910	#152
	100,000	2,348	140	1,086	-	-	3,574	#152
	125,000	3,013	140	1,086	-	-	4,239	#154 Ψ
$50,000	$100,000	$2,348	$140	$1,759	-	-	$4,247	#130
	150,000	3,678	140	1,759	-	-	5,577	#146
	200,000	5,007	140	1,759	-	-	6,906	#149
$75,000	$150,000	$3,678	$140	$2,233	-	-	$6,051	#101
	250,000	6,336	140	2,233	-	-	8,709	#136
	350,000	8,995	140	2,233	-	-	11,368	#143
SAN ANTONIO								
$25,000	$75,000	$1,332	$143	$1,037	-	-	$2,512	#134
	100,000	2,049	143	1,037	-	-	3,229	#146
	125,000	2,766	143	1,037	-	-	3,946	#151
$50,000	$100,000	$2,049	$143	$1,679	-	-	$3,871	#117
	150,000	3,483	143	1,679	-	-	5,305	#137
	200,000	4,917	143	1,679	-	-	6,739	#147
$75,000	$150,000	$3,483	$143	$2,132	-	-	$5,758	#87
	250,000	6,351	143	2,132	-	-	8,626	#133
	350,000	9,219	143	2,132	-	-	11,494	#144
THE WOODLANDS								
$25,000	$75,000	$1,354	$140	$955	-	-	$2,449	#129
	100,000	2,067	140	955	-	-	3,162	#143
	125,000	2,778	140	955	-	-	3,873	#149

*There are 163 cities in this book. The city with the lowest tax burden for an income/home value combination is given the #1 rating; the city with the highest total tax burden is given the #163 rating.

Income	Home Value	Property Tax & Other Fees	Personal Property Tax & Auto Fees	Sales Tax	Local Income Tax	State Income Tax	Total Tax Burden	Rank * From #1- #163
THE WOODLANDS continued								
$50,000	$100,000	$2,067	$140	$1,546	-	-	$3,753	#106
	150,000	3,493	140	1,546	-	-	5,179	#133
	200,000	4,923	140	1,546	-	-	6,609	#144
$75,000	$150,000	$3,493	$140	$1,963	-	-	$5,596	#81
	250,000	6,352	140	1,963	-	-	8,455	#130
	350,000	9,211	140	1,963	-	-	11,314	#141

*There are 163 cities in this book. The city with the lowest tax burden for an income/home value combination is given the #1 rating; the city with the highest total tax burden is given the #163 rating.

Austin

Austin has no local income tax but does levy a sales tax.

Most purchases are taxed at 8.25%. Major consumer categories taxed at a different rate: None. Major consumer categories that are exempt from sales tax include: Drugs, groceries and medical services.

Within the city limits of Austin, the property tax rate is .025319. Homes are assessed at 100% of market value. There are various exemptions off the city, community college, county and school district portions of the property tax. Property tax does not cover garbage pickup; the additional fee is approximately $204 per year. This amount also includes a solid waste fee and an anti-litter fee.

Austin has no personal property tax for individuals.

Our couples relocating to Austin must pay a registration fee of $72 per automobile, a title fee of $13 per automobile and a new resident fee of $90 per automobile at the time of registration. Thereafter, on an annual basis, our couples will pay a registration fee which includes a county road and bridge fee, per automobile.

Brownsville

Brownsville has no local income tax but does levy a sales tax.

Most purchases are taxed at a rate of 8.25%. Major consumer categories taxed at a different rate: None. Major consumer categories that are exempt from sales tax include: Drugs, groceries and medical services.

Within the city limits of Brownsville, the property tax rate is .02787088. Homes are assessed at 100% of market value. There are various exemptions off the city, county and school district portions of the property tax. Property tax does not cover garbage pickup; the additional fee is approximately $175 per year. Residents also pay approximately $54 per year for street maintenance and $30 per year for environmental fees.

Brownsville has no personal property tax for individuals.

Our couples relocating to Brownsville must pay a registration fee of $59 per automobile, a county road and bridge fee of $10 per automobile, a title fee of $13 per automobile and a new resident fee of $90 per automobile at the time of registration. Thereafter, on an annual basis, our couples will pay a registration fee and a county road and bridge fee, per automobile.

Dallas

Dallas has no local income tax but does levy a sales tax.

Most purchases are taxed at a rate of 8.25%. Major consumer categories taxed at a different rate: None. Major consumer categories that are exempt from sales tax include: Drugs, groceries and medical services.

In the Dallas Independent School District, the property tax rate is .02720697. Homes are assessed at 100% of market value. There are various exemptions off the city, community college, county, hospital and school district portions of the property tax. Property tax does not cover garbage pickup; the additional fee is approximately $148 per year.

Dallas has no personal property tax for individuals.

Our couples relocating to Dallas must pay a registration fee of $59 per automobile, a county road and bridge fee of $10 per automobile, an application fee of $13 per automobile, a new resident fee of $90 per automobile and an automated system enhancement fee of $1 per automobile at the time of registration. Thereafter, on an annual basis, our couples will pay a registration fee, a county road and bridge fee, and an automated system enhancement fee, per automobile.

Georgetown

Georgetown has no local income tax but does levy a sales tax.

Most purchases are taxed at a rate of 7.25%. Major consumer categories taxed at a different rate: None. Major consumer categories that are exempt from sales tax include: Drugs, groceries and medical services.

In the Sun City neighborhood of Georgetown, the property tax rate is .0244609. Homes are assessed at 100% of market value. There are exemptions off the school, farm and road, city and county portions of the property tax. Property tax does not cover garbage pickup; the additional fee, which includes recycling, is approximately $141 per year. There is also a stormwater drainage fee of approximately $27 per year. Property tax does not include the homeowners association fee for Sun City. The additional fee is approximately $725 per year, and benefits to homeowners include landscaping, club memberships, residential activities, and swimming and health facilities. We have not included the homeowners association fee in our calculations since it does not apply to all residents of Georgetown.

Georgetown has no personal property tax for individuals.

Our couples relocating to Georgetown must pay a registration fee of $59 per automobile, a county road and bridge fee of $12 per automobile, an application fee of $13 per automobile, a new resident fee of $90 per automobile and an automated system enhancement fee of $1 per automobile at the time of registration. Thereafter, on an annual basis, our couples will pay a registration fee, a county road and bridge fee, and an automated system enhancement fee, per automobile.

Houston

Houston has no local income tax but does levy a sales tax.

Most purchases are taxed at a rate of 8.25%. Major consumer categories taxed at a different rate: None. Major consumer categories that are exempt from sales tax include: Drugs, groceries and medical services.

In the Spring Branch Independent School District, the property tax rate is .03175353. Homes are assessed at 100% of market value. There are various exemptions off the city, county, community college and school district portions of the property tax. Property tax includes garbage pickup.

Houston has no personal property tax for individuals.

Our couples relocating to Houston must pay a registration fee of $59 per automobile, a county road and bridge fee of $12 per automobile, an application fee of $13 per automobile, a new resident fee of $90 per automobile and an automated system enhancement fee of $1 per automobile at the time of registration. Thereafter, on an annual basis, our couples will pay a registration fee, a county road and bridge fee, and an automated system enhancement fee, per automobile.

Kerrville

Kerrville has no local income tax but does levy a sales tax.

Most purchases are taxed at a rate of 8.25%. Major consumer categories taxed at a different rate: None. Major consumer categories that are exempt from sales tax include: Drugs, groceries and medical services.

Within the city limits of Kerrville, the property tax rate is .026586. Homes are assessed at 100% of market value. There are exemptions off the various components of the property tax. Property tax does not cover garbage pickup; the additional fee is approximately $149 per year.

Kerrville has no personal property tax for individuals.

Our couples relocating to Kerrville must pay a registration fee of $59 per automobile, a county road and bridge fee of $10 per automobile, an application fee of $13 per automobile, a new resident fee of $90 per automobile and an automated system enhancement fee of $1 per automobile at the time of registration. Thereafter, on an annual basis, our couples will pay a registration fee, a county road and bridge fee, and an automated system enhancement fee, per automobile.

San Antonio

San Antonio has no local income tax but does levy a sales tax.

Most purchases are taxed at a rate of 7.875%. Major consumer categories taxes at a different rate: None. Major consumer categories that are exempt from sales tax include: Drugs, groceries and medical services.

In the Alamo Heights School District, the property tax rate is .02868117. Homes are assessed at 100% of market value. There are exemptions off the various components of the property tax. Property tax does not cover garbage pickup; the additional fee is approximately $126 per year. This fee includes environmental fees, brush pickup and recycling fees.

San Antonio has no personal property tax for individuals.

Our couples relocating to San Antonio must pay a registration fee of $59 per automobile, a county road and bridge fee of $12 per automobile, an application fee of $13 per automobile, a new resident fee of $90 per automobile and an automated system enhancement fee of $1 per automobile at the time of registration. Thereafter, on an annual basis, our couples will pay a registration fee, a county road and bridge fee, and an automated system enhancement fee, per automobile.

The Woodlands

The Woodlands has no local income tax but does levy a sales tax.

Most purchases are taxed at a rate of 7.25%. Major consumer categories taxed at a different rate: None. Major consumer categories that are exempt from sales tax include: Drugs, groceries and medical services.

In the Alden Bridge neighborhood of The Woodlands, the property tax rate is .02859. Homes are assessed at 100% of market value. There are exemptions off the various components of the property tax. There is a homeowners association fee (rate) of .0057 of assessed home valuation. Homeowner benefits due to this fee include landscaping and maintenance, fire and emergency medical response, special programs, residential activities, and swimming and health facilities. The association fee also covers garbage pickup.

The Woodlands has no personal property tax for individuals.

Our couples relocating to The Woodlands must pay a registration fee of $59 per automobile, a county road and bridge fee of $10 per automobile, an application fee of $13 per automobile and a new resident fee of $90 per automobile at the time of registration. Thereafter, on an annual basis, our couples will pay a registration fee, a county road and bridge fee, and an automated system enhancement fee, per automobile.

• Texas' Best Retirement Towns •

Georgetown, Texas

Georgetown, 25 miles north of the state capital of Texas, may not be as well known as the town of the same name outside Washington, DC, but it also boasts an exceptionally pretty, resident-friendly, restored downtown. A few years ago its residents celebrated the town's 150th anniversary.

As if its Hill Country location, historical heritage as a cattle drive stopover, and proximity to the big city amenities of Austin were not enough incentive for relocating retirees, Del Webb Corp. set a Sun City master-planned community on its outskirts in 1995.

Harold and Jean Steadman had retired to Buchanan Dam, TX. When they heard Sun City was coming to Georgetown, they immediately registered to buy one of the first homes in the new community. "Health care, planned programs and outings, clean air, and a low crime rate get high marks," Harold says. "There are so many different things to do and opportunities to get involved. We'll never leave.

"This is my rest home," he adds.

Population: 26,400 in city, 235,000 in county.

Climate: High   Low
January   59   39
July   95   74

Cost of living: Below average (specific index not available).

Average price of a new home: $193,500

Security: 17.3 crimes per 1,000 residents, lower than the national average of 42.7 crimes per 1,000 residents.

Information: Georgetown Chamber of Commerce, P.O. Box 346, Georgetown, TX 78627-0346, (512) 930-3535 or www.georgetownchamber.org.

Kerrville, Texas

Set in the rolling terrain of the Texas Hill Country and bisected by the gentle Guadalupe River, the quiet town of Kerrville can be a surprise and relief to newcomers. With about one-third of its residents qualifying as senior citizens, Kerrville has all the desirable trappings, including a veterans hospital, liberal arts college (Schreiner University), master-planned country clubs and manufactured-housing communities, miles of hiking and biking trails and a low cost of living.

Elton "Al" Donaubauer was director of financial development at the University of Arkansas when he came down to Kerrville to speak to the Rotary Club. He liked what he saw of the people and surroundings, and 10 years later, he and wife Mauryne left Fayetteville to retire to the town they remembered so fondly.

What brought them here? "Climate was one thing," Al says. "Next to San Diego, it's the best year-round climate in the country. And the warm, friendly people — some of the best we've ever met. Cultural activities at Schreiner University were also high on the list," he adds.

Population: 19,818 in city, 42,623 in county.

Climate: High   Low
January   61   33
July   94   68

Cost of living: Below average (specific index not available).

Average price of a new home: $133,500

Security: 36.6 crimes per 1,000 residents, lower than the national average of 42.7 crimes per 1,000 residents.

Information: Kerrville Area Chamber of Commerce, 1700 Sidney Baker St., Suite 100, Kerrville, TX 78028, (830) 896-1155 or www.kerrvilletx.com.

Rio Grande Valley, Texas

The Rio Grande Valley of Texas covers an area larger than some states, lies farther south than most of the state of Florida, and its largest city, Brownsville, is at roughly the same latitude as Key West.

Its semitropical setting produces a climate conducive to prodigious growth of citrus fruits and vegetables, palms and bougainvillea. The wide, sandy beaches of South Padre Island and the fairways of numerous golf courses invite full-time residents and winter Texans alike to spend their days outdoors.

Mel and Sally Reeves leave Wichita, KS, each year at the first of November and head south to their home in Harlingen, where they live until the end of April. "Harlingen is a great place to spend the winter," Mel says. "An average day is filled with sunshine, and the coldest month of the year, January, has an average temperature of 60 degrees. We rarely spend a day indoors. We're golfers, but we have friends who go boating, fishing and hunting throughout the winter."

"We like to slip across the border into Matamoros to eat, shop and get a taste of Mexican culture," Sally says. "And South Padre Island is primarily a resort community, so it's a great place to hang out and soak up some sand and sun," she adds.

Population: 160,000 in Brownsville, 72,419 in Harlingen, and 120,000 in McAllen.

Climate: High   Low
January   68   48
July   94   74

Cost of living: 95 in Brownsville, 93 in Harlingen and 92 in McAllen, based on national average of 100.

Average price of a new home: $116,000

Security: 66.6 crimes per 1,000 residents, higher than the national average of 42.7 crimes per 1,000 residents.

Information: Harlingen Area Chamber of Commerce, 311 E. Tyler St., Harlingen, TX 78550, (800) 531-7346 or www.harlingen.com. Brownsville Chamber of Commerce, 1600 E. Elizabeth St., Brownsville, TX 78520, (956) 542-4341 or www.brownsvillechamber.com. McAllen Chamber of Commerce, 10 N. Broadway, McAllen, TX 78501, (956) 682-2871 or www.mcallenchamber.com.

San Antonio, Texas

Whether you've been to San Antonio or not, you probably "Remember the Alamo," having heard the phrase as a child. Once you visit, you aren't likely to forget any part of this memorable city. Even with more than a million inhabitants, it still exudes a small-town resort atmosphere and is popular with vacationers from across the country.

Market Square, with its farm market and dozens of arts and crafts shops, and the River Walk, a 2.5-mile waterway lined with restaurants, shops and parks, join the Alamo as landmarks of this enchanting city.

Ray and Barbara Clark were stationed near San Antonio while he served in the military. They returned to Indiana after his discharge to run a family business but vowed they would someday retire in Texas. Twenty-five years later they finally made it happen, and once here they promise not to leave again.

"It's beautiful country," Ray says. "The cost of living is much less than the Midwest. With no income tax, you're taxed on what you spend. It has tremendous medical facilities, and with the highway network, it's easy to travel. I'm having the time of my life — relaxing."

Population: 1,190,000 in city, 1,400,000 in county.

Climate:

	High	Low
January	61	38
July	95	75

Cost of living: 90, based on national average of 100.

Average price of a new home: $129,000

Security: 72.3 crimes per 1,000 residents, higher than the national average of 42.7 crimes per 1,000 residents.

Information: Greater San Antonio Chamber of Commerce, 602 E. Commerce St., P.O. Box 1628, San Antonio, TX 78296, (210) 229-2100 or www.sachamber.org.

The Woodlands, Texas

This unincorporated, master-planned community just 27 miles north of Houston has 65,000 inhabitants who share the dual benefits of a rural environment and the best of 21st-century ingenuity. Six villages, each with its own architectural style, community center, dining and shopping facilities, keep traffic flow to a minimum and neighborliness to a maximum. Only minutes away, a town center and mall with more than 400 retail and commercial businesses provides all of the goods and services residents need.

Tom and Marliese Jordan moved from the San Francisco Bay area to be near their daughter, who was already living in The Woodlands. They bought in the village of Windsor Hills, a 55-and-over community "full of friendly people, with a clubhouse that has become the center of our social life," Marliese says.

"The Woodlands is a wonderful place to live. It's not congested, is safe and has very little traffic so it's easy to get around. I'm trying to get a girlfriend from San Francisco to move here," she says.

Population: 65,000 in city, 200,000 in county.

Climate:

	High	Low
January	61	41
July	94	73

Cost of living: Below average (specific index not available).

Average price of a new home: $250,000

Security: 30 crimes per 1,000 residents in Montgomery County, lower than the national average of 42.7 crimes per 1,000 residents.

Information: South Montgomery County Woodlands Chamber of Commerce, 1400 Woodloch Forest Drive, Suite 500, The Woodlands, TX 77380, (281) 367-5777 or www.smcwcc.org.

UTAH

Tax Heavens O	Tax Hells Ψ	Top Retirement Towns
None	None	St. George

Utah has a state income tax and a state sales tax.

The state income tax rate is graduated from 2.3% to 7% depending upon income bracket. For married couples filing jointly, the rate is 2.3% for the first $1,500 of taxable income; the rate is 3.3% on the next $1,500 of taxable income; the rate is 4.2% on the next $1,500 of taxable income; the rate is 5.2% on the next $1,500 of taxable income; the rate is 6% on the next $1,500 of taxable income; and the rate is 7% on taxable income above $7,500.

Major tax credits or rebates include: Credit for taxes paid to other states. Our couples do not qualify for this program.

The state sales tax rate is 4.75%, but local governments can add to this amount.

Our couples relocating to the cities listed below must pay a registration fee of $36 per automobile; an annual uniform fee, which is based on the age of the vehicle, of $150 per automobile; and in Salt Lake City, an air pollution control fee of $3 per automobile at the time of registration. Thereafter, on an annual basis, our couples will pay a renewal fee, an annual uniform fee, and in Salt Lake City, an air pollution control fee. Recreational vehicles and motorcycles are also subject to an annual uniform fee, which is 1.5% of the taxable value of the vehicle.

St. George

St. George has no local income tax but does levy a sales tax.

Most purchases are taxed at a rate of

UTAH TAX TABLE

Instructions

1. Find the Income in the far left column closest to your anticipated retirement income.
2. Find the Home Value closest to the value of the home where you will live in retirement.
3. Follow that row to your estimated Total Tax Burden at age 65 and beyond.

Income	Home Value	Property Tax & Other Fees	Personal Property Tax & Auto Fees	Sales Tax	Local Income Tax	State Income Tax	Total Tax Burden	Rank* From #1- #163
ST. GEORGE								
$25,000	$75,000	$609	$349	$994	-	-	$1,952	#52
	100,000	767	349	994	-	-	2,110	#42
	125,000	926	349	994	-	-	2,269	#32
$50,000	$100,000	$768	$349	$1,554	-	$906	$3,577	#85
	150,000	1,084	349	1,554	-	906	3,893	#46
	200,000	1,401	349	1,554	-	906	4,210	#35
$75,000	$150,000	$1,084	$349	$1,943	-	$3,564	$6,940	#130
	250,000	1,718	349	1,943	-	3,564	7,574	#98
	350,000	2,351	349	1,943	-	3,564	8,207	#66
SALT LAKE CITY								
$25,000	$75,000	$703	$355	$1,009	-	-	$2,067	#71
	100,000	900	355	1,009	-	-	2,264	#56
	125,000	1,096	355	1,009	-	-	2,460	#51
$50,000	$100,000	$900	$355	$1,578	-	$906	$3,739	#104
	150,000	1,292	355	1,578	-	906	4,131	#66
	200,000	1,685	355	1,578	-	906	4,524	#51
$75,000	$150,000	$1,292	$355	$1,974	-	$3,564	$7,185	#135
	250,000	2,078	355	1,974	-	3,564	7,971	#116
	350,000	2,863	355	1,974	-	3,564	8,756	#85

*There are 163 cities in this book. The city with the lowest tax burden for an income/home value combination is given the #1 rating; the city with the highest total tax burden is given the #163 rating.

6.25%. Major consumer categories taxed at a different rate include: Food away from home, which is taxed at a rate of 7.25%. Major consumer categories that are exempt from sales tax include: Drugs, medical supplies, and medical services.

Within the city limits of St. George, the property tax rate is .01152. Homes are assessed at 55% of market value. There is a state tax relief program that has four components: circuit breaker property tax credit available to residents 65 or older with a gross income below $22,422; indigent tax relief available to residents 65 or older with a gross income below $22,422; veteran's exemption; and blind exemption. Our couples do not qualify for these programs. Property tax does not cover garbage pickup; the additional fee is approximately $116 per year. There is also a drainage fee of $18 per year.

Salt Lake City

Salt Lake City has no local income tax but does levy a sales tax.

Most purchases are taxed at a rate of 6.35%. Major consumer categories taxed at a different rate include: Food away from home, which is taxed at a rate of 7.35%. Major consumer categories that are exempt from sales tax include: Drugs, medical supplies and medical services.

Within the city limits of Salt Lake City, the property tax rate is .0142820. Homes are assessed at 55% of market value. There is a state tax relief program that has four components: circuit breaker property tax credit available to residents 65 or older with a gross income below $22,422; indigent tax relief available to residents 65 or older with a gross income below $22,422; veteran's exemption; and blind exemption. Our couples do not qualify for these programs. Property tax does not cover garbage pickup; the additional fee is approximately $114 per year.

• Utah's Best Retirement Town •

St. George, Utah

Twenty-five years ago, few people outside of Utah had ever heard of St. George — even though Mormon leader Brigham Young had directed its settlement in the mid-1800s and had a winter home there.

Once a quiet village built around the stark white St. George Temple and set among the sandstone cliffs of southwest Utah, it has become a thriving, booming retirement and tourist destination, transportation hub and major new job market.

Clean air, blue skies and a moderate climate invite year-round golf and outdoor activities — though summer temperatures can reach a hot, dry 100 degrees. Deep river gorges and tall mountain peaks provide diversity and scenic beauty to the surrounding landscape and a playground for amateur archaeologists to practice their avocation.

Chris and Polly Snider of Raleigh, NC, visited friends in St. George for several years and "couldn't wait for the next visit," Chris says. "We knew we didn't want to live anyplace but southwest Utah. We've hiked and climbed in all of the state and national parks in the area, and there's still incredible beauty waiting to be discovered in the valleys and canyons we haven't visited."

"It's getting busier and more crowded, but there's lots of room for growth," Polly says. "It's big country around here — come on out."

Population: 52,000 in city, 85,000 in county.

Climate:

	High	Low
January	53	26
July	102	66

Cost of living: 93, based on national average of 100.

Average price of a new home: $154,900

Security: 35.7 crimes per 1,000 residents, lower than the national average of 42.7 crimes per 1,000 residents.

Information: St. George Chamber of Commerce, 97 E. St. George Blvd., St. George, UT 84770, (435) 673-1587 or www.stgeorgechamber.com.

VERMONT

Tax Heavens O
None

Tax Hells Ψ
None

Top Retirement Towns
None

Vermont has a state income tax and a state sales tax.

The state income tax rate is 24% of federal tax liability.

Major tax credits or rebates include: Credit for taxes paid to other states, credit for elderly or disabled and renter rebate. Our couples do not qualify for these programs. There is also a homeowner property tax rebate and an additional property tax rebate if household income is $47,000 or less. All of our couples qualify for the homeowner property tax rebate and some of our couples qualify for the additional property tax rebate.

The state sales tax rate is 5%.

VERMONT TAX TABLE

Instructions

1. Find the Income in the far left column closest to your anticipated retirement income.
2. Find the Home Value closest to the value of the home where you will live in retirement.
3. Follow that row to your estimated Total Tax Burden at age 65 and beyond.

Income	Home Value	Property Tax & Other Fees	Personal Property Tax & Auto Fees	Sales Tax	Local Income Tax	State Income Tax[†]	Total Tax Burden	Rank[*] From #1- #163
BURLINGTON								
$25,000	$75,000	$2,019	$86	$712	-	($529)	$2,288	#106
	100,000	2,571	86	712	-	(1,083)	2,286	#59
	125,000	3,124	86	712	-	(1,635)	2,287	#35
$50,000	$100,000	$2,571	$86	$1,150	-	$763	$4,570	#142
	150,000	3,677	86	1,150	-	72	4,985	#126
	200,000	4,783	86	1,150	-	(626)	5,393	#104
$75,000	$150,000	$3,677	$86	$1,460	-	$2,197	$7,420	#143
	250,000	5,889	86	1,460	-	803	8,238	#123
	350,000	8,100	86	1,460	-	(591)	9,055	#98

[†]Property tax rebate is issued as a reduction of income tax due or as a refund if the credit is greater than the tax liability.
[*]There are 163 cities in this book. The city with the lowest tax burden for an income/home value combination is given the #1 rating; the city with the highest total tax burden is given the #163 rating.

Burlington

Burlington has no local income tax and does not levy an additional sales tax.

Most purchases are taxed at the state rate of 5%. Major consumer categories taxed at a different rate include: Food away from home, which is taxed at a rate of 9%. Major consumer categories that are exempt from sales tax include: Groceries, medical supplies, medical services and drugs.

Within the city limits of Burlington, the property tax rate is .022114. Homes are assessed at 100% of market value. Property tax does not cover garbage pickup; the additional fee is approximately $360 per year.

Burlington has no personal property tax for individuals.

Our couples relocating to Burlington may be subject to a use tax per automobile depending on the amount of tax paid in the state in which the vehicle was purchased. If sales tax of at least 6% was paid in another state at the time of purchase, no additional tax is due. If less than 6% was paid, the owner is required to pay the difference. We've assumed our couples have paid tax greater than or equal to the use tax. Our couples must pay a registration fee of $43 per automobile, a title fee of $10 per automobile and a lien fee of $5 per automobile at the time of registration. Thereafter, on an annual basis, our couples will pay a renewal fee per automobile.

VIRGINIA

Tax Heavens O	Tax Hells ψ	Top Retirement Towns
Williamsburg	None	Abingdon
		Charlottesville
		Williamsburg

Virginia has a state income tax and a state sales tax.

The state income tax rate is graduated from 2% to 5.75% depending upon income bracket. For married couples filing jointly, the rate is 2% on the first $3,000 of taxable income; the rate is 3% on the next $2,000 of taxable income; the rate is 5% on the next $12,000 of taxable income; and the rate is 5.75% on taxable income above $17,000.

In calculating the tax, there is no deduction for federal income tax paid. Federal, state and private pensions are not exempt. Social Security benefits are exempt. There is a $5,000 standard deduction from adjusted gross income for married couples filing jointly. There is an $800 personal exemption from adjusted gross income per person plus an $800 personal exemption from adjusted gross income per person for residents age 65 or older. There is an age deduction from income of $6,000 per person age 62-64 or $12,000 per person age 65 or older.

Major tax credits or rebates include: Credit for income taxes paid to other states and low-income tax credit, which our couples do not qualify for, and a spouse tax adjustment credit, which one of our couples qualifies for.

The state sales tax rate is 3.5%, but local governments can add to this amount.

Our couples relocating to the cities

VIRGINIA TAX TABLE

Instructions

1. Find the Income in the far left column closest to your anticipated retirement income.
2. Find the Home Value closest to the value of the home where you will live in retirement.
3. Follow that row to your estimated Total Tax Burden at age 65 and beyond.

Income	Home Value	Property Tax & Other Fees	Personal Property Tax & Auto Fees	Sales Tax	Local Income Tax	State Income Tax	Total Tax Burden	Rank* From #1-#163
ABINGDON								
$25,000	$75,000	$855	$291	$760	-	-	$1,906	#42
	100,000	1,105	291	760	-	-	2,156	#45
	125,000	1,355	291	760	-	-	2,406	#47
$50,000	$100,000	$1,105	$291	$1,195	-	$84	$2,675	#13
	150,000	1,605	291	1,195	-	84	3,175	#13
	200,000	2,105	291	1,195	-	84	3,675	#12
$75,000	$150,000	$1,605	$291	$1,483	-	$1,053	$4,432	#31
	250,000	2,605	291	1,483	-	1,053	5,432	#20
	350,000	3,605	291	1,483	-	1,053	6,432	#20
CHARLOTTESVILLE								
$25,000	$75,000	$868	$529	$743	-	-	$2,140	#87
	100,000	1,145	529	743	-	-	2,417	#75
	125,000	1,423	529	743	-	-	2,695	#70
$50,000	$100,000	$1,145	$529	$1,170	-	$84	$2,928	#27
	150,000	1,700	529	1,170	-	84	3,483	#28
	200,000	2,255	529	1,170	-	84	4,038	#29
$75,000	$150,000	$1,700	$529	$1,455	-	$1,053	$4,737	#49
	250,000	2,810	529	1,455	-	1,053	5,847	#34
	350,000	3,920	529	1,455	-	1,053	6,957	#33

*There are 163 cities in this book. The city with the lowest tax burden for an income/home value combination is given the #1 rating; the city with the highest total tax burden is given the #163 rating.

VIRGINIA TAX TABLE

Instructions

1. Find the Income in the far left column closest to your anticipated retirement income.
2. Find the Home Value closest to the value of the home where you will live in retirement.
3. Follow that row to your estimated Total Tax Burden at age 65 and beyond.

Income	Home Value	Property Tax & Other Fees	Personal Property Tax & Auto Fees	Sales Tax	Local Income Tax	State Income Tax	Total Tax Burden	Rank* From #1- #163
RICHMOND								
$25,000	$75,000	$1,209	$610	$775	-	-	$2,594	#141
	100,000	1,566	610	775	-	-	2,951	#134
	125,000	1,924	610	775	-	-	3,309	#128
$50,000	$100,000	$1,566	$610	$1,219	-	$84	$3,479	#75
	150,000	2,281	610	1,219	-	84	4,194	#77
	200,000	2,996	610	1,219	-	84	4,909	#73
$75,000	$150,000	$2,281	$610	$1,512	-	$1,053	$5,456	#79
	250,000	3,711	610	1,512	-	1,053	6,886	#71
	350,000	5,141	610	1,512	-	1,053	8,316	#70
WILLIAMSBURG								
$25,000	$75,000	$405	$450	$775	-	-	$1,630	#19
	100,000	540	450	775	-	-	1,765	#14
	125,000	675	450	775	-	-	1,900	#9 ⭕
$50,000	$100,000	$540	$450	$1,219	-	$84	$2,293	#4 ⭕
	150,000	810	450	1,219	-	84	2,563	#2 ⭕
	200,000	1,080	450	1,219	-	84	2,833	#2 ⭕
$75,000	$150,000	$810	$450	$1,512	-	$1,053	$3,825	#10 ⭕
	250,000	1,350	450	1,512	-	1,053	4,365	#4 ⭕
	350,000	1,890	450	1,512	-	1,053	4,905	#4 ⭕

*There are 163 cities in this book. The city with the lowest tax burden for an income/home value combination is given the #1 rating; the city with the highest total tax burden is given the #163 rating.

listed below must pay a title fee of $10 per automobile and a registration fee of $27 per automobile at the time of registration. Thereafter, on an annual basis, our couples will pay a renewal fee per automobile.

Abingdon

Abingdon has no local income tax but does levy a sales tax.

Most purchases are taxed at a rate of 4.5%. Major consumer categories taxed at a different rate include: Groceries, which are taxed at a rate of 4%, and food away from home, which is taxed at a rate of 8.5%. Major consumer categories that are exempt from sales tax include: Drugs and medical services.

Within the town of Abingdon, the property tax rate is .01. Homes are assessed at 100% of market value. There is a senior citizen exemption for homeowners age 65 or older with gross

income of $12,000 or less and net worth of $30,000 or less, excluding home value. Property tax does not cover garbage pickup; the additional fee is approximately $105 per year.

Abingdon has a personal property tax rate of .021. Personal property is assessed at 100% of loan value. Mobile homes, however, are taxed at the property tax rate of .01 and assessed at 100% of market value. There is a personal property tax relief of 47.5% off the first $20,000 of assessed value for automobiles. No tax is due for automobiles valued at $1,000 or less. Items subject to the tax include: Automobiles, boats, trailers, motorcycles, airplanes and farm equipment.

Charlottesville

Charlottesville has no local income tax but does levy a sales tax.

Most purchases are taxed at a rate of

4.5%. Major consumer categories taxed at a different rate include: Groceries, which are taxed at a rate of 4%, and food away from home, which is taxed at a rate of 7.5%. Major consumer categories that are exempt from sales tax include: Drugs and medical services.

Within the city limits of Charlottesville, the property tax rate is .0111. Homes are assessed at 100% of market value. There is a senior citizen exemption for homeowners age 65 or older with gross income of $22,000 or less and net worth of $75,000 or less, excluding home value. Property tax does not cover garbage pickup; the additional fee is approximately $35 per year.

Charlottesville has a personal property tax rate of .0420. Personal property is assessed at 100% of NADA loan value. Mobile homes, however, are taxed at the property tax rate of .0111 and assessed at 100% of market value. There is a personal property tax relief of 47.5% off the first $20,000 of assessed value for automobiles. No tax is due for vehicles valued at $1,000 or less. Items subject to the tax include: Automobiles, boats, trailers, motorcycles, airplanes and farm equipment.

Richmond

Richmond has no local income tax but does levy a sales tax.

Most purchases are taxed at a rate of 4.5%. Major consumer categories taxed at a different rate include: Groceries, which are taxed at a rate of 4%, and food away from home, which is taxed at a rate of 9.5%. Major consumer categories that are exempt from sales tax include: Drugs and medical services.

Within the city limits of Richmond, the property tax rate is .0143. Homes are assessed at 100% of market value. There is a senior citizen exemption for homeowners age 65 or older with gross income of $20,000 or less and net worth of $100,000 or less, excluding home value. Property tax does not cover garbage pickup; the additional fee is approximately $136 per year.

Richmond has a personal property tax rate of .0370. Personal property is assessed at 100% of NADA trade-in value. Mobile homes, however, are taxed at the property tax rate of .0143 and assessed at 100% of market value. There is a personal property tax relief of 47.5% off the first $20,000 of assessed value for automobiles. No tax is due for automobiles valued at $1,000 or less. Items subject to the tax include: Automobiles, boats, trailers, motorcycles, airplanes and farm equipment.

Williamsburg

Williamsburg has no local income tax but does levy a sales tax.

Most purchases are taxed at a rate of 4.5%. Major consumer categories taxed at a different rate include: Groceries, which are taxed at a rate of 4%, and food away from home, which is taxed at a rate of 9.5%. Major consumer categories that are exempt from sales tax include: Drugs and medical services.

Within the city limits of Williamsburg, the property tax rate is .0054. Homes are assessed at 100% of market value. There is a senior citizen exemption for homeowners age 65 or older with gross income of $20,000 or less and net worth of $75,000 or less, excluding home value. Property tax includes garbage pickup.

Williamsburg has a personal property tax rate of .0350. Personal property is assessed at 100% of loan value. Mobile homes, however, are taxed at the property tax rate of .0054 and assessed at 100% of market value. There is a personal property tax relief of 47.5% off the first $20,000 of assessed value for automobiles. No tax is due for automobiles valued at $1,000 or less. Items subject to the tax include: Automobiles, boats, trailers, motorcycles, airplanes and farm equipment.

• Virginia's Best Retirement Towns •

Abingdon, Virginia

Until recent years, the oldest town west of the Blue Ridge Mountains, chartered in 1778, was little-known outside the region because of its isolated, hard-to-reach location in the mountains of southwest Virginia. The former Martha Washington College for Women and renowned Barter Theatre, one of the longest-running theaters in America, were the primary attractions bringing visitors to its doors.

The opening of Interstate 81 allowed the region to be discovered by more travelers. Today Abingdon's 20-block historic district, William King Regional Arts Center, 1832 Martha Washington Inn, Barter Theatre, the annual Virginia Highlands Festival and nearby Mount Rogers National Recreation Area, site of the highest mountains in Virginia, draw tourists from across the Southeast and beyond.

Carl and Lou Atwater were accustomed to driving up Interstate 81 from their home in Nashville to attend stage productions at the old Barter Theatre, and they wasted no time after retirement making the move a permanent one. "We liked the size of the town, its historic past and lively present. There's a lot going on here," Lou says. "You can watch artists at work, attend plays at the Barter, dine in some really unique downtown restaurants or shop at Dixie Pottery, among others," she says.

"Or go hiking on Mount Rogers in the fall while the leaves are turning. You'll see some of the prettiest mountains in the country," Carl adds.

Population: 7,500 in city, 48,000 in county.

Climate:

	High	Low
January	43	24
July	84	64

Cost of living: Below average (specific index not available.)

Average price of a new home: $139,900

Security: 35.2 crimes per 1,000 residents, lower than the national average of 42.7 crimes per 1,000 residents.

Information: Washington County Chamber of Commerce, 179 E. Main St., Abingdon, VA 24210, (540) 628-8141 or www.washingtonvachamber.org.

Charlottesville, Virginia

Tucked into the scenic Shenandoah Valley with the undulating peaks and valleys of the Blue Ridge Mountains to the west and flatlands of the Tidewater Region falling away to the east, this town is blessed with natural and man-made amenities.

They include the University of Virginia, architecturally crafted by President Thomas Jefferson, and a beautifully restored, pedestrian-friendly downtown mall. Charlottesville has an outstanding historical legacy, having served as the home of three American presidents, and an excellent location conducive to rural escapes in less than 30 minutes and forays into busy Washington, DC, in about two hours.

A widely traveled couple, Brian and Jean Mandeville of Minneapolis, MN, retired to Charlottesville "hoping to find new opportunities in the next step on life's journey," Brian says. "We fell in love with Charlottesville — the size of the town, its four-season climate, its topography, the general environment, charm and heritage."

"And the people," Jean adds. "The wonderful, grand, friendly, well-mannered people."

Population: 40,500 in city, 80,000 in county.

Climate:

	High	Low
January	43	26
July	87	66

Cost of living: Below average (specific index not available).

Average price of a new home: $149,500

Security: 60.6 crimes per 1,000 residents, higher than the national average of 42.7 crimes per 1,000 residents.

Information: Charlottesville Regional Chamber of Commerce, P.O. Box 1564, Charlottesville, VA 22902, (804) 295-3141 or www.cvillechamber.org.

Williamsburg, Virginia

If you're a dyed-in-the-wool history buff and would like to live in the shadow of the nation's beginnings, this is the place to be. In 1607, America's first permanent English colony was started in Jamestown. In 1781, the decisive battle for the nation's independence was fought — and won — at Yorktown. And Williamsburg, the third point in this historic triangle, was the political and economic center of the Virginia Colony. Today, it is a restored, living replica of the town's past.

A 7,600-strong student body at the College of William and Mary helps enliven the spirit of the community, while Colonial Williamsburg attracts a steady stream of visitors from around the world, ensuring economic stability and prosperity for the area.

"In two words, it's wonderful," says Arlene Geldreich. She and husband Richard retired to Ford's Colony, four miles outside of Williamsburg, in 1994 after living in Ohio, California and New Jersey. "You can do anything your heart desires. The community offers everything and it has the cleanest air we've ever lived in," she adds.

"It's a great location for travel to the beach, mountains or major city," says Richard. "The entire peninsula is a historic treasure. Come take a look."

Population: 15,000 plus about 7,600 students in city, 58,000 in York County and 48,000 in James City County.

Climate:

	High	Low
January	48	27
July	88	67

Cost of living: Average (specific index not available).

Average price of a new home: $252,000

Security: 39.2 crimes per 1,000 residents, lower than the national average of 42.7 crimes per 1,000 residents.

Information: Williamsburg Area Chamber of Commerce, P.O. Box 3620, Williamsburg, VA 23187-3620, (800) 368-6511 or www.williamsburgcc.com.

WASHINGTON

<table>
<tr><td>

Tax Heavens O

Friday Harbor
Oak Harbor

</td><td>

Tax Hells Ψ

None

</td><td>

Top Retirement Towns

Port Townsend
San Juan Islands
Sequim
Whidbey Island

</td></tr>
</table>

Washington has no state income tax but does have a state sales tax.

Major tax credits or rebates: None. The state sales tax rate is 6.5%, but local governments can add to this amount.

Since car registration and renewal fees differ within the state, see city information for details.

WASHINGTON TAX TABLE

Instructions

1. Find the Income in the far left column closest to your anticipated retirement income.
2. Find the Home Value closest to the value of the home where you will live in retirement.
3. Follow that row to your estimated Total Tax Burden at age 65 and beyond.

Income	Home Value	Property Tax & Other Fees	Personal Property Tax & Auto Fees	Sales Tax	Local Income Tax	State Income Tax	Total Tax Burden	Rank* From #1-#163
FRIDAY HARBOR								
$25,000	$75,000	$587	$66	$1,014	-	-	$1,667	#22
	100,000	767	66	1,014	-	-	1,847	#17
	125,000	920	66	1,014	-	-	2,000	#13
$50,000	$100,000	$1,255	$66	$1,642	-	-	$2,963	#29
	150,000	1,715	66	1,642	-	-	3,423	#26
	200,000	2,176	66	1,642	-	-	3,884	#22
$75,000	$150,000	$1,715	$66	$2,084	-	-	$3,865	#11
	250,000	2,636	66	2,084	-	-	4,786	#9 O
	350,000	3,557	66	2,084	-	-	5,707	#10 O
OAK HARBOR								
$25,000	$75,000	$450	$66	$1,093	-	-	$1,609	#16
	100,000	633	66	1,093	-	-	1,792	#16
	125,000	788	66	1,093	-	-	1,947	#10 O
$50,000	$100,000	$1,229	$66	$1,770	-	-	$3,065	#36
	150,000	1,746	66	1,770	-	-	3,582	#32
	200,000	2,263	66	1,770	-	-	4,099	#33
$75,000	$150,000	$1,746	$66	$2,247	-	-	$4,059	#13
	250,000	2,779	66	2,247	-	-	5,092	#14
	350,000	3,813	66	2,247	-	-	6,126	#14
PORT TOWNSEND								
$25,000	$75,000	$540	$66	$1,080	-	-	$1,686	#25
	100,000	749	66	1,080	-	-	1,895	#21
	125,000	927	66	1,080	-	-	2,073	#16

*There are 163 cities in this book. The city with the lowest tax burden for an income/home value combination is given the #1 rating; the city with the highest total tax burden is given the #163 rating.

Income	Home Value	Property Tax & Other Fees	Personal Property Tax & Auto Fees	Sales Tax	Local Income Tax	State Income Tax	Total Tax Burden	Rank* From #1 - #163
PORT TOWNSEND continued								
$50,000	$100,000	$1,461	$66	$1,748	-	-	$3,275	#55
	150,000	2,068	66	1,748	-	-	3,882	#45
	200,000	2,676	66	1,748	-	-	4,490	#47
$75,000	$150,000	$2,068	$66	$2,220	-	-	$4,354	#25
	250,000	3,283	66	2,220	-	-	5,569	#26
	350,000	4,498	66	2,220	-	-	6,784	#28
SEATTLE								
$25,000	$75,000	$608	$202	$1,167	-	-	$1,977	#58
	100,000	815	202	1,167	-	-	2,184	#47
	125,000	991	202	1,167	-	-	2,360	#44
$50,000	$100,000	$1,462	$202	$1,889	-	-	$3,553	#82
	150,000	2,035	202	1,889	-	-	4,126	#64
	200,000	2,607	202	1,889	-	-	4,698	#60
$75,000	$150,000	$2,035	$202	$2,397	-	-	$4,634	#42
	250,000	3,180	202	2,397	-	-	5,779	#31
	350,000	4,325	202	2,397	-	-	6,924	#31
SEQUIM								
$25,000	$75,000	$578	$66	$1,080	-	-	$1,724	#27
	100,000	812	66	1,080	-	-	1,958	#24
	125,000	1,012	66	1,080	-	-	2,158	#26
$50,000	$100,000	$1,419	$66	$1,748	-	-	$3,233	#50
	150,000	2,003	66	1,748	-	-	3,817	#39
	200,000	2,588	66	1,748	-	-	4,402	#40
$75,000	$150,000	$2,003	$66	$2,220	-	-	$4,289	#22
	250,000	3,172	66	2,220	-	-	5,458	#21
	350,000	4,341	66	2,220	-	-	6,627	#23

*There are 163 cities in this book. The city with the lowest tax burden for an income/home value combination is given the #1 rating; the city with the highest total tax burden is given the #163 rating.

Friday Harbor

Friday Harbor has no local income tax but does levy a sales tax.

Most purchases are taxed at a rate of 7.7%. Major consumer categories taxed at a different rate: None. Major consumer categories that are exempt from sales tax include: Medical services, drugs and groceries.

Within the city limits of Friday Harbor, the property tax rate is .00920764. Homes are assessed at 100% of market value. There is a homeowner's exemption available to homeowners age 61 or older with a gross income of $30,000 or less. This exemption exempts the homeowner from excess levies, resulting in a property tax rate of .00721422; there are various other statewide exemptions that are available to homeowners age 61 or older with gross income below $24,000.

Property tax does not cover garbage pickup; the additional fee is approximately $255 per year. Homeowners also pay a storm water utilities fee, which averages $79 per year.

Friday Harbor has no personal property tax for individuals.

Our couples relocating to Friday Harbor must pay a combined transfer and registration fee of $60 per automobile at the time of registration. Thereafter, on an annual basis, our couples will pay a renewal fee per automobile.

Oak Harbor

Oak Harbor has no local income tax but does levy a sales tax.

Most purchases are taxed at a rate of 8.3%. Major consumer categories taxed at a different rate: None. Major consumer categories that are exempt from sales tax include: Medical services, drugs and groceries.

Within the city limits of Oak Harbor, the property tax rate is .0103377. Homes are assessed at 100% of market value. There is a homeowner's exemption available to homeowners age 61 or older with a gross income of $30,000 or less. This exemption exempts the homeowner from excess levies, resulting in a property tax rate of .00729671; there are various other statewide exemptions that are available to homeowners age 61 or older with gross income below $24,000. Property tax does not cover garbage pickup; the additional fee is approximately $195 per year.

Oak Harbor has no personal property tax for individuals.

Our couples relocating to Oak Harbor must pay a registration fee of

$61 per automobile at the time of registration. Thereafter, on an annual basis, our couples will pay a renewal fee per automobile.

Port Townsend

Port Townsend has no local income tax but does levy a sales tax.

Most purchases are taxed at a rate of 8.2%. Major consumer categories taxed at a different rate: None. Major consumer categories that are exempt from sales tax include: Medical services, drugs and groceries.

Within the city limits of Port Townsend, the property tax rate is .01214877. Homes are assessed at 100% of market value. There is a homeowner's exemption available to homeowners age 61 or older with a gross income of $30,000 or less. This exemption exempts the homeowner from excess levies, resulting in a property tax rate of .008385633; there are various other statewide exemptions that are available to homeowners age 61 or older with gross income below $24,000. Property tax does not cover garbage pickup; the additional fee is approximately $174 per year. Homeowners also pay a storm water utilities fee, which averages $72 per year.

Port Townsend has no personal property tax for individuals.

Our couples relocating to Port Townsend must pay a combined transfer and registration fee of $61 per automobile at the time of registration. Thereafter, on an annual basis, our couples will pay a renewal fee per automobile.

Seattle

Seattle has no local income tax but does levy a sales tax.

Most purchases are taxed at a rate of 8.8%. Major consumer categories taxed at a different rate: Food away from home, which is taxed at a rate of 9.3%. Major consumer categories that are exempt from sales tax include: Medical services, drugs and groceries.

Within the city limits of Seattle, the property tax rate is .01145. Homes are assessed at 100% of market value. There is a homeowner's exemption available to homeowners age 61 or older with a gross income of $30,000 or less. This exemption exempts the homeowner from excess levies, resulting in a property tax rate of .00830; there are various other statewide exemptions that are available to homeowners age 61 or older with gross income below $24,000. Property tax does not cover garbage pickup; the additional fee is approximately $193 per year. Homeowners also pay a yard waste fee of $51 per year and a storm water drainage fee of $73 per year.

Seattle has no personal property tax for individuals.

Our couples relocating to Seattle must pay a registration fee of $134 for the Explorer and $124 for the Cutlass at the time of registration. These include a license fee of $30 per automobile, a local fee of $15 per automobile, a Regional Transit Authority (RTA) excise tax based upon the year, make and model of the automobile of $58 for the Explorer and $48 for the Cutlass, an inspection fee of $15 per automobile and other miscellaneous fees of $16 per automobile. Thereafter, on an annual basis, our couples will pay a license fee, a local fee, a filing fee and an RTA excise tax, per automobile.

Sequim

Sequim has no local income tax but does levy a sales tax.

Most purchases are taxed at a rate of 8.2%. Major consumer categories taxed at a different rate: None. Major consumer categories that are exempt from sales tax include: Medical services, drugs and groceries.

Within the city limits of Sequim, the property tax rate is .01168853. Homes are assessed at 100% of market value. There is a homeowner's exemption available to homeowners age 61 or older with a gross income of $30,000 or less. This exemption exempts the homeowner from excess levies, resulting in a property tax rate of .00937350; there are various other statewide exemptions that are available to homeowners age 61 or older with gross income below $24,000. Property tax does not cover garbage pickup; the additional fee is approximately $250 per year.

Sequim has no personal property tax for individuals.

Our couples relocating to Sequim must pay a registration fee of $61 per automobile at the time of registration. Thereafter, on an annual basis, our couples will pay a renewal fee per automobile.

• Washington's Best Retirement Towns •

Port Townsend, Washington

The busy harbor, with colorful sails wafting in a gentle breeze, was once the lifeblood of this seafaring town. A variety of housing sites overlook the town and bay, offering spectacular views of the distant Strait of Juan de Fuca and nearby Admiralty Inlet. Navy and merchant ships navigate slowly through inlet waters as they pass to berths in Puget Sound.

The town has a mystic quality, perhaps emanating from its past, when old sea captains quaffed ale in its taverns and braved rough seas, bent on establishing the center of shipping and commerce in the Northwest. But part of the creative energy flows from a large, active retiree population as they apply varied and considerable talents to the task of improving their adopted home.

Philip and Janet Flynn spent 35 years in Sacramento and more than a year in Victoria, Canada, before they found just the perfect spot for their dream home — "a 330-foot lot fronting Admiralty Inlet, where every ship entering Puget Sound passes directly in front of our home," Philip says.

"We have wonderful weather here in the rain shadow of the Olympic Mountains, and a spectacular view," Janet says. "Port Townsend is clean, there's little traffic and it's practically crime-free. Shopping was a happy surprise," she adds. "We have a wonderful market just 10 minutes away."

Population: 8,200 in city, 25,000 in county.

Climate:	High	Low
January	46	37
July	72	51

Cost of living: Above average (specific index not available).

Average price of a new home: $172,000

Security: 40.9 crimes per 1,000 residents, lower than the national average of 42.7 crimes per 1,000 residents.

Information: Port Townsend Chamber of Commerce, 2437 E. Sims Way, Port Townsend, WA 98368, (360) 385-7869 or www.ptchamber.org.

San Juan Islands, Washington

Friday Harbor, with about 1,800 residents, is the largest settlement in the San Juans, a cluster of islands in northwest Washington. A two-and-a-half-hour ferry ride out of Anacortes is the scourge of the islands for the impatient traveler and the salvation for those who cherish isolation.

The little ferry dockage is only a few blocks long, comprised of restaurants, motels and tourist shops. Hospital facilities are available on the mainland via helicopter for a small annual fee.

A low crime rate, excellent weather, friendly people and seclusion are cited as the major reasons people live here, and many are protective of their lifestyle. "It's time to pull up the drawbridge," says Dick Fales. "Please tell people it rains a lot," says Eugene Richey. Both men cherish the safety and solitude of the islands.

Population: 1,800 in Friday Harbor. Total population of the San Juan Islands is 14,000.

Climate:

	High	Low
January	44	35
July	70	50

Cost of living: Above average (specific index not available).

Average price of a new home: $265,000

Security: 17.9 crimes per 1,000 residents in San Juan County, lower than the national average of 42.7 crimes per 1,000 residents.

Information: San Juan Island Chamber of Commerce, P.O. Box 98, Friday Harbor, WA 98250, (360) 378-5240 or www.sanjuanisland.org. Orcas Island Chamber of Commerce, P.O. Box 252, Eastsound, Orcas Island, WA 98245-0252, (360) 376-3766 or www.orcasisland.org. Lopez Island Chamber of Commerce, P.O. Box 102, Lopez, WA 98261, (360) 468-4664 or www.lopezisland.com.

Sequim, Washington

Nestled between the 8,000-foot peaks of the Olympic Mountains and the picturesque Strait of Juan de Fuca, Sequim (pronounced Skwim) is strategically located along the northern gateway to remote reaches of Washington's Olympic Peninsula. This quaint seaside hamlet, where mammoths and mastodons once grazed, has become a magnet for relocating retirees. Catalysts are the scenic beauty of the area combined with the upbeat, positive outlook of its people.

Byron and Barbara Nelson retired to Sequim five years ago and are enjoying their lifestyle more every day. "It's a unique, wonderful community with a serene, peaceful, friendly atmosphere and incredibly clean air," Byron says. "I can stand at my back door and watch a herd of elk grazing in the distance."

Population: 4,200 in city; 65,000 in county.

Climate:

	High	Low
January	46	32
July	71	52

Cost of living: Above average (specific index not available).

Average price of a new home: $139,500

Security: 47.4 crimes per 1,000 residents, higher than the national average of 42.7 crimes per 1,000 residents.

Information: Sequim-Dungeness Chamber of Commerce, P.O. Box 907, Sequim, WA 98382-0907, (800) 737-8462 or www.cityofsequim.com.

Whidbey Island, Washington

Accessed by highway from the north, or a one-and-a-half-hour ferry ride from Port Townsend to the south, Whidbey Island especially appeals to those seeking refuge from the faster-paced life on the mainland. Its landscape is distinguished by blue-water coves, green farmlands, towering oaks and Douglas firs.

Oak Harbor, the largest of the island's towns, has a medical clinic, small community college, hospital and enough outlets for basic goods and services to require few trips to the mainland for supplies.

Picturesque Coupeville, in the center of the island, is encompassed by Ebey's Landing National Historic Reserve. Peaceful little Langley, near the southern tip, is popular with tourists, art aficionados and those who come to dine in its award-winning restaurants.

Ed and Marie Parr tired of shoveling snow and scoured the Northwest before settling on Langley. Ed found his golf course, Marie her low-maintenance home, and both enjoy the view of the waterways and islands around Whidbey. They find time to share stories with "a wonderful mix" of neighbors at an island coffee shop.

Population: 1,300 in Langley, 1,700 in Coupeville, 21,000 in Oak Harbor and 78,200 in county.

Climate:

	High	Low
January	45	35
July	66	52

Cost of living: Above average (specific index not available).

Average price of a new home: $181,000 in Oak Harbor, $175,000 in Coupeville and $210,000 in Langley.

Security: 15.5 crimes per 1,000 residents, lower than the national average of 42.7 crimes per 1,000 residents.

Information: Langley-South Whidbey Chamber of Commerce, P.O. Box 403, Langley, WA 98260, (360) 221-5676 or www.whidbey.com/langley. Central Whidbey Chamber of Commerce, P.O. Box 152, Coupeville, WA 98239, (360) 678-5434 or www.whidbey.net/coup. Greater Oak Harbor Chamber of Commerce, P.O. Box 883, Oak Harbor, WA 98277, (360) 675-3755 or www.oakharborchamber.org.

WEST VIRGINIA

Tax Heavens O
None

Tax Hells Ψ
None

Top Retirement Towns
None

West Virginia has a state income tax and does levy a state sales tax.

The state income tax rate is graduated from 3% to 6.5% depending upon income bracket. For married couples filing jointly, the rate is 3% on the first $10,000 of taxable income; the rate is 4% on the next $15,000 of taxable income; the rate is 4.5% on the next $15,000 of taxable income; the rate is 6% on the next $20,000 of taxable income; and the rate is 6.5% for taxable income above $60,000.

In calculating the tax, there is no deduction for federal income tax paid. Federal, state and private pensions are not exempt, although there is a deduction of up to $2,000 from certain federal and state pensions. Social Security benefits subject to federal tax are not exempt. There is an exemption allowance of $2,000 per person from adjusted gross income. There is an exclusion of up to $8,000 of any source of income from adjusted gross income per person for persons age 65 or older.

Major tax credits of rebates include: Credit for income taxes paid to other states.

The state sales tax rate is 6%.

WEST VIRGINIA TAX TABLE

Instructions

1. Find the Income in the far left column closest to your anticipated retirement income.
2. Find the Home Value closest to the value of the home where you will live in retirement.
3. Follow that row to your estimated Total Tax Burden at age 65 and beyond.

Income	Home Value	Property Tax & Other Fees	Personal Property Tax & Auto Fees	Sales Tax	Local Income Tax	State Income Tax	Total Tax Burden	Rank* From #1-#163
CHARLESTON								
$25,000	$75,000	$499	$453	$949	-	$41	$1,942	#50
	100,000	727	453	949	-	41	2,170	#46
	125,000	954	453	949	-	41	2,397	#46
$50,000	$100,000	$727	$453	$1,485	-	$758	$3,423	#70
	150,000	1,182	453	1,485	-	758	3,878	#44
	200,000	1,637	453	1,485	-	758	4,333	#39
$75,000	$150,000	$1,182	$453	$1,849	-	$2,318	$5,802	#92
	250,000	2,092	453	1,849	-	2,318	6,712	#64
	350,000	3,002	453	1,849	-	2,318	7,622	#45

*There are 163 cities in this book. The city with the lowest tax burden for an income/home value combination is given the #1 rating; the city with the highest total tax burden is given the #163 rating.

Charleston

Charleston has no local income tax and does not levy an additional sales tax.

Most purchases are taxed at the state rate of 6%. Major consumer categories taxed at a different rate: None. Major consumer categories that are exempt from sales tax include: Drugs and medical services.

Within the Charleston District, the property tax rate is .015166 for Class II (owner-occupied) property. Homes are assessed at 60% of market value. There is a homestead exemption of $20,000 off assessed value available to homeowners if at least one is age 65 or older. Property tax does not cover garbage pickup; the additional fee is approximately $120 per year if gross income is above $18,000 and $60 per year if gross income is below $18,000.

Charleston has a personal property tax rate of .007578 for Class I items; a rate of .015156 for Class II items; and a rate of .030312 for Class IV items. Personal property is assessed at 60% of face value for Class I; 60% of replacement cost for Class II; and 60% of loan value for Class IV.

Items subject to the personal property tax include: Class I — notes, stocks, bonds, farm equipment and farm animals; Class II — owner-occupied residences and bona fide farms including mobile homes; Class IV — everything not in classes I and II inside of municipalities. If property is inside city limits, this would include vehicles, satellite dishes, pets, watercraft, aircraft, trailers, campers, motorcycles and other real estate. There is a homestead exemption of $20,000 off assessed value available to homeowners if at least one is age 65 or older for Class II items only. The Class I personal property tax is sometimes referred to as an intangibles tax in other states, and we do not include it in our calculations. (See Intangibles Tax in Introduction.) We've assumed automobiles are the only items owned by our couples that are subject to personal property tax.

Our couples relocating to Charleston must pay a 5% privilege tax based on the NADA loan value of the automobile. The privilege tax for the Explorer is $640 and $440 for the Cutlass. Our couples must also pay a title fee of $10 per automobile, a lien fee of $5 per automobile and a registration fee of $30 per automobile at the time of registration. Thereafter, on an annual basis, our couples will pay a renewal fee per automobile.

WISCONSIN

Tax Heavens O	Tax Hells Ψ	Top Retirement Towns
None	Madison	Door County
	Milwaukee	Eagle River

Wisconsin has a state income tax and a state sales tax.

The state income tax is graduated from 4.73% to 6.75% depending upon income bracket. For married couples filing jointly, the rate is 4.73% on the first $10,390 of taxable income; the rate is 6.33% on the next $10,390 of taxable income; the rate is 6.55% on the next $135,070 of taxable income; and the rate is 6.75% on taxable income above $155,850.

In calculating the tax, there is no deduction for federal income tax paid. Federal and state pensions are not generally exempt from tax, although Wisconsin does exempt pensions received by persons who were members of, or retired from, certain governmental retirement systems prior to January 1, 1964. Private pensions are not exempt. Some Social Security benefits subject to federal tax are not exempt from tax. There is a sliding-scale standard deduction for married couples filing jointly that starts at $12,970 and decreases until it is completely phased out at Wisconsin adjusted gross income of $81,148. There is a personal exemption of $600 per person from Wisconsin adjusted gross income. There is also an exemption of $200 per person for persons age 65 or older.

Major tax credits or rebates include: Credit for income taxes paid to other states and itemized deduction credit, which our couples do not qualify for; working families tax credit, which one of our couples qualifies for; and school property tax credit and married couple credit, which our couples qualify for.

The state sales tax rate is 5%, but local governments can add to this amount.

Our couples relocating to the cities listed below must pay a plate fee of $45 per automobile, a title fee of $22 per automobile and a lien filing fee of $4 per automobile. Thereafter, on an annual basis, our couples will pay a renewal fee per automobile.

WISCONSIN TAX TABLE

Instructions

1. Find the Income in the far left column closest to your anticipated retirement income.
2. Find the Home Value closest to the value of the home where you will live in retirement.
3. Follow that row to your estimated Total Tax Burden at age 65 and beyond.

Income	Home Value	Property Tax & Other Fees	Personal Property Tax & Auto Fees	Sales Tax	Local Income Tax	State Income Tax†	Total Tax Burden	Rank* From #1-#163
EAGLE RIVER								
$25,000	$75,000	$1,493	$90	$724	-	-	$2,307	#110
	100,000	1,990	90	724	-	-	2,804	#120
	125,000	2,488	90	724	-	-	3,302	#127
$50,000	$100,000	$1,990	$90	$1,173	-	$1,516	$4,769	#152
	150,000	2,985	90	1,173	-	1,443	5,691	#148
	200,000	3,980	90	1,173	-	1,443	6,686	#146
$75,000	$150,000	$2,985	$90	$1,489	-	$3,316	$7,880	#153
	250,000	4,975	90	1,489	-	3,316	9,870	#150
	350,000	6,965	90	1,489	-	3,316	11,860	#148
MADISON								
$25,000	$75,000	$1,857	$90	$724	-	-	$2,671	#146
	100,000	2,476	90	724	-	-	3,290	#148
	125,000	3,095	90	724	-	-	3,909	#150

†School property tax credit is taken as a reduction of state income tax due.
*There are 163 cities in this book. The city with the lowest tax burden for an income/home value combination is given the #1 rating; the city with the highest total tax burden is given the #163 rating.

Income	Home Value	Property Tax & Other Fees	Personal Property Tax & Auto Fees	Sales Tax	Local Income Tax	State Income Tax†	Total Tax Burden	Rank* From #1-#163
MADISON continued								
$50,000	$100,000	$2,476	$90	$1,173	-	$1,450	$5,189	#157 Ψ
	150,000	3,714	90	1,173	-	1,443	6,420	#157 Ψ
	200,000	4,952	90	1,173	-	1,443	7,658	#157 Ψ
$75,000	$150,000	$3,714	$90	$1,489	-	$3,316	$8,609	#158 Ψ
	250,000	6,190	90	1,489	-	3,316	11,085	#156 Ψ
	350,000	8,666	90	1,489	-	3,316	13,561	#155 Ψ
MILWAUKEE								
$25,000	$75,000	$2,173	$90	$741	-	-	$3,004	#153
	100,000	2,883	90	741	-	-	3,714	#155 Ψ
	125,000	3,593	90	741	-	-	4,424	#156 Ψ
$50,000	$100,000	$2,883	$90	$1,200	-	$1,443	$5,616	#160 Ψ
	150,000	4,303	90	1,200	-	1,443	7,036	#160 Ψ
	200,000	5,722	90	1,200	-	1,443	8,455	#160 Ψ
$75,000	$150,000	$4,303	$90	$1,523	-	$3,316	$9,232	#160 Ψ
	250,000	7,142	90	1,523	-	3,316	12,071	#162 Ψ
	350,000	9,981	90	1,523	-	3,316	14,910	#162 Ψ
STURGEON BAY								
$25,000	$75,000	$1,431	$90	$724	-	-	$2,245	#102
	100,000	1,908	90	724	-	-	2,722	#112
	125,000	2,385	90	724	-	-	3,199	#116
$50,000	$100,000	$1,908	$90	$1,173	-	$1,519	$4,690	#149
	150,000	2,862	90	1,173	-	1,443	5,568	#145
	200,000	3,816	90	1,173	-	1,443	6,522	#142
$75,000	$150,000	$2,862	$90	$1,489	-	$3,316	$7,757	#152
	250,000	4,770	90	1,489	-	3,316	9,665	#149
	350,000	6,678	90	1,489	-	3,316	11,573	#145

†School property tax credit is taken as a reduction of state income tax due.

*There are 163 cities in this book. The city with the lowest tax burden for an income/home value combination is given the #1 rating; the city with the highest total tax burden is given the #163 rating.

Eagle River

Eagle River has no local income tax but does levy a sales tax.

Most purchases are taxed at a rate of 5.5%. Major consumer categories taxed at a different rate: None. Major consumer categories that are exempt from sales tax include: Drugs, groceries and medical services.

Within the city limits of Eagle River, the effective property tax rate is .01990. Homes are assessed at 100% of market value. There is a sliding-scale homestead property tax credit available for residents with household income of $20,290 or less. Property tax includes garbage pickup.

Eagle River has no personal property tax for individuals.

Madison

Madison has no local income tax but does levy a sales tax.

Most purchases are taxed at a rate of 5.5%. Major consumer categories taxed at a different rate: None. Major consumer categories that are exempt from sales tax include: Drugs, groceries and medical services.

Within the city limits of Madison, the effective property tax rate is .02476. Homes are assessed at 100% of market value. There is a sliding-scale homestead property tax credit available for residents with household income of $20,290 or less. Property tax includes garbage pickup.

Madison has no personal property tax for individuals.

Milwaukee

Milwaukee has no local income tax but does levy a sales tax.

Most purchases are taxed at a rate of 5.6%. Major consumer categories taxed at a different rate: Food away from home, which is taxed at a rate of 5.85%. Major consumer categories that are exempt from sales tax include: Drugs, groceries and medical services.

Within the city limits of Milwaukee, the effective property tax rate is .02839. Homes are assessed at 100% of market value. There is a sliding-scale homestead property tax credit available for residents with household income of $20,290 or less. Property tax covers a portion of garbage collection; the additional fee is $44 per year.

Milwaukee has no personal property tax for individuals.

Sturgeon Bay

Sturgeon Bay has no local income tax but does levy a sales tax.

Most purchases are taxed at a rate of 5.5%. Major consumer categories taxed at a different rate: None. Major consumer categories that are exempt from sales tax include: Drugs, groceries and medical services.

Within the city limits of Sturgeon Bay, the effective property tax rate is .01908. Homes are assessed at 100% of market value. There is a sliding-scale homestead property tax credit available for residents with household income of $20,290 or less. Property tax includes garbage pickup.

Sturgeon Bay has no personal property tax for individuals.

• Wisconsin's Best Retirement Towns •

Door County, Wisconsin

Cold winters aside, retirees who make Door County their home say it offers everything they could want for a fulfilled retirement lifestyle. The peninsula has 250 miles of shoreline dotted with more than 40 islands, most accessible to boaters and fishermen. History buffs will find dozens of museums and attractions, many on the National Register of Historic Places, in the quaint villages and towns that fill the coves and inlets of Door County.

The Peninsula Players, American Folklore Theatre, Peninsula Music Festival and dozens of art galleries and studios are some of the groups and venues bringing the performing and visual arts to receptive audiences.

Surprisingly, many retirees like winters best. "The real people of the Door are here in winter," says Fran Burton, who moved here with husband Paul from Kansas.

George and Barbara Larsen, from Sheboygan, WI, love the beautiful, quiet winters here, and Ted and Agnes Kubicz, from northern Illinois, have found that winters are the perfect time to finish a good book.

Population: 9,636 in Sturgeon Bay, the county's only city, and 26,967 in Door County.

Climate:

	High	Low
January	23	9
July	80	60

Cost of living: Above average (specific index not available).
Average price of a new home: $239,900
Security: 19.8 crimes per 1,000 residents, lower than the national average of 42.7 crimes per 1,000 residents.
Information: Door County Chamber of Commerce, 1015 Green Bay Road, P.O. Box 406, Sturgeon Bay, WI 54235-0406, (800) 527-3529 or www.door countyvacations.com.

Eagle River, Wisconsin

This small, backwoods town rests on the banks of its namesake river, connected to the northeast Wisconsin countryside by a chain of 28 navigable lakes. The most popular and often fastest way into town is by boat for many of its residents.

The six-block business district is getting a facelift, and an economic restructuring committee is working to keep local shoppers from having to drive 25 miles to Rhinelander to spend their grocery dollars.

Mid-80s summer temperatures bring hordes of tourists, fishermen and recreational boaters into the area. When autumn arrives, the heavily forested landscape of maples and birch takes on a reddish-golden hue, but an early winter quickly turns the leaves brown and ski trails white for cross-country skiers and snowmobilers. Ice fishermen drive their pickups and vans onto frozen area lakes for a chance to snag a hungry muskie, walleye or northern pike.

Jim and Sandra Slagle lived in Minnesota and Kenosha, WI, before retiring to Eagle River. "It's a quiet little town, only a mile square, but it has a lot going on." Jim says. "The snowmobile derby and ice fishing bring in winter visitors. Bicycling, kayaking and canoeing are favorite summertime sports. Most importantly, we have good neighbors and good churches," he adds.

Population: 1,645 in city, 18,000 in county.

Climate:

	High	Low
January	25	10
July	85	60

Cost of living: Average (specific index not available).
Average price of a new home: $162,500
Security: 54.7 crimes per 1,000 residents, higher than the national average of 42.7 crimes per 1,000 residents.
Information: Eagle River Area Chamber of Commerce, P.O. Box 1917, Eagle River, WI 54521, (800) 359-6315 or www. eagleriver.org.

WYOMING

Tax Heavens O
Cheyenne
Jackson

Tax Hells ψ
None

Top Retirement Towns
Jackson Hole

Wyoming has no state income tax but does have a state sales tax. Major tax credits or rebates include: None.

The state sales tax rate is 4%, but local governments can add to this amount.

Our couples relocating to the cities listed below must pay a county fee per automobile based on the year and MSRP of the vehicle. The county fee is $295 for the Explorer and $245 for the Cutlass. Our couples must also pay a title fee of $6 per automobile, a Vehicle Identification Number (VIN) inspection fee of $5 per automobile, a lien fee of $10 per automobile and a state fee of $15 per automobile at the time of registration. Thereafter, on an annual basis, our couples will pay a county fee and a state fee, per automobile.

WYOMING TAX TABLE

Instructions

1. Find the Income in the far left column closest to your anticipated retirement income.
2. Find the Home Value closest to the value of the home where you will live in retirement.
3. Follow that row to your estimated Total Tax Burden at age 65 and beyond.

Income	Home Value	Property Tax & Other Fees	Personal Property Tax & Auto Fees	Sales Tax	Local Income Tax	State Income Tax	Total Tax Burden	Rank* From #1- #163
CHEYENNE								
$25,000	$75,000	$675	$462	$783	-	-	$1,920	#48
	100,000	852	462	783	-	-	2,097	#40
	125,000	1,029	462	783	-	-	2,274	#33
$50,000	$100,000	$852	$462	$1,223	-	-	$2,537	#8 O
	150,000	1,206	462	1,223	-	-	2,891	#7 O
	200,000	1,560	462	1,223	-	-	3,245	#6 O
$75,000	$150,000	$1,206	$462	$1,532	-	-	$3,200	#2 O
	250,000	1,913	462	1,532	-	-	3,907	#2 O
	350,000	2,621	462	1,532	-	-	4,615	#3 O
JACKSON								
$25,000	$75,000	$659	$462	$939	-	-	$2,060	#70
	100,000	799	462	939	-	-	2,200	#49
	125,000	939	462	939	-	-	2,340	#40
$50,000	$100,000	$799	$462	$1,468	-	-	$2,729	#16
	150,000	1,079	462	1,468	-	-	3,009	#9 O
	200,000	1,358	462	1,468	-	-	3,288	#8 O
$75,000	$150,000	$1,079	$462	$1,838	-	-	$3,379	#4 O
	250,000	1,638	462	1,838	-	-	3,938	#3 O
	350,000	2,197	462	1,838	-	-	4,497	#2 O

*There are 163 cities in this book. The city with the lowest tax burden for an income/home value combination is given the #1 rating; the city with the highest total tax burden is given the #163 rating.

Cheyenne

Cheyenne has no local income tax but does levy a sales tax.

Most purchases are taxed at a rate of 5%. Major consumer categories taxed at a different rate: None. Major consumer categories that are exempt from sales tax include: Drugs, medical supplies and medical services.

Within the city limits of Cheyenne, the property tax rate is .0745. Homes are assessed at 9.5% of market value. Property tax does not cover garbage pickup; the additional fee is approximately $144 per year.

Cheyenne has no personal property tax for individuals.

Jackson

Jackson has no local income tax but does levy a sales tax.

Most purchases are taxed at a rate of 6%. Major consumer categories taxed at a different rate: None. Major consumer categories that are exempt from sales tax include: Drugs, medical supplies and medical services.

Within the city limits of Jackson, the property tax rate is .058847. Homes are assessed at 9.5% of market value. Property tax does not cover garbage pickup; the additional fee is approximately $240 per year.

Jackson has no personal property tax for individuals.

• Wyoming's Best Retirement Town •

Jackson Hole, Wyoming

"If you're looking for cold winters, an out-of-doors lifestyle and out-of-sight real estate prices, we've got it all here in Jackson Hole," says Joe Bennett. He and wife Gainor moved here from Salt Lake City after vacationing in the area over many years.

Jackson Hole, a 60-mile-long valley in the Teton Mountain Range that stretches between the town of Jackson and the south entrance of Yellowstone National Park, has been everything the Bennetts expected it to be. They ski the high slopes of the Tetons, fish for trout in the cold rapids of the Snake River as it flows by their home, and go bicycling along quiet country roads on the mountain-ringed valley floor.

Summer weather is just about perfect in Jackson Hole, attracting more tourists than can be found during ski season. And the town's popularity with celebrities and other wealthy vacation-home owners has resulted in more fine restaurants than you'd find in towns many times the size.

"There are lots of indoor cultural amenities, too," Joe says. "We enjoy the Little Theater productions, Grand Teton Music Festival and exhibits at the Wildlife Art Museum. This town has a lot of artisans and a very active arts community."

Population: 5,500 in city, 15,000 in county.

Climate:

	High	Low
January	28	2
July	79	41

Cost of living: Above average (specific index not available).

Average price of a new home: $325,000

Security: 37.7 crimes per 1,000 residents in Teton County, and 60.4 crimes per 1,000 residents in Jackson, compared to the national average of 42.7 crimes per 1,000 residents.

Information: Jackson Hole Chamber of Commerce, P.O. Box 550, Jackson, WY 83001, (307) 733-3316 or www.jackson holechamber.com.

WASHINGTON, DC

Tax Heavens ❍
None

Tax Hells Ψ
Washington, DC

Top Retirement Towns
None

Washington, DC, has an income tax and a sales tax.

The income tax rate is graduated from 5% to 9.5% depending upon income bracket. For married couples filing jointly with taxable income of up to $10,000, the rate is 5%; the rate is 7.5% on the next $10,000 of taxable income; and the rate is 9.5% on taxable income above $20,000.

In calculating the tax, there is no deduction for federal income tax paid. Federal, District of Columbia and private pensions are not exempt, though there is a $3,000 exemption per person from federal and District of Columbia pensions. Social Security benefits are exempt. There is a $2,000 standard deduction from adjusted gross income for married couples filing jointly. There is a $2,740 personal exemption from adjusted gross income for married couples filing jointly and there is a $1,370 personal exemption per person from

adjusted gross income for persons age 65 or older.

Major tax credits or rebates include: Credit for income taxes paid to other states, low-income credit, and property tax credit if gross income is less than $20,000. Our couples do not qualify for these programs.

Most purchases are taxed at a rate of 5.75%. Major consumer categories taxed at a different rate include: Food away from home, which is taxed at a rate of 10%. Major consumer categories that are exempt from sales tax include: Drugs and groceries.

Within the city limits of Washington, DC, the property tax rate is .0096. Homes are assessed at 100% of market value. There is a homestead exemption of $30,000 off assessed value available to all homeowners. There is a reduction of 50% of property taxes due available to homeowners age 65 or older with Washington, DC, adjusted gross income

of less than $100,000. Property tax includes garbage pickup.

Washington, DC, has no personal property tax for individuals.

Our couples relocating to Washington, DC, must pay an excise tax of 7% of fair market value for the Explorer and 6% of fair market value for the Cutlass. The excise tax due is $1,187 for the Explorer and $713 for the Cutlass. Our couples must also pay a tags fee per automobile based on the weight of the vehicle. The fee is $88 for the Explorer and $55 for the Cutlass. Our couples must also pay a title fee of $20 per automobile, an inspection fee of $25 per automobile and a lien fee of $15 per automobile at the time of registration. Thereafter, on an annual basis, our couples will pay a tags fee and excise tax per automobile, plus a $25 inspection fee per automobile every other year.

WASHINGTON, DC, TAX TABLE

Instructions

1. Find the Income in the far left column closest to your anticipated retirement income.
2. Find the Home Value closest to the value of the home where you will live in retirement.
3. Follow that row to your estimated Total Tax Burden at age 65 and beyond.

Income	Home Value	Property Tax & Other Fees	Personal Property Tax & Auto Fees	Sales Tax	Local Income Tax	State Income Tax	Total Tax Burden	Rank* From #1- #163
WASHINGTON, DC								
$25,000	$75,000	$216	$2,067	$864	$382	-	$3,529	#159 Ψ
	100,000	336	2,067	864	382	-	3,649	#154 Ψ
	125,000	456	2,067	864	382	-	3,769	#146
$50,000	$100,000	$336	$2,067	$1,383	$2,059	-	$5,845	#161 Ψ
	150,000	576	2,067	1,383	2,059	-	6,085	#155 Ψ
	200,000	816	2,067	1,383	2,059	-	6,325	#138
$75,000	$150,000	$576	$2,067	$1,743	$4,292	-	$8,678	#159 Ψ
	250,000	1,056	2,067	1,743	4,292	-	9,158	#142
	350,000	1,536	2,067	1,743	4,292	-	9,638	#111

*There are 163 cities in this book. The city with the lowest tax burden for an income/home value combination is given the #1 rating; the city with the highest total tax burden is given the #163 rating.

Ranking of Total Tax Burdens for Retirees
Earning $25,000 and Owning a Home Valued at $75,000

Rank	City, State	Total Tax	Rank	City, State	Total Tax
1	ANCHORAGE, AK	$ 184	83	HENDERSONVILLE, NC	$2,127
2	WILMINGTON, DE	712	(TIE) 84	LEESBURG, FL	2,129
3	BEND, OR	1,186	(TIE) 84	ORLANDO, FL	2,129
4	HONOLULU, HI	1,259	86	WAYNESVILLE, NC	2,137
5	GRANTS PASS, OR	1,318	87	CHARLOTTESVILLE, VA	2,140
6	ASHLAND, OR	1,336	88	CHARLESTON, SC	2,146
7	NEW YORK CITY, NY	1,359	89	GAINESVILLE, GA	2,156
8	LINCOLN CITY, OR	1,385		**AVERAGE**	**$2,163**
9	OMAHA, NE	1,398	(TIE) 90	OCALA, FL	2,168
10	SAVANNAH, GA	1,430	(TIE) 90	PUNTA GORDA, FL	2,168
11	EUGENE, OR	1,456	92	HOUSTON, TX	2,180
12	PORTLAND, OR	1,468	93	BRADENTON, FL	2,184
13	DALLAS, TX	1,492	94	PARIS, TN	2,186
14	BILLINGS, MT	1,549	95	CARLSBAD, CA	2,208
15	SANTA FE, NM	1,570	96	VERO BEACH, FL	2,218
16	OAK HARBOR, WA	1,609	97	MARYVILLE, TN	2,232
17	BATON ROUGE, LA	1,627	98	MIAMI, FL	2,234
18	LEXINGTON, KY	1,628	99	LOS ANGELES, CA	2,239
19	WILLIAMSBURG, VA	1,630	(TIE) 100	PENSACOLA, FL	2,243
20	BUFFALO, NY	1,636	(TIE) 100	ATLANTA, GA	2,243
21	NATCHITOCHES, LA	1,640	102	STURGEON BAY, WI	2,245
22	FRIDAY HARBOR, WA	1,667	103	WINTER HAVEN, FL	2,247
23	SYRACUSE, NY	1,676	104	FLAGSTAFF, AZ	2,261
24	NAPLES, FL	1,681	105	EUFAULA, AL	2,283
25	PORT TOWNSEND, WA	1,686	106	BURLINGTON, VT	2,288
26	JACKSONVILLE, FL	1,690	107	OKLAHOMA CITY, OK	2,294
27	SEQUIM, WA	1,724	108	MINNEAPOLIS, MN	2,295
28	COEUR D'ALENE, ID	1,740	109	SCOTTSDALE, AZ	2,296
29	ST. SIMONS ISLAND, GA	1,770	110	EAGLE RIVER, WI	2,307
30	DENVER, CO	1,786	111	SAN FRANCISCO, CA	2,311
31	THOMASVILLE, GA	1,790	112	CHICAGO, IL	2,312
32	BOISE, ID	1,812	113	EDENTON, NC	2,315
33	PORTSMOUTH, NH	1,817	114	PRESCOTT, AZ	2,316
34	BEAUFORT, SC	1,852	115	DADE CITY, FL	2,321
35	LAS CRUCES, NM	1,857	116	BOSTON, MA	2,331
(TIE) 36	VICKSBURG, MS	1,869	117	OXFORD, MS	2,332
(TIE) 36	MYRTLE BEACH, SC	1,869	118	TAMPA, FL	2,333
38	HILTON HEAD, SC	1,893	119	SIERRA VISTA, AZ	2,341
39	HOT SPRINGS, AR	1,897	(TIE) 120	PALM DESERT, CA	2,358
40	CLEMSON, SC	1,898	(TIE) 120	FORT LAUDERDALE, FL	2,358
41	DETROIT, MI	1,904	122	SAN JUAN CAPISTRANO, CA	2,364
42	ABINGDON, VA	1,906	123	TUCSON, AZ	2,376
(TIE) 43	LOUISVILLE, KY	1,911	124	SARASOTA, FL	2,384
(TIE) 43	NEW ORLEANS, LA	1,911	125	CINCINNATI, OH	2,399
45	LONGBOAT KEY, FL	1,914	126	GAINESVILLE, FL	2,407
(TIE) 46	FAIRHOPE, AL	1,915	127	ASHEVILLE, NC	2,442
(TIE) 46	BRANSON, MO	1,915	128	SIOUX FALLS, SD	2,448
48	CHEYENNE, WY	1,920	129	THE WOODLANDS, TX	2,449
49	AUSTIN, TX	1,932	130	TEMECULA, CA	2,451
50	CHARLESTON, WV	1,942	131	HATTIESBURG, MS	2,452
51	RUIDOSO, NM	1,943	132	BREVARD, NC	2,454
(TIE) 52	KEY WEST, FL	1,952	133	ST. PETERSBURG, FL	2,492
(TIE) 52	ST. GEORGE, UT	1,952	134	SAN ANTONIO, TX	2,512
54	ORMOND BEACH, FL	1,953	135	LAS VEGAS, NV	2,524
55	SIESTA KEY, FL	1,955	136	WICHITA, KS	2,546
56	DELAND, FL	1,961	137	CAMDEN, ME	2,570
57	SANIBEL ISLAND, FL	1,974	138	PHOENIX, AZ	2,572
58	SEATTLE, WA	1,977	139	CHAPEL HILL, NC	2,577
59	GREEN VALLEY, AZ	1,993	140	RENO, NV	2,587
60	FORT COLLINS, CO	2,023	141	RICHMOND, VA	2,594
61	BALTIMORE, MD	2,024	142	GEORGETOWN, TX	2,612
62	COLUMBUS, OH	2,030	143	WILMINGTON, NC	2,642
63	PINEHURST, NC	2,033	144	LITTLE ROCK, AR	2,665
64	BOCA RATON, FL	2,038	145	OJAI, CA	2,666
65	SAN DIEGO, CA	2,042	146	MADISON, WI	2,671
(TIE) 66	NORTH FORT MYERS, FL	2,043	147	HARTFORD, CT	2,716
(TIE) 66	ST. AUGUSTINE, FL	2,043	148	FARGO, ND	2,751
68	CLEVELAND, OH	2,051	149	MEMPHIS, TN	2,820
69	LAKELAND, FL	2,055	150	LANCASTER, PA	2,861
70	JACKSON, WY	2,060	151	CAPE COD, MA	2,902
(TIE) 71	JUPITER, FL	2,067	152	KERRVILLE, TX	2,910
(TIE) 71	SALT LAKE CITY, UT	2,067	153	MILWAUKEE, WI	3,004
73	PETOSKEY, MI	2,074	154	DES MOINES, IA	3,013
74	GREENVILLE, SC	2,079	(TIE) 155	NEWARK, NJ	3,073
75	AIKEN, SC	2,088	(TIE) 155	PHILADELPHIA, PA	3,073
76	MOUNT DORA, FL	2,099	157	BROWNSVILLE, TX	3,147
77	ALBUQUERQUE, NM	2,108	158	NEW HAVEN, CT	3,254
78	NEW BERN, NC	2,110	159	WASHINGTON, DC	3,529
79	CAPE MAY, NJ	2,113	160	INDIANAPOLIS, IN	3,530
80	TOMS RIVER, NJ	2,115	161	CELEBRATION, FL	3,699
81	KANSAS CITY, MO	2,125	162	PITTSBURGH, PA	3,979
82	VENICE, FL	2,126	163	PROVIDENCE, RI	4,491

Ranking of Total Tax Burdens for Retirees
Earning $25,000 and Owning a Home Valued at $100,000

Rank	City, State	Total Tax	Rank	City, State	Total Tax
1	ANCHORAGE, AK	$ 184	83	ORMOND BEACH, FL	$2,514
2	WILMINGTON, DE	1,161	84	PRESCOTT, AZ	2,515
3	HONOLULU, HI	1,259	85	AUSTIN, TX	2,516
4	BEND, OR	1,487		**AVERAGE**	**$2,524**
5	NEW YORK CITY, NY	1,528	86	MARYVILLE, TN	2,526
6	BILLINGS, MT	1,613	87	NORTH FORT MYERS, FL	2,537
7	PETOSKEY, MI	1,626	88	LOS ANGELES, CA	2,551
8	GRANTS PASS, OR	1,636	89	BOCA RATON, FL	2,562
9	ASHLAND, OR	1,657	90	DELAND, FL	2,563
10	SAVANNAH, GA	1,666	91	VENICE, FL	2,564
11	OMAHA, NE	1,718	92	LAKELAND, FL	2,572
12	SANTA FE, NM	1,720	93	OKLAHOMA CITY, OK	2,574
13	LINCOLN CITY, OR	1,744	94	SIERRA VISTA, AZ	2,582
14	WILLIAMSBURG, VA	1,765	95	EDENTON, NC	2,586
15	EUGENE, OR	1,779	96	PUNTA GORDA, FL	2,591
16	OAK HARBOR, WA	1,792	97	SAN FRANCISCO, CA	2,595
17	FRIDAY HARBOR, WA	1,847	98	JUPITER, FL	2,603
18	PORTLAND, OR	1,861	99	ST. AUGUSTINE, FL	2,629
19	BATON ROUGE, LA	1,869	100	SAN JUAN CAPISTRANO, CA	2,631
20	LEXINGTON, KY	1,871	101	PALM DESERT, CA	2,638
21	PORT TOWNSEND, WA	1,895	102	LEESBURG, FL	2,645
22	NATCHITOCHES, LA	1,930	103	ORLANDO, FL	2,647
23	DENVER, CO	1,950	104	MOUNT DORA, FL	2,658
24	SEQUIM, WA	1,958	105	BOSTON, MA	2,660
25	BRANSON, MO	1,963	106	TUCSON, AZ	2,686
26	DALLAS, TX	2,003	107	OXFORD, MS	2,688
(TIE) 27	FAIRHOPE, AL	2,005	108	TOMS RIVER, NJ	2,707
(TIE) 27	MYRTLE BEACH, SC	2,005	109	ATLANTA, GA	2,710
29	COEUR D'ALENE, ID	2,008	110	BRADENTON, FL	2,711
30	NAPLES, FL	2,014	111	VERO BEACH, FL	2,718
(TIE) 31	BEAUFORT, SC	2,022	(TIE) 112	OCALA, FL	2,722
(TIE) 31	HILTON HEAD, SC	2,022	(TIE) 112	STURGEON BAY, WI	2,722
33	BALTIMORE, MD	2,024	114	BREVARD, NC	2,744
34	CLEMSON, SC	2,026	115	TEMECULA, CA	2,749
35	ST. SIMONS ISLAND, GA	2,045	116	HOUSTON, TX	2,775
36	THOMASVILLE, GA	2,070	117	ASHEVILLE, NC	2,789
37	BOISE, ID	2,083	118	CHICAGO, IL	2,793
38	LAS CRUCES, NM	2,085	119	MINNEAPOLIS, MN	2,794
39	BUFFALO, NY	2,093	120	EAGLE RIVER, WI	2,804
40	CHEYENNE, WY	2,097	121	LAS VEGAS, NV	2,809
41	HOT SPRINGS, AR	2,105	122	SARASOTA, FL	2,819
42	ST. GEORGE, UT	2,110	123	PENSACOLA, FL	2,821
43	RUIDOSO, NM	2,138	124	SIOUX FALLS, SD	2,840
44	VICKSBURG, MS	2,152	125	PHOENIX, AZ	2,853
45	ABINGDON, VA	2,156	126	WINTER HAVEN, FL	2,855
46	CHARLESTON, WV	2,170	127	WICHITA, KS	2,856
47	SEATTLE, WA	2,184	128	HATTIESBURG, MS	2,861
48	JACKSONVILLE, FL	2,198	129	CINCINNATI, OH	2,867
49	JACKSON, WY	2,200	130	RENO, NV	2,888
50	LOUISVILLE, KY	2,210	131	WILMINGTON, NC	2,912
51	GREEN VALLEY, AZ	2,213	132	MIAMI, FL	2,919
52	PORTSMOUTH, NH	2,239	133	OJAI, CA	2,929
53	FORT COLLINS, CO	2,240	134	RICHMOND, VA	2,951
54	DETROIT, MI	2,245	135	CHAPEL HILL, NC	2,955
55	PINEHURST, NC	2,257	136	TAMPA, FL	2,970
56	SALT LAKE CITY, UT	2,264	137	CAMDEN, ME	2,973
(TIE) 57	SYRACUSE, NY	2,278	138	DADE CITY, FL	2,985
(TIE) 57	AIKEN, SC	2,278	139	FORT LAUDERDALE, FL	2,990
59	BURLINGTON, VT	2,286	140	LITTLE ROCK, AR	3,005
60	GREENVILLE, SC	2,306	141	GAINESVILLE, FL	3,079
61	SIESTA KEY, FL	2,308	142	ST. PETERSBURG, FL	3,112
62	KEY WEST, FL	2,312	143	THE WOODLANDS, TX	3,162
63	CHARLESTON, SC	2,317	144	GEORGETOWN, TX	3,223
64	SAN DIEGO, CA	2,321	145	HARTFORD, CT	3,226
65	LONGBOAT KEY, FL	2,330	146	SAN ANTONIO, TX	3,229
66	NEW ORLEANS, LA	2,335	147	MEMPHIS, TN	3,244
67	HENDERSONVILLE, NC	2,364	148	MADISON, WI	3,290
68	CLEVELAND, OH	2,368	149	FARGO, ND	3,307
69	NEW BERN, NC	2,370	150	CAPE COD, MA	3,308
70	EUFAULA, AL	2,377	151	LANCASTER, PA	3,471
71	PARIS, TN	2,401	152	KERRVILLE, TX	3,574
(TIE) 72	WAYNESVILLE, NC	2,402	153	DES MOINES, IA	3,623
(TIE) 72	COLUMBUS, OH	2,402	154	WASHINGTON, DC	3,649
74	CAPE MAY, NJ	2,407	155	MILWAUKEE, WI	3,714
75	CHARLOTTESVILLE, VA	2,417	156	PHILADELPHIA, PA	3,734
76	ALBUQUERQUE, NM	2,443	157	BROWNSVILLE, TX	3,844
77	SANIBEL ISLAND, FL	2,450	158	NEW HAVEN, CT	3,866
78	KANSAS CITY, MO	2,460	159	NEWARK, NJ	3,984
79	GAINESVILLE, GA	2,469	160	CELEBRATION, FL	4,115
80	FLAGSTAFF, AZ	2,472	161	INDIANAPOLIS, IN	4,249
81	CARLSBAD, CA	2,475	162	PROVIDENCE, RI	4,809
82	SCOTTSDALE, AZ	2,513	163	PITTSBURGH, PA	4,959

Ranking of Total Tax Burdens for Retirees
Earning $25,000 and Owning a Home Valued at $125,000

Rank	City, State	Total Tax	Rank	City, State	Total Tax
1	ANCHORAGE, AK	$ 184	83	DETROIT, MI	$2,848
2	HONOLULU, HI	1,259	84	OKLAHOMA CITY, OK	2,853
3	WILMINGTON, DE	1,609	85	EDENTON, NC	2,857
4	BILLINGS, MT	1,613	86	LOS ANGELES, CA	2,864
5	NEW YORK CITY, NY	1,697	87	SAN FRANCISCO, CA	2,879
6	BEND, OR	1,789	88	SYRACUSE, NY	2,880
7	SANTA FE, NM	1,871		**AVERAGE**	**$2,893**
8	PETOSKEY, MI	1,885	89	SAN JUAN CAPISTRANO, CA	2,898
9	WILLIAMSBURG, VA	1,900	90	PALM DESERT, CA	2,917
10	OAK HARBOR, WA	1,947	91	SANIBEL ISLAND, FL	2,926
11	GRANTS PASS, OR	1,955	92	BOSTON, MA	2,989
12	ASHLAND, OR	1,979	93	TUCSON, AZ	2,996
13	FRIDAY HARBOR, WA	2,000	94	VENICE, FL	3,003
14	SAVANNAH, GA	2,003	95	PUNTA GORDA, FL	3,015
15	BALTIMORE, MD	2,024	96	NORTH FORT MYERS, FL	3,030
16	PORT TOWNSEND, WA	2,073	97	BREVARD, NC	3,034
17	FAIRHOPE, AL	2,095	98	OXFORD, MS	3,043
18	EUGENE, OR	2,101	99	TEMECULA, CA	3,046
19	LINCOLN CITY, OR	2,102	100	ORMOND BEACH, FL	3,074
20	BATON ROUGE, LA	2,112	101	BOCA RATON, FL	3,085
21	LEXINGTON, KY	2,113	102	LAKELAND, FL	3,088
22	DENVER, CO	2,114	103	LAS VEGAS, NV	3,094
23	MYRTLE BEACH, SC	2,142	104	AUSTIN, TX	3,125
24	HILTON HEAD, SC	2,150	105	PHOENIX, AZ	3,134
25	CLEMSON, SC	2,154	106	ASHEVILLE, NC	3,137
26	SEQUIM, WA	2,158	107	JUPITER, FL	3,140
27	BRANSON, MO	2,162	108	LEESBURG, FL	3,160
28	OMAHA, NE	2,165	(TIE) 109	DELAND, FL	3,165
29	BEAUFORT, SC	2,193	(TIE) 109	ORLANDO, FL	3,165
30	NATCHITOCHES, LA	2,220	(TIE) 109	WICHITA, KS	3,165
31	PORTLAND, OR	2,254	112	ATLANTA, GA	3,178
32	ST. GEORGE, UT	2,269	113	WILMINGTON, NC	3,182
33	CHEYENNE, WY	2,274	114	RENO, NV	3,190
34	COEUR D'ALENE, ID	2,277	115	OJAI, CA	3,192
35	BURLINGTON, VT	2,287	116	STURGEON BAY, WI	3,199
(TIE) 36	HOT SPRINGS, AR	2,313	(TIE) 117	MOUNT DORA, FL	3,215
(TIE) 36	LAS CRUCES, NM	2,313	(TIE) 117	ST. AUGUSTINE, FL	3,215
38	ST. SIMONS ISLAND, GA	2,319	119	VERO BEACH, FL	3,218
39	RUIDOSO, NM	2,333	120	SIOUX FALLS, SD	3,233
40	JACKSON, WY	2,340	121	BRADENTON, FL	3,239
41	NAPLES, FL	2,347	122	SARASOTA, FL	3,253
42	THOMASVILLE, GA	2,351	123	HATTIESBURG, MS	3,269
43	BOISE, ID	2,353	124	CHICAGO, IL	3,273
44	SEATTLE, WA	2,360	125	OCALA, FL	3,275
45	DALLAS, TX	2,392	126	TOMS RIVER, NJ	3,300
46	CHARLESTON, WV	2,397	127	EAGLE RIVER, WI	3,302
47	ABINGDON, VA	2,406	128	RICHMOND, VA	3,309
48	GREEN VALLEY, AZ	2,433	129	CHAPEL HILL, NC	3,333
49	VICKSBURG, MS	2,434	130	CINCINNATI, OH	3,335
50	FORT COLLINS, CO	2,456	131	LITTLE ROCK, AR	3,345
51	SALT LAKE CITY, UT	2,460	132	HOUSTON, TX	3,374
52	AIKEN, SC	2,467	133	CAMDEN, ME	3,376
53	EUFAULA, AL	2,471	134	MINNEAPOLIS, MN	3,396
54	PINEHURST, NC	2,481	135	PENSACOLA, FL	3,398
55	CHARLESTON, SC	2,489	136	WINTER HAVEN, FL	3,464
56	CAPE MAY, NJ	2,500	137	MIAMI, FL	3,603
57	LOUISVILLE, KY	2,509	138	TAMPA, FL	3,608
58	GREENVILLE, SC	2,532	139	FORT LAUDERDALE, FL	3,621
59	BUFFALO, NY	2,550	140	DADE CITY, FL	3,650
60	SAN DIEGO, CA	2,599	141	MEMPHIS, TN	3,667
61	HENDERSONVILLE, NC	2,602	142	CAPE COD, MA	3,715
62	PARIS, TN	2,616	143	ST. PETERSBURG, FL	3,731
63	NEW BERN, NC	2,630	144	HARTFORD, CT	3,737
(TIE) 64	SIESTA KEY, FL	2,662	145	GAINESVILLE, FL	3,751
(TIE) 64	PORTSMOUTH, NH	2,662	146	WASHINGTON, DC	3,769
66	WAYNESVILLE, NC	2,667	147	GEORGETOWN, TX	3,835
67	KEY WEST, FL	2,671	148	FARGO, ND	3,862
68	FLAGSTAFF, AZ	2,682	149	THE WOODLANDS, TX	3,873
69	CLEVELAND, OH	2,686	150	MADISON, WI	3,909
70	CHARLOTTESVILLE, VA	2,695	151	SAN ANTONIO, TX	3,946
71	JACKSONVILLE, FL	2,707	152	LANCASTER, PA	4,080
72	PRESCOTT, AZ	2,714	153	DES MOINES, IA	4,232
73	SCOTTSDALE, AZ	2,731	154	KERRVILLE, TX	4,239
74	CARLSBAD, CA	2,742	155	PHILADELPHIA, PA	4,396
75	LONGBOAT KEY, FL	2,747	156	MILWAUKEE, WI	4,424
76	NEW ORLEANS, LA	2,759	157	NEW HAVEN, CT	4,477
77	COLUMBUS, OH	2,775	158	CELEBRATION, FL	4,532
78	ALBUQUERQUE, NM	2,779	159	BROWNSVILLE, TX	4,540
79	GAINESVILLE, GA	2,782	160	NEWARK, NJ	4,896
80	KANSAS CITY, MO	2,795	161	INDIANAPOLIS, IN	4,986
81	MARYVILLE, TN	2,819	162	PROVIDENCE, RI	5,376
82	SIERRA VISTA, AZ	2,824	163	PITTSBURGH, PA	5,939

Ranking of Total Tax Burdens for Retirees
Earning $50,000 and Owning a Home Valued at $100,000

Rank	City, State	Total Tax	Rank	City, State	Total Tax
1	ANCHORAGE, AK	$ 184	(TIE) 83	LOS ANGELES, CA	$3,568
2	WILMINGTON, DE	2,042	(TIE) 83	GAINESVILLE, FL	3,568
3	PORTSMOUTH, NH	2,239	85	ST. GEORGE, UT	3,577
4	WILLIAMSBURG, VA	2,293	86	HATTIESBURG, MS	3,582
5	MYRTLE BEACH, SC	2,452	87	ASHLAND, OR	3,602
(TIE) 6	BEAUFORT, SC	2,469	88	SAN JUAN CAPISTRANO, CA	3,606
(TIE) 6	HILTON HEAD, SC	2,469	89	PALM DESERT, CA	3,613
8	CHEYENNE, WY	2,537	90	SAN FRANCISCO, CA	3,631
9	CLEMSON, SC	2,562	91	TAMPA, FL	3,633
10	DENVER, CO	2,591	92	COEUR D'ALENE, ID	3,634
(TIE) 11	NAPLES, FL	2,621		**AVERAGE**	**$3,639**
(TIE) 11	SAVANNAH, GA	2,621	93	LINCOLN CITY, OR	3,644
13	ABINGDON, VA	2,675	94	PENSACOLA, FL	3,651
(TIE) 14	THOMASVILLE, GA	2,676	95	FORT LAUDERDALE, FL	3,667
(TIE) 14	DALLAS, TX	2,676	96	FLAGSTAFF, AZ	3,676
16	JACKSON, WY	2,729	97	EUGENE, OR	3,679
17	ST. SIMONS ISLAND, GA	2,739	98	ST. PETERSBURG, FL	3,682
18	GREENVILLE, SC	2,753	99	SCOTTSDALE, AZ	3,692
19	AIKEN, SC	2,814	100	BOISE, ID	3,708
20	SANTA FE, NM	2,831	101	BUFFALO, NY	3,710
21	NATCHITOCHES, LA	2,842	102	TEMECULA, CA	3,724
22	BATON ROUGE, LA	2,851	103	COLUMBUS, OH	3,725
(TIE) 23	FORT COLLINS, CO	2,853	104	SALT LAKE CITY, UT	3,739
(TIE) 23	CHARLESTON, SC	2,853	105	PRESCOTT, AZ	3,747
25	SIESTA KEY, FL	2,878	(TIE) 106	SIERRA VISTA, AZ	3,753
26	VICKSBURG, MS	2,883	(TIE) 106	THE WOODLANDS, TX	3,753
27	CHARLOTTESVILLE, VA	2,928	108	PORTLAND, OR	3,761
28	NEW YORK CITY, NY	2,930	109	CLEVELAND, OH	3,792
29	FRIDAY HARBOR, WA	2,963	110	GEORGETOWN, TX	3,814
30	LONGBOAT KEY, FL	2,964	111	TOMS RIVER, NJ	3,820
31	SANIBEL ISLAND, FL	2,982	112	HOT SPRINGS, AR	3,825
32	JACKSONVILLE, FL	2,993	113	TUCSON, AZ	3,843
33	NORTH FORT MYERS, FL	3,026	114	LOUISVILLE, KY	3,846
34	KEY WEST, FL	3,029	115	OJAI, CA	3,864
35	BOCA RATON, FL	3,051	116	MIAMI, FL	3,866
36	OAK HARBOR, WA	3,065	117	SAN ANTONIO, TX	3,871
37	LAKELAND, FL	3,090	118	EUFAULA, AL	3,893
38	JUPITER, FL	3,092	119	CHICAGO, IL	3,963
39	VENICE, FL	3,134	120	MEMPHIS, TN	3,981
40	ORLANDO, FL	3,136	121	SYRACUSE, NY	4,008
41	HONOLULU, HI	3,137	122	PHOENIX, AZ	4,052
42	PARIS, TN	3,138	123	PINEHURST, NC	4,061
43	PUNTA GORDA, FL	3,161	124	BRANSON, MO	4,105
44	AUSTIN, TX	3,189	125	NEW BERN, NC	4,143
45	LAS CRUCES, NM	3,191	126	HENDERSONVILLE, NC	4,168
46	BRADENTON, FL	3,200	127	WAYNESVILLE, NC	4,175
47	GREEN VALLEY, AZ	3,208	128	CINCINNATI, OH	4,224
48	OCALA, FL	3,211	129	DETROIT, MI	4,243
49	GAINESVILLE, GA	3,222	130	KERRVILLE, TX	4,247
50	SEQUIM, WA	3,233	131	CAMDEN, ME	4,260
51	CAPE MAY, NJ	3,244	132	HARTFORD, CT	4,365
52	ORMOND BEACH, FL	3,258	133	WICHITA, KS	4,376
53	MARYVILLE, TN	3,263	134	EDENTON, NC	4,390
54	ST. AUGUSTINE, FL	3,270	135	FARGO, ND	4,400
55	PORT TOWNSEND, WA	3,275	136	OKLAHOMA CITY, OK	4,414
56	VERO BEACH, FL	3,288	137	BOSTON, MA	4,491
57	SAN DIEGO, CA	3,295	138	NEW HAVEN, CT	4,505
58	NEW ORLEANS, LA	3,304	139	BROWNSVILLE, TX	4,517
59	RUIDOSO, NM	3,318	140	BREVARD, NC	4,548
60	BILLINGS, MT	3,336	141	ASHEVILLE, NC	4,562
61	FAIRHOPE, AL	3,342	142	BURLINGTON, VT	4,570
62	LEESBURG, FL	3,343	143	LITTLE ROCK, AR	4,627
63	WINTER HAVEN, FL	3,344	144	OMAHA, NE	4,657
64	DELAND, FL	3,372	145	KANSAS CITY, MO	4,666
65	SIOUX FALLS, SD	3,377	146	LANCASTER, PA	4,681
66	BEND, OR	3,387	(TIE) 147	CELEBRATION, FL	4,685
67	SARASOTA, FL	3,389	(TIE) 147	WILMINGTON, NC	4,685
68	LAS VEGAS, NV	3,400	149	STURGEON BAY, WI	4,690
69	OXFORD, MS	3,409	150	CHAPEL HILL, NC	4,728
70	CHARLESTON, WV	3,423	151	NEWARK, NJ	4,747
71	ATLANTA, GA	3,445	152	EAGLE RIVER, WI	4,769
72	HOUSTON, TX	3,448	153	BALTIMORE, MD	4,802
73	CARLSBAD, CA	3,450	154	MINNEAPOLIS, MN	4,810
74	DADE CITY, FL	3,474	155	CAPE COD, MA	5,139
(TIE) 75	RENO, NV	3,479	156	DES MOINES, IA	5,163
(TIE) 75	RICHMOND, VA	3,479	157	MADISON, WI	5,189
77	ALBUQUERQUE, NM	3,498	158	PHILADELPHIA, PA	5,509
78	MOUNT DORA, FL	3,510	159	INDIANAPOLIS, IN	5,563
79	LEXINGTON, KY	3,511	160	MILWAUKEE, WI	5,616
80	PETOSKEY, MI	3,528	161	WASHINGTON, DC	5,845
81	GRANTS PASS, OR	3,536	162	PITTSBURGH, PA	6,492
82	SEATTLE, WA	3,553	163	PROVIDENCE, RI	6,622

Ranking of Total Tax Burdens for Retirees
Earning $50,000 and Owning a Home Valued at $150,000

Rank	City, State	Total Tax	Rank	City, State	Total Tax
1	ANCHORAGE, AK	$ 184	83	SARASOTA, FL	$4,258
2	WILLIAMSBURG, VA	2,563	84	VERO BEACH, FL	4,287
3	HILTON HEAD, SC	2,725	85	OCALA, FL	4,318
4	MYRTLE BEACH, SC	2,726	86	TEMECULA, CA	4,319
5	BEAUFORT, SC	2,810	87	EUGENE, OR	4,324
6	CLEMSON, SC	2,819	88	COEUR D'ALENE, ID	4,350
7	CHEYENNE, WY	2,891	89	LINCOLN CITY, OR	4,361
8	DENVER, CO	2,919	90	LEESBURG, FL	4,374
9	JACKSON, WY	3,009	91	ORMOND BEACH, FL	4,379
10	PORTSMOUTH, NH	3,084	92	ATLANTA, GA	4,380
11	WILMINGTON, DE	3,120	93	OJAI, CA	4,390
12	SANTA FE, NM	3,132	94	HATTIESBURG, MS	4,399
13	ABINGDON, VA	3,175		AVERAGE	$4,401
14	AIKEN, SC	3,192	95	AUSTIN, TX	4,408
15	CHARLESTON, SC	3,197	96	CLEVELAND, OH	4,427
16	GREENVILLE, SC	3,205	97	BOISE, ID	4,431
17	HONOLULU, HI	3,220	98	ST. AUGUSTINE, FL	4,441
18	THOMASVILLE, GA	3,238	99	LOUISVILLE, KY	4,444
19	FORT COLLINS, CO	3,286	100	TUCSON, AZ	4,462
20	NAPLES, FL	3,287	101	COLUMBUS, OH	4,470
21	ST. SIMONS ISLAND, GA	3,288	102	BRANSON, MO	4,502
22	SAVANNAH, GA	3,296	103	PINEHURST, NC	4,509
23	BATON ROUGE, LA	3,336	104	PORTLAND, OR	4,547
24	NEW YORK CITY, NY	3,380	105	WINTER HAVEN, FL	4,561
25	NATCHITOCHES, LA	3,422	106	DELAND, FL	4,576
26	FRIDAY HARBOR, WA	3,423	107	PHOENIX, AZ	4,613
27	VICKSBURG, MS	3,448	108	MOUNT DORA, FL	4,625
28	CHARLOTTESVILLE, VA	3,483	109	HENDERSONVILLE, NC	4,643
29	FAIRHOPE, AL	3,522	110	HOUSTON, TX	4,646
30	PARIS, TN	3,568	111	TOMS RIVER, NJ	4,656
31	PETOSKEY, MI	3,573	112	NEW BERN, NC	4,663
32	OAK HARBOR, WA	3,582	113	WAYNESVILLE, NC	4,705
33	SIESTA KEY, FL	3,585	114	DADE CITY, FL	4,804
34	LAS CRUCES, NM	3,647	115	PENSACOLA, FL	4,807
35	GREEN VALLEY, AZ	3,648	116	MEMPHIS, TN	4,827
36	RUIDOSO, NM	3,708	117	CHICAGO, IL	4,875
37	KEY WEST, FL	3,748	118	TAMPA, FL	4,908
38	LONGBOAT KEY, FL	3,797	119	GAINESVILLE, FL	4,912
39	SEQUIM, WA	3,817	120	DETROIT, MI	4,916
40	DALLAS, TX	3,841	121	ST. PETERSBURG, FL	4,921
41	GAINESVILLE, GA	3,848	122	BUFFALO, NY	4,929
42	MARYVILLE, TN	3,849	123	FORT LAUDERDALE, FL	4,930
43	SAN DIEGO, CA	3,852	124	EDENTON, NC	4,933
44	CHARLESTON, WV	3,878	125	OKLAHOMA CITY, OK	4,973
45	PORT TOWNSEND, WA	3,882	126	BURLINGTON, VT	4,985
46	ST. GEORGE, UT	3,893	127	WICHITA, KS	4,994
47	BILLINGS, MT	3,917	128	GEORGETOWN, TX	5,037
48	SANIBEL ISLAND, FL	3,934	129	CAMDEN, ME	5,067
49	LAS VEGAS, NV	3,970	130	BREVARD, NC	5,129
50	CAPE MAY, NJ	3,981	131	BOSTON, MA	5,149
51	CARLSBAD, CA	3,984	132	CINCINNATI, OH	5,160
52	BEND, OR	3,990	133	THE WOODLANDS, TX	5,179
53	LEXINGTON, KY	3,995	134	WILMINGTON, NC	5,225
54	PUNTA GORDA, FL	4,008	135	MIAMI, FL	5,235
55	JACKSONVILLE, FL	4,010	136	ASHEVILLE, NC	5,257
56	VENICE, FL	4,011	137	SAN ANTONIO, TX	5,305
57	NORTH FORT MYERS, FL	4,013	138	LITTLE ROCK, AR	5,307
58	EUFAULA, AL	4,081	139	KANSAS CITY, MO	5,336
59	RENO, NV	4,082	140	HARTFORD, CT	5,387
60	FLAGSTAFF, AZ	4,096	141	CHAPEL HILL, NC	5,484
61	BOCA RATON, FL	4,098	142	FARGO, ND	5,511
62	OXFORD, MS	4,120	143	CELEBRATION, FL	5,519
63	LAKELAND, FL	4,124	144	OMAHA, NE	5,551
64	SEATTLE, WA	4,126	145	STURGEON BAY, WI	5,568
65	SCOTTSDALE, AZ	4,127	146	KERRVILLE, TX	5,577
66	SALT LAKE CITY, UT	4,131	147	SYRACUSE, NY	5,614
67	SAN JUAN CAPISTRANO, CA	4,140	148	EAGLE RIVER, WI	5,691
68	PRESCOTT, AZ	4,145	149	NEW HAVEN, CT	5,728
69	NEW ORLEANS, LA	4,152	150	LANCASTER, PA	5,899
70	SIOUX FALLS, SD	4,162	151	BROWNSVILLE, TX	5,910
71	JUPITER, FL	4,165	152	BALTIMORE, MD	5,930
72	ALBUQUERQUE, NM	4,169	153	CAPE COD, MA	5,953
(TIE) 73	PALM DESERT, CA	4,172	154	MINNEAPOLIS, MN	6,046
(TIE) 73	ORLANDO, FL	4,172	155	WASHINGTON, DC	6,085
75	GRANTS PASS, OR	4,173	156	DES MOINES, IA	6,381
76	LOS ANGELES, CA	4,193	157	MADISON, WI	6,420
77	RICHMOND, VA	4,194	158	NEWARK, NJ	6,552
78	SAN FRANCISCO, CA	4,199	159	PHILADELPHIA, PA	6,832
79	SIERRA VISTA, AZ	4,237	(TIE) 160	INDIANAPOLIS, IN	7,036
80	HOT SPRINGS, AR	4,241	(TIE) 160	MILWAUKEE, WI	7,036
81	ASHLAND, OR	4,245	162	PROVIDENCE, RI	7,757
82	BRADENTON, FL	4,255	163	PITTSBURGH, PA	8,452

Ranking of Total Tax Burdens for Retirees Earning $50,000 and Owning a Home Valued at $200,000

Rank	City, State	Total Tax	Rank	City, State	Total Tax
1	ANCHORAGE, AK	$1,071	83	LOUISVILLE, KY	$5,042
2	WILLIAMSBURG, VA	2,833	84	CLEVELAND, OH	5,062
3	HILTON HEAD, SC	3,133	85	LINCOLN CITY, OR	5,078
4	MYRTLE BEACH, SC	3,204	86	TUCSON, AZ	5,082
5	CLEMSON, SC	3,231	87	HENDERSONVILLE, NC	5,118
6	CHEYENNE, WY	3,245	88	SARASOTA, FL	5,127
7	DENVER, CO	3,246	89	BOCA RATON, FL	5,145
8	JACKSON, WY	3,288	90	LAKELAND, FL	5,158
9	BEAUFORT, SC	3,303	91	PHOENIX, AZ	5,175
10	HONOLULU, HI	3,402	92	NEW BERN, NC	5,183
11	SANTA FE, NM	3,433		**AVERAGE**	**$5,187**
12	ABINGDON, VA	3,675	93	ORLANDO, FL	5,208
13	FAIRHOPE, AL	3,702	94	COLUMBUS, OH	5,214
14	CHARLESTON, SC	3,708	95	HATTIESBURG, MS	5,216
15	FORT COLLINS, CO	3,719	96	WAYNESVILLE, NC	5,235
16	AIKEN, SC	3,737	97	JUPITER, FL	5,237
17	THOMASVILLE, GA	3,799	98	COEUR D'ALENE, ID	5,244
18	BATON ROUGE, LA	3,821	99	VERO BEACH, FL	5,287
19	NEW YORK CITY, NY	3,830	100	BRADENTON, FL	5,310
20	ST. SIMONS ISLAND, GA	3,836	101	ATLANTA, GA	5,316
21	GREENVILLE, SC	3,840	(TIE) 102	BOISE, ID	5,333
22	FRIDAY HARBOR, WA	3,884	(TIE) 102	PORTLAND, OR	5,333
23	PORTSMOUTH, NH	3,929	104	BURLINGTON, VT	5,393
24	NAPLES, FL	3,953	105	LEESBURG, FL	5,406
25	SAVANNAH, GA	3,971	106	OCALA, FL	5,425
26	PARIS, TN	3,998	107	EDENTON, NC	5,475
27	NATCHITOCHES, LA	4,002	108	ORMOND BEACH, FL	5,499
28	VICKSBURG, MS	4,014	109	OKLAHOMA CITY, OK	5,532
29	CHARLOTTESVILLE, VA	4,038	(TIE) 110	ST. AUGUSTINE, FL	5,613
30	PETOSKEY, MI	4,050	(TIE) 110	WICHITA, KS	5,613
31	GREEN VALLEY, AZ	4,088	112	AUSTIN, TX	5,627
32	RUIDOSO, NM	4,098	113	MEMPHIS, TN	5,673
33	OAK HARBOR, WA	4,099	114	BREVARD, NC	5,709
34	LAS CRUCES, NM	4,103	115	MOUNT DORA, FL	5,741
35	ST. GEORGE, UT	4,210	116	WILMINGTON, NC	5,765
36	WILMINGTON, DE	4,244	117	WINTER HAVEN, FL	5,778
37	EUFAULA, AL	4,268	118	DELAND, FL	5,780
38	SIESTA KEY, FL	4,292	119	CHICAGO, IL	5,788
39	CHARLESTON, WV	4,333	120	BOSTON, MA	5,806
40	SEQUIM, WA	4,402	121	TOMS RIVER, NJ	5,832
41	SAN DIEGO, CA	4,409	122	HOUSTON, TX	5,868
42	CAPE MAY, NJ	4,420	123	CAMDEN, ME	5,873
43	MARYVILLE, TN	4,435	124	ASHEVILLE, NC	5,952
44	KEY WEST, FL	4,468	125	PENSACOLA, FL	5,963
45	GAINESVILLE, GA	4,474	126	LITTLE ROCK, AR	5,987
46	LEXINGTON, KY	4,479	127	KANSAS CITY, MO	6,006
47	PORT TOWNSEND, WA	4,490	128	CINCINNATI, OH	6,097
48	BILLINGS, MT	4,497	129	DETROIT, MI	6,124
(TIE) 49	FLAGSTAFF, AZ	4,517	130	DADE CITY, FL	6,134
(TIE) 49	CARLSBAD, CA	4,517	131	BUFFALO, NY	6,149
51	SALT LAKE CITY, UT	4,524	132	ST. PETERSBURG, FL	6,160
52	LAS VEGAS, NV	4,539	133	TAMPA, FL	6,183
53	PRESCOTT, AZ	4,542	134	FORT LAUDERDALE, FL	6,193
54	SCOTTSDALE, AZ	4,562	135	CHAPEL HILL, NC	6,239
55	BEND, OR	4,593	136	GAINESVILLE, FL	6,256
56	LONGBOAT KEY, FL	4,631	137	GEORGETOWN, TX	6,260
57	HOT SPRINGS, AR	4,657	138	WASHINGTON, DC	6,325
58	SAN JUAN CAPISTRANO, CA	4,674	139	CELEBRATION, FL	6,353
59	RENO, NV	4,685	140	OMAHA, NE	6,445
60	SEATTLE, WA	4,698	141	HARTFORD, CT	6,471
61	SIERRA VISTA, AZ	4,720	142	STURGEON BAY, WI	6,522
62	PALM DESERT, CA	4,731	143	MIAMI, FL	6,604
63	SAN FRANCISCO, CA	4,767	144	THE WOODLANDS, TX	6,609
64	GRANTS PASS, OR	4,811	145	FARGO, ND	6,622
65	LOS ANGELES, CA	4,818	146	EAGLE RIVER, WI	6,686
66	OXFORD, MS	4,831	147	SAN ANTONIO, TX	6,739
67	ALBUQUERQUE, NM	4,840	148	CAPE COD, MA	6,767
68	PUNTA GORDA, FL	4,855	149	KERRVILLE, TX	6,906
69	SANIBEL ISLAND, FL	4,886	150	NEW HAVEN, CT	6,951
70	VENICE, FL	4,887	151	LANCASTER, PA	7,118
71	ASHLAND, OR	4,888	152	BALTIMORE, MD	7,136
72	BRANSON, MO	4,898	153	SYRACUSE, NY	7,219
73	RICHMOND, VA	4,909	154	BROWNSVILLE, TX	7,304
74	TEMECULA, CA	4,913	155	MINNEAPOLIS, MN	7,314
75	OJAI, CA	4,916	156	DES MOINES, IA	7,601
76	SIOUX FALLS, SD	4,947	157	MADISON, WI	7,658
77	PINEHURST, NC	4,956	158	PHILADELPHIA, PA	8,114
78	EUGENE, OR	4,969	159	NEWARK, NJ	8,350
79	NORTH FORT MYERS, FL	5,000	160	MILWAUKEE, WI	8,455
80	NEW ORLEANS, LA	5,001	161	INDIANAPOLIS, IN	8,508
81	DALLAS, TX	5,007	162	PROVIDENCE, RI	8,893
82	JACKSONVILLE, FL	5,027	163	PITTSBURGH, PA	10,412

Ranking of Total Tax Burdens for Retirees Earning $75,000 and Owning a Home Valued at $150,000

Rank	City, State	Total Tax	Rank	City, State	Total Tax
1	ANCHORAGE, AK	$ 184	83	TUCSON, AZ	$5,617
2	CHEYENNE, WY	3,200	84	CARLSBAD, CA	5,631
3	PORTSMOUTH, NH	3,287	85	GAINESVILLE, GA	5,693
4	JACKSON, WY	3,379		**AVERAGE**	**$5,724**
5	NAPLES, FL	3,632	86	HATTIESBURG, MS	5,724
6	HILTON HEAD, SC	3,651	87	SAN ANTONIO, TX	5,758
7	MYRTLE BEACH, SC	3,652	88	PETOSKEY, MI	5,762
8	BEAUFORT, SC	3,736	89	SAN JUAN CAPISTRANO, CA	5,787
9	CLEMSON, SC	3,807	(TIE) 90	PHOENIX, AZ	5,796
10	WILLIAMSBURG, VA	3,825	(TIE) 90	NEW YORK CITY, NY	5,796
11	FRIDAY HARBOR, WA	3,865	92	CHARLESTON, WV	5,802
12	SIESTA KEY, FL	3,988	93	TOMS RIVER, NJ	5,805
13	OAK HARBOR, WA	4,059	94	PALM DESERT, CA	5,819
14	PARIS, TN	4,068	95	LOS ANGELES, CA	5,868
15	GREENVILLE, SC	4,131	96	SAN FRANCISCO, CA	5,889
16	KEY WEST, FL	4,179	97	CELEBRATION, FL	5,922
17	AIKEN, SC	4,180	98	TEMECULA, CA	5,966
18	CHARLESTON, SC	4,185	99	SANTA FE, NM	5,998
19	LONGBOAT KEY, FL	4,200	100	OJAI, CA	6,008
20	SANIBEL ISLAND, FL	4,279	101	KERRVILLE, TX	6,051
21	DENVER, CO	4,284	102	CHICAGO, IL	6,074
22	SEQUIM, WA	4,289	103	BEND, OR	6,105
23	DALLAS, TX	4,315	104	COLUMBUS, OH	6,133
24	MARYVILLE, TN	4,349	105	LEXINGTON, KY	6,144
25	PORT TOWNSEND, WA	4,354	106	CLEVELAND, OH	6,162
26	NORTH FORT MYERS, FL	4,358	107	GRANTS PASS, OR	6,288
27	JACKSONVILLE, FL	4,384	108	ATLANTA, GA	6,311
28	LAS VEGAS, NV	4,387	109	HOT SPRINGS, AR	6,345
29	PUNTA GORDA, FL	4,411	110	ASHLAND, OR	6,382
30	VENICE, FL	4,414	111	BROWNSVILLE, TX	6,384
31	ABINGDON, VA	4,432	112	EUGENE, OR	6,439
32	BOCA RATON, FL	4,443	113	COEUR D'ALENE, ID	6,472
33	WILMINGTON, DE	4,458	114	LINCOLN CITY, OR	6,476
34	LAKELAND, FL	4,469	115	BRANSON, MO	6,478
35	RENO, NV	4,499	(TIE) 116	LOUISVILLE, KY	6,509
36	JUPITER, FL	4,510	(TIE) 116	LAS CRUCES, NM	6,509
37	ORLANDO, FL	4,517	118	PINEHURST, NC	6,519
38	SIOUX FALLS, SD	4,527	119	BOISE, ID	6,553
39	BRADENTON, FL	4,600	120	RUIDOSO, NM	6,621
40	FORT COLLINS, CO	4,628	121	HENDERSONVILLE, NC	6,653
41	BATON ROUGE, LA	4,632	122	NEW BERN, NC	6,660
42	SEATTLE, WA	4,634	123	PORTLAND, OR	6,662
43	SARASOTA, FL	4,661	124	WAYNESVILLE, NC	6,702
44	OCALA, FL	4,663	125	BOSTON, MA	6,742
45	NATCHITOCHES, LA	4,671	126	FARGO, ND	6,787
46	GREEN VALLEY, AZ	4,688	127	BUFFALO, NY	6,811
47	VERO BEACH, FL	4,690	128	BILLINGS, MT	6,839
48	ORMOND BEACH, FL	4,724	129	CINCINNATI, OH	6,852
49	CHARLOTTESVILLE, VA	4,737	130	ST. GEORGE, UT	6,940
50	THOMASVILLE, GA	4,742	131	EDENTON, NC	6,943
51	FAIRHOPE, AL	4,751	132	LANCASTER, PA	6,973
(TIE) 52	LEESBURG, FL	4,777	133	ALBUQUERQUE, NM	6,996
(TIE) 52	VICKSBURG, MS	4,777	134	BREVARD, NC	7,139
54	ST. AUGUSTINE, FL	4,786	(TIE) 135	CAMDEN, ME	7,185
55	CAPE MAY, NJ	4,790	(TIE) 135	SALT LAKE CITY, UT	7,185
56	ST. SIMONS ISLAND, GA	4,852	137	HARTFORD, CT	7,201
57	AUSTIN, TX	4,882	138	DETROIT, MI	7,214
58	WINTER HAVEN, FL	4,906	139	WILMINGTON, NC	7,222
59	DELAND, FL	4,921	140	ASHEVILLE, NC	7,254
60	MOUNT DORA, FL	5,028	141	WICHITA, KS	7,285
61	HOUSTON, TX	5,120	142	LITTLE ROCK, AR	7,346
62	DADE CITY, FL	5,149	143	BURLINGTON, VT	7,420
63	PENSACOLA, FL	5,238	144	OKLAHOMA CITY, OK	7,424
64	GAINESVILLE, FL	5,257	145	KANSAS CITY, MO	7,426
65	FORT LAUDERDALE, FL	5,275	146	CHAPEL HILL, NC	7,481
66	FLAGSTAFF, AZ	5,277	147	NEW HAVEN, CT	7,542
67	SCOTTSDALE, AZ	5,291	148	SYRACUSE, NY	7,545
68	TAMPA, FL	5,296	149	CAPE COD, MA	7,546
69	ST. PETERSBURG, FL	5,324	150	NEWARK, NJ	7,686
70	MEMPHIS, TN	5,327	151	OMAHA, NE	7,756
71	PRESCOTT, AZ	5,346	152	STURGEON BAY, WI	7,757
72	HONOLULU, HI	5,351	153	EAGLE RIVER, WI	7,880
73	SAVANNAH, GA	5,392	154	DES MOINES, IA	8,121
74	SIERRA VISTA, AZ	5,401	155	INDIANAPOLIS, IN	8,291
75	EUFAULA, AL	5,431	156	PHILADELPHIA, PA	8,535
(TIE) 76	NEW ORLEANS, LA	5,445	157	MINNEAPOLIS, MN	8,571
(TIE) 76	OXFORD, MS	5,445	158	MADISON, WI	8,609
78	GEORGETOWN, TX	5,454	159	WASHINGTON, DC	8,678
79	RICHMOND, VA	5,456	160	MILWAUKEE, WI	9,232
80	SAN DIEGO, CA	5,499	161	BALTIMORE, MD	9,292
81	THE WOODLANDS, TX	5,596	162	PROVIDENCE, RI	9,769
82	MIAMI, FL	5,609	163	PITTSBURGH, PA	9,865

Ranking of Total Tax Burdens for Retirees
Earning $75,000 and Owning a Home Valued at $250,000

Rank	City, State	Total Tax	Rank	City, State	Total Tax
1	ANCHORAGE, AK	$1,958	83	TEMECULA, CA	$7,155
2	CHEYENNE, WY	3,907	84	HOT SPRINGS, AR	7,177
3	JACKSON, WY	3,938	85	MOUNT DORA, FL	7,260
4	WILLIAMSBURG, VA	4,365	86	BRANSON, MO	7,270
5	HILTON HEAD, SC	4,467		**AVERAGE**	**$7,296**
6	MYRTLE BEACH, SC	4,608	87	BEND, OR	7,310
7	CLEMSON, SC	4,631	88	AUSTIN, TX	7,321
8	BEAUFORT, SC	4,722	89	DELAND, FL	7,329
9	FRIDAY HARBOR, WA	4,786	90	WINTER HAVEN, FL	7,339
10	PARIS, TN	4,928	91	HATTIESBURG, MS	7,359
11	DENVER, CO	4,939	92	RUIDOSO, NM	7,401
12	NAPLES, FL	4,963	93	PINEHURST, NC	7,414
13	PORTSMOUTH, NH	4,978	94	LAS CRUCES, NM	7,422
14	OAK HARBOR, WA	5,092	95	CLEVELAND, OH	7,432
15	FAIRHOPE, AL	5,111	96	PENSACOLA, FL	7,549
16	CHARLESTON, SC	5,208	97	GRANTS PASS, OR	7,563
17	AIKEN, SC	5,270	98	ST. GEORGE, UT	7,574
18	GREENVILLE, SC	5,401	99	CELEBRATION, FL	7,589
19	SIESTA KEY, FL	5,402	100	HENDERSONVILLE, NC	7,603
20	ABINGDON, VA	5,432	101	COLUMBUS, OH	7,622
21	SEQUIM, WA	5,458	102	ASHLAND, OR	7,667
22	FORT COLLINS, CO	5,494	103	NEW BERN, NC	7,700
23	MARYVILLE, TN	5,521	104	LOUISVILLE, KY	7,705
24	LAS VEGAS, NV	5,526	105	EUGENE, OR	7,729
25	GREEN VALLEY, AZ	5,568	106	WAYNESVILLE, NC	7,762
26	PORT TOWNSEND, WA	5,569	107	HOUSTON, TX	7,800
27	BATON ROUGE, LA	5,601	(TIE) 108	FORT LAUDERDALE, FL	7,802
28	KEY WEST, FL	5,618	(TIE) 108	ST. PETERSBURG, FL	7,802
29	RENO, NV	5,705	110	DADE CITY, FL	7,808
30	HONOLULU, HI	5,716	111	TAMPA, FL	7,846
31	SEATTLE, WA	5,779	112	CHICAGO, IL	7,899
32	EUFAULA, AL	5,806	113	GEORGETOWN, TX	7,900
33	NATCHITOCHES, LA	5,831	114	LINCOLN CITY, OR	7,909
34	CHARLOTTESVILLE, VA	5,847	115	GAINESVILLE, FL	7,945
35	THOMASVILLE, GA	5,865	116	SALT LAKE CITY, UT	7,971
36	LONGBOAT KEY, FL	5,867	117	BILLINGS, MT	8,000
37	VICKSBURG, MS	5,909	118	EDENTON, NC	8,028
38	ST. SIMONS ISLAND, GA	5,948	119	BOSTON, MA	8,057
39	SIOUX FALLS, SD	6,097	120	TOMS RIVER, NJ	8,133
40	PUNTA GORDA, FL	6,104	121	ATLANTA, GA	8,182
41	FLAGSTAFF, AZ	6,119	122	PORTLAND, OR	8,233
42	PRESCOTT, AZ	6,141	123	BURLINGTON, VT	8,238
43	SCOTTSDALE, AZ	6,161	124	COEUR D'ALENE, ID	8,260
44	VENICE, FL	6,166	125	BREVARD, NC	8,300
45	SANIBEL ISLAND, FL	6,184	126	WILMINGTON, NC	8,302
46	CAPE MAY, NJ	6,252	127	ALBUQUERQUE, NM	8,338
47	NORTH FORT MYERS, FL	6,333	128	MIAMI, FL	8,347
48	SIERRA VISTA, AZ	6,367	129	BOISE, ID	8,358
49	SARASOTA, FL	6,399	130	THE WOODLANDS, TX	8,455
50	JACKSONVILLE, FL	6,418	131	WICHITA, KS	8,523
51	LAKELAND, FL	6,536	132	OKLAHOMA CITY, OK	8,542
52	BOCA RATON, FL	6,537	133	SAN ANTONIO, TX	8,626
53	ORLANDO, FL	6,589	134	ASHEVILLE, NC	8,644
54	PETOSKEY, MI	6,591	135	LITTLE ROCK, AR	8,706
55	SANTA FE, NM	6,599	136	KERRVILLE, TX	8,709
56	SAN DIEGO, CA	6,612	137	CINCINNATI, OH	8,725
57	DALLAS, TX	6,647	138	KANSAS CITY, MO	8,766
58	JUPITER, FL	6,654	139	CAMDEN, ME	8,798
59	VERO BEACH, FL	6,689	140	CHAPEL HILL, NC	8,992
60	NEW YORK CITY, NY	6,696	141	FARGO, ND	9,009
61	CARLSBAD, CA	6,698	142	WASHINGTON, DC	9,158
62	WILMINGTON, DE	6,706	143	BROWNSVILLE, TX	9,171
63	BRADENTON, FL	6,710	144	CAPE COD, MA	9,174
64	CHARLESTON, WV	6,712	145	BUFFALO, NY	9,250
65	SAVANNAH, GA	6,742	146	LANCASTER, PA	9,411
66	LEESBURG, FL	6,841	147	DETROIT, MI	9,468
67	SAN JUAN CAPISTRANO, CA	6,855	148	OMAHA, NE	9,544
68	TUCSON, AZ	6,856	149	STURGEON BAY, WI	9,665
69	OXFORD, MS	6,867	150	EAGLE RIVER, WI	9,870
70	OCALA, FL	6,878	151	HARTFORD, CT	9,965
71	RICHMOND, VA	6,886	152	NEW HAVEN, CT	9,988
72	PHOENIX, AZ	6,920	153	BALTIMORE, MD	10,498
73	PALM DESERT, CA	6,937	154	DES MOINES, IA	10,559
74	GAINESVILLE, GA	6,946	155	SYRACUSE, NY	10,756
75	ORMOND BEACH, FL	6,964	156	MADISON, WI	11,085
76	MEMPHIS, TN	7,019	157	MINNEAPOLIS, MN	11,107
77	SAN FRANCISCO, CA	7,025	158	PHILADELPHIA, PA	11,179
78	OJAI, CA	7,060	159	INDIANAPOLIS, IN	11,235
79	LEXINGTON, KY	7,112	160	NEWARK, NJ	11,271
80	LOS ANGELES, CA	7,118	161	PROVIDENCE, RI	12,040
81	ST. AUGUSTINE, FL	7,130	162	MILWAUKEE, WI	12,071
82	NEW ORLEANS, LA	7,142	163	PITTSBURGH, PA	13,785

Ranking of Total Tax Burdens for Retirees Earning $75,000 and Owning a Home Valued at $350,000

Rank	City, State	Total Tax	Rank	City, State	Total Tax
1	ANCHORAGE, AK	$3,732	83	MEMPHIS, TN	8,712
2	JACKSON, WY	4,497	84	NEW BERN, NC	8,740
3	CHEYENNE, WY	4,615	85	SALT LAKE CITY, UT	8,756
4	WILLIAMSBURG, VA	4,905	86	JUPITER, FL	8,799
5	HILTON HEAD, SC	5,283	87	BRADENTON, FL	8,819
6	CLEMSON, SC	5,455	88	WAYNESVILLE, NC	8,822
7	FAIRHOPE, AL	5,471	89	GRANTS PASS, OR	8,837
8	MYRTLE BEACH, SC	5,564	90	NEW ORLEANS, LA	8,839
9	DENVER, CO	5,595		**AVERAGE**	**$8,888**
(TIE) 10	BEAUFORT, SC	5,707	91	LOUISVILLE, KY	8,902
(TIE) 10	FRIDAY HARBOR, WA	5,707	92	LEESBURG, FL	8,904
12	PARIS, TN	5,788	93	ASHLAND, OR	8,953
13	HONOLULU, HI	6,081	94	WILMINGTON, DE	8,954
14	OAK HARBOR, WA	6,126	95	DALLAS, TX	8,978
15	EUFAULA, AL	6,181	96	HATTIESBURG, MS	8,993
16	CHARLESTON, SC	6,230	97	EUGENE, OR	9,019
17	NAPLES, FL	6,294	98	BURLINGTON, VT	9,055
18	AIKEN, SC	6,360	99	OCALA, FL	9,092
19	FORT COLLINS, CO	6,361	100	COLUMBUS, OH	9,111
20	ABINGDON, VA	6,432	101	EDENTON, NC	9,113
21	GREEN VALLEY, AZ	6,448	102	BILLINGS, MT	9,161
22	BATON ROUGE, LA	6,572	103	ORMOND BEACH, FL	9,205
23	SEQUIM, WA	6,627	104	CELEBRATION, FL	9,257
24	LAS VEGAS, NV	6,665	105	LINCOLN CITY, OR	9,343
25	PORTSMOUTH, NH	6,668	106	BOSTON, MA	9,372
26	GREENVILLE, SC	6,670	107	WILMINGTON, NC	9,382
27	MARYVILLE, TN	6,694	108	BREVARD, NC	9,461
28	PORT TOWNSEND, WA	6,784	109	ST. AUGUSTINE, FL	9,473
29	SIESTA KEY, FL	6,815	110	MOUNT DORA, FL	9,491
30	RENO, NV	6,911	111	WASHINGTON, DC	9,638
31	SEATTLE, WA	6,924	112	OKLAHOMA CITY, OK	9,660
32	PRESCOTT, AZ	6,936	113	ALBUQUERQUE, NM	9,679
33	CHARLOTTESVILLE, VA	6,957	114	CHICAGO, IL	9,724
34	FLAGSTAFF, AZ	6,960	115	DELAND, FL	9,738
35	THOMASVILLE, GA	6,987	116	AUSTIN, TX	9,759
36	NATCHITOCHES, LA	6,991	117	WICHITA, KS	9,761
37	SCOTTSDALE, AZ	7,031	118	WINTER HAVEN, FL	9,773
38	VICKSBURG, MS	7,040	119	PORTLAND, OR	9,804
39	ST. SIMONS ISLAND, GA	7,044	120	PENSACOLA, FL	9,860
40	KEY WEST, FL	7,057	121	ASHEVILLE, NC	10,034
41	SANTA FE, NM	7,201	122	COEUR D'ALENE, ID	10,049
42	SIERRA VISTA, AZ	7,333	123	ATLANTA, GA	10,053
43	LONGBOAT KEY, FL	7,534	124	LITTLE ROCK, AR	10,066
44	NEW YORK CITY, NY	7,596	125	KANSAS CITY, MO	10,106
45	CHARLESTON, WV	7,622	126	BOISE, ID	10,164
46	SIOUX FALLS, SD	7,667	127	ST. PETERSBURG, FL	10,280
47	CAPE MAY, NJ	7,700	128	FORT LAUDERDALE, FL	10,328
48	SAN DIEGO, CA	7,725	129	GEORGETOWN, TX	10,346
49	CARLSBAD, CA	7,765	130	TAMPA, FL	10,396
50	PUNTA GORDA, FL	7,798	131	CAMDEN, ME	10,411
51	VENICE, FL	7,919	132	TOMS RIVER, NJ	10,463
52	SAN JUAN CAPISTRANO, CA	7,923	133	DADE CITY, FL	10,468
53	HOT SPRINGS, AR	8,009	134	CHAPEL HILL, NC	10,503
54	PHOENIX, AZ	8,044	135	CINCINNATI, OH	10,598
55	PALM DESERT, CA	8,056	136	GAINESVILLE, FL	10,634
56	BRANSON, MO	8,063	137	HOUSTON, TX	10,715
57	LEXINGTON, KY	8,081	138	CAPE COD, MA	10,801
58	SANIBEL ISLAND, FL	8,088	139	MIAMI, FL	11,086
59	SAVANNAH, GA	8,092	140	FARGO, ND	11,231
60	TUCSON, AZ	8,095	141	THE WOODLANDS, TX	11,314
61	OJAI, CA	8,113	142	OMAHA, NE	11,332
62	SARASOTA, FL	8,137	143	KERRVILLE, TX	11,368
63	SAN FRANCISCO, CA	8,161	144	SAN ANTONIO, TX	11,494
64	RUIDOSO, NM	8,181	145	STURGEON BAY, WI	11,573
65	GAINESVILLE, GA	8,199	146	BUFFALO, NY	11,689
66	ST. GEORGE, UT	8,207	147	LANCASTER, PA	11,848
67	OXFORD, MS	8,289	148	EAGLE RIVER, WI	11,860
68	NORTH FORT MYERS, FL	8,307	149	DETROIT, MI	11,884
69	PINEHURST, NC	8,309	150	BROWNSVILLE, TX	11,958
70	RICHMOND, VA	8,316	151	NEW HAVEN, CT	12,435
71	LAS CRUCES, NM	8,334	152	BALTIMORE, MD	12,910
72	TEMECULA, CA	8,344	153	DES MOINES, IA	12,997
73	LOS ANGELES, CA	8,368	154	HARTFORD, CT	13,325
74	JACKSONVILLE, FL	8,453	155	MADISON, WI	13,561
75	BEND, OR	8,516	156	MINNEAPOLIS, MN	13,643
76	HENDERSONVILLE, NC	8,553	157	PHILADELPHIA, PA	13,824
77	PETOSKEY, MI	8,558	158	SYRACUSE, NY	13,967
78	LAKELAND, FL	8,604	159	INDIANAPOLIS, IN	14,179
79	BOCA RATON, FL	8,631	160	PROVIDENCE, RI	14,311
80	ORLANDO, FL	8,661	161	NEWARK, NJ	14,900
81	VERO BEACH, FL	8,688	162	MILWAUKEE, WI	14,910
82	CLEVELAND, OH	8,702	163	PITTSBURGH, PA	17,705

TAX HEAVEN OR HELL

How do the cities we've profiled stack up against each other tax-wise? The following charts show our 10 Tax Heavens and Hells for each of nine income/home categories. Find the category that most closely matches the income and home value you anticipate for yourself in retirement.

If you don't see a city you're interested in, check the full ranking for each income/home value category — from #1 to #163 — in the preceding pages.

Our charts do not take into account cost-of-living factors in the areas we examined. For instance, Honolulu appears in several Tax Heaven charts, but residents there face very high real estate prices. Our charts rank cities solely by the tax burdens you will incur living there.

You may be surprised to see that not all of our Tax Heaven slots have been filled by cities from states with no state income tax. Florida, the top retirement state, has no state income tax, but only one of the 31 Florida cities we profile

Tax Heavens ○ ○ ○

$25,000 Income/$75,000 Home

	TAX
1. ANCHORAGE, AK	$ 184
2. WILMINGTON, DE	712
3. BEND, OR	1,186
4. HONOLULU, HI	1,259
5. GRANTS PASS, OR	1,318
6. ASHLAND, OR	1,336
7. NEW YORK CITY, NY	1,359
8. LINCOLN CITY, OR	1,385
9. OMAHA, NE	1,398
10. SAVANNAH, GA	1,430

$25,000 Income/$100,000 Home

	TAX
1. ANCHORAGE, AK	$ 184
2. WILMINGTON, DE	1,161
3. HONOLULU, HI	1,259
4. BEND, OR	1,487
5. NEW YORK CITY, NY	1,528
6. BILLINGS, MT	1,613
7. PETOSKEY, MI	1,626
8. GRANTS PASS, OR	1,636
9. ASHLAND, OR	1,657
10. SAVANNAH, GA	1,666

$25,000 Income/$125,000 Home

	TAX
1. ANCHORAGE, AK	$ 184
2. HONOLULU, HI	1,259
3. WILMINGTON, DE	1,609
4. BILLINGS, MT	1,613
5. NEW YORK CITY, NY	1,697
6. BEND, OR	1,789
7. SANTA FE, NM	1,871
8. PETOSKEY, MI	1,885
9. WILLIAMSBURG, VA	1,900
10. OAK HARBOR, WA	1,947

$50,000 Income/$100,000 Home

	TAX
1. ANCHORAGE, AK	$ 184
2. WILMINGTON, DE	2,042
3. PORTSMOUTH, NH	2,239
4. WILLIAMSBURG, VA	2,293
5. MYRTLE BEACH, SC	2,452
6. BEAUFORT, SC (TIE)	2,469
HILTON HEAD, SC (TIE)	2,469
8. CHEYENNE, WY	2,537
9. CLEMSON, SC	2,562
10. DENVER, CO	2,591

$50,000 Income/$150,000 Home

	TAX
1. ANCHORAGE, AK	$ 184
2. WILLIAMSBURG, VA	2,563
3. HILTON HEAD, SC	2,725
4. MYRTLE BEACH, SC	2,726
5. BEAUFORT, SC	2,810
6. CLEMSON, SC	2,819
7. CHEYENNE, WY	2,891
8. DENVER, CO	2,919
9. JACKSON, WY	3,009
10. PORTSMOUTH, NH	3,084

$50,000 Income/$200,000 Home

	TAX
1. ANCHORAGE, AK	$1,071
2. WILLIAMSBURG, VA	2,833
3. HILTON HEAD, SC	3,133
4. MYRTLE BEACH, SC	3,204
5. CLEMSON, SC	3,231
6. CHEYENNE, WY	3,245
7. DENVER, CO	3,246
8. JACKSON, WY	3,288
9. BEAUFORT, SC	3,303
10. HONOLULU, HI	3,402

$75,000 Income/$150,000 Home

	TAX
1. ANCHORAGE, AK	$ 184
2. CHEYENNE, WY	3,200
3. PORTSMOUTH, NH	3,287
4. JACKSON, WY	3,379
5. NAPLES, FL	3,632
6. HILTON HEAD, SC	3,651
7. MYRTLE BEACH, SC	3,652
8. BEAUFORT, SC	3,736
9. CLEMSON, SC	3,807
10. WILLIAMSBURG, VA	3,825

$75,000 Income/$250,000 Home

	TAX
1. ANCHORAGE, AK	$1,958
2. CHEYENNE, WY	3,907
3. JACKSON, WY	3,938
4. WILLIAMSBURG, VA	4,365
5. HILTON HEAD, SC	4,467
6. MYRTLE BEACH, SC	4,608
7. CLEMSON, SC	4,631
8. BEAUFORT, SC	4,722
9. FRIDAY HARBOR, WA	4,786
10. PARIS, TN	4,928

$75,000 Income/$350,000 Home

	TAX
1. ANCHORAGE, AK	$3,732
2. JACKSON, WY	4,497
3. CHEYENNE, WY	4,615
4. WILLIAMSBURG, VA	4,905
5. HILTON HEAD, SC	5,283
6. CLEMSON, SC	5,455
7. FAIRHOPE, AL	5,471
8. MYRTLE BEACH, SC	5,564
9. DENVER, CO	5,595
10. BEAUFORT, SC (TIE)	5,707
FRIDAY HARBOR, WA (TIE)	5,707

shows up as a Tax Heaven (and for only one of our income/home value categories). Why? Florida makes up for a lack of state income tax by collecting more revenue via sales and property taxes. More Florida cities surface in the tax-friendliest half of the rankings, though.

Across the board, our top Tax Heaven is Anchorage, AK — although most retirees will think twice about moving there to save on their tax bills.

If you're looking for a warm-weather home, you will be pleased to know that many Sunbelt states are tax-kind to senior citizens. Among the best are cities in Alabama, Florida, Georgia, New Mexico, South Carolina, Tennessee and Virginia. Take care to note that there are sometimes sharp differences between cities in these states (particularly true with Florida).

In general, taxes are highest in the Northeast and Midwest. Our Tax Hell charts include cities from Connecticut, Indiana, Iowa, Minnesota, New Jersey, New York, Pennsylvania, Rhode Island and Wisconsin, as well as the District of Columbia. Again, some cities in these states fare better than others.

Tax Hells ψ ψ ψ

$25,000 Income/$75,000 Home

	TAX
1. PROVIDENCE, RI	$4,491
2. PITTSBURGH, PA	3,979
3. CELEBRATION, FL	3,699
4. INDIANAPOLIS, IN	3,530
5. WASHINGTON, DC	3,529
6. NEW HAVEN, CT	3,254
7. BROWNSVILLE, TX	3,147
8. PHILADELPHIA, PA (TIE)	3,073
NEWARK, NJ (TIE)	3,073
10. DES MOINES, IA	3,013

$25,000 Income/$100,000 Home

	TAX
1. PITTSBURGH, PA	$4,959
2. PROVIDENCE, RI	4,809
3. INDIANAPOLIS, IN	4,249
4. CELEBRATION, FL	4,115
5. NEWARK, NJ	3,984
6. NEW HAVEN, CT	3,866
7. BROWNSVILLE, TX	3,844
8. PHILADELPHIA, PA	3,734
9. MILWAUKEE, WI	3,714
10. WASHINGTON, DC	3,649

$25,000 Income/$125,000 Home

	TAX
1. PITTSBURGH, PA	$5,939
2. PROVIDENCE, RI	5,376
3. INDIANAPOLIS, IN	4,986
4. NEWARK, NJ	4,896
5. BROWNSVILLE, TX	4,540
6. CELEBRATION, FL	4,532
7. NEW HAVEN, CT	4,477
8. MILWAUKEE, WI	4,424
9. PHILADELPHIA, PA	4,396
10. KERRVILLE, TX	4,239

$50,000 Income/$100,000 Home

	TAX
1. PROVIDENCE, RI	$6,622
2. PITTSBURGH, PA	6,492
3. WASHINGTON, DC	5,845
4. MILWAUKEE, WI	5,616
5. INDIANAPOLIS, IN	5,563
6. PHILADELPHIA, PA	5,509
7. MADISON, WI	5,189
8. DES MOINES, IA	5,163
9. CAPE COD, MA	5,139
10. MINNEAPOLIS, MN	4,810

$50,000 Income/$150,000 Home

	TAX
1. PITTSBURGH, PA	$8,452
2. PROVIDENCE, RI	7,757
3. MILWAUKEE, WI (TIE)	7,036
INDIANAPOLIS, IN (TIE)	7,036
5. PHILADELPHIA, PA	6,832
6. NEWARK, NJ	6,552
7. MADISON, WI	6,420
8. DES MOINES, IA	6,381
9. WASHINGTON, DC	6,085
10. MINNEAPOLIS, MN	6,046

$50,000 Income/$200,000 Home

	TAX
1. PITTSBURGH, PA	$10,412
2. PROVIDENCE, RI	8,893
3. INDIANAPOLIS, IN	8,508
4. MILWAUKEE, WI	8,455
5. NEWARK, NJ	8,350
6. PHILADELPHIA, PA	8,154
7. MADISON, WI	7,658
8. DES MOINES, IA	7,601
9. MINNEAPOLIS, MN	7,314
10. BROWNSVILLE, TX	7,304

$75,000 Income/$150,000 Home

	TAX
1. PITTSBURGH, PA	$9,865
2. PROVIDENCE, RI	9,769
3. BALTIMORE, MD	9,292
4. MILWAUKEE, WI	9,232
5. WASHINGTON, DC	8,678
6. MADISON, WI	8,609
7. MINNEAPOLIS, MN	8,571
8. PHILADELPHIA, PA	8,535
9. INDIANAPOLIS, IN	8,291
10. DES MOINES, IA	8,121

$75,000 Income/$250,000 Home

	TAX
1. PITTSBURGH, PA	$13,785
2. MILWAUKEE, WI	12,071
3. PROVIDENCE, RI	12,040
4. NEWARK, NJ	11,271
5. INDIANAPOLIS, IN	11,235
6. PHILADELPHIA, PA	11,179
7. MINNEAPOLIS, MN	11,107
8. MADISON, WI	11,085
9. SYRACUSE, NY	10,756
10. DES MOINES, IA	10,559

$75,000 Income/$350,000 Home

	TAX
1. PITTSBURGH, PA	$17,705
2. MILWAUKEE, WI	14,910
3. NEWARK, NJ	14,900
4. PROVIDENCE, RI	14,311
5. INDIANAPOLIS, IN	14,179
6. SYRACUSE, NY	13,967
7. PHILADELPHIA, PA	13,824
8. MINNEAPOLIS, MN	13,643
9. MADISON, WI	13,561
10. HARTFORD, CT	13,325

To make the right retirement reloca
And now you can — wit

You've got to have good information to make a good decision. And if you're wondering where to retire – one of the most important decisions you'll ever make – you need the best information available.

That's why the editors of *Where to Retire* magazine have commissioned this unique and informative series of *Special Reports*. They're practical, in-depth analyses of the most important issues involved in retirement relocation, in an easy-to-read format.

Every *Special Report* is meticulously researched data, hard facts and unbiased reporting. No outside advertising is accepted.

Best of all, we've managed to keep the price for each *Special Report* to a very manageable $3.95, plus $2.25 total postage and handling no matter how many *Special Reports* you order. ■

SR 1 — How to Plan and Execute A Successful Retirement Relocation

See what 200 relocated retirees said when asked, "If you could move again, what would you do differently?" You'll save the small price of this report many times over with the first common mistake you avoid.

Our author has heard all the first-hand accounts of moves gone awry and will steer you away from the relocation potholes. We'll tell you how to find and negotiate with a moving company, what to expect to pay and how to avoid being gouged. We'll tell you when to move, what to take and what to leave behind. Step-by-step, we'll walk you through a careful and cost-efficient shutdown at your current address and get you up and running in your new home quickly and as inexpensively as possible. $3.95.

SR 4 — Should You Retire to a Manufactured Home?

Explore this popular but controversial lifestyle option if you're looking for top value for your housing dollar.

We'll tell you how manufactured homes have changed, how they compare to site-built homes and how safe they are from high winds and fire. We'll cover zoning restrictions, financing options and price appreciation over time.

We'll tell you who lives in manufactured homes and examine various options including land-lease and resident-owned communities, home-land packages and subdivisions. We'll tell you how to shop for a manufactured home, including how to be sure your home meets national standards. And we will advise you how to figure the *total* cost of ownership.

Finally, we'll cover the purchase, delivery, siting and inspection of your new home, including consumer protection laws and how to ensure you're getting what you paid for. Illustrated, $3.95.

SR 7 — America's 100 Best Master-Planned Communities

In this special issue of Where to Retire dated Summer 2001, we evaluated nearly 500 planned communities throughout the United States to uncover the very best options for active retirees. All of these communities are still building new homes, but their amenities and shared facilities (clubhouses, golf courses, health clubs, restaurants, etc.) are complete and operating. They are located in coastal towns, mountains, deserts and lakeside from Florida to Washington state, from the Northeast to the desert Southwest. We included luxury, high-end communities and affordable, site-built and manufactured-home developments. Best of all, you're not just buying a new home in any of these developments...you're buying the new retirement lifestyle. $3.95.

SR 5 — Retiring Outside the United States

More than 350,000 retired Americans live outside the country, in places like Mexico, Uruguay, Costa Rica and Portugal. They go for three reasons: climate, a lower cost of living that translates into a higher standard of living, and the excitement of residing and traveling in a foreign country. Many go early in retirement, spend several years and then return home.

Sound interesting? Then you won't want to miss this informative primer on retiring abroad. We'll tell you how to determine if you'd be happy retiring abroad, how to find the country and town that best suit your lifestyle and how to adjust to everyday life in a new country. We'll discuss eight popular — and economical — foreign retirement spots and provide sources for additional information you might need. Finally, we'll tell you the most common (and costly) mistakes you could make in the process of moving abroad and how to avoid them. $3.95.

on, you've got to have all the facts.
imited-edition *Special Reports*.

SR 6 — Discounts for Travelers 50 and Beyond

Good news for anyone who loves to travel! When you turn 50, you're automatically eligible for an impressive array of travel discounts. What's more, the older you get, the greater the number of airlines, hotels and others willing to offer you those savings. And when you hit 65, every age-related discount in the entire travel industry can be yours for the asking.

But you'll have to know where to look and whom to ask. That's why we produced this insider's guide to finding and getting discounts from airlines, hotels, rental car companies, theme parks, cruise lines and national parks. Also includes invaluable advice on when and how to use discount travel clubs, how to save 50% traveling off-season, how to get a rebate on every airline ticket and more. Whether traveling to check out retirement sites, on business or strictly for pleasure, this guide can save you hundreds of dollars on your first trip. $3.95.

SR 8 — America's Most Affordable Retirement Towns

Would you like to pay less for everything from groceries and restaurants to movies and health care? Would you jump at the chance to trade your current house for one 50 percent larger, at no extra cost?

Many retirees succeed in slashing their cost of living when they relocate. They enjoy a higher standard of living in retirement because their dollar simply goes further in their new home town.

We considered nearly 200 retirement meccas in this country, from well-known to undiscovered, before compiling this list of 25 affordable towns that are also great for retirement. Each town profile includes interviews with relocated retirees and vital information on climate, housing cost, taxes, crime rate, overall cost of living, health care, educational opportunities and more. $3.95.

SR 19 — How to Get the Most Out of Social Security

Did you know that two people of identical age, earnings history, marital status and life expectancy can receive lifetime Social Security benefits which differ by $25,000 — or more — solely on the basis of when they asked for their retirement benefits to begin? It's true, which is why the date you pick to start Social Security is one of the most important decisions you will ever make. This report will help you make the correct decision and show you:
♦ How to get every dollar you deserve from Social Security ♦ How to avoid or reduce taxes you pay on Social Security ♦ Income that won't affect your benefits ♦ Who should start Social Security at age 62 and who should wait until age 70 ♦ Who can get disability benefits ♦ Techniques of thieves and shysters who target Social Security recipients ♦ How to get an estimate of future benefits from the Social Security Administration — free ♦ How to know if you've started Social Security too early — and what to do about it ♦ Who is eligible for Supplemental Security Income ♦ How to apply for benefits for a loved one who can't handle his or her own finances ♦ How to get benefits based on your ex-spouse's earnings ♦ And much, much more.

Whether retirement is a distant dream, just around the corner or even if you're already receiving benefits, we'll show you how to maximize your benefits and avoid the mistakes that can cost you thousands of dollars. $3.95.

Practical, in-depth analyses of the most important issues involved in retirement relocation.
ORDER TODAY!

YES! I want to make the right relocation decision. I enclose $3.95 for each report ordered, plus $2.25 total for postage and handling or $4 for Canadian delivery. Please send me each *Special Report* checked below. (Texas residents add 8.25% sales tax.)

☐ SR 1   ☐ SR 5   ☐ SR 8
☐ SR 4   ☐ SR 6   ☐ SR 19
          ☐ SR 7

Name _____

Address _____

City _____ State _____ Zip _____

Clip and mail this coupon, along with a check or money order payable to:

Number of reports_____ x $3.95 = _____
Plus postage & handling _____ $2.25
(Texas residents add 8.25% sales tax.) _____
Total enclosed _____

Vacation Publications
1502 Augusta Dr.-Suite 415
Houston, TX 77057

Allow 4-6 weeks for delivery.

9 Great Books to Help You
Make the Best Move of Your Life

■ America's 100 Best Places to Retire
Undiscovered and Low-Cost Edens
Edited by Richard Fox

From the editors of Where to Retire magazine. Learn about climate, cost of living, home prices, taxes, crime and health care in America's best retirement spots. Meet the retirees who've made the move and hear how they like their new hometown. Includes top picks in every region and highlights unknown and inexpensive retirement meccas. **$16.95**

(ALL NEW SECOND EDITION)

■ Where to Retire in Florida
Retirement Areas in the Sunshine State
Richard & Betty Fox

Don't move to Florida without reading this book! This interesting and informative guide covers 99 Florida cities and towns, including a new look at longtime hotspots and many undiscovered havens. Provides information on taxes, costs of living, health care, climate, recreation and crime rates, with a rating of each town's potential for retirement living from both male and female perspectives. **$16.95**

(ALL NEW SECOND EDITION)

■ Retirement Migration in America
Size, Trends and Economic Impact
Charles F. Longino Jr., Ph.D.

380,000 Americans retire out of state every year, generating billions in sales for everything from real estate to health care and revitalizing rural America. This book quantifies the economic impact on every state and county in America for economic development agencies, developers, financial institutions and others who want to know where America's retirees are moving. **$39.95**

■ Choose the Southwest
Retirement Discoveries for Every Budget
John Howells

Profiles 50 areas in Nevada, Utah, Colorado, Arizona, New Mexico and West Texas and includes all the basic data about costs of living, real estate, medical care, climate, recreation, culture and crime and safety. **$14.95**

■ Choose Mexico
Live Well on $600 a Month
John Howells & Don Merwin

Mexico is a huge bargain for U.S. retirees. If you want to retire south of the border, you'll want the book recommended by Mexican consulates. It describes the best places to settle and covers housing, finances, health care, legal requirements, shopping and recreation. **$12.95**

■ Choose Costa Rica
A Guide to Retirement & Investment
John Howells

A vacation favorite, Costa Rica's low prices and liberal immigration laws attract an increasing number of Americans. Howells covers costs, medical care, housing, recreation, legal requirements and investment opportunities. Bonus section on Guatemala. **$14.95**

■ Where to Retire House Plans
200 Beautiful and Efficient Designs for Retirement Lifestyles

Thinking of building your retirement dream house? Check out this selection of award-winning designs from Lifestyle HomeDesign, a leading home plan service. Front view and floor plans for 200 beautiful homes ideal for retirement lifestyles. All styles and budgets. Order complete blueprints for any house you like, saving up to 90% of the cost of custom plans, or simply scan for ideas. **$5.95**

■ Choose the Pacific Northwest
Includes Washington, Oregon and British Columbia
John Howells

A close look at one of America's most desirable retirement areas, including housing, safety, climate, health care, transportation, entertainment, culture and recreation. **$12.95**

■ Where to Retire
Best and Most Affordable Places
John Howells

This book covers cities and towns in 23 states — from Virginia, the Carolinas and Florida to California, the Pacific Northwest and Hawaii. A wealth of information on climate, living costs, health care, crime rates, taxes and lifestyle. Places for snowbirds and RVers are noted. **$17.95**

30-DAY MONEY-BACK GUARANTEE

Yes! Please send me the books marked below. My payment is enclosed.

☐ *America's 100 Best Places to Retire* $16.95 _____
☐ *Where to Retire in Florida* $16.95 _____
☐ *Retirement Migration in America* $39.95 _____
☐ *Choose the Southwest* $14.95 _____
☐ *Choose Mexico* $12.95 _____
☐ *Choose Costa Rica* $14.95 _____
☐ *Where to Retire House Plans* $5.95 _____
☐ *Choose the Pacific Northwest* $12.95 _____
☐ *Where to Retire* $17.95 _____

Plus shipping/handling @ $2.50 per title
($4 U.S. per title for Canadian delivery) ➤ _____

Texas residents add 8.25% sales tax. _____

TOTAL enclosed _____

Clip and mail this coupon, along with a check or money order payable to:

Vacations To Go
1502 Augusta Dr. - Suite 415
Houston, TX 77057

Allow 4-6 weeks for delivery.
Send to:

_____
NAME

_____
ADDRESS

_____
CITY/STATE/ZIP

For delivery within 10 days, call (800) 338-4962 and order by credit card.

Open 8:30-5:30, Monday-Friday, CST

NOTES

NOTES

NOTES